When Words Are Inadequate

OXFORD STUDIES IN DANCE THEORY

Mark Franko, Series Editor

When Words Are Inadequate

Modern Dance and Transnationalism in China

NAN MA

OXFORD
UNIVERSITY PRESS

OXFORD
UNIVERSITY PRESS

Oxford University Press is a department of the University of Oxford. It furthers
the University's objective of excellence in research, scholarship, and education
by publishing worldwide. Oxford is a registered trade mark of Oxford University
Press in the UK and certain other countries.

Published in the United States of America by Oxford University Press
198 Madison Avenue, New York, NY 10016, United States of America.

Library of Congress Cataloging-in-Publication Data
Names: Ma, Nan (Chinese literature teacher) author.
Title: When Words are Inadequate : Modern Dance and Transnationalism in China / Nan Ma.
Other titles: Modern Dance and Transnationalism in China
Description: New York : Oxford University Press, [2023] |
Series: Oxford studies in dance theory series |
Includes bibliographical references and index.
Identifiers: LCCN 2022050269 (print) | LCCN 2022050270 (ebook) |
ISBN 9780197575307 (hardcover) | ISBN 9780197575314 (paperback) |
ISBN 9780197575338 (epub) | ISBN 9780197575345 (ebook) | ISBN 9780197575321
Subjects: LCSH: Modern dance—China—History. | Dance—China—History. |
Transnationalism. | Performance art—China—History. |
Duncan, Isadora, 1877-1927. | Wigman, Mary, 1886-1973. |
Classification: LCC GV1691 .M273 2023 (print) | LCC GV1691 (ebook) |
DDC 792.80951—dc23/eng/20221101
LC record available at https://lccn.loc.gov/2022050269
LC ebook record available at https://lccn.loc.gov/2022050270

DOI: 10.1093/oso/9780197575307.001.0001

Paperback printed by Marquis, Canada
Hardback printed by Bridgeport National Bindery, Inc., United States of America

For my family

Contents

Series Editor Foreword

Mark Franko

This is the first monograph in the English language to study Chinese modern dance of the early to mid-twentieth century from a transnational perspective. As such, it fills a gaping hole separating the historical advent of dance modernism in the early twentieth century from existing studies of "modern Chinese dance" in the second half of the twentieth century. This book is therefore an event of some importance.

Author Nan Ma overturns the idea that dance modernism was a strictly Western phenomenon. In so doing, she "decenters" Western dance historiography while also taking certain Western influences on Chinese dance into account. Throughout she situates the modernist theories and practices of Chinese artists in analytical and historical Chinese frameworks. Thus, as Ma herself notes, she avoids the pitfalls of both Eurocentrism and Sinocentrism. Her perspective is truly global and can serve as a model for future studies in cognate areas because she avoids facile ideological postures. She is actively engaged with Chinese studies as well with dance studies, which gives her research a transdisciplinary depth and breadth. The analytical picture that emerges is truly global in all its dimensions, and this book should therefore contribute to the growing literature on alternative modernities from a global perspective.

The book introduces the stories of Yu Rongling, Wu Xiaobang, Dai Ailian, and Guo Mingda by carefully documenting their activities in both China and the West. Ma links each Chinese artist to a Western canonical counterpart: Isadora Duncan, Mary Wigman, Rudolf Laban, and Alwin Nikolais, respectively. Ma discusses Chinese modern dancers as transnational and transcultural agents who transformed and reconceptualized modern dance in well-contextualized Chinese contexts. The trope of expressing the inexpressible (dance and language), bridging the present with a pre-historical past, and the formation of classicism and "ethnic" dance in national and nationalizing contexts are all articulated here in conjunction with the pressures and effects of these artists' border crossings. Ma's focus is intensely transnational and geopolitical, and her methodology is bound to be influential on future studies.

Acknowledgments

This book is developed from my PhD dissertation, which would not have been possible without my mentors at the University of Wisconsin–Madison. My advisor, Professor Nicole Huang, then at the Department of East Asian Languages and Literature, encouraged my first step of writing on dance as a literary student who did not (and still does not) dance, and her constant support and intellectual guidance helped me through my most difficult times in graduate school. I always look up to her as a model for being a scholar and teacher. My co-advisor, Professor Steve C. Ridgely, introduced me to the scholarship of modern Japanese literature and culture and urged me to learn Japanese, which turned out to be essential to this project. I also thank him for the many hours he spent with me discussing and editing earlier versions of the chapters. It was Professor Rania Huntington who, with her expertise and patience, walked me through the fields of traditional Chinese theaters and late Qing literature, both of which are relevant to several chapters of this book. She, together with Professor William H. Nienhauser, Jr., provided me with the best classical Chinese literature training I could ever imagine. I feel truly fortunate to have Professor Jill H. Casid as my teacher of visual culture. Attending her seminars led me to confront challenging theoretical questions in my project, and through her teaching and writing she demonstrated perfectly how critical rigor could be welded with creative imagination in interdisciplinary research. I owe great debts to Andrea Harris, my dance history professor, who carried on UW-Madison's rich legacy of dance studies passed down from Margaret H'Doubler and Sally Banes. At Lathrop Hall, where the first university dance degree program in the United States was born in 1926, Professor Harris familiarized me with twentieth-century dance history, without which I would have never become confident as a literary student doing research on dance. Pleasant and productive conversations with Professor Jin-Wen Yu at the Dance Department and Professor Shuxing Fan at the Department of Theater and Drama showed me fresh perspectives of artists, to whom I extend my heartfelt gratitude. I am deeply thankful to Professor Naomi McGloin for handholding me through the years of learning Japanese and spending long hours with me discussing my translation of Japanese materials for this project. For friendship, I thank Daisy Yan Du, Hai Liu, Lu Liu, Xiang Lü, Yuli Na, Laura Jo-han Wen, and Chen Wu, among others.

I completed my dissertation and more than half of this book project at Swarthmore College, where I was a visiting instructor at the department of modern languages and literatures from 2013 to 2015. My Swarthmore colleagues exhibited genuine interest in my research and great patience for me as a new academic transitioning from graduate school to a faculty position. Haili Kong's rich knowledge of modern Chinese literature and history ensured our conversations were always informative and never dull. I am grateful for his support of my teaching and his regular gentle reminders, which sustained my writing momentum. The late Alan Berkowitz made my working at Swarthmore a truly enjoyable and precious experience. His work on the portrayal and practice of Taoist reclusion in early medieval China inspired chapter 3 of this book, as reflected in the chapter's title. I will never forget his graceful way of balancing teaching, writing, and life. Lala Zuo generously offered me much-needed advice on teaching at a top library arts college. It was her friendship that accompanied me throughout this demanding stage of my career and beyond. I am also thankful to Pallabi Chakravorty, Ju-hui Chiu, William Gardner, Wol-A Kang, Jyun-hong Lu, Kirsten Speidel, and Qian Sun for true camaraderie.

I extend my sincerest gratitude to my wonderful colleagues at Dickinson College, who have become my role models and dependable friends. Rae Yang helped me navigate various teaching, research, and service responsibilities, and the life in Carlisle in general. David Strand has been a great mentor, and his scholarship set the bar high for my research. I can always expect from Neil Diamant refreshingly sharp insights, and his impressive productivity and rigorous writing have been an inspiration for me since day one. Alex Bates is the one I constantly turn to when I encounter difficulties in work and life. Shawn Bender, our department chair for the past few years, was most instrumental in my finishing the book. In 2019, he first organized a workshop within our department, during which Alex, David, and he himself provided invaluable feedback on the introductory chapter and the book proposal. He then invited three external scholar-readers to come to Dickinson and presided over a one-day workshop to discuss each draft chapter in detail. It is fair to say that without Shawn's continuous support, the book would have been completed much later and of lower quality. For friendship and support, I also thank Qing Bai, Dengjian Jin, Akiko Meguro, Wei Ren, Sarah Skaggs, Evan Young, and Rui Zhang.

I am deeply indebted to Liang Luo at University of Kentucky, Ke Ren at College of the Holy Cross, and Emily Wilcox at William & Mary, who read earlier versions of the manuscript and attended my book workshop at Dickinson. Their insightful and detailed comments were indispensable in shaping the book into its current form. Liang's work on modern Chinese theater is an exemplar I try to emulate all the time, and her warm encouragement went a long way in boosting my morale throughout the writing process. Ke, a rigorous historian friend, always pointed me to the right primary and secondary sources whenever asked. Emily, for her path-breaking work on Chinese dance, has become one of my major interlocutors in this book project, and her consistent enthusiasm for my research motivated every phase of my writing. Her decade-long friendship, radiant energy, and unreserved generosity are what I treasure the most.

Credits go to Chinese dance scholars and their associates, including, to name only a few, Jiang Dong, Luo Bin, Feng Bihua, Ye Jin, and Ye Mingming, who were students, colleagues, relatives, or acquaintances of the main dancers under study in the book. They always leveraged their knowledge, resources, and networks to help me with my questions and requests. Their kindness guaranteed the timely completion of this project.

Almost two decades ago, as a fresh graduate from Peking University preoccupied with German Romantic literature, I did not have the slightest idea that I would later spend ten years drafting a book on dance. It was my graduate study of aesthetics at Tsinghua University that seeded my interest in dance. My advisor Professor Xiao Ying pointed out to me for the first time that both Western and Chinese aestheticians reserved a special place for dance in their art theories. Li Qiong—a professionally trained dancer, my classmate, roommate, friend, and "elder sister"—convinced me to join her in watching many dance concerts and performances in Beijing and shared with me her experiences and expertise as a dancer. To Professor Xiao and Li Qiong I extend my belated thanks for their encouraging me to enter the most fantastic world of dance.

For other opportunities to share work in progress, I am grateful to all participants of the following events who gave me helpful feedback. A preliminary version of chapter 4 was presented at the annual conference of the Association for Asian Studies held in Washington D.C. in 2018, and earlier versions of chapter 2 at the Stanford-Berkeley Graduate Students Conference on Modern Chinese Studies in 2013, at the CHINOPERL Conference in Philadelphia in 2014, and at the Mellon Summer Seminar in Dance Studies at Northwestern University in 2015. Special thanks go to Susan Manning, organizer of the 2015 Mellon dance seminar, who warmly introduced me to the amazing community of dance scholars and showed continued interest in and support for my research since then. Mark Franko, series editor of Oxford's Studies in Dance Theory, read an earlier version of the introduction and offered critical input that reshaped the introductory chapter. A paper developed from a section of chapter 3 was shared at the "Dancing East Asia" Conference at University of Michigan in 2017 and later appeared in *Corporeal Politics: Dancing East Asia*, edited by Kathrine Mezur and Emily Wilcox (University of Michigan Press, 2020). An earlier version of chapter 2 has been published in the journal *Modern Chinese Literature and Culture* 28, no. 1 (2016). I thank the anonymous reviewers for useful comments and the editors of these publications for permission to reprint here. At Oxford University Press, I am extremely thankful to Norman Hirschy, Lauralee Yeary, and Paloma Escovedo, whose professional and thoughtful support helped me through the prolonged process of writing a book amid all the chaos of the COVID pandemic, and to my anonymous readers for tremendously valuable feedback that improved this project.

The research of this project was generously funded by the Chancellor's Scholarship for Trans-Asian Studies (2011) and the International Summer Fieldwork Fellowship (2013) granted by the University of Wisconsin-Madison; the Faculty Research Grant (2013-2015) by Swarthmore College; the Faculty Conference Travel Fund (2018), Scholarly Project Fund (2016, 2018), and Publication Costs Fund (2022) by Dickinson College; and the Asia Library Travel Grant (2019) by the University of Michigan. For library assistance during my archival research, I deeply thank Liangyu Fu at the Asia Library of the University of Michigan.

At last, I wish to thank my incredible family: Xiaolu Wang, husband, friend, colleague, logistics provider, intellectual interlocutor, and first reader; my parents and parents-in-law, who supported me in countless, selfless ways throughout the years; Eileen, my understanding daughter, who reminds me of the purpose of doing all this; and Coco and Cola, my two puppies who taught me positivity and how to have fun.

Introduction

The Chinese Case of Modern Dance

In the June of 1926, Beijing, John Van Antwerp MacMurray (1881–1960), American minister to the Republic of China (1912–1949) from 1925 to 1929, used a newly marketed, highly compact Cine-Kodak 16mm motion-picture camera to shoot a three-minute silent sequence of a Chinese woman performing a "sword dance" in an outdoor setting (figure I.1).[1] The woman, who is middle aged, wearing ancient-style Han-Chinese theatrical dress and headwear, dances confidently against a regal background of the signature architectures of the old imperial capital: a white-marble fence, grand palace walls, gatehouses, and the Temple of Heaven towering behind. Despite its combative theme as connoted by the use of two prop swords, the dance is not violent at all, but instead smooth, elegant, and light in mood, which may be best described by the Chinese idiom "like gliding clouds and flowing water." There is virtually no jerking, jumping, contrasting, exertive, or expansive movement, and the rhythm is steady, at a medium pace. The woman first dances with one hand holding both swords, such that it appears as if there is only one blade. Then, she splits the swords, each hand holding one, and raises and intersects them overhead to form a cross. After a short freeze in this pose, in a slightly acrobatic manner, she starts to wield the two swords—sometimes synced and sometimes not—in curvy, linear, circular, and spinning patterns. The traces of the flying blades weave out a domed space surrounding the dancer, who in turn moves trippingly in curvy, linear, and circular routes on the stone-paved ground.

The modern camera's gaze, being a symbol of the West's technological supremacy and perhaps driven by the Westerner's Orientalist curiosity, seems to frame the imperial, religious architectures of collapsed dynasties, the dancer, and her dance into an essentialized representation of an exotic other, belonging to a mysterious Chinese tradition located in the past. Indeed, the *Sword Dance* might be seen as "traditional." Its costume, props, and choreography were all inspired by a dance episode performed by Mei

When Words Are Inadequate. Nan Ma, Oxford University Press. © Oxford University Press 2023.
DOI: 10.1093/oso/9780197575307.003.0001

Figure I.1 Yu Rongling performing *Sword Dance*, Beijing, 1926. Image courtesy of the Seeley G. Mudd Manuscript Library at Princeton University.

Lanfang 梅蘭芳 (1894–1961)—the great male performer who specialized in playing the female leading roles (*dan* 旦) of traditional Chinese theater—in *Ba wang bie ji* 霸王別姬 (the heroic king's farewell to his concubine, figure I.2), which was a well-known work of Peking Opera, a popular genre that culminated a centuries-long Chinese theatrical tradition.[2] Moreover, the female dancer's method of composition, namely, distilling and adapting codified movement convention from traditional theaters into dance vocabulary and stand-alone choreography, is similar to (if not as systematic as) that adopted by choreographers from generations later in the 1950s to create so-called Chinese classical dance (*Zhongguo gudian wu* 中國古典舞), a still evolving dance genre that supposedly represents the essence of the Chinese dance tradition.[3]

However, this filmed dance is not as "classical" or "Chinese" as it may seem; it was inextricably intertwined with the global rise of dance modernism, and modernism in performance genres in general, since the turn of the century thanks to an international network of artistic exchanges that bridged China and the West. In the early 1910s, Mei Lanfang and his colleagues started to modernize Peking Opera by highlighting female visuality and sensuality

Figure I.2 Mei Lanfang performing *Ba wang bie ji* (The heroic king's farewell to his concubine), ca. 1922. Image courtesy of the Mei Lanfang Memorial Library.

through incorporating rich dance moves and dance-enhancing costume and lighting designs into stage performance, including the dance episode in *Ba wang bie ji* that inspired *Sword Dance*.[4] His reform was partly influenced by the groundbreaking innovations of the American dancer Loie Fuller (1862–1928), considered in Western dance historiography one of the founding figures of modern dance.[5] In turn, Mei's performance during his 1935 European tour famously impressed Bertolt Brecht and stimulated the latter's influential conception of the "alienation effect."[6] Moreover, in September

Figure I.3 Denishawn dancer Anne Douglas rehearsing *General Wu's Farewell to His Wife*, China, 1926. Image courtesy of the Music Division, Library of Congress.

1926, just three months after the filming of *Sword Dance*, Ruth St. Denis and Ted Shawn, pioneers of American modern dance and leaders of their dance troupe Denishawn, began their second tour in China, during which they performed in Shanghai two works with Chinese themes: *Wu shuai bie qi* 吳帥 別妻 (General Wu's farewell to his wife, figure I.3) and *Bai yu guanyin* 白玉 觀音 (White Jade Avalokitesvara, or *White Jade*, figure I.4). Mei contributed directly to the choreography of the former—the American version of *Ba*

Figure I.4 Ruth St. Denis performing *White Jade*, 1926. Image courtesy of the Music Division, Library of Congress.

wang bie ji—during DeniShawn's previous Chinese tour in October 1925 (when the American dancers watched Mei performing his original version of the sword dance).[7] The Chinese woman's filmed *Sword Dance* and another work of hers, *Guanyin wu* 觀音舞 (Avalokitesvara dance, figure I.5), correspond neatly to these two American modern dance works in terms of themes and sources.[8] It seems that the Chinese dancer had been striving to posit her choreographies as part of global dance modernism—instead of some purely "classical" Chinese dance—in an emulating, competing, and mutual-borrowing relationship with Western early modern dance. This Chinese dancer in focus is Yu Rongling 裕容齡 (ca. 1888–1973).

Even more revealing is the fact that Yu was among the earliest students of Isadora Duncan (ca. 1877–1927) in Paris around the turn of the century, which coincided with the rise to international fame of the iconic American modern dance pioneer. Yu later transformed the "Greek dance" (or early modern dance as known today) she learned from Duncan into her version of "Chinese dance," classical and modern at once. While it is difficult

Figure I.5 Yu Rongling performing *Guanyin wu* (Avalokitesvara dance), 1926.
This photo appeared in Yu's memoir published in the Chinese dance journal
Wudao 舞蹈, no. 2 (March 1958), p. 45.

to pinpoint the formal connections between Duncan's Greek dance and
Yu's choreography with more than twenty years in between, possible traces
of Duncan's influence may still be discernible in the costume, choreography, and setting of the filmed *Sword Dance*. Unlike the thick long dress in
Mei's *Ba wang bie ji* that completely covers the performer's feet, Yu's dress is
shorter (above the ankles) and lighter so that it shows all her footwork and
generates a flowy effect closer to that of Duncan's "Greek tunic" (though not

as revealing as the latter). Compared with Mei's version, Yu's dance steps, with heels often raised above the ground, have a slightly bouncy, "upward" quality that is absent in the original Peking Opera version but present in Duncan's early dancing (though Yu wears shoes, unlike Duncan's bare feet).[9] Moreover, quite radically, Yu not only decouples the actor from the dramatic role to become a female soloist, which is itself a modernist transmutation,[10] but also decontextualizes the sword dance from both its original narrative structure and the theatrical stage, and brings it into an open, monumental space with Temple of Heaven as background, to be reframed and recorded by the Westerner's motion-picture camera. This is a cross-cultural, intermedial, modernist gesture that seems to point to and perhaps also challenge the earlier iconic images, captured in photographs or words, of Duncan in "Greek tunic" and in dancing poses against the Parthenon and other ancient Greek and Egyptian temples as backdrop—a typical gesture of modern dance that keeps referencing and rewriting its own history.[11]

The example above epitomizes some key questions this book tries to answer. What new insights can be gained into global dance modernism of the twentieth century by highlighting the case of modern dance in China, a country that is still deemed peripheral to the early modern dance revolutions centered on the United States and Europe? To what extent can the Chinese case complicate our understanding of the boundaries between modern, classical, national, and ethnic dances in the colonial and postcolonial context of wars and revolutions, travels and migrations, and gender, racial, ethnic, and cultural politics? Conversely, by reinserting the global genre of modern dance—admitting the genre's lack of coherency and unity—into the current constellation of China studies, especially modernist studies of Chinese literature and arts, is it possible to uncover distinct patterns of the intermedial dynamics between the bodily dance and the other more language- or representation-centered artistic mediums in China? Can such an intervention provide fresh historical perspectives on the theoretical relationship between dance and language, expression and representation, the corporeal and the textual, and the performative and the discursive?

In striving to answer these questions, this book provides a transnational and transcultural history of modern dance written from and beyond the perspective of China. On the one hand, it contributes to the dance scholarship on the early to mid-twentieth-century global dissemination of modern dance, in which China is typically missing from the picture, by excavating the Chinese contributions to this movement. On the other hand, it extends the horizon of China studies, where modern dance is largely missing, by rewriting the cultural history of modern China from a *bodily movement*-based perspective through the lens of global dance modernism. The book explores the intertwined relationships between performance and representation, choreography and politics, and nation-building and global modernisms. In situating modern dance within an intermedial circuit of literary and artistic forms, it demonstrates how the genre constituted an alternative and complement to other sibling arts in participating in China's various revolutions, reforms, wars, and political movements in the twentieth century.

Dancers as Transnational and Transcultural Agents

This book's transnational and transcultural nature is immediately manifest in the lives and careers of the four major dancer-choreographers under study. Yu Rongling, the Eurasian daughter of a top-rank Late Qing, Manchu diplomat, first learned traditional Japanese dance in Tokyo, then studied early modern dance with Duncan in Paris in the early 1900s, brought it back to the imperial court of the crumbling Qing Empire (1636–1912), and further created its Chinese counterpart under the auspices of Empress Dowager Cixi 慈禧 (1835–1908). Wu Xiaobang 吳曉邦 (1906–1995), known as "father of China's new dance," first studied ballet and modern dance in Tokyo from the late 1920s to early 1930s with Takata Seiko 高田原世子 (1895–1977) and later with Eguchi Takaya 江口隆哉 (1900–1977)—both of whom learned modern dance in Europe and/or the United States—and then became the first professional dancer in modern China who later transformed the modern dance he learned in Japan into "China's new dance." Dai Ailian 戴愛蓮 (1916–2006), the widely regarded "mother of modern Chinese dance," was born as a subject of the British Empire into a third-generation Cantonese immigrant family in Trinidad; at age fourteen Dai moved to London to study ballet and later the central European school of modern dance; she went to China in the early 1940s at the height of the Second World War; melded the theory and methodology of modern dance into her study, adaptation, and creation of ethnic dances in China; and eventually became a Chinese citizen. Guo Mingda 郭明達 (ca. 1916–2014), who left Republican China for the United States in 1947, obtained his master's degree in dance education from the University of Iowa (1947–1950), pursued a doctorate in dance education at New York University (1951–1954), learned various schools of

Euro-American modern dance, studied dance and choreography with Alwin Nikolais (1910–1993) at the Henry Street Playhouse in New York for four years (1952–1955), and returned to socialist China in 1955.

Since the earliest defining moments of modern dance, Chinese artists had been actively participating in its production, performance, and discourse on international and domestic stages. In addition to the example of Mei Lanfang, as shown later in the book, Yu Rongling was involved in Isadora Duncan's early universalist conception of modern dance and later reoriented it toward a national one; Wu Xiaobang requestioned the relationship between dance, literature, and music by integrating literary narrative and music back into *Ausdruckstanz* (expressionist dance, which stresses the independence and purity of dance from other mediums) of Mary Wigman (1886–1973); Dai Ailian participated in the formation, application, and dissemination of Labanotation, the "universal" symbolic system for notating dance and bodily movement initiated by Rudolf von Laban (1879–1958); Guo Mingda translated, integrated, and reinterpreted histories and theories of various schools of Western modern dance and played an instrumental role in preserving the modern dance discourse in socialist China—during a time when modern dance was banned—and in reviving the genre in the Reform Era of the 1980s.

Asian contributions like these to modern dance had long been neglected in Western dance historiography until recently.[12] Even for those works that touch upon the West–Asia intercultural exchanges in the history of early modern dance, the focus is usually on Japan and India, while China is largely left out of the picture.[13] The case of modern dance demonstrates Sinophone scholar Shu-mei Shih's argument that "modernism never traveled one way from a point of origin to a place of destination. But it was consistently described as such due to the imbalance of discursive power between China and the West."[14] It seems that, after all, the claimed "universal metakinesis" (in John Martin's terms) of modern dance cannot escape the gravity of the discursive hegemony of the West.[15] A major motivation of this book is thus to take a step in the direction of redressing this "imbalance of discursive power" by recuperating these Chinese contributions to modern dance in the twentieth century.

However, Shih also warns against the fallacy of simply replacing Eurocentrism with some version of Sinocentrism.[16] To abolish Eurocentrism without installing any other singular "-centrism," literary scholar Susan Friedman proposes a radical "planetary turn" for modernist studies that re-posits modernity (and modernism) "as a geohistorical condition that is multiple, contradictory, interconnected, polycentric, and recurrent . . . across the globe."[17] Following Freidman's call, this book challenges the still largely Eurocentric historiography of modern dance by reinserting China into the transnational and transcultural network of artistic exchange that fostered the rise of modern dance as a global phenomenon in the early twentieth century.[18] It foregrounds the Chinese case as a nexus of negotiation, adaptation, and evolvement, yet without either essentializing modern dance in China as a coherent genre that is fundamentally different from the modern dance of the West and Japan or simply treating it as some secondary or tertiary derivatives of the more "authentic" Western counterparts. That is, this book demonstrates how the development of modern dance in China intersected, overlapped, and interacted with other centers of dance modernism around the world—including Japan, France, the United States, Germany, and Britain—and thus further complicates the binary conceptions of center/periphery and West/East.

To rectify the "imbalance of discursive power" in dance historiography by no means suggests that one can then assume away the historical imbalance of power in the global geopolitical terrains that modulated the transnational circulation and local developments of modern dance. The two-way crossings between China and the West were almost always asymmetric and unequal, and the "imbalance of power" was the very historical condition under which the border-crossings happened. For example, the international travels of Yu Rongling with her diplomat father to Tokyo and Paris were the direct results of the Qing Empire's humiliating defeats against Japan in the First Sino-Japanese War (1894–1895) and against the "Eight-Nation Alliance" during the Boxer Uprising (1899–1900), respectively. Wu Xiaobang's study of modern dance in Tokyo from the late 1920s to the mid-1930s took place under the gathering war clouds that eventually turned into Japan's total invasion of China in the Second Sino-Japanese War (1937–1945). Dai Ailian's travels from Trinidad to London and then to China via Hong Kong, her experiences of studying ballet and modern dance, and her perception and conception of world dances, Oriental dances, and Chinese dances were all enabled and conditioned by the material and cultural infrastructures of the colonial hierarchies of the British Empire. What motivated Guo Mingda to go to the United States to study dance in the first place was his hope to transform and strengthen the Chinese nation by introducing advanced physical and dance education from the West. As a result, these artists all more or less endorsed the superiority and authority of Western modernism and, to a varying extent, embodied and reinforced Eurocentrism.

Therefore, this book is both a reproduction and, more importantly, a criticism of the Eurocentric conception of modernism in the case of modern Chinese dance (to be more clearly defined in the next section). It is a reproduction of such because it recognizes the powerful influence of the world colonial hierarchies in structuring the Chinese dancer-choreographers' experiences of traveling internationally and domestically, studying and adapting modern dance, and creating their own versions of modern Chinese dance. The book is also a criticism of such because it shows how the dancer-choreographers exploited and reoriented the paradoxes inherent to the Eurocentric logic of universality claimed by modern dance and creatively combined those with a wide range of Chinese and non-Chinese sources and resources to create its Chinese counterparts, and the discourses thereof, as a means to address personal, national, artistic, and political urgencies at different times of the twentieth century.

Similarly, this book is also both a reproduction and criticism of the Sinocentric conception of "Chineseness" in modern Chinese dance. On the one hand, all the dancer-choreographers discussed in this book had seriously tried to justify the Chineseness of their dance in relation to "China" as a central, yet fluid, geopolitical and cultural construct at various historical junctures. On the other hand, the Chineseness being constructed in modern Chinese dance had always been fractured and unstable, because the dancer-choreographers located Chineseness in very different aspects of Chinese dance (such as the symbolic, the thematic, the spiritual, or the formal), and different times (past or present), places (coastal metropolises, inland, or borderlands), and ethnicities (Han or other ethnic groups), complicated further by the ever-changing domestic and international politics and the large-scale dislocation, migration, and relocation of people during wars and political turmoils.[19] More importantly, the construction of Chineseness in modern Chinese dance had always been enmeshed inextricably within the discourses and praxes of cosmopolitanism, modernism, (anti-)colonialism, and diaspora, all beyond China's national borders and with China being only one of many centers.

Taken together, this book demonstrates that both modernism and Chineseness in modern Chinese dance were "multiple, contradictory, interconnected, polycentric, and recurrent" in nature. Dance has always been, and will continue to be, a murky, generative, and transformative ground for the power struggle, negotiation, and collaboration across the boundaries between the personal, the local, the national, and the universal.

Modern Dance and Modern Chinese Dance

Throughout the book, I use the term "modern dance" in accord with its most common meaning in dance studies. Historically, this somewhat ambiguous category refers retrospectively to various Euro-American dance reform practices beginning around the turn of the century that were typically posited as the artistic antithesis to the "'unnatural' and 'degenerate' movements of ballet and the 'modern' social dancing."[20] The surge of dance modernism was tied with the converged interest across artistic and industrial fields in objectifying bodily movement, which gave rise to the belief that if personality could be removed from dance, bodily movement, in its own physical form, would obtain autonomous significance as some aesthetic "absolute" that could project the "vision of universal subjectivity" and justify the autonomy of dance.[21] The identity of modern dance started to coalesce in the 1930s through the discursive project of John Martin (1893–1985), the influential American dance critic, to define the genre by specifying the communicative property of its medium. Martin argued that bodily movement alone could express universal emotion through what he called "metakinesis" (or kinesthesia), a physio-psychological process whereby the spectator could supposedly feel the physical and emotional state of the dancer empathetically by watching the latter's bodily movement. Therefore, through kinesthesia, modern dance promised to challenge language- and representation-based paradigms of meaning making and communication.[22]

Current dance scholarship has begun to extensively question and critique these standard assumptions about early modern dance—that is, the promotion of "natural" movement against existing codified conventions (e.g., classical ballet), the autonomy of bodily movement, and the universality of kinesthesia—from historical and theoretical perspectives that are often centered on gender, racial, and class politics as well as cross-genre and intermedial dynamics.[23] This book, in the same spirit, will use the Chinese case to show that the development of modern dance in China, from the very beginning, did not simply follow but also complicated these assumptions in various ways under vastly different historical conditions.

According to Western dance historiography, there were two major origins of modern dance. The first was a group of loosely connected pioneering American female dancers who rose to fame on European stages several decades apart.[24] The three most famous dancers among them were Loie Fuller, Isadora Duncan, and Ruth St. Denis. The second was the central European school of modern dance, which strived to theorize and systematize the methods of analyzing, composing, performing, and recording dances based on the "natural law of bodily movement."[25] The most representative individuals of this school were Laban and Wigman. As in Yu's example and further demonstrated in the book, Chinese pioneers of modern dance had direct or indirect interactions with the careers of these founding figures.

Despite its focus on modern dance, this book, at various points, touches on the history of ballet, the "invented" Chinese classical dance, and modernized ethnic folk dance in China. The last two concert dance genres together are typically called the "Chinese dance" (*Zhongguo wu* 中國舞) by Chinese dance scholars.[26] Both genres are thought of as "Chinese" because they drew heavily from, respectively, traditional Chinese theatrical movement conventions and the folk dance forms of various ethnic minorities that are constituents of the overarching "Chinese nation," even though both genres were influenced by the aesthetics and training regime of Soviet ballet and character dance (balletized European national folk dances). They were also modern, which is often implied, because these concert dance genres had not come into being until the mid-1940s and 1950s and, in principle, could be distinguished from historical dance forms existing in China long before the "modern era" (1919–1949, according to the official periodization in Chinese historiography.[27]

In her groundbreaking 2019 book, *Revolutionary Bodies: Chinese Dance and the Socialist Legacy*, Emily Wilcox critically examines the historical creation of Chinese dance in the twentieth century by providing a comprehensive historical background, analyzing a large number of dance works from a variety of genres, and covering major Chinese dancer-choreographers.[28] While Wilcox largely treats the introduced modern dance as a genre distinct from and competing against Chinese dance, this book regards the Chinese development of modern dance as integral to the origin of (modern) Chinese dance. This is due to two reasons. First, modern dance, along with ballet, were the two major dance genres imported to China that triggered the evolution of the hybrid identity of Chinese dance. Chinese classical dance and ethnic folk dance were, to some extent, anachronistic constructs both competing with and borrowing from modern dance and ballet. These concert dance genres are in constant conversation, competition, collaboration, and hybridization (as in Yu's *Sword Dance*). Thus, the boundaries between them are far from rigid or time-invariant. The Chinese development of modern dance compellingly demonstrates the transcultural and transnational origin of (modern) Chinese dance and the underlying struggles for the discursive authority over the definitions of universality, nationality, the modern, and tradition. Second, the major pioneers discussed in this book were all first trained in modern dance and ballet, and then later ventured into the realms of Chinese classical dance and/or ethnic folk dances. As a result, the abovementioned cross-genre issues find their varying embodiments in the careers of these figures who themselves crossed and blurred the boundaries of various genres. Therefore, for the purpose of this book, I use the somewhat cumbersome and ambiguous term "modern Chinese dance" to refer to Chinese dance (Chinese classical dance and ethnic folk dance), ballet, and modern dance developed in twentieth-century China (though ballet is discussed only occasionally).[29] By focusing on the early development of modern dance in China, this book builds on and contributes to the emergent English scholarship of Chinese dance studies by showing that Chinese dance—a heterogenous genre that took shape mainly in the 1950s—has deep roots in the global dissemination of modern dance since the early 1900s onward, and thus significantly extends the historical horizon of the subfield.[30]

Historian Edward Dickinson points out that the rise of early modern dance in pre-WWI Europe was first and foremost a marketing success that relied on the infrastructure and techniques of modern marketing.[31] The marketers, often modern dancers themselves, usually positioned their choreography and performances in the field of mass culture, which differed from, yet bridged, both high and popular cultures.[32] The Chinese pioneers of modern dance faced similar "marketing" issues, but were confronted by even greater challenges against a different historical background and thus chose a different set of strategies. Unlike in the West, when modern dance and ballet first arrived in China in the early twentieth century, there were, for artistic dance (regardless of genre), no professional training institutions, production organizations, performance platforms, or consumer bases, let alone a recognizable or legitimate identity as an independent art form or performance genre.[33] However, like in the West, imported social and popular dances in, for instance, cabarets, revues, circuses, magic shows, and films had established their own market niches in several treaty-port cities. These dance forms "biased" the popular perception of concert dance toward something more like fashionable social skills or "vulgar" and "decadent" commercial diversion—or the "leg business" as they were called in the West.[34] By focusing on modern dance, yet in relation to these popular dance forms, this book can better investigate the personal experiences, dilemmas, and strategies of the individual artists involved in the long and challenging campaign of establishing modern dance as a legitimate and independent serious art in China, on the one hand, and as a useful instrument for social transformation, nation-building, and mass mobilization by appealing to the masses, on the other. Therefore, by examining the possibilities and limits of the agency of artists in the field of cultural politics, this book also seeks to converse with the growing literature on the convergence of, and the tension between, the avant-garde and the popular, modernism and leftism.[35]

The development of modern dance in China, and modern Chinese dance in general, was not isolated from the other art forms. As a new genre in China, modern dance, from the very beginning, had to keep reestablishing and re-justifying itself as an independent and legitimate genre, in a web of relations to other more well-established yet constantly evolving art forms, such as literature, film, visual arts, music, and theater. This book, at various places, discusses the unique difficulties and opportunities faced by dance practitioners, and their strategies, successful or not, to navigate through this web of relations to find the rightful, though often precarious, position for dance. Thus, this book, which is intended to intersect cultural, historical, and modernist studies, greatly benefits from and contributes to the existing scholarship on these sibling arts, including word-based literature.[36]

Dance and Words

> [W]hen we bristle with rage, or start with fright, or resort to gesticulation when at a loss for an adequately expressive word, we are practicing the beginnings of dance.
> —John Martin, *Introduction to the Dance*, 1965[37]

Here, Martin conceptualizes (modern) dance as an alternative, immediate means of expression that bypasses words and language. Although, ironically, the success of Martin's career and his historical reputation were built primarily upon language in the form of dance review and criticism, he expressed his "distrust" of language as early as in the 1930s: "In the present period of civilization an excessive evaluation is placed upon literacy . . . Nothing has meaning until it is translated into words; there is no substance in an emotional reaction, no validity in a muscular response; there is only language."[38]

Martin was not alone in distrusting words among his generation. Dance scholar Gabriele Brandstetter observes that this distrust reflects a widespread cultural crisis since around 1900—variously called the crisis of language, of knowledge, of meaning, and of representation, "namely as an expression of a complex cognitive problem, which called into question the self-evident communicability of sensual experiences and their experience of sense or meaning through symbolic representation."[39] This crisis was closely linked to the conditions of "modernity," summarized by Charles Baudelaire as "the ephemeral, the fugitive, the contingent," which also capture the key features of dance, especially modern dance.[40] Thus, the kinesthetic of dance, as put by modernist scholar Carrie Preston, "highlights one of the central motifs of modernism: the desire to make sense of the body, to account for and somehow encompass bodily experiences in art, and to figure movement in words, sculpture, painting, and other media."[41] Many intellectuals, writers, and artists then turned to dance to look for inspirations for their reflection on the nature of the respective artistic mediums they worked with, in confrontation with the "new media," such as photography and film.[42] For example, dance modernism, as literary scholar Susan Jones shows, played an instrumental role in the emergence of a modernist sensibility among well-known poets, from Stéphane Mallarmé to Ezra Pound, to "the embeddedness of physical movement in the very material of language itself."[43] Art historian Nell Andrea also demonstrates that, at the time of the historical avant-garde, famous painters and filmmakers worked in collaboration with dancer-choreographers to test and break down the limits of various art forms, a concerted endeavor unified by an "urge" toward abstraction, in order to "bridge the gulf between art and life."[44] This "urge to abstraction" was paradoxically directed toward the goal of creating art lived in the present through the muscular perception of movement—best exemplified by the corporeal medium of dance, in which the artist becomes the art, and ideals become embodied.[45] Brandstetter even argues that dance rose "from its position at the bottom rungs of art's hierarchy to the top," becoming "a key symbol of modernity and the central medium of all arts seeking to reflect the new technological age as an era defined by movements."[46]

For Martin (and others), through kinesthesia, dance—unlike music, which can ultimately be reduced to symbolic notes written in ink on paper, or film, which must be mediated by modern technology—becomes the only candidate for the universal and immediate means of communication that precludes the necessity of translation.[47] However, there are two major contradictions in Martin's argument. First, historically, this universalist project of American modern dance was motivated by a nationalist cultural ambition. As dance historian Susan Manning observes, despite its universalist claims, the practice of early modern dance always relied on "essentialized national identities."[48] During a time when America, the "land of assimilation," rose to a world superpower in the early twentieth century, Martin sought to replace the European conception of national culture, which privileged a representational literary heritage and a shared language formed in the past, with a new one that saw in modern dance an embodied, becoming, performative, future-oriented, and self-creating American nationhood.[49] Second, theoretically, Martin's conception of the immediacy of modern dance and kinesthesia is built on, in Franko's terms, a "primitive" expression theory that is not immediate in nature.[50] In Martin's view, in order for the dancer's various emotional states to be "felt" correctly by the spectator, the dancer must first encode—supposedly in some "spontaneous" and thus natural and universal way—each emotional state ("anger" or "fright") into corresponding bodily movement ("bristle" or "start") that can then be automatically and empathetically decoded by the spectator through kinesthesia. Therefore, the functioning of Martin's kinesthesia depends on a "very rudimentary semiology" that is, though not fully representational, "no longer immediate in communication."[51] In other words, although Martin intends to use kinesthesia to cut through language and representation to achieve *immediate* communication in dance, his theorized expressive mechanism follows a *mediated* logic similar to that of language and representation.

The two contradictions in Martin's theory of modern dance—universality versus nationality, immediacy versus mediacy—both find their counterparts in the history of modern Chinese dance. This book treats these two pairs of polarities as the extremes of two "orthogonal," conceptual axes for organizing the narrative of the book, which attempts to capture the dynamics through which the rise and fall of various forces competing, struggling, or collaborating along these two axes shaped the landscape of dance in China. Whereas the previous sections have discussed the universality-nationality dimension, the rest of this section focuses on the immediacy-mediacy axis in a Chinese context.

> Poetry is where intention goes. Being within one's heart, it is intention; coming out in words, it is poetry. Emotion stirs within, and then takes shape in words. When words are inadequate, one sighs [to express] it. When sighing is inadequate, one sings it. When singing is inadequate, unconsciously one's hands swing and feet stamp [to express] it.
> —"The Great Preface" to *The Book of Poetry* (*Shi jing* 詩經), ca. 1st century AD.[52]

This ancient passage from "The Great Preface" to *The Book of Poetry* has been regarded as a major classical source with lasting influence on both Chinese literary theory and dance theory.[53] In the last sentence, there are two verbs describing the unconscious movements of hands and feet, respectively, *wu* 舞 (swing) and *dao* 蹈 (stamp), which in modern Chinese coalesce into a compound word, *wudao* 舞蹈, for dance. This passage is comparable on several levels to that by Martin on the "beginnings of dance" quoted earlier. Both propose some "primitive" expression theory about how intention/emotion ("anger" and "fright" in Martin's) becomes externalized through bodily means ("bristle" and "start" in Martin's), treat unconscious or spontaneous bodily reactions to emotion as the foundation for dance, and situate the theory of dance in relation to words and language. However, there is a major difference between the two: whereas Martin posits dance as an alternative to language and, as implied, to other mediums, the Chinese counterpart imbricates words, dance, and other mediums into a hierarchical chain of expression that works in sequence to bring out emotion. The result is a poetic order of expressive mediums that can be characterized as a series of concentric circles: intention/emotion is at the center; words occupy the privileged innermost circle closest to intention/emotion; nothing can be expressed through any other medium without words first trying to translate and release a welling-up of feelings, which becomes "poetry"; what words cannot express is then passed on to other mediums in outer circles sequentially, with dance being placed at the outermost, corresponding to the least immediate medium.

This difference between Martin's model of expression and its Chinese counterpart needs to be understood within the historical contexts of *The Book of Poetry* and its "Great Preface," two texts written centuries apart. *The*

Book of Poetry is an anthology of 305 poems dated from twelfth to seventh century BC, compiled and edited by Confucius (551–479 BC), according to traditional belief. It has been widely regarded as the "fountainhead" of the millennia-long Chinese literary tradition and enshrined as the first of the "six classics" (*liu jing* 六經) of the Confucian school.[54] During and before Confucious' time, poetry, as is believed, was not a purely literary genre, but an integrative art form that had a performative dimension, including music/singing and dancing/gesturing, alongside words—not unlike the belief that, in ancient Greece, poetry, music, and dance were all fused together.[55] Yet, "The Great Preface" was written centuries later around first century AD; by that time the original musical and dancing components of the collected poems had been long lost, and Confucianism already elevated to the status as the official, orthodox ideology.[56] Given this background, one of the goals of "The Great Preface" was to formulate a poetics that establishes the dominant status of words in the Confucian literary orthodoxy over music and dance (both of which had been considered as integral to poetry)—a goal opposite to Martin's to promote dance against language.

Partly because of this long Confucian literary tradition that privileged words over other mediums, "poetry" gradually became associated predominantly with "words" in Chinese.[57] In contrast, dance, now semantically separated from poetry, was exiled to the margins (even more so than music/singing), as some residual unconscious. This marginalization of dance in the expressive hierarchy is also reflected in contemporary Chinese dance historiography. According to the official narrative, by the late imperial era (the Ming and Qing dynasties, 1368–1911), dance, as an independent art form that once enjoyed its heyday in the Tang dynasty (618–907 AD), had declined and eventually disappeared from China's "historical stage" and become largely absorbed into *xiqu* 戲曲 (traditional Chinese theaters), and the practitioners of *xiqu* and folk arts "who were good at dancing" became the major carriers of the marginalized Chinese dance tradition.[58]

Ironically, in the contemporary Chinese dance field, dance scholars and critics often quote the same passage from "The Great Preface," which was originally intended to marginalize dance, as a theoretical justification of dance as a privileged art form.[59] This reversion is made possible by the very logic underlying the construction of the Confucian poetics, which is predicated on negativity—the inadequacy of artistic mediums, including words. Words, though occupying the central position, *cannot* monopolize meaning because of their inadequacy: as flowing from the center to the margins across various mediums, "emotion/intention" *spills over* in a cascading manner. It is this "spillover" that gives the margins an edge that could be used to deconstruct the Confucian concentric order and subvert the center. In the modern reinterpretation of this text, only with the final unconscious participation of hands and feet can the mind be able to communicate its deepest urge through the body. Compared with other artistic mediums, dance represents the most heightened and general life response that transcends words and other art forms. For example, in *Wudao biaoyan xinlixue* 舞蹈表演心理學 (The psychology of dance performance), a 2013 textbook of the Beijing Dance Academy—the most prestigious academic institution of dance in China, the author states that

> The body is the carrier of the subject, and also the only hinge that connects the subject and the object. Hence . . . the body is expression, the body is the most expressive [medium], and the expressive power of the body surpasses all. As it is said, *since words are inadequate, hands swing and feet stamp [to express] it.*[60]

That is, in the contemporary Chinese discursive field of dance, the power struggle between words and the body overthrows the Confucian poetic order from within. Moreover, it is the theory of modern dance that partly motivates this reinterpretation—this quote and a discussion of Martin's conception of kinesthesia appear on the same page of the textbook. The valorization in modern dance of the body in motion and its connection to the unconscious furnishes the theoretical ground for reversing the order in the Confucian concentric hierarchy: due to the inadequacy of all other mediums, especially language, the distance between dance and emotion, which is depicted as the greatest among all mediums, is now paradoxically used to justify the status of dance as the "last resort"—and thus the most fundamental and immediate means—for expressing emotion.

However, modern dance in China, unlike its Western modernist counterpart, never truly generated systematic discourse on the autonomy of the genre until the 1980s. Rather, it was almost always entangled with other mediums and genres, to varying extents, in both practice and discourse, as if foreshadowed by the Confucian poetic order: regardless of their relative status in the hierarchy, all mediums must work *together* to achieve the full expression of emotion. Instead of treating this "lack" of autonomy as a sign of "underdeveloped" modernism in the Chinese case of modern dance, a major goal of this book is to demonstrate and explain, both historically and theoretically, that this intermediality or transmediality was an effective yet friction-fraught strategy adopted by Chinese dancer-choreographers to formulate and promote dance modernism during the first eight decades of the twentieth-century, a time in China characterized by a deep sense of urgency due to successive wars, revolutions, national crises, and socio-political upheavals.

Choreography and Writing

Like other studies of dance history of earlier eras, the dances and dancing bodies under examination are recorded primarily in the form of text and secondarily in visual representations.[61] For most of the dance works discussed, with a few exceptions (like Yu's *Sword Dance*), there are only photographic documentation and verbal descriptions and testimonies that help preserve some information of their performances as historical, now absent, events. Therefore, in some sense, this is a dance history without dance—or a re-textualization of dances and bodies preserved in textual and other forms. Even though this is common practice in dance history, upon which many dance scholars have reflected, it is worthwhile to briefly revisit this paradox that entails the problematization of the word/dance binary, since this transmediality is a main theme throughout the book.[62] The key lies in the conceptual connection between another pair: choreography and writing, the simultaneously corporeal and intellectual laboring processes that generate and/or record the respective signs.

Throughout the book, I use the word "choreography" in two senses: first, the artistic process of composing and arranging the movement of a body or bodies in space-time, or the resulting composition of this process (choreography as composing/composed dance); second, the original meaning of the word—the method and process of writing dance in symbolic notations, or the resulting written notation of such a process (choreography as writing/written dance).[63] Both forms of choreography—as composing/composed dance and as writing/written dance—are the objects of study in this book, and both forms, especially the second, have an affinity with the concepts of writing and texts.[64]

Even for the first form, choreography may still be conceptualized as the art of "writing" meaning onto space-time through the kinetic laboring body, with dance being the ephemeral trace of writing.[65] Jacques Derrida regards choreography as a special form of generalized writing: "we say 'writing' for all that gives rise to an inscription in general, whether it is literal or not and even if what it distributes in space is alien to the voice: cinematography, *choreography*, of course, but also pictorial, musical, sculptural 'writing.' "[66] Mark Franko also argues that the possibility of conceiving choreography as writing is enabled by the connection that "the very concept of dance depends in some measure on the notion of a *trace* in which the body, language as sign, and the gesture of drawing coincide as the very definition of what *dancing* means."[67] It is in this sense that writing dance history without dance through this transmediality can be fruitful in revealing the inter-dynamics between different mediums.

Writing may also be conceptualized as an act of choreography. Dance scholar SanSan Kwan justifies writing as a special form of choreography by borrowing anthropologist Sally Ann Ness's idea that writing is in some sense a somatic process of "dis-membering" and "re-membering" the bodily experiences of the writer, and thus a form of choreography.[68] Just like choreography, writing in general is, in Kwan's words, a "piercing together of various moving parts into a consciously designed whole" in the narrative space-time.[69] Susan Foster demonstrates performatively that "choreographic devices"—such as the "bodied" experiences and memories of the writer and the order, sequence, and structure of dance—can be used as the "organizational force" and "template" for shaping, or "choreographing," the writing about dance.[70] That is, the text of a dance history may be seen as a product of iterative, transmedial (re)choreographing/(re)writing. To challenge the binaries of dance/text and choreography/writing is by no means to reduce one to the other; rather, it is to, in Foster's words, "assume the disparity between the verbal and danced, not only accepting the fact of dance's disappearance but celebrating the opportunity to resurrect it on written page" in an interactive, nonlinear, not one-to-one corresponding way.[71]

This transmediality between dance, text, and other mediums does not just constitute the core theoretical challenge and justification of this book but also has historical and substantive significance, because all the major dancer-choreographers discussed in this book were aware of and explored and exploited this transmediality in various ways. For example, Yu Rongling created her at once "new" and "old" Chinese dance through a transmedial relation with ancient Chinese paintings and traditional theater. Wu Xiaobang developed his "new dance" by bringing modern dance into an intricate intermedial entanglement with literary narrative, music, theater, and Chinese classical philosophical texts. Both Dai Ailian's conception of her Chinese dance and her project of collecting, synthesizing, and disseminating Chinese ethnic dances were ultimately transmediated by written dance notations. As literary and dance scholar Lucia Ruprecht observes, the "gestural imaginary" of dance is "transmitted through discourse, comes to a standstill in media of arrest, and is reset into motion by media of movement."[72]

The primary sources used include (1) the dancer-choreographers' autobiographies (or biographies), writings, photos, and verbal descriptions of their dance works and careers; (2) memoirs of their friends, collaborators, and students; and (3) archives, video recordings (in some rare cases), and relevant newspaper and journal articles in the period under study. The potential retrospective and/or ideology-related biases, errors, and gaps of the first two categories may be, to some extent, balanced and checked by the third. The project's reliance on personal accounts of dancers and those close to them as primary texts is partly due to the difficulty of recovering from conventional historical sources transnational and intercultural encounters of the early twentieth century, especially those involving young people and the transient art form of dance. However, this is also a deliberate choice. The dancer-choreographers' personal narratives provide a "first-person" perspective, often retrospective, on their strategies and trajectories—both corporeal and discursive—to establish, negotiate, and justify the identities of themselves and their dance within different challenging historical environments. This agency of dancer-choreographers and its limits, inseparable from their personal experiences and sense-making, are a major focus of study for this interpretive, not just empirical, project. Moreover, commentaries and memoirs of spectators and those close to the dancer-choreographers—which corroborate, complement, or contradict the first-person accounts—are not seen merely as other fragmentary, subjective, and distorted versions of representation of the staged, historical, and life events under study. Rather, those texts in some sense have become part of the events. Commentators, argues dance scholar Kate Elswit, actively participate in the cultural production, not just reflection, of the performance event, since they draw upon their own widespread varieties of expertise and experience (as writers, composers, actors, painters, or just ordinary spectators) concerning what the staged event is and how it fits into the particular cultural context.[73] Those commentaries are "archives of watching," characterized by "dispersion," registering how a single event proliferates and transforms into "multiple possible responses through a process that is creative, affective, and translative, but always within a constellation of possibilities."[74] This book further applies this observation to the career and life, not just staged, events of the dancer-choreographers, who were in various ways influenced by the avant-garde idea of unifying art and life.

Admittedly, the meanings contained in these texts and photos are unstable and uncertain at best. Yet this limitation needs not be seen as necessarily debilitating, because it constitutes an opportunity to explore the entanglement—transmediation, appropriation, antagonism, or alliance—among dance, texts, and other mediums. Even a historical photograph's "stilling of [dance] movement," according to Ruprecht's interpretation of Walter Benjamin's reading of Bertolt Brecht's epic theater, not only captures but also *performs* a gestural function of dance, which momentarily interrupts movement flow in dance, allows for a suspenseful arrested moment of self-reflection and proliferating possibilities, and thus constitutes the medium's critical potentiality.[75] Through this intermedial cross-mapping and interweaving, despite the partiality and uncertainty in each single medium, one may discover some visual or mental paradigms shared across mediums—as Brandstetter puts it, "the *patterns* that form the deep underlying structure that shapes the foundation of dance" may become apparent when they overlap and intersect with comparable phenomena in other textual and artistic mediums.[76] This transmedial "reading" of dance (as shifting bodily signs in the nonverbal symbolic realm) and of literary text (as systems of signs seeking to signify bodily presence in its representational deferment) could bridge the performative and the discursive, the corporeal and the textual.[77]

Chapter Outlines

The historical period covered by this book spans from the turn of the century to the 1980s. It starts with the travel of Yu Rongling's modern dance from Paris to the Late Qing imperial court of Empress Dowager Cixi, and its adaptation and evolution into the, at once modern and classical, "Chinese dance," which evidences the powerful influence of modern dance as a border-crossing bodily medium. The book (excluding the epilogue) ends with Dai Ailian's long transnational, transcultural, and transmedial journey of promoting the dance notation system Labanotation in China, using it to record, study, and adapt ethnic-minority dances in China's borderlands, and disseminating the written Chinese dances on the international discursive stage of dance studies in the 1990s. That is, in the book's narrative order, the balance of the word-dance relation shifts from tilting toward "dance" at the beginning to tilting toward "words" (dance notation) at the end. In between, the book demonstrates that the power struggles among different individuals, art forms, parties (or Parties), discourses, and ideologies make the tilting of the balance exhibit a "teetering" pattern. However, this book is not a century-long comprehensive history of modern dance in China, but instead covers key historical moments, individuals, organizations, and dance works in thematic chapters. Yet it takes up critical questions about the word-dance relation in a roughly chronological order, which emphasizes the continuity of this history from the Late Qing, the Republican period, to the socialist era.

Chapter 1 follows the international travel of Yu Rongling in the early 1900s, who transformed Isadora Duncan's "Greek dance" into its Chinese counterpart. It shows that, on the one hand, Western modern dance, at its very beginning, incorporated the "Oriental body" within itself, rather than simply treating it as some exotic other. On the other hand, Yu's "Chinese dance" cannot be understood as some "invented tradition" created by the local as some "old" way to resist the "new" way imposed by colonial powers, because it exposes and exploits the paradox inherent in the very logic of dance modernism: modern dance is, in the words of Yu, "both inventing the new and reviving the old." The chapter further demonstrates that this paradox is caused by a particular mode of corporeal modernity underlying the philosophy of early modern dance, which is characterized by the blurred boundaries between the past and the future, the universal and the national. This mode of corporeal modernity enabled early modern dance and the cosmopolitan women performing it to cross various borders of race, culture, nation, and time. However, it can also be appropriated and re-articulated by the local to handle anxieties about perceived differences and particularities that sprang from all these border-crossings within a global colonial hierarchy. Therefore, this chapter contributes to the rethinking of the origin of modernism and feminism as global and multiple, instead of exclusively Western, in nature and of the evolving late Qing court as part of global modernity, rather than simply a "backward" and "reclusive" monarchy.

Chapter 2 examines the life, career, choreographies, and performances of Wu Xiaobang in Tokyo, Shanghai, and beyond in the 1930s and 1940s and his strategies to adapt the theory and methodology of the central European modern dance he learned in Japan into "China's new dance." While chapter 1 focuses on the relatively static concept of corporeality, chapter 2 leverages the more dynamic concept of *kinesthesia*, a word combining movement (*kine*) and sensation (*aesthesia*), which refers to the contagious nature of bodily movement and the human consciousness of movement. The theoretical significance of kinesthesia lies in its potential of transforming the spectators off stage into quasi-participants of the performance on stage and thus blurs the distinction between the "active" performer(s) and the "passive" audience, which had political and practical implications for the role of modern dance in an age of mass mobilization and war. Moreover, early modern dance often promoted kinesthesia as a bodily means to challenge the hegemonic system of language- and representation-based paradigms. However, Wu did not pit kinesthesia against language or narrative, but instead incorporated elements of these, along with properties of other artistic mediums, into his dance. I argue that this strategy of transmediation, which I call "reverse integration," was partly caused by the status of modern dance being a "latecomer" in the Chinese field of other more well-established modern art forms, striving to establish its legitimacy and independence in relation to those more powerful arts. It was also the result of the somewhat conflicting dual goals of modern dance in China—to position itself as an urban high art, on the one hand, and, on the other hand, as a useful tool for mass enlightenment and mobilization during a time of national crisis, revolution, and total war.

Chapter 3 follows Wu's artistic endeavor into the late 1950s of the early socialist era. While the previous chapters focus more on the transnational, transcultural, and transmedial aspects of dance, this chapter pays particular attention to its "trans-temporal" dimension. By that time, Wu's new dance had fallen out of political favor due to its "bourgeois ideology." As a response, Wu developed "resistive" strategies to continue his modernist endeavor in the socialist regime. Specifically, he looked into Chinese literary and philosophical classics of the past to create the paradoxical "classical new dance" 古典新舞 (*gudian xin wu*) as a disguised haven to harbor his modernist ideas. Wu's classical new dance was the antithesis of Chinese classical dance that was contemporaneously being developed and based mainly on Chinese theatrical tradition. The invention of classical dance was part of a much larger national project, demanded by the Chinese Communist Party, to create "national forms" in literature and arts by resorting to traditional and folk forms. One of the main purposes of this cultural-political project was to use the national forms in the making as a means to interpellate the bourgeois and West-leaning intellectuals and artists into subjection to the new regime. Wu's classical new dance was a circuitous modernist critique of both invented tradition and national forms, and thus a deflection of the interpellation of the state, by denying any codified form in dance—the very premise underlying national forms and invented tradition. Moreover, Wu also appropriated the millennia-old, Chinese intellectual ideal of "reclusion" in his classical new dance to construct an individual-based, spiritual utopia characterized by a slow temporality and reclusive spatiality to resist the collectivist, material utopian movement of the Great Leap Forward Campaign (1958–1960) with an ever-accelerating temporality and all-encompassing spatiality. However, this resistance is conflicted in nature: Wu's expansive embracement of spirituality is at the cost of the body's physicality in his dance. Therefore, this chapter sheds light on the possibilities and limits of the agency of artists in negotiating the relative independence of art within and against the ideological control of the socialist state.

Chapter 4 shifts the focus to Dai Ailian, the first dancer who had devotedly collected ethnic minority dances in the southwestern borderlands of China and further adapted them for stage in the mid-1940s. In the existing historiography, Dai's life and career are subsumed within a triumphant, linear narrative of "homecoming" and "root-searching" through dance. A consequence is that the account of the origin of China's modern ethnic dances has become a predominantly nationalist and nativist one, predicated on a "Chinese identity" coherent and stable across space-time. To challenge this perspective, building on and extending Emily Wilcox's analysis of Dai's diasporic experiences, this chapter recasts Dai's life and career and the origin of China's modern ethnic dance into an alternative framework of "multi-diaspora" along the geopolitical borders between "empires" (the British Empire and China). Dai's multi-diasporic anxieties and aspirations, as an undercurrent, capitalized and rode on the nationalist mainstream and vice versa, yet often with a vector of diverging momentums. This multi-diasporic undercurrent suggests that the emergence of Chinese ethnic dance in the mid-1940s was not just a nationalist response to the political imperatives of China. It was also an outgrowth of the extensive global circuit of intercultural transactions conditioned by the world colonial hierarchy. However, dance per se turned out to be inadequate in addressing the precarity of Dai's multi-diasporic experiences. Ethnic dances, in the case of Dai, must be first (trans) mediated by labanotation to enter Dai's negotiation of gender, racial, and national identities on both domestic and international stages. That is, Dai's adaptation of ethnic dances was fundamentally informed and mediated by the theory, methodology, and symbols of modern dance, and by distributing

Chinese ethnic dances in Labanotation on the international stage, Dai for the first time expanded Laban's vision of "a literature of dance" into "a world literature of dances."

The epilogue introduces Guo Mingda, a male dancer-choreographer and theorist of modern dance. It shows that Guo's modern dance endeavors provided an important "(anti-)American link" that connected the end of modern/new dance in socialist China in 1960 and the revival of modern dance in the early 1980s, with the Cultural Revolution (1966–1976) in between.

In summary, on the one hand, in referencing the concentric Confucian poetic order, the narrative progression of the chapters roughly follows a "centripetal," margin-to-center route on the dance-word dimension, starting from weighing toward the dancing body at the beginning, shifting to the intertwinement among dance, words, and other mediums in the middle, and to weighing toward the word-like written dance notation at the end. On the other hand, on the geo-spatial dimension, the book follows the opposite "centrifugal," center-to-margin route: although almost all chapters cover transnational travels of dancers and dances, in the domestic part, the book starts from the Forbidden City in the imperial capital Beijing in the north, moving to coastal cities in the east and south, to inland cities in the south and west, and to the remote borderlands in the southwest, with Beijing being a major center, among others, of gravity.

1

Traveling "Princess" and Dancing "Diplomat"

Yu Rongling, Corporeal Modernity, and Isadora Duncan

Paris, 1901, shortly after the Exposition Universelle and the Boxer Uprising (1899–1900), Yu Rongling 裕容齡 (ca. 1888–1973), around age fourteen, the fifth and youngest child of Yu Geng (aka Yu Keng 裕庚), the Qing minister to France, started to take "Greek dance" classes with the twenty-three-year-old Isadora Duncan (ca. 1877–1927), which would last intermittently for about two years.[1] Duncan, who arrived in Paris from London a year earlier, just opened her dance studio and began to teach dance lessons (figure 1.1). By that time, Duncan had commenced her experiment on "Greek dance" (later known as early modern dance), often performing in the semi-private salons of her patrons, a close circle of wealthy noble American Grecophile expatriates.[2] Though yet to make a name for her dance, Duncan had already become a controversial figure in the Parisian upper-class society, as she danced in ancient Greek-style tunic that highlighted "her lightly-clad, bare-limbed female body."[3]

Sometime around 1902, Yu Rongling took a major role, as a certain "goddess" from Greek mythology, in one of Duncan's Greek dramatic dances performed either publicly or semi-publicly in Paris.[4] A teenaged girl from the Manchu court of the Qing Empire—characteristically depicted by the Western press as backward, conservative, and xenophobic—danced gracefully as a Greek goddess, barefoot and thinly clad, in front of a Parisian upper-class audience. This dancing cosmopolitan figure, characterized by temporal, racial, and geo-cultural hybridity, could be norm-defying for an audience who at the turn of the century had just witnessed the end of the Victorian era. Note that about a mere year earlier, when Duncan first performed in Parisian salons, her solo body and simple tunic shocked her unprepared elite audiences "accustomed to very different styles of dance and performance"

When Words Are Inadequate. Nan Ma, Oxford University Press. © Oxford University Press 2023. DOI: 10.1093/oso/9780197575307.003.0002

Figure 1.1 Isadora Duncan dancing in the Amphitheatre of Dionysus, Athens, 1904. Photographed by Raymond Duncan. Image courtesy of the Jerome Robbins Dance Division, The New York Public Library for the Performing Arts, Astor, Lenox, and Tilden Foundations.

(such as Anna Pavlova's classical ballet and Loïe Fuller's skirt dance), let alone the broader audiences at high art theaters.[5]

In association with Duncan, who made significant contributions to first-wave feminism by establishing herself, through solo expression, as "a type for the independent, creative, 'new woman' of modernism,"[6] such a dancing image of Yu Rongling would seem even more out of place back in the patriarchal Qing Empire, ruled, ironically, by a powerful matriarch, Empress

Dowager Cixi 慈禧太后 (1835–1908). Many upper-class Chinese women then still stayed mostly in the inner quarters of households, with their feet bound. *Nüjie zhong* 女界钟 (The Women's Bell), the book that marks the beginning of the systematic advocacy for women's rights in China, would be published by Jin Tianhe 金天翮 (1873–1947) a year later in 1903. Qiu Jin 秋瑾 (1875–1907), the famous nationalist-feminist revolutionary, would not travel to Japan until 1904, and her friend Lü Bicheng 呂碧城 (1883–1943), the well-known cosmopolitan feminist, would begin her journey to the United States and Europe as late as in 1918. He-Yin Zhen 何殷震 (ca. 1884–1920?), a prominent anarchist-feminist writer, would go to Tokyo in 1907 and found the Society for the Restoration of Women's Rights in the same year.[7] Fictions featuring well-educated activist Chinese "new women" traveling around the globe would not flourish until a couple of years later—for example, the popular novel *Niehai hua* 孽海花 (Flower in a Sea of Karma), would be written by Zeng Pu 曾樸 (1871–1935) in 1904.

In 1903, because of the Yu children's cosmopolitan background, mastery of foreign languages and knowledge, and good reputation among the trusted Qing ministers, Empress Dowager Cixi ordered Rongling and her elder sister Deling 德齡 (1885–1944, known as Princess Der Ling in the West) to serve as "ladies in waiting" and in fact personal consultants on foreign affairs. In the imperial palace, Rongling stayed for about four years (and Deling two years).[8] The Yu sisters experienced the last days of the crumbling empire at its very heart, and they formed a close relationship with Cixi (figure 1.2). The empress dowager was so fond of the energetic cosmopolitan girls that she bestowed upon them the tile of *junzhu* 郡主—a princess-rank title.[9]

However, Rongling and her sister were not mere onlookers; what they brought with them into the Forbidden Palace was part of a world that was still quite foreign to the people living in the palace (mainly women and eunuchs), including Western fashion, etiquette, knowledge, technology, thoughts, and arts. Among these, Cixi was fascinated by Western dance.[10] According to Deling's account, after hearing out the outline of Duncan's philosophy with great interest, Cixi expressed her enthusiasm in meeting Duncan in person.[11] Although this hoped-for meeting never materialized, the Yu sisters did create some sort of connection between the two famous women—who might seem to live in two different worlds—in the rise of global modernities around the turn of the century.

Knowing that Rongling was good at Western dancing, Cixi asked Rongling to study and revive the Chinese dance tradition that had long been lost in

Figure 1.2 From left to right: Louisa Pierson, Yu Deling (Princess Der Ling), Cixi, Yu Rongling, Summer Palace, Beijing, ca. 1903. Photographed by Yu Xunling. Image courtesy of the Freer Gallery of Art and Arthur M. Sackler Gallery Archives, Smithsonian Institution.

history. Under Cixi's patronage, Rongling created several works of "Chinese dance." Rongling performed these dance works, along with Western dances, in front of Cixi and other royal and noble women and court ladies, which greatly pleased the empress dowager.[12] Rongling carried on this project of reviving the Chinese dance, on and off, as a personal effort, after the fall of the Qing dynasty, at least into the late 1920s. This may be seen as the inception of a much larger and enduring national project of inventing the Chinese classical dance.[13]

Then, why, in the case of dance, could Yu Rongling—a girl from the "conservative," "backward," and "misogynistic" Far East—stand so naturally at the international frontier (and center) of avant-garde art in Paris at the turn of the century, when, in other fields of art and literature back in China, the influence of modernism and feminism, though having germinated, had yet to burgeon at full speed?[14] Why was Cixi, stereotyped as the narrow-minded xenophobic old empress dowager, so fascinated by Western dance in general and Duncan's modern dance in particular that she enthusiastically sponsored Rongling's initial effort to create its Chinese counterpart? Is this "Chinese dance" a continued development of modern dance guided by its (proto)modernist and feminist ideology, or an abrupt departure and retreat from this ideology into the illusion of a long-lost national tradition? How does the transcultural metamorphosis of Rongling (and her sister) and her dance inform our understanding of the origin of modernism and feminism as global and multiple, rather than exclusively Western, in nature?[15]

The key to the answers, as I argue, lies in a particular mode of "corporeal modernity" represented by Duncan's philosophy of early modern dance. I borrow the term corporeal modernity from Fran Martin and Ari Larissa Heinrich's formulation in *Embodied Modernities: Corporeality, Representation, and Chinese Cultures*.[16] The original concept refers to, first, how representations of the body in various media played an important role in the discourse on modernity in twentieth-century China, and second, how modern science, technology, and ideology shaped the representations of the body and body culture in China. Here, I extend this conceptualization of corporeal modernity to further emphasize that corporeality is not just about the body or body culture per se, or the representations thereof, but also an *interpersonal-level* communicative channel and site of perception, articulation, and negotiation during interactions between individual bodies—a corporeal process fundamental to the formation of the modern subject in the colonial or semi-colonial context.

The concept of corporeal modernity is pertinent to this study for two reasons. First, Duncan's feminist philosophy of modern dance, which had great influence on Yu Rongling and her choreography, is predicated on a particular mode of corporeal modernity. Instead of basing her conception of the human body mainly on modern medical and anatomical knowledge, Duncan paradoxically goes back in time to search for the Greek ideal of the body and further graft that ideal onto the theory of evolution. While existing dance scholarship has extensively examined in Duncan's dance philosophy and choreography both the bi-directional temporality and the role of evolution theory, this study further demonstrates how a bi-directional temporality that points to the past and the future *at once* is compatible with the unidirectional, linear logic of evolution.[17] As elaborated later, on the one hand, the "masculine" theory of evolution, which supposedly applies to all organic bodies, supplies a universal corporeal-temporal basis for the (proto-)modernist—with, paradoxically, an "antimodern-classicist" twist— and feminist philosophy of Duncan's dance. On the other hand, Duncan imposes feminist agency (or "will," in Duncan's, Nietzsche's, and the evolutionist Ernest Haeckel's term) upon the trajectory of evolution, by twisting the unidirectional temporal order of the evolution of the (female) body, first backward, to the particular locus of ancient Greece as a middle point, then forward, to link the past to the future. In such a two-step switching, Duncan's appropriation of Haeckel's evolution theory can accommodate bidirectionality in a unidirectional temporal framework, preserving a linear logic of evolutionary progress while creating room for feminist agency. The resulting corporeal modernity is characterized by the blurred boundaries between the past and the future, the universal and the particular.

Second, this mode of corporeal modernity enables early modern dance and the women performing it to cross various borders of race, culture, nation, and time by leveraging the associated spatio-temporal universality and evolutionary "truth." However, it can also be easily appropriated and re-articulated by the local as a means to handle the anxieties about perceived differences and particularities that spring from all these border-crossings happening under a global colonial hierarchy viewed more and more in terms of social Darwinism, by providing a possibility, though perhaps illusive, of exerting agency over the course of evolution.

Therefore, this mode of corporeal modernity underlying the fascinating polymorphic images and international travels of Yu Rongling and her modern dance provides a unique prism to examine one aspect of the final "clashes"—non-violent, permeating, generative, yet full of anxieties—between the West and the very core of the Qing Empire, namely, Cixi's court. At that time, what the retrospective term "modernity" denotes was perceived in China more as relative geopolitical and cultural differences under an imposed colonial hierarchy than as a universal temporal division between the backward and the advanced, the old and the new, a division to be finally reified by the May Fourth Movement almost two decades later. The main players involved in these peaceful clashes under study were predominantly women, be they Chinese or Western, Manchu or Han, or in-between. Their firsthand experiences thus registered the responses, dilemmas, creativity, and agency of elite women who once stood close to or at the centers of power. With old worldviews challenged and borders crossed, new views, however blurry and instable, began to take shape. The original perspective of the self could no longer be taken for granted, and the foreign other's point of view must be considered.[18] The cosmopolitan background of Rongling and her sister "lubricated" this dynamic, with their ability to embrace and switch

between multiple identities and perspectives. This generative and transformative process was two-directional, rather than a one-way traffic from the West
to China. Yu Rongling, pupil of Duncan, actively participated in the creation
of Western modern dance and the modernism and feminism it embodied,
while Empress Dowager Cixi, by having the cosmopolitan girls serve at her
inner court, invited part of the Western world into the heart of her empire.

On the one hand, the origin of Western modern dance was not exclusively Western in nature; the early modern dance incorporated the "Oriental
bodies" within it from the very beginning, rather than simply treating them
as some exotic other. On the other hand, the birth of the "Chinese dance" was
not purely Chinese either, but a transnational and transcultural product of
global modernism. Moreover, this modernity of Chinese dance cannot be
entirely explained as some "invented tradition" that the local created as some
"old way" to resist the "new way" imposed by Western colonial powers, because it betrays, appropriates, and exploits the paradoxical nature of modernism in the case of dance: as pointed out by Yu Rongling, modernism is
both "reviving the old" and "creating the new," both highlighting the national and promoting the universal.[19] As demonstrated later, the cosmopolitan experiences and international travels of Yu facilitated the interaction
between Western modern dance and Chinese dance, at once modern and
classical, since their births; the two had been in a competing and mutual-
borrowing, if asymmetric, relationship ever since.

While existing scholarship on late Qing culture has investigated a similar
process happening in the larger late Qing society mainly through the lens of
language and literature, the case of Yu Rongling and her dance highlights its
bodily dimension, which is relatively understudied.[20] The "clashes" addressed
here were, in large part, encounters between different female bodies and were
mediated, first and foremost, through and on the site of bodies, not languages; in fact, language obstacles often existed in international contacts.
Thus, one needs to view and understand the transnational and transcultural
metamorphosis of Yu Rongling and her dance in terms of this corporeality.

This chapter also contributes to the recent revisionist scholarship on the
role of Empress Dowager Cixi as an active facilitator and participant, instead of a reactionary, in the socio-cultural transformation of the late Qing
Empire.[21] More specifically, it extends the line of research on Cixi's engagement in the production of arts—for instance, music, theater, literature, painting, calligraphy, and photography—by including the corporeal
art of dance.[22] Through modern dance, the chapter attempts to establish an

indirect link between Cixi (and her imperial court) and the Western historical avant-garde, modernism, and feminism, and shed light on how Cixi may have conceived the role of dance in the cultural politics of China on the competitive international stage.

The following sections will first highlight the cosmopolitan experiences of Yu Rongling, tracing her transnational and transcultural travels from China to Paris and her experiences of studying and performing modern dance with Isadora Duncan, showing how her hybrid cosmopolitan identity may have been appropriated by both Duncan's (proto-)modernist and feminist ideology and the Parisian audiences' tastes of Oriental exoticism and queer eroticism. By teasing out the relation between Duncan's theory of corporeal modernity and evolution, the chapter demonstrates that Duncan's Hellenistic approach in her early career to modernism and feminism employs a pseudo-atavist logic of modernity, which proposes that the corporeal modernity of the human (especially female) body can only be achieved by going back to the past through the feminist agency of modern dance, and how Yu Rongling's cosmopolitan background fits into this logic. The second half of this chapter follows Yu Rongling's steps from Paris back to Cixi's imperial court, which brought about a series of cultural clashes. Corporeality became a central channel and site for perceiving, understanding, and negotiating these clashes. Situated within this context, the chapter further argues that Yu Rongling and Cixi appropriated the paradoxical logic in the corporeal modernity of Duncan's dance to serve a (proto-)nationalist purpose in the process of creating the "Chinese classical dance," which from the very beginning had been a transnational and transcultural modern product with a temporality pointing to both the past and the future.

Note that this chapter relies heavily on the Yu sisters' memoirs, autobiographies, and biographies, which should not be taken word for word. For example, Deling's *Two Years in the Forbidden City* was published six years after she left Cixi's court and Rongling's *Qing gong suo ji* 清宮瑣記 (Miscellaneous Records of the Qing Palace) almost half a century later. Moreover, Deling's memoirs are all in English and thus influenced by the author's stylized translation and rendition catering to the targeted foreign readership, not to mention her own personal and emotional investments in those memories.[23] Even though I conducted cross-checking among different sources whenever possible, it is more reasonable to treat those primary sources as mediated and mediating texts that are subject to textual analysis, instead of as objective historical records. Nevertheless, it is valuable to see those mediated events and conversations through the subjective eyes of the Yu sisters, because their personal, cosmopolitan experiences mediating between Cixi's court and the West are the very focus of this chapter, and the more or less distorted images in their eyes are also the "object" under study here.

The Cosmopolitan Children

In some sense, Yu Rongling was more "ideal" than the above-mentioned real or fictional late Qing feminist icons in representing the miracle of "total communication," a term used by Ying Hu to denote the speedy and effortless acquisition of foreign languages and knowledge by the heroines in late Qing novels.[24] Total communication was virtually a given fact for Yu Rongling rather than a fictional utopia. All children of the Yu family were multilingual—Rongling herself was fluent in Chinese, English, French, and Japanese at a young age, and about eight years of her childhood were spent abroad, with traveling experiences in Japan and almost all major European countries. Western newspapers widely reported in 1902 that Rongling, as young as at age twelve, started to work as "her father's assistant" at the Qing legation in Paris and "wrote all the important communications which passed between M. Delcasse [Théophile Delcassé, French foreign minister from 1898 to 1905] and the Chinese legation."[25] Even before they left China, the Yu family, as described by one of their foreign acquaintances, was "a noisy family of English-speaking children."[26]

Furthermore, whereas almost all the Chinese feminist icons, real or fictional, were more or less troubled by a feeling of self-loathing due to a deep sense of cultural, racial, and gender inferiority, Rongling and her siblings were radiant with remarkable confidence, which is best demonstrated by the Greek goddess she danced elegantly under the gaze of the Parisian audience. Thus, unlike Lü Bicheng who, as Grace Fong argues, espoused a version of cosmopolitanism that emphasizes the cultivated detachment and distance from any restrictive form of cultural identity and political affiliation, the young Rongling and her siblings represent the other side of cosmopolitanism, as characterized by easy and playful embracing and switching between multiple roles and identities (figure 1.3).[27] Xunling 勛齡, Rongling's elder brother, quickly became a social favorite in the Parisian diplomatic circles due to his European-like physical features and upbringing, and created

Figure 1.3 Yu Rongling (left) and Deling dressed for Carneval in Paris, ca. 1900. Photographed by Charles Chusseau-Flaviens. Image courtesy of the George Eastman House.

a sensation by marrying a French girl.[28] Rongling herself, at that time known as "Miss Nellie Yu-Keng" in the Western press, became a "unique figure in Paris society," who "enjoys a popularity in the French capital that makes her an object of envy to many a young Frenchwomen moving in the same circle of society" and was described by a French newspaper as "a charming Chinese girl who is Parisian in all but name."[29] A 1903 *New York Times* article reports that "Miss Nellie Yu-Keng . . . speaks English and French . . . She is described as extremely pretty and possessing all the charm and grace of a modern Parisienne. [She] can hardly fail to be a popular acquisition to diplomatic society."[30] Another 1904 article in *The Washington Times* says that the Yu sisters "have no horror of the 'foreign devil,' and, indeed, were quite ready to flirt furiously with him when they lived with their mother in Paris, and took Parisian society by storm."[31]

Moreover, unlike those feminist icons, most of whom lived on the margins of the late Qing society (many were "criminals," in fiction or reality, wanted by the government), the Yu family had close connections and direct access to centers of power, both abroad and in China. Due to his charisma, diplomatic craftiness, and foreign-friendliness, Yu Geng gained respect from and maintained a good rapport with the ruling classes and royal houses of Japan and European countries, which also opened the doors for his children to these power centers.[32] As a result, the Yu children had been very active in important diplomatic occasions from a young age. For instance, Deling was received by Emperor Meiji and Empress Haruko of Japan at age eleven, and the whole family, as secret Roman Catholics, was blessed by Pope Leo XIII in an audience particularly arranged for them in the Vatican.[33] The debut party of Deling, at which Rongling was also likely to be present, was hosted by French President Emile Loubert, honoring King Oscar II of Sweden, who announced the young lady's formal entry into society.[34] Back in China, the names of powerful supporters and friends (either Han or Manchu) of the Yu family were also stellar. Among them were Zhang Zhidong 張之洞, Li Hongzhang 李鴻章, Ronglu 榮祿, Prince Qing 慶親王, and, behind all these, the ultimate ruler Empress Dowager Cixi.[35]

This unique combination of atypical "traits" among Rongling and her siblings was a direct outgrowth of their unusual family background. Rongling is widely recognized as the "first Chinese who studied Japanese and Euro-American dance" in the Chinese dance historiography.[36] However, what is suppressed by this alleged "Chineseness" is her complicated lineage and cultural identity. Rongling's father Yu Geng was an elite member of the hereditary Han-martial Plain White Banner (*Hanjun zheng bai qi* 漢軍正白旗) with probably both Manchu and Han ancestors, a secretly baptized Christian, a pro-West reformist, and an open-mined and tolerant father who, according to Deling, admitted that at heart "I am more like a foreigner"—an attitude more or less shared by his children.[37] He insisted his young daughters receive the same education as their brothers, learning Chinese classics and studying Western languages and knowledge with foreign missionaries,

with seemingly more weight placed on the latter (Rongling's literacy in foreign languages seems to be at a higher level than classical Chinese).[38] It seems
that Yu Geng had a cosmopolitan vision for his daughters' futures.

Besides a "heretic" father, Rongling and her siblings also had an unusual mother. Louisa Pierson, the beloved wife of Yu Geng, was a Eurasian
born probably out of wedlock, daughter of a "mysterious" American merchant from Boston, Massachusetts, who owned a business in Shanghai.[39]
Therefore, the cosmopolitan spirit of the Yu sisters was partly cultivated by
their strong-willed parents with a hybrid cultural and racial background,
and the Yu sisters, throughout their lives, continued to consciously maintain
this cosmopolitan image through self-promotion and self-stylization in the
forms of writing, public speech, and choreography. In fact, the experiences
of the Yu family, though far from representative of the average Chinese
household, were an embodiment of a larger historical process of various
border-crossings—race, ethnicity, culture, and nationality—that had been
happening in the late Qing world, which was characterized by a severe imbalance of power. The international travels of Rongling and her siblings
throughout their childhood was a direct consequence of the disastrous
failures of the Qing Empire in wars against colonial powers. Yu Geng was
first appointed as the Qing minister to Japan (1895–1899) to deal with the
aftermath of the First Sino-Japanese War (1894–1895), and then the minister
to France (1899–1903) in the wake of the Boxer Uprising, which brought his
family to Paris, where they bore the brunt of the diplomatic crisis engendered
by the bloody upheavals at home.[40] These international experiences, together
with their unique family background, shaped Rongling and her siblings into
cosmopolitan children.

Dancing in Paris with Isadora

Yu Geng did succeed in bringing his cosmopolitan vision for his daughters
into reality. Louisa, due to her taste in fashions and arts, American lineage,
and diplomatic status, had wide social connections with the "vaguely demi-
monde artist-aristocrat circles" in Paris.[41] It was through these connections
that the Yu family quickly blended themselves into the Parisian society,
making acquaintance at parties with painters, writers, composers, and finally
the famous modern dancer Isadora Duncan. Ignoring the warnings given by
the Parisian "society leaders" about the controversial reputation of Duncan

and her dance, Louisa chose to send her daughters to Duncan's dance studio rather than other "safer" options like ballet schools, because she was determined to expose her daughters to the most up-to-date trends of arts and fashions in the world.[42]

Rongling and her sister Deling were among the very first students with whom Duncan experimented her new "Greek" philosophy of dance creation and education being developed around the turn of the century.[43] During the two or three years (1901–1903) when the Yu sisters intermittently studied and danced with Duncan, the female bodies were a constant focus of mutual gaze, perception, and conversation between the two parties involved.[44] Those years were crucial to Duncan and her modern dance, because it was during this period that she created her first mature modern dance works, established a coherent theory for her modern dance, and started to gain international fame. Thus, the bodily experiences of Rongling and Deling, who witnessed and participated in this process, provide a lens to examine the origin of Western modern dance, which incorporated Oriental bodies (actually with mixed lineage, as in the case of the Yu sisters) within it, rather than constructing them purely as some exotic other standing for what the self is not. This incorporation was, as demonstrated below, through careful selection and investment.

Although part of the reason why Duncan offered dance classes in Paris was to make her economic ends meet, she maintained her "idiosyncratic" standard in selecting students. On the first day of class, Duncan led Rongling and Deling, together with other more than twenty girls who were all prospective students, to run in circles in her dance studio, accompanied by the piano played by Duncan's mother. Rongling was asked to stop after just finishing the first round. She became nervous, thinking that she had been eliminated in the process, but it turned out later that she and her sister had passed Duncan's test. Duncan offered to teach the Yu sisters in private lessons, rather than in regular classes.[45] The Yu sisters' descriptions of Duncan's method and criteria for selecting pupils are consistent with both Duncan's basis of choreography, "derived from running, skipping, and other common movements,"[46] and her "aesthetic gymnastic" trainings received during her childhood in Oakland, California, which "included dancelike exercises including skipping, follow-stepping, change-stepping, and galloping."[47] All these activities were rooted in Delsartism, a umbrella term capturing a variety of "physical culture" practices, "from elocution to gymnastics to statue-posing," which were imported to and became widely popular in the United States in the late

nineteenth century and can all be loosely traced back to the French performance theorist François Delsarte (1811–1871).[48]

Rongling was talented in dance, which had been manifest since a very
young age, when she spontaneously danced to the music played by one
of her language teachers.[49] However, there might be something else, in
addition to her talent, that helped the Yu sisters easily pass Duncan's test.
As Manchu girls, Rongling and Deling were not allowed to have their
feet bound, and because of their father's tolerance, the energetic and active girls often engaged in such bold activities and mischief as climbing
trees and wading in ponds.[50] Duncan, by observing their way of running,
may have been impressed by this boldness and physical energy, agility,
and coordinated ability, which were in accord with Duncan's modern (yet
paradoxically "classist") and feminist vision of the natural and healthy female body.

The selection did not stop there. After the Yu sisters were admitted to
Duncan's class, Deling recalled, Duncan closely examined them "as a sci-
entist studies the antics of newly discovered creatures."[51] Duncan was
contemplating how to fit the Oriental bodies into her Greek dance. Before
long Duncan made her decision: Rongling, who was "taller, more willowy,
and more conventionally beautiful" than Deling, was "more appropriate
for Duncan's 'Greek interpretations,'" while the plumper Deling was to be
assigned other roles in future performances, such as a Pan-like figure, possibly a dancing role in some version of Duncan's choreography *Pan and Echo*
(ca. 1903).[52]

The Yu sisters, together with other two girls who also passed Duncan's
test, began to take dance classes with Duncan.[53] The class met three times
a week, one and a half hours each time, divided into three sections.[54] Due
to Duncan's frequent international travel during the period and her own
admission that "she was not a teacher," many of the lessons were probably
taught by Duncan's elder sister Elizabeth, who had been deeply involved in
Duncan's dance career.[55] Then, the greatest strengths of Duncan's teaching
were her inspiring personality and the charismatic presence of her own
body. As remembered by Deling, during the classes she found it "difficult
not to go into rhapsodies over the glorious body of Duncan."[56] Rongling,
even more than half a century later, could still vividly recall with admira-
tion a scene of Duncan's dancing body—"Duncan, in her white tunic with
a tint of light green, . . . as if a beauty dances trippingly in the moonlight,
just like a natural painting, making us enthralled and longing."[57]

While the entrance test was about running, the dance training started with walking. Duncan taught the girls how to walk up stairs gracefully, presumably in a "natural," rather than affected, manner. Based on the Yu sisters' descriptions, the training seems to start from dance moves not far from daily body movements, such as rhythmic walking, running, jumping, and posing, which is consistent with Duncan's emphasis on natural body movement and matches Duncan's own teaching notes.[58] This basic training stage lasted for about a year to "soften" the girls' bodies until they gained "absolute control" of them.[59]

The training was by no means "natural" or effortless—it was more like military drilling. The hard-working Duncan explained to each girl her mistakes in each move and asked her to repeat until perfection. To ensure this, Duncan broke down a single dance move into a series of poses and, just like the technique of slow motion in cinematography, asked the girls to swing "gradually from one pose to the other," insisting that they "must fall instantly into the exact pose," a training method called "posing"—or more precisely, "statue-posing" or "living statues"—which was a hallmark of Delsartean practice at that time.[60] Duncan "spared no effort or expense" to bring the point home to the girls that to dance and pose elegantly "means to practice, practice . . . until the head aches and the heart aches, and even the soul perspires with the endless effort. For a single awkward posture is . . . monstrous. Even the people in the last row can see *that*!"[61] To make her point vivid, Duncan often let the Yu sisters observe her regular classes from the perspective of audience, to see how she pointed out and corrected the mistakes of each student.[62] Therefore, as recalled by Deling, "[a] thousand beginnings, all wrong, until finally we caught the right one, which we probably forgot again when the next day came, but gradually, through labor and heartache, mastering the little things that led, in their sum total, to mastery of ourselves."[63] That is, in order to appear "natural" and "improvised" in the Duncan-style dancing to create an illusion of "spontaneity," one has to go through long-term, painstaking technical repetition to internalize those movements as "second nature"—a Duncan paradox well documented by dance historians.[64]

Probably after the first stage of training, Duncan started to let the girls to engage in "real dancing." As Deling recalled, instead of molding every student according to a predetermined standard movement repertoire as in ballet training, Duncan "created dances for her pupils, building the dance around the individual," which finally led to coherent dance works such as the "Greek dramatic dance" depicted at the beginning of the chapter.[65] Deling's observation confirms Duncan's documented emphasis on preserving "a creative individuality" for each student, even when they are dancing together, "forming part of a whole, under group inspiration."[66]

According to Deling, Duncan sometimes took her students to the Louvre and Versailles to study the "sculptured works of the masters," as an important means to reinforce the ideas of "perfect poses" she taught in class. The figures of human bodies were often the main topic of conversations during their wandering around. Duncan would explain to the girls "every important detail" of the masterpieces, "over and over again, seemingly without end." Deling once told Duncan that she wished she could see Duncan's body taking the place of the great naked statues. Duncan replied humorously: "I'd like to have their fashions generally adopted. You know how I feel about clumsy conventional clothes!"[67] On another occasion, Duncan also told the girls that "I do not *live* in ordinary dress. I cover my body because the law demands it. Silly, the law!"[68]

Then, how should we understand Duncan's "Nudism" in her philosophy of Greek dance, and the role of the Oriental bodies incorporated in it? What are the particular mode of corporeal modernity and the underlying power relations embodied in this transnational and transcultural origin of modern dance? What did the spatially and temporally hybrid figure of Rongling—a thinly clad girl from the Far East dancing as a Greek goddess in front of a Parisian audience—mean to Duncan, the audience, and the girls themselves? The clues may be found in Duncan's manifesto of her early modern dance *The Dance of the Future*.[69]

The Dance of the Future and the Body of the Orient

The Dance of the Future is a public speech delivered by Duncan in Berlin in 1903, in which she for the first time systematically presented her philosophy of modern dance. As the time of the speech coincides with the ending of the Yu sisters' three-year study with Duncan, *The Dance of the Future* may be seen as a summary of Duncan's theoretical contemplation on the pedagogy and choreography of modern dance during that three-year period preceding the speech. Therefore, it sheds light onto the role of Rongling and Deling, and the Oriental body they represented, in the origin of modern dance.

Duncan's philosophy of modern dance brought forth a particular mode of corporeal modernity based on evolutionism. Unlike the conception of the human body based on medical science that treats the body as an absolute given object, for Duncan, who was also greatly influenced by Nietzsche, the human body is still in the middle of "crossing" over an abyss "between beast and Higher Man."[70] However, the current position of the human (especially female) body on this evolutionary trajectory, according to Duncan, has dangerously deviated from the right (or natural) path due to the suppression of the female body by the current state of civilization.

Thus, in order to cross from the "bad" present over to the "good" future along the right evolutionary path, the female body had to first return to the "ideal" past of ancient Greece supposedly free of suppression, through modern dance. This is the twisted temporality of evolution—characterized by the pattern "present→past→future" with the ahistorical and romanticized past as a central link—that underlies the corporeal modernity in Duncan's feminist philosophy of early modern dance. This mode of corporeal modernity exhibits blurred boundaries between the past and future, the universal and the national, the constant and the variable, engendering instable meanings that are subject to multiple interpretations. The cosmopolitan background and Oriental body of Rongling, as demonstrated later, fit well into this corporeal modernity of Duncan's modern dance.

The importance of evolution in Duncan's theory is evident from the beginning of *The Dance of the Future*.

> A woman once asked me why I dance with bare feet and I replied, "Madam, I believe in the religion of the beauty of the human foot"—and the lady replied, "But I do not" and I said, "Yet you must, Madam, for the expression and intelligence of the human foot is one of the greatest triumphs of the *evolution of man*." "But," said the lady, "I do not believe in the evolution of man;" At this said I "My task is at an end. I refer you to my most revered teachers Mr. Charles Darwin and Mr. Ernest Haeckel"—"But," said the lady, "I do not believe in Darwin and Haeckel." At this point I could think of nothing more to say. So you see, that to convince people, I am of little value and ought not to speak.[71]

In this amusing conversation, or failure thereof, used by Duncan to open her speech, the bare feet of the female body is presented as a fetish for the "greatest triumphs of the evolution of man." The dramatized impossibility of conversation between Duncan and the "lady" is a reflection of Duncan's own anxiety in her uphill battle of legitimizing and promoting modern dance. The lady might stand for several things. The first and foremost is the aesthetic and disciplinary tradition of ballet—the "natural" bare feet of Duncan form a sharp contrast to the deformed *pointe* feet bound in ballet shoes. For Duncan, not just the feet, but the whole body of any well-trained ballet dancer, is deformed due to "incorrect dress and incorrect movement."[72] More generally, Duncan challenges the prohibitions and constraints imposed on the female body by the Victorian apparel, as represented by heavy layers of clothing, binding corset, and tight laces.[73]

Interestingly, what paralleled Duncan's foot fetish was a Western Christian obsession with the Han-Chinese foot binding.[74] In Duncan's view, the bound feet of Chinese women might as well serve as a negative counterpart of the bare feet—the deformation resulting from foot binding, from the Western perspective, was even more abhorrent than that from ballet training.[75]

However, unlike those Western missionary activists who advocated the abolishment of foot-binding within a "masculine missionary hierarchy" and a Christian framework, Duncan, in the most general sense, opposed *any* form of constraint and oppression inflicted upon the female body, which went well beyond Christianity.[76] By promoting the Greek nudism as the highest form of natural beauty, Duncan strived to purge the Original Sin branding the Christian female body and undo the body-soul divide enforced since the biblical age of Garden of Eden—"Man, arrived at the end of civilization, will have to return to nakedness, not to the unconscious nakedness of the savage, but to the conscious and acknowledged nakedness of the mature Man, whose body will be the harmonious expression of his spiritual being."[77]

Moreover, by advancing an evolutionary interpretation of the Greek body tradition, Duncan redirected the time arrow pointing to the past forward, toward a universal "new woman" dancing triumphantly in a higher stage of human evolution. That is, Duncan's philosophy of modern dance is not just about liberating the female body *as it is* (or *was*); rather, its goal is to "restart" the natural evolution of women that has supposedly been arrested since the advent of the Christian civilization. Thus, for Duncan, modern dance "is a question of race, of the development of the female sex to beauty and health, of the *return to the original strength and to natural movements of woman's body.* It is a question of the development of perfect mothers and the birth of healthy and beautiful children. The dancing school of the future is to develop and to show the ideal form of woman."[78] It is in this sense that "returning" to the past represented by ancient Greece, on the one hand, becomes a necessary path to the future and to the corporeal modernity of the "female sex," and on the other hand is a primary means to exert feminist agency upon the iron law of evolution by twisting its unidirectional temporality. The "past," no longer a forever-lost Golden Age to be lamented or the counterpart of "modernity" to be left behind, is rescued by Duncan's modern dance as a bridge crossing over the evolutionary abyss separating the present and the future of women. As Duncan claims, "the dance of the future is the dance of the past."[79]

Duncan's evolutionary interpretation of her Greek dance not only recycles the past into modernity, but also challenges the boundaries of nations and cultures. For Duncan, the Greek dance "is *not* a national or characteristic art but has been and will be the art of *all humanity for all time*. Therefore dancing naked upon the earth I naturally fall into Greek positions, for Greek positions are only earth positions."[80] Clearly, Duncan claims both temporal and spatial universality—albeit Eurocentric—for her Greek dance, which supposedly transcends temporal, national, and cultural borders.

This context might shed light on the possible role of the cosmopolitan Yu Rongling and her Oriental body in Duncan's agenda. On the one hand, the body of Rongling, a girl from the "backward" Qing Empire, could be a symbol for "Chinese Women" in general, who serve as a stronger negative counterpart than Western Women to Duncan's evolved New Woman. On the other hand, Rongling is not just a Chinese Woman—her cosmopolitan experiences provide an "interface" through which the Oriental body may be transformed and assimilated into the universal body of Duncan's New Woman. The "Greek" grace played out perfectly by Rongling becomes compelling proof of Duncan's universalist claim—even the Chinese body, allegedly most astray from the right evolutionary path, can be saved and brought back on track through modern dance, thus forcefully showing that Greek dance is "the art of all humanity for all time" and "Greek positions are only earth positions."

However, Duncan's universalist interpretation and exploitation of the Greek dance and the Oriental body is precarious. The very gesture of "returning" to the past cannot automatically guarantee a magical jump to the future but implies the danger of being stuck in the past. The assimilation of the other and the universalization of the particular entail the intrinsic risk of exoticizing the self and particularizing the universal. Moreover, despite Haeckel's introducing the "will" into evolution theory, embracing evolutionism itself precludes stability of meaning, as what is the "fittest" can never be predetermined, but always exists in a state of "to become," subject to the selection by nature through trial and error in the "unending ever increasing evolution, wherein are no ends and no stops."[81]

This instability may have been well exploited by the Parisian audience viewing Rongling's performance of the Greek dance. Unlike Duncan, who strived to incorporate the "Chinese body" from the Far East into her universalist interpretation of the Greek dance, in the mind of the Parisian audience, the Far East was not that far from the "Greece" in the first place—they both belong to the Orient.[82] At that time, as recalled by Rongling, fantasies of ancient Greece were widespread in Paris. Body images copied from Greek artifacts were on items for sale all over the marketplace (such as postcards).[83] However, these Parisian fantasies were much less universalist Hellenistic ones (as Duncan's) than Orientalist (i.e., exotic and erotic) ones. As Emily Apter points out, "[t]his conflation of Greece and the orient was of course particularly common in turn-of-the-century art, literature, opera, dance and theatre; syncretistic otherness was the fashion, spawning a wild hybridity of styles—Egypto-Greek, Greco-Asian, Biblical-Moorish."[84] Moreover, such an Orientalist approach to Greece was often seen as a cipher for queer eroticism.[85] Therefore, despite Duncan's longtime effort to shed eroticism from and establish a "chaste" image for her dance in the eyes of the general public—a goal largely achieved later in her career—the hybrid "Greco-Asian" image of Rongling, instead of being interpreted as the proof of the universality of Duncan's "Greek positions," may have been consumed as an Oriental exotic and (queer) erotic commodity by some of the at-the-turn-of-the-century Parisian elite audiences.[86] On the receptive side, Duncan's return to ancient Greece, to some extent, lost its forward-seeking evolutionary potentiality, and the self became exoticized (and eroticized) and the universal particularized.

In fact, Duncan herself was quite aware of these risks. In a passage addressing "a misunderstanding that might easily arise," Duncan clarifies: "[f]rom what I have said you might conclude that my intention is to return to the dances of the old Greeks or that I think that the dance of the future will be a revival of the antique dances or even of those of the primitive tribes. No, the dance of the future will be a new movement, a consequence of the entire evolution which mankind has passed through. To return to the dances of the Greeks would be as impossible as it is unnecessary. We are not Greeks and cannot therefore dance Greek dances."[87] Duncan also emphasizes that the universality of her modern dance is not a Procrustean bed, but instead promotes the development of individuality and particularity.[88] She implicitly admits that each country has its own unique "ideal of the beauty of form and movement,"[89] and even hints that the dance of the ancient "Greek" is but one among several other legitimate representatives of the "dance of the past," such as those of the "Egyptian" and "early Italian."[90]

However, these dialectical, and even contradictory, qualifications and clarifications made by Duncan do not eliminate those risks of reversing her universalist claims, but in fact betray them, foregrounding the problematics intrinsic to her philosophy of modern dance. Any act of border-crossing, be it temporal or spatial, always entails the possibility of a reverse crossing, and thus generates instability in meaning and opens up the space for multiple interpretations and appropriations. This point may be seen more clearly in Yu Rongling's creation of the "Chinese classical dance" in Cixi's imperial court after traveling back to the disintegrating Qing Empire.

Corporeal Modernity in the "Forbidden Palace"

The service of the Yu sisters in the imperial palace ordered by Cixi was part of a response of the Qing court to the repeated failures in struggles against colonial powers. Although the socio-economic and cultural landscapes of many Chinese cities, especially treaty ports, had been fundamentally changed due to constant interaction with foreign presence, Cixi's court remained semi-reclusive around the turn of the century. The knowledge and impressions about the empress dowager and her court formed in the West were largely based on hearsays that mixed facts with stories, limited, fragmented, and distorted at the best, and it was equally true the other way around.[91] This situation gradually became intolerable for the Qing court, since Cixi had to involve herself and her court more personally and deeply in dealing with foreign affairs, as necessitated by the deepening of the semi-colonial status of China—a direct result of the First Sino-Japanese War (1894–1895) and the more recent Boxer Uprising.[92]

No longer could she sit comfortably behind the curtain. The empress dowager had to reveal more of herself and her court to the outside world. Her imperial women and court ladies needed to attend banquets on invitation by the wives of foreign ambassadors, and Cixi herself, as a hostess showing hospitality, had to open her forbidden palace to host feasts in return and present herself in meetings with foreign visitors on various occasions, catching up with the international standards of diplomacy (figure 1.4).[93] That is why Cixi's court needed the Yu sisters, with their corporeal knowledge of foreign languages, manners, and customs.

Figure 1.4 Empress Dowager Cixi with foreign envoys' wives in Leshoutang, Summer Palace, Beijing, ca. 1903. Photographed by Yu Xunling. Image courtesy of the Freer Gallery of Art and Arthur M. Sackler Gallery Archives, Smithsonian Institution.

This decision by Cixi should be understood in the larger context of the "information order," as termed by the historian Jenny Huangfu Day, of the late Qing Empire.[94] Since the founding of the Zongli Yamen 總理衙門 (similar to the foreign ministry in Western governments) in the mid-1860s, the Qing government had been sending out investigatory and diplomatic missions, and later resident ministers to major foreign powers.[95] By 1895, the year when Yu Geng was appointed as minister to Japan, the Qing diplomatic network of overseas offices had boasted twelve legations and twelve consulates.[96] In addition to their diplomatic duties, Qing diplomats like Yu Geng "worked as the empire's distant information managers by researching, documenting, and interpreting the West for a range of domestic readership," routinely reporting to the throne generated knowledge in various written forms such as "letters, journals, reports, proposals, and memorials," which "touched nearly all aspects of the empire's foreign relations and international affairs."[97] Yet this spawning information network might have several shortcomings, especially from the perspective of Cixi. First, information formed and flowed relatively slowly through this bureaucratic hierarchy before reaching the throne and thus might be subject to constant selection, distortion, and manipulation along this complex communication channel by various agents with different, and often conflicting, interests.[98] Second, the knowledge was mediated by classical written Chinese, often in the form of boilerplate-like official documents, that suffered from all kinds of inaccuracies entailed by the process of translation and encoding/decoding; those written forms thus cannot efficiently and precisely relay detailed, direct, corporeal experiences and knowledge needed for ritual-like diplomatic occasions on which the empress dowager and her court ladies must "perform" in person.[99] Third, the information order was all staffed with male officials typically lacking "feminine" sensitivity, who were not best suited for conveying such intimate corporeal knowledge to the empress dowager due to institutional and gender reasons.[100] Therefore, the cosmopolitan Yu sisters became the ideal candidates who could serve as a more direct and personal bridge between Cixi and the foreign world that cut through the thickly bureaucratic, men-dominated imperial information order.

The cultural "clash" between the West and the Qing court was, first and foremost, a corporeal one embodied by elite women, Western, Chinese, and in-between. Since Cixi was the sponsor of Yu Rongling's dance, some discussion of this bodily clash can foreground the corporeal context within which the transnational and transcultural dance practices and creations of Rongling took place.

The corporeal—body features, clothes, manners—seems to become a constant focus of attention for all the parties involved. This focus on the corporeal should not be quickly dismissed as some characteristically trivial female "obsession" of vanity. Rather, it highlights the bodily aspect of the dynamics of identity (trans)formation. Through the self-conscious switching, comparing, and negotiating between different perspectives, the self and the other were being redefined and transformed, and a new kind of (inter)subjectivity gradually emerged, which was distinctively corporeal and modern. This bodily (inter)subjectivity had subtle connection with evolutionary thinking. Andrew F. Jones, by analyzing literary texts and visual cultural materials, highlights the problematic of agency and the risk of atavism inherent in evolutionary or developmental thinking—defined as the vernacular, often "scientifically imprecise or inaccurate," popularization of the theory of evolution in the "popular media and everyday discourse."[101] By focusing more directly on the corporeal, I next show how these "risks" associated with evolutionary thinking might provide a corporeal-temporal framework to transform the body into a site of mediation, negotiation, and change.

Although the Yu sisters served as interpreters on diplomatic occasions, the role of language was often limited. Those occasions—state banquets, formal lunches, and dinners—necessitated simultaneous one-to-one or small group interactions among many people, which rendered complete translation impossible. Even possessing some knowledge of the native language of the other party in interaction was ineffective for communication, as misunderstanding was common.[102] During one such lunch, a foreign woman spoke in heavily accented Chinese to a Qing princess for a long time, but the princess thought she was speaking in some foreign language, and the same foreign woman mistook the German a Qing court woman spoke for Chinese.[103] It seems that in this kind of socialization, language lost its efficacy in communication.

Instead, the corporeal became the focus of attention for both parties in interaction. In some sense, even the linguistic was mediated by and understood *as* the corporeal. According to Deling, a Qing court lady once naively asked the Yu sisters whether one acquires a foreign language by drinking the water of that country.[104] In this episode, learning foreign languages is conceived as a corporeal experience, as represented by the bodily act of "drinking." Physical appearance, makeup, dresses, facial expressions, etiquette, bodily manners, all these corporeal features constitute the main channel through which each party in interaction strives to present the favorable image of the self to the other and infer relevant information—such as taste, status, upbringing, intention, and personality—from the other.[105]

During the first few months following their entry into the imperial court, the curly-haired Yu sisters were ordered by the empress dowager to be dressed in the latest styles of Paris. Interestingly, this supposedly "private" event received coverage by the Western press. A 1904 *The Washington Times* article, titled "French Styles the Vogue in China," reports that Cixi "ordered the Pekin princesses to take lessons in the art of wearing the latest French fashions from the charming daughter[s] of Yu Keng [Geng]," and the "lessons" seem to be a success, as it turned out that "[in] fact, there is little in the way of Western frivolity that the Pekin princesses cannot pick up."[106] It is possible that this "private" imperial "Paris fashion show" had become a "public relation" event to signal to the Western world Cixi's willingness to reform and modernize in the wake of the Boxer Uprising.

Cixi, a lover of beauty, now finally got a chance to have a close look at the high fashion of the West. While the hybrid image of Yu Rongling covered by Greek tunic back in Paris served as a persuasive advertisement for Duncan's universalist Hellenistic interpretation of ancient Greece and (perhaps inadvertently) catered for the Orientalist exotic and (queer) erotic appetite of the Western audiences, now the cosmopolitan Yu sisters in the fashionable Stamler and Jeanne gowns became a magnifying glass for Cixi and her court ladies to scrutinize, compare, and reflect upon the states of corporeality of Western and Chinese women.[107] After closely examining the heavy layers of the apparel, especially the whale-bone and steel-made corsets, Cixi commented that it is indeed "pitiable" for Western women to bind their waists with steel bars to the extent that they can hardly breathe, and this is "no better than" foot binding.[108] Being aware of the fact that the bound feet of Chinese women had become the laughingstock of foreigners, Cixi, who as a Manchu deemed foot binding abhorrent, turned out to be on the same side as Isadora Duncan for criticizing Victorian clothing for its "barbarian" oppression of the female body. This is perhaps partly why Cixi was so interested in Duncan's philosophy of modern dance, as its universalist claims can be readily appropriated to "equalize" Western and Chinese women based on a "no-better-than" argument, at least on the corporeal dimension.

Cixi was however no true follower of Duncan—she would certainly frown upon the "Nudism" in Duncan's philosophy. According to Deling, after seeing an oil portrait of Deling dressed in a usual European evening dress, Cixi was very much shocked by the revealing garb "without sleeves and without collars" and "laughed and exclaimed" that "[e]verything seems to go backwards in foreign countries."[109] The same comment would also apply to Duncan's even-more-revealing Greek tunic, and Cixi may be indeed partly right about the fact that exposing the female body can be used as a gesture of returning to the past. Underlying Cixi's comment, as related by Deling, is a clear sense of linear temporality, similar to that of evolutionary thinking, which was appropriated to establish a sense of cultural superiority by interpreting the Western fashion as a kind of cultural atavism.[110] The same logic exists in Cixi's remarks on the physical features of Western women— she thought they were unattractive because of their hairy faces and cat-like colored eyes, which has an undertone of biological atavism.[111]

Biased as they seem, these comments of Cixi, which are mediated by Deling's English text, should not be simply seen as a narrow-minded, egocentric, and racist defense of the superiority of, among other things, the Chinese female corporeality. Rather, they are informed and transformed by a constant awareness of the self being viewed and judged, with no less if not more bias, by the foreign other, real or imagined. After every diplomatic meeting, Cixi always asked the Yu sisters to report everything about what the foreign visitor(s) thought of the audience, the food, the decoration, and most importantly, Cixi herself.[112] When foreign visitors were present at a luncheon, Cixi would order the other imperial women to sit down to eat with her at the table, even though the court rules strictly forbade this, because she was afraid that following the rules on such occasions would make the foreign visitors "think we are barbarians" and "form a wrong impression."[113] Partly due to the pressure of this foreign gaze, Cixi (and some of the imperial women and court ladies) even began to use foreign-made cosmetics, drink coffee, and adopt the etiquette of hand shaking.[114] After noticing that some of her foreign guests "did not behave very well," Cixi returned that gaze: "They [the foreigners] seem to think we are only Chinese and do not know anything, and look down upon us. I notice these things very quickly and am surprised to see people who claim to be well educated and civilized acting the way they do. I think we whom they call barbarians are much more civilized and have better manners."[115]

If the distinction between the barbarous and the civilized, the primitive and the evolved, the backward and the advanced is so blurred and fluid in the realm of the corporeal and subject to different interpretations, and if the corporeal is governed by the logic of evolution, then the final authority to judge does not rest in the hands of foreigners, or Chinese, or anyone, but rather in some indefinite future to be determined by "natural selection." It is in this indeterminacy that the possibility of agency lies, illusive as it may seem with hindsight. In Deling's account, Cixi once compared herself with Queen Victoria of Britain: "Although I have heard much about Queen Victoria and read a part of her life which someone has translated into Chinese, still I don't think her life was half so interesting and eventful as mine. My life is not finished yet and *no one knows what is going to happen in the future*. I may surprise the foreigners some day with something extraordinary and do something quite contrary to anything I have yet done."[116]

From this perspective provided by Deling's narrative, Cixi and the Chinese corporeality she defended should not be dismissed as the "old" to be buried in the past, nor should the Western counterparts be regarded as the "new" that was predestined to prevail in the future. Instead, the very act of comparing, emulating, and competing compels Cixi, along with whatever she represents, and the Western counterparts into the same evolutionary space-time, whose future fates are only to be adjudicated by the law of natural selection. It is in this sense that this new (inter)subjectivity (new, because both the self and the other are being constantly transformed in this process) activated in the evolutionary space-time may be retrospectively called "modern."

The same corporeal consciousness may well apply to the case of dance. If the dance of "the Greeks," "the Egyptian," or "the early Italian" can be regarded as valid candidates to represent "the dance of the past" and, further, "the dance of the future," why cannot the dance of the Chinese? By simply asking this question, the universalist logic of Duncan's modern dance is reversed into a (proto-)nationalist one. Since this pursuit was informed by the linear temporality of evolutionary competition, "the dance of the Chinese" created thereby cannot simply be old or traditional, but must at the same time be new and modern, just like Duncan's Greek dance, which, as Rongling once commented, "can be said to be creating the new, and as well reviving the old."[117]

"Reviving the Old" and "Creating the New"

The motivation for Cixi to order Yu Rongling to create "Chinese dance" was unlikely to be purely artistic or entertaining. Given the perceived importance of the corporeal in her dealing with foreigners, Cixi probably reserved a place for dance in her diplomatic agenda. Yu Geng first sensed the utility of dance in diplomacy when he was at the post of Qing minister to Japan (1895–1899). His wife Louisa once received a visit of a Japanese countess, during which Rongling, then no more than eleven, against Louisa's will volunteered to perform a classical Japanese dance *Tsurukame* 鶴亀 (crane-tortoise) she learned from a Japanese servant without her parents' knowledge. Rongling's performance greatly impressed the countess, as well as Yu Geng, who heard about the countess' praise afterward. Realizing that dance may be useful in the diplomatic life of his family, he hired a professional Japanese dancer to teach Rongling at the legation.[118] After Yu Geng arrived in Paris as Qing minister to France, he put his idea about the socio-diplomatic function of dance into practice by hosting fancy balls at the Chinese legation for the Parisian diplomatic circles and attending balls held elsewhere, in which the Yu children were active participants (figure 1.3).[119]

It is possible that Cixi was aware of these dancing activities—both artistic and social dances—of the Yu family abroad.[120] As shown below, due to gender issues, Cixi preferred artistic dance to social dance, which led her to invest in the former eventually. This decision linked the origin of "Chinese dance," whether classical or modern, to Duncan's modern dance in a relation of emulation, differentiation, and competition.

When the Yu sisters served at her court, according to an anecdote Deling recorded, Cixi once asked Deling: "What is dancing? Someone told me that two people hold hands and jump all over the room. If that is the case I don't see any pleasure in it at all. Do you have to jump up and down with men?"[121] After hearing out Deling's explanation of all kinds of social dances popular in the Western societies, Cixi ask the Yu sisters to give her some demonstration. The two girls danced a waltz accompanied by a large gramophone found in Cixi's bedroom. Cixi commented that the dance was "very pretty, and just like the girls used to do centuries ago in China," but she thought it would be very inappropriate in China for a man to dance with a girl, let alone with his arm around the girl's waist. Still, through switching between foreign and Chinese perspectives, according to Deling, Cixi admitted that "[i]t shows that they [the foreigners] are broader minded than us."[122] A similar episode was widely circulated in Western newspapers in 1903: Rongling and Deling once "danced a minuet dressed as a French peasant boy and girl. On the same evening four Chinese princesses went through a quadrille, the empress looking on with evident pleasure."[123] In the news report, this episode is contrasted with that "[i]t is only about three years since the dowager empress of China loathed foreigners and everything foreign" (referring to Cixi's role in the 1900 war against the Eight-Nation Alliance during the Boxer Uprising), which is intended to stress the speed of the "modernization" of Cixi's court. It is possible that Cixi used this social dance episode as part of a "public relation" maneuver to repair the international image of her court and herself damaged three years earlier.

Deling once also performed for Cixi a "Greek dance" Duncan had taught her, though, following Louisa's advice, in costume having "plenty of lining, so that it would not be *too* transparent." Cixi thought the dance was beautiful and said: "I should like very much to see her [Duncan]. I wonder if you could persuade her to come to China."[124]

Cixi was seemingly drawn more to Duncan's artistic dance than social dance, because the former was more gender "appropriate" and more in accord with Cixi's conception of dance as what "the girls used to do centuries ago in China." When watching the Yu sisters' performances of Western dances, what was in Cixi's mind seems to be the long-lost dance tradition in China, which eventually motivated her to order Rongling to resurrect it. This project was partly motivated by, and emulated and competed with, Duncan's effort to revive the dance of the ancient Greeks, which, as elaborated above, had already blurred various temporal, racial, and cultural boundaries and been subject to local appropriations and reinterpretations. Although Cixi's agenda of "reviving the old" was unlikely to be guided by Duncan's universalist and evolutionist vision, the very motivation of emulating and competing with early modern dance alone determined the resurrected (or created, more precisely) Chinese dance to be a modern product. As demonstrated below, not just the motivation, but also the sources, elements, and methods used to create the "Chinese dance," and even the venue and situation of its first performance, were both Chinese and foreign, old and new.

On an occasion where Cixi and Louisa discussed Western and Chinese arts, as recalled by Rongling, the empress dowager said: "Long ago at the end of the Ming dynasty, there was an imperial secondary wife with the surname Tian who could dance very well, but unfortunately it has been lost. I have always wanted the princesses of the royal houses to study dance, but could never find the right person. Now that Rongling knows how to dance, let her study in the palace!"[125] Following Cixi's order, just like Duncan, who invented Greek dance by observing the body figures in various forms of ancient Greek artifacts displayed in museums, Rongling, by studying the images of dancing beauties portrayed in ancient Chinese paintings in the imperial art collections and discussing musical matters with the court eunuch musicians, created at least three Chinese dances—Hehua xianzi wu 荷花仙子舞 (Dance of the Lotus Blossom Fairy), Shan wu 扇舞 (Fan Dance), and Ruyi wu 如意舞 (Ruyi Dance, where ruyi is a jade mascot meaning good fortune and pleasure).[126]

It is likely that Rongling might have also incorporated motifs, postures, and moves inspired by Peking Opera, classical Japanese dance, and Duncan's modern dance and ballet. For example, the fairy theme of Lotus Blossom Fairy resembles those of typical Western ballets, and the prop fan in the Fan Dance was also characteristic of the classical Japanese dance Tsurukame she learned in Tokyo.[127] Moreover, as Cixi was a lover of Peking Opera, Rongling had many chances to watch the performances of famous actors, and the court musicians were all accompanists of the opera.[128]

While it is unclear whether, and to what extent, Rongling directly borrowed formal elements from Duncan's modern dance, it can be reasonably inferred that Duncan's teaching had significant influence on Rongling's choreography. Unlike the training of classical Japanese dance, Western ballet, or Peking Opera, the primary goal of which is to let the apprentice master the well-developed dance moves of the existing repertoire, Duncan's instruction offered greater opportunity to expose her students to the more intellectual and creative process of choreography.[129]

Duncan, as Deling puts it, was a "mistress of dance-creation," creating dance for each girl according to her own individuality. The Yu sisters often had the chance to observe how Duncan choreographed new dances by "interpreting" the music, a spiritual process phrased by Duncan as "I have to create as I do."[130] Their long walks, observations, and conversations with Duncan in the Louvre and Versailles would be another opportunity for Rongling to learn this rare and intimate feat, through which the static postures of the great sculptures and paintings, with "every important detail" explained "over and over again," were animated into Duncan's legendary dances. As Duncan states in *The Dance of the Future*, "I shall not teach the children to imitate my movements, but to make their own, I shall not force them to study certain definite movements, I shall help them to develop those movements which are natural to them."[131] This exposure to Duncan's choreographic practice, an invaluable experience that was hard to get elsewhere, conceivably left a deep imprint in Rongling's creative mind, with which she could breathe life into the portraits of ancient beauties and alchemize dance elements from different cultural sources into "Chinese" dance movements "natural" to her.[132]

Rongling's first dance performance in the imperial palace was triggered by a diplomatic crisis. In February 1904, the Russo-Japanese War (1904–1905) broke out after the failure of diplomatic negotiation.[133] Awkwardly caught in the middle of the struggle between two expansionist powers, Russia and Japan, over the Far East hegemony, the weaker Qing Empire had to embarrassingly choose a neutral stance in this war rampaging on Chinese soil. The empress dowager was troubled by a sense of personal and national humiliation and became sullen. In order to cheer Cixi up, Rongling was urged to hold a dance concert in the palace on the third day of the fifth lunar month (June 16, 1904), which was probably the first formal concert of an individual dancer held in modern China (not including those held in foreign concessions).[134]

Three dances, all chosen by Cixi herself, were in the concert program. The first was a Spanish dance, the second the *Ruyi* dance, and the last a Greek dance. Because there were both Western and Chinese dances, two bands were oddly arranged by the sides of the "stage"—the red-carpet covered courtyard of the *Lei Shou Tang* 樂壽堂 (Hall of Happiness and Longevity) in the *Yihe Yuan* 頤和園 (Garden of Nurtured Harmony, or Summer Palace). While the Chinese band consisted of court accompanists of Peking Opera, the Western music band was transported from Tianjin by Yuan Shikai 袁世凱 (1859–1916), future president of the Republic of China and briefly the emperor. The costume for the two Western dances was carried by Rongling back to Beijing when her family left Paris, and that for the Chinese *Ruyi* dance was particularly tailored as per Cixi's order. Besides the empress dowager, in the audience were Emperor Guangxu 光緒 (then thirty-three years old), the other imperial women, court ladies, and the wives and daughters of princes.[135]

No detail about the dances is available, except for the costume. For the Spanish dance, presumably fast-paced and passionate, Rongling donned a long yellow satin dress, a shawl with red tassels covering her shoulders, with two large red flowers attached to the sides of her hair. In sharp contrast to this "Spanish" costume and that of the "Greek dance" (figure 1.5), for the *Ruyi* dance, Rongling was clad in the formal Manchu *qizhuang* 旗裝 (literally, "flag dress")—more specifically, a *mangpao* 蟒袍 (literally, "python robe"), an all-covering long red dress embroidered with dragon-like patterns. Her hair was braided in the Manchu style *erbatou* 二把頭 (literally, "two barred head") with two red tassels dangling on the sides (figure 1.6). The prop *ruyi*, instead of using the real jade one (too unwieldy and hard to decorate), was made of paper and bound with red satin, to be presented to the empress dowager at the end of the dance as a gesture of paying homage.[136]

The concert ended with the "Greek dance" (figure 1.5).[137] Based on the style of the architecture in the background, the picture was probably taken at Yu's concert location—the front door of the *Le shou tang* in the Summer Palace. It can be seen from the picture that the costume is of Egyptian style, instead of the Greek tunic characteristic of Duncan's dance. It might be the case that since there was no Greek tunic available, Rongling instead chose the Egyptian costume brought back from Paris; the hybrid "Egypto-Greek" style was "particularly common" on the turn-of-the-century Parisian stage, with which Rongling must have been familiar.[138] In any case, Cixi probably did not care much about the differences, but conflated them under a single

Figure 1.5 Yu Rongling performing a "Greek dance" in the Summer Palace, Beijing, 1904. This photo appeared in Yu's memoir published in the Chinese dance journal *Wudao* 舞蹈, no. 2 (March 1958), p. 44.

label of "Greek dance." The performance was successful, which greatly delighted Cixi.

However, this performance should not be simply treated as some mindless court entertainment. This concert of Rongling, in addition to its diverting function, may be interpreted as a rehearsal of introducing the newly (re) born "Chinese dance" into the competitive corporeal stage of world dances. Cixi's choices of the three national dances deserve some deliberation. The

Figure 1.6 Yu Rongling in Manchu-style costume for performing the *Ruyi* dance, Summer Palace, Beijing, 1904. This photo appeared in Yu's biography published in the Chinese academic journal *Zongheng* 纵横, no. 5 (1999), p. 49.

new Chinese dance accounted for only one of the three items in the program, while foreign dances constituted the majority. Clearly, Cixi was not interested in Chinese dance per se, but rather the Chinese dance *in relation to* Western dances, especially the early modern dance (or Greek dance), which she had probably watched once before (performed by Deling).

The ordering of the dances is informative. The Greek dance was the last one, corresponding to the last act of a typical Peking Opera performance called *zhouzi* 軸子 (literally, the "axis")—an insignificant act during which the seasoned audience would leave for home. Rongling's *Ruyi* dance was arranged next to last, mirroring the second act from the last in Peking Opera called *yazhou* 壓軸 (the one "on top of the axis"), which was the most important act, usually performed by the leading actor in a troupe. Being a dedicated fan and major sponsor of Peking Opera and instrumental in its formation, Cixi seems to use this arrangement to suggest that the creation of Chinese dance was intended to challenge and compete with the early modern dance. Thus, this act of Rongling may be read as a means for Cixi to demonstrate the potential superiority of the Chinese female corporeality—"I think we whom they call barbarians are much more civilized and have better manners." Although "they," the foreigners, were not present in person, their imagined gaze was probably lurking by the stage.

Beneath the surface of the stark difference between the image of Rongling dancing in the skimpy Greek tunic and that of the same girl moving gracefully in the head-to-toe Manchu *qizhuang* was hidden a long-neglected connection between Isadora Duncan and Empress Dowager Cixi, between early modern dance and Chinese dance, and between the Western corporeality and its Chinese counterpart, which were in constant interaction and transformation. Yu Rongling, with her multi-racial, cosmopolitan identities and experiences, and border-crossing dance, played a non-negligible role in establishing and facilitating this corporeal connection and interaction.

"Greek dance" Meets Chinese Revolution

In November of 1926, the dance troupe of the Isadora Duncan School in Moscow (Duncan moved to Moscow in 1921) began their Chinese tour— that was twenty two years after Rongling's dance concert in the imperial palace, eighteen years after Cixi's death, fifteen years after the demise of the Qing Empire, five months after John Van Antwerp MacMurray filmed Rongling's *Sword Dance* (see "Introduction"), one month after Denishawn's performance in Shanghai, and when the Northern Expedition of the Great Revolution led by the Guangzhou Nationalist government was sweeping across southern China. Led by Irma Duncan (1897–1977), one of the six "Isadorables" (Duncan's major disciples and adopted daughters), the tour received considerable media coverage in China.[139] News reports and reviews written by Chinese and foreign intellectuals—for example, the famous

dramatist Tian Han 田漢, writer Yu Dafu 郁達夫, and the Prussian philosopher Alfred Westharp (countryman of Irma Duncan and good friend of the
Chinese philosopher Liang Shuming 梁漱溟)—appeared in several major
print media, reflecting on the nature and potential socio-cultural roles of
modern dance in China.[140]

What is of particular interest here is Tian Han's response to Irma's performance at the Odeon Theater in Shanghai. The near-sighted artist could not
see the performance on stage clearly—in his eyes was only *the movement
of shade and colour*" that were "so simple and pure, so natural, and so powerful."[141] Yet this in fact gave Tian a vantage point to peek at the "essence" of
Irma's dance. As he talked to Irma,

> "Yours is really a kind of movement, but not the so-called dance. You are
> not a bright star among many dancing girls; you are virtually a commander
> of the Red Army on stage! Your teacher is known for reviving the ancient
> Greek dance, but I saw in your dance drama not so much ancient Greece as
> modern Russia! The resistance of the oppressed, the triumph of life! . . ."[142]

"Quite so, Mr. Tien," Replied Irma.[143] Tian continues in his essay,

> Among those who had seen Ruth St. Denis' dancing and then came to
> see Irma Duncan's dancing, there must be someone who would say their
> [Irma's] dancing is overly non-technical, overly simple. In fact, this kind
> of technique that does not pursue techniques, and this simplicity danced
> out of complexity, are the greatest characteristics of the New arts: "the New
> artists are not jewelers carving gems; they are blacksmiths. Their weapons
> are iron hammers." You have a look at Irma's *Blacksmith*! They are truly the
> unifier of life and art. Irma explains that the essence of her dance is distilled
> from the "*unconscious movement*" of our daily life. This word in particular
> proves that their art is consistent with the mainstream modern literature.
> Ah, the embodiment of bitterness and depression! The manifestation of the
> unconscious! Aren't these what we are doing? Irma's dancing, dressed in red
> and barefooted, raising her arm with a battle cry, leading her troops to fight
> toward where evil hides, flying and dancing toward a bright realm, is the
> dance of modern people.[144]

What was filtered through Tian's nearsighted eyes turned out to be quite
farsighted—he spotted in her modern dance a paradoxical convergence of

the abstract modern dance *movement* (as in "the movement of shade and colour") and the international socialist/leftist *movement* (as in the revolutionary movement of the Red Army) galvanized by the Russian Bolshevik Revolution. This convergence would become a main refrain in the development of modern dance in China throughout the decades to come.[145] The world of international modern dance was about to experience a profound "leftist turn" in the 1930s—the "decorative, exotic female representations popularized by St. Denis" (or those of Rongling's) would be rejected, as would be "the maternal representations of 'Women' that Duncan's later choreography constructed."[146] Tian accurately predicted both developments in the passage above.

However, what was not mentioned by Tian is the tension between the elitist "feminine" modernism and the populist socialism/leftism in Irma's dance, which may be best illustrated by the stark contrast between the Greek tunic (figure 1.7) and the proletarian themes in some of her choreographies. As the title of Irma's *Blacksmith* (mentioned by Tian Han in the quote above) suggests, this dance may be seen as the Duncan Moscow school's avant-gardist effort to transform the elitist modern femininity defined in Duncan's

Figure 1.7 Duncan's Moscow school on tour in China, 1926. In the center: Irma Duncan. The photo appeared in Ilya Ilyich Schneider, *Isadora Duncan: The Russian Years*, tran. David Magarshack (New York: Harcourt, Brace & World, Inc., 1968), following p. 200.

earlier choreography by fusing such femininity with the militant image of the proletarian blacksmith, which resulted in a dissonant combination. Yet, the feminine details of the costume and the female body were conveniently filtered out, inadvertently or not, by Tian's bad sight; what remained were only the "barefoot" and the color "red" that Tian interpreted as the symbols of the proletarian. This tension between modernism and leftism/socialism is the main thread for the next two chapters. Note that highlighting this tension does not mean to go "backward" to reinforce the division between the two. Rather, its purpose is to emphasize that the relationship between them is characterized by *both* convergence and dissonance.

2

Transmediating Kinesthesia

Wu Xiaobang, Mary Wigman via Tokyo, and Modern Dance in Wartime China

In the spring of 1929, the twenty-three-year-old Wu Xiaobang 吳曉邦 (1906–1995), who grew up in a wealthy landlord and financial capitalist family in Suzhou (62 miles northwest of Shanghai) but secretly joined the Communist Youth's League, set off for Tokyo, where he began to study violin and Western music (figure 2.1). Prior to his education in music, Wu was at first a student of finance, then a bank intern, a student of law, a military cadet, a soldier of the Great Revolution (1924–1927), and a middle school history teacher.[1] As with his previous endeavors, the fickle young bourgeois' enthusiasm in music was short-lived. One day early in his time in Japan, Wu watched the dance *A Group of Ghosts* performed by the students of Waseda University in Tokyo. Wu was so shocked by the power of the performance that he could not sleep for several nights. The dance, accompanied by the rhythmic knocks of a Buddhist wooden fish, brought to life the images of various ghosts—vampires, people who starved to death, and those who died in injustice—lost and wandering in a silent night. In Wu's own account, this dark dance struck him because it "forcefully embodied the miseries of the oppressed," which made him settle down in dance as his life-long pursuit.[2]

From 1929 to 1936, Wu studied modern dance in Tokyo, first with Takata Seiko 高田原世子 (1895–1977) and then briefly with Eguchi Takaya 江口隆哉 (1900–1977), both Japanese who had learned modern dance in Western countries. From the mid-1930s Wu became the first professional dancer-choreographer in modern China and later spent more than two decades transforming the modern dance—especially the central European school represented by Rudolf von Laban (1870–1958) and Mary Wigman (1886–1973)—that he learned via Japan into what came to be referred to as "China's new dance" (*Zhongguo xin wudao* 中国新舞蹈). This endeavor emulated the various "new" art movements in Chinese literature, theater, music, painting, and cinema promoted by the Chinese May Fourth intellectuals and later

When Words Are Inadequate. Nan Ma, Oxford University Press. © Oxford University Press 2023.
DOI: 10.1093/oso/9780197575307.003.0003

Figure 2.1 Wu Xiaobang (on the right) and his Japanese violin teacher, Tokyo, ca. 1929. Image courtesy of the China Dancers Association.

the leftist and left-leaning artists in the first few decades of the twentieth century.[3] In creating a new identity for dance in China, touring the whole country to disseminate his art, establishing studios and schools to educate many among the first generation of professional dancers, and publishing books on dance aesthetics, pedagogy, histories, as well as critical reviews, Wu, "father of China's new dance," stands as a distinct figure in the cultural history of modern China.

Given Wu's importance in the history of modern Chinese dance, the story of his viewing *A Group of Ghosts* can be compared to the groundbreaking narration in the "Preface to *Outcry*" (*Nahan* zixu 呐喊自序, 1923) by Lu Xun 鲁迅 (1881–1936), the single most monumental figure in the literary and intellectual history of modern China. About two decades earlier, during the Russo-Japanese War (1904–1905) rampaging on Chinese soil, around the same time that Yu Rongling held her first dance concert in the Qing court for Empress Dowager Cixi and other royals (see chapter 1), the young Lu Xun, also about twenty-three, was studying medicine at the Sendai Medical College in Japan. According to Lu Xun's account, one day, a professor showed the class some "photographic slides" of scenes from the ongoing war. Lu Xun watched that a suspected Chinese "spy" was bound and to be beheaded by a Japanese soldier, surrounded by a Chinese crowd, "all physically strong bodies, yet displaying expressions of apathy . . . who had come to appreciate the spectacle."[4] He then realized that citizens that are ignorant and mentally weak, "no matter how healthy and sturdy their bodies, can serve as nothing more than subject matter for or spectators of meaningless public displays," and thus the top priority should not be studying medicine but to "transform their spirits" through literature.[5] This is the epiphany Lu Xun describes as initiating his writing career, the narration of which has been canonized as one of the genesis moments of modern Chinese literature.

In both narrated events, the abrupt changes of life courses were stimulated by visual images in which the body, and the theme of death, figure saliently. Yet Lu Xun and Wu followed seemingly opposite paths. Lu Xun chose the mind over the body in abandoning medicine for words, since he believed in the supreme power of literature for mass enlightenment and social transformation. In contrast, Wu devoted himself to the wordless movement of the body, as he saw in the dancing body similar transformative potential yet with a unique strength—to "forcefully embody the miseries of the oppressed." To establish literature as the privileged medium for nation-building and reforming the Chinese "national character" (guominxing 國民性), Lu Xun dramatized the dichotomy between words and the body and imposed a hegemonic hierarchy on them. However, although sharing political concerns with Lu Xun, Wu clearly posed with his dancing body a challenge to the dichotomy. As I demonstrate in what follows, the dancing body, literary narrative, and other mediums are closely yet uneasily intertwined with each other in Wu's choreography. This transmedial entanglement is crucial to understanding the significance and the particular role of Wu and his dance in the field of the "new" and leftist literary and art movements in 1930s China during a time of national crisis and war.[6] Moreover, it provides a unique Chinese case of transnational and transmedial strategies employed by modern dance practitioners, for the dance studies literature on the global dissemination of the genre in the early twentieth century.

To better explicate the relationship between modern dance and other literary and art forms in China, I next highlight two conditions under which the transnational travel of Wu's modern dance occurred. The first concerns the timing of this travel. At first glance, the story of modern dance told here seems similar to those of sibling arts—a group of Chinese students went abroad, often in Japan, to learn modern Western arts and brought them back to China to reform the "old" and establish the "new"—with the exception that Wu was alone in his generation in seriously studying dance. However, there are complications in this parallel. By the time Wu introduced modern dance to China in the mid-1930s, the May Fourth movement was fifteen years in the past, and the various new literary and art forms it had introduced were already well established and had begun to wield considerable influence in both the discourses and praxes of enlightenment, nation-building, and revolution. Moreover, under the shadows of gathering war clouds, the new arts had started to join forces in the cause of mass mobilization for the total war against Japan. Thus, in historical conditions that differed from the May Fourth era, the main task for Wu and his dance, as a latecomer with relative disadvantage, was to strategically carve out a niche within the landscape of these more established arts through collaboration, differentiation, and competition, to establish a legitimate and independent status for dance.

The second condition concerns the ideology underlying early twentieth-century modern dance's emphasis on *kinesthesia* as the primary means for meaning making and communication. Kinesthesia, combining movement (*kine*) and sensation (*aesthesia*)—the sensation of movement or the so-called sixth sense—highlights the contagious nature of human bodily movement.[7] More specifically, as theorized by the founding figures of modern dance, it is the physio-psychological empathy one person feels for another person when watching the movements of the latter. In the discourse of modern dance, kinesthesia is exalted as a kind of direct bodily communication, supposedly *unmediated* by language or other forms of representation. Kinesthetic empathy does not require the spectator to enact the observed bodily movement; rather, it entails only an automated physio-psychological process in which the observed movements and related experiences are simulated in the spectator's muscular, neural, and cognitive systems. The influential American dance critic John Martin argues that while all dance forms resort to kinesthesia in varying degrees, modern dance, "instead of employing the cumulative resources of academic tradition" as ballet does, "cuts through directly to the source of all dancing"—"the inherent contagion of bodily movement," that is, kinesthesia.[8]

The idea of kinesthesia fitted uniquely in the cultural context of 1930s China. It challenges the common conception of the body as some passive medium of representation, in which external meanings are inscribed. For example, in contemporaneous discourses of social reform and nation-building, Chinese intellectuals, writers, and artists often use the trope of "the body as a metaphor" for the Chinese nation, which is constantly being abused and exploited by domestic reactionary and foreign imperialist enemies and thus needs to be saved; another widely employed trope is "the body as a fetish," onto which anxieties of intellectuals to reform and modernize the Chinese subjecthood are projected, as in Lu Xun's case.[9] In contrast, kinesthesia, by turning the body into a dynamic engine for meaning making and communication (not merely a mimetic medium for representation), reveals the body's potential of exerting its own critical agency, which, in Wu's vision, could prove useful in the greater politico-artistic movement. Moreover, kinesthesia potentially transforms the spectators offstage into quasi-participants in the performance and, as a result, reshapes the entire performing and viewing experience into a quasi-Nietzschean ritual that blurs the distinction between an active performer and a passive audience and therefore "offers a communal experience and alters community."[10] It is by promoting kinesthesia—which promises to undo the dichotomies between the mind and the body, perception and action, art as object/spectacle and as lived experience—that modern dance offers a possibility of kinesthetic universality capable of transcending various barriers. This, as demonstrated later, became a highly valuable strength of modern dance in wartime China.

However, this alleged kinesthetic universality is never unconditional. The arrival of Wu's dance in 1930s China could be characterized by a fundamental mismatch: on one side was the perceived status of modern dance as a "postliterate" urban high art that resists incorporation into forms of mass media; on the other side was the overarching imperative in China toward using the arts for enlightening and mobilizing the largely illiterate masses for the cause of national salvation, a goal that is hard to accomplish without the use of language, narrative, and mass media.[11] It may seem that dance in general, as a non-literary and non-textual form, is compatible with and even has some advantage in the task of reaching an illiterate audience. However, modern dance as an abstract and often nonrepresentational form prevents it from being a ready and reliable vehicle for promulgating precise political messages with unambiguous meaning, as is required in mass mobilization. Andrea Hewitt argues that the rise of modern dance and the promotion of

kinesthesia in the early twentieth century can be seen as a "postliterate" reaction against language/text- and representation-based paradigms.[12] Mark
Franko further generalizes that "dance itself in the West is the ultimate project
of relativizing meaning."[13] Moreover, advocating the "unmediated" nature of
kinesthesia, early modern dance had the tendency to resist the technologies
of mass mediation. For example, Isadora Duncan (1877–1927) "refused to be
filmed by a motion picture camera, believing that the technology distorted
her practice as a dancer and distanced her from the audience," because the
camera, as an inserted medium, attenuates the direct bodily effect of kinesthesia and objectified her unique and ephemeral art into a mass-replicable
commodity.[14] Also, as discussed in greater detail later, in order to claim its
"purity" and autonomous status, early modern dance practitioners—Mary
Wigman, for example—tended to avoid using framing literary narrative and
even accompanying music, in contrast to ballet.

How to reconcile the two more or less conflicting goals—to establish
modern dance as both a serious high art and a useful tool in the cause of
national salvation and mass mobilization—was crucial for modern dance
to attain a legitimate and autonomous status in China. Wu's choice was to
abandon the paths of his foreign mentors who focused on the formal purity of kinesthesia. Instead, he insisted that dance should be an art with
both "integrativeness" (*zonghexing* 綜合性) and "independence" (*dulixing*
獨立性) that incorporates traits of literature, music, and painting, and
emphasized that this is the lynchpin of the development of artistic dance in
China.[15] As a result, Wu pursued an approach that I call "reverse integration."
That is, dance, which was originally integrated into other arts (theater, for
example), claims its independence by reversely integrating elements of those
arts (such as literary narrative and music) into its kinesthesia, rather than
excluding them from it. Reverse integration, as demonstrated later, was by
no means a frictionless process; it was fraught with dilemmas and diverging
momentums. Nevertheless, modern dance did succeed in establishing its
niche in both the intellectual discourses and cultural praxes in late 1930s
China by providing a unique bodily alternative and complement to other artistic mediums.

This chapter contributes to the growing literature on the intersection of
the avant-garde and the popular, modernism and leftism, and the corresponding intermedial and cross-genre hybridization and fertilization, in
Republican-era literature and arts in general and performance arts in particular, which is typically situated in a transnational and transcultural

context.[16] However, Wu and his modern dance constitute an atypical case of these general "border-crossing" trends in the period under study: unlike the other arts, artistic/aesthetic dance in China, be it modern or traditional, had achieved neither a widely recognized independent elite status nor a popular one; it remained largely obscure in the field of arts. In China's treaty-port cities, while Western-styled social and popular dances had flourished, ballet as a high art had very limited influence (mainly initiated in the early 1920s by the "White Russians" in exile after the 1917 Bolshevik Revolution).[17] Because modern dance, since its birth, had positioned itself as the antithesis of both social/popular dance and ballet in terms of ideology and practice, it was very difficult for the newcomer to capitalize on the existing influence and audience bases of those genres.[18] Moreover, the kinesthetic property of modern dance—without meaning grounded in verbal or visual forms of representation—further aggravated these problems. As a result, the challenges facing the other new arts in the preceding decades became doubled in the case of modern dance, which shaped the genre's evolution in China in some unique ways. Thus, the case of dance further complicates our understanding of these "border-crossing" trends.

The remainder of this chapter unfolds in four sections. Section one traces Wu's learning, choreographing, and performing experiences in Tokyo and Shanghai to contextualize the problems in the transnational travel of modern dance to China. Section two focuses on Wu's discursive effort to overcome these problems and to establish modern dance as a legitimate and independent art in China. This section pays particular attention to Wu's translingual struggle centering on the naming of dance, underlying which are two major problems: the tension between the somatic and kinetic aspects of modern dance, and the uneasy relation between dance as a "latecomer" and other more established art forms. Section three addresses Wu's choreographic strategy of reverse integration. By examining one dimension of reverse integration—the incorporation of elements of narrative and speech into dance—this section highlights through close analysis of two of Wu's modern dance works the fraught relation between kinesthesia and language. The last section shifts the focus to another dimension of reverse integration—the incorporation of songs and music. It demonstrates how Wu drew on the trend in leftist "mass music" by using military themes to facilitate the communication of kinesthesia and extend the influence of his modern dance during a period of war and mass mobilization. At the same time, however, Wu seems to deliberately keep his dance from being identified entirely with the themes of mass mobilization and war. This ambivalence results from the dual goals of modern dance in China—to build up its general significance in the cause of national salvation, and to establish itself as an independent serious art at the same time.

Between Tokyo and Shanghai

In the winter of 1929, Wu Xiaobang began his dance study in Tokyo with the prominent female dancer Takada Seiko. Takada, together with many other well-known Japanese modern dance pioneers, was first trained in Western ballet in the 1910s at the opera division of the Imperial Theater in Tokyo, but later became dissatisfied with the ballet system.[19] From 1922 to 1924, Takada studied dance in the United States and Europe, where she was deeply influenced by various schools of modern dance, including that of Isadora Duncan. Although the training methods Takada used in her teaching were based on ballet, she did not use any barre in training and seems to have deemphasized pointe technique in her choreography.[20]

From 1929 to 1936, Wu went back and forth between Tokyo and Shanghai three times, studying with Takada for more than four years. During the first of two interludes in Shanghai (November 1931–September 1932), Wu opened a dance school; in a second interlude (winter 1934–October 1935), he founded a dance research institute, taught some short-term students, choreographed several dances for a musical drama (yue ju 樂劇) and a spoken drama (hua ju 話劇), and held a public concert of his dance works composed in Tokyo. The time Wu spent in Shanghai was relatively short (less than one year for each stay), and none of his activities there can be said to have been successful. He spent a great deal of money maintaining his dance schools but had only a few uncommitted students, and he sold just one ticket for his first public dance concert.[21]

Nevertheless, the two interludes in Shanghai are important, because these provided him with opportunities to test, reflect on, adjust, and negotiate the positions of his dance in two vastly different cultural-political worlds in East Asian. By the 1930s, in Japan, various artistic dance genres, including modern dance, had become an important and active force in the artistic arena in major cities with a large audience base.[22] Dance had become a standard course in the curricula of elementary and secondary schools. As recalled by Wei Bu 韋布 (who took Takada's dance classes together with Wu and became an accomplished film producer later), advertisements for performances of well-known dancers were commonly found in Tokyo newspapers. When Takada held a dance concert in 1936 at the Hibiya Auditorium, one of the largest theaters in Tokyo, there were no empty seats, a stark contrast to the single ticket sold at Wu's first public concert a year earlier in Shanghai.[23] The contrast reflects the huge gap between the status that modern dance obtained in Japan and China, respectively.

In the October of 1935, Wu went to Japan for the third time; this time, Wu started to pay more attention to other schools of modern dance in Japan. In July 1936, Wu took a three-week course on central European modern dance taught by Eguchi Takaya (1900–1977), who later became a hugely influential dancer, choreographer, theorist, and educator in Japan.[24] Eguchi also once studied dance at Takada's dance institute together with Wu, but in 1931, he went to Germany to pursue an apprenticeship with Mary Wigman, one of the most important figures in the history of modern dance, student and colleague of Rudolf Laban, the founder of central European modern dance.[25]

Unlike other modern dance schools of the time that relied mainly on the idiosyncratic genius of individual artists, the founders of the central European School strove to rationalize and systemize the "natural law" of human bodily movement and the general method of composing dance works from scratch. By relating the moving human body with the polyhedral space it spans, Laban invented a system of movement analysis, grounded in the faith that bodily movements, even unconscious ones, are to some extent analyzable, predictable, and recordable.[26] Laban called this law of movement "natural" because he abstracted and generalized it from everyday activities of people into a universal topological system—the Greek geometry of the Platonic Solids. According to Laban, any bodily movement can be seen as a series of patterned transitions from one Platonic Solid to another, with each solid corresponding to a particular body configuration in space contained in the solid's interior (see also chapter 4).[27] Wigman, in her *Ausdruckstanz* (expressionist dance), developed a general method of creating bodily movements for each dance work through improvisation driven by the artist's inner desire to express, a method that paradoxically reinstalled the creative agency of the dancer-choreographer at the center of Laban's somewhat deterministic natural law of bodily movement.[28]

Both Laban's "natural law" and Wigman's methodology of dance composition were the foci of the three-week course taught by Eguchi. Included in the course contents are an introduction to the major parts of the human body; the instinctive and habitual movements of the body; the various forms and forces of movements; the primary, auxiliary, and oscillating movements; and the rhythms of movements.[29] To familiarize the students with all these concepts, Eguchi first taught various movements of each single joint, and then the movements of two and more joints, and at last the movements involving the body as a whole. That is, based on the "natural law," Eguchi's training method first breaks down the holistic body and its movement into parts and categories, assigns hierarchical roles and functions to them, rebuilds their interconnections, and then reintegrates them into a holistic and organic "Gestalt"—something, as a whole, more than the sum of all its parts.[30] According to Eguchi's account, even before he went to Germany, he had preliminarily formed a very similar vision of dance analysis and composition; only after he watched Wigman's training routine did he realized that his former exploration was ten years late and not nearly as deep and thoughtful as the Laban-Wigman system.[31] This movement theory and training method were very different from those based on ballet. As Wu recalls, ballet training focused only on some parts of the body, while Eguchi's training emphasized the movements of every part. Wu was not used to it at first, and felt pain all over his body, especially in his chest and abdomen.[32]

A feature of Eguchi's course is that there was a session called "theories and techniques for the practice of composition," in which students were required to create their own dance movements according to the "natural law."[33] Unlike other dance training systems, which usually force students to practice the existing formal vocabulary, codes, and repertoire for many years before they are permitted to choreograph their own dances, Eguchi's method, inherited from that of Wigman, put each student, at the very beginning, into the position of an "inventor" who creates new movements for each dance work based on personal experiences and inner inspirations.[34] For Eguchi and his students, it was an imperative to continually create novel movements and avoid codification or formularization of dance moves.[35]

Central European modern dance appealed greatly to Wu. The appeal derived first from its claimed systematic and scientific nature in terms of both the theory and methodology of dance composition and training. By that time, Wu had already read about Duncan's modern dance, which he knew was different from ballet, but he "had no idea at all about how to proceed."[36] After years of ballet-based training, Wu realized that he was still trapped in the arts of the nineteenth century and "felt clueless when he had to express the characters of modern people in the twentieth century."[37] The central

European school provided a flexible framework that, in Wu's view, could be readily appropriated to systematically "invent" the dance movements of "modern people." Moreover, for Wu, it made available an alternative training method much simpler than that of ballet. This simplicity was highly desirable, especially in China, because it could facilitate the dissemination of modern dance in the urgent times of revolution, war, and mass mobilization. As proved by his later teaching practices, using this method, Wu often needed only a few weeks or months to train students who had barely danced previously so that they could mount a public dance performance of considerable scale and complexity.[38]

What Wu learned from Eguchi in the three-week workshop became the theoretical and methodological basis of his dance choreography and teaching practices for the rest of his life.[39] In October 1936, Wu finished his dance study in Tokyo, went back to Shanghai, reopened his dance research institute, and began to fully devote himself to the cause of promoting and establishing modern dance as a legitimate and independent art in China. However, Wu's early dance works composed in Japan (discussed later), even those with a clear Chinese theme, were largely the outgrowth of the particular urban culture of Tokyo. To search for inspiration, Wu frequently attended concerts, plays, and art exhibitions in Tokyo, and sometimes stood in front of the gate of the Shinjuku Railway Station for days to "observe the passengers coming and going, trying to get a glimpse of their inner secrets through their expressions and manner of walking."[40] Unsurprisingly, when Wu "transplanted" his dance works from Tokyo to Shanghai with its quite different urban culture and sociopolitical environment, "maladaptation" occurred—Wu's only audience was a small group of elite literary and artistic circles, many of whom had studied abroad.[41] Thus, how to adapt his modern dance to fit the new environment of China became a major concern for Wu.

Between the Kinetic and the Somatic

Isadora Duncan wrote in her globally circulated 1927 autobiography *My Life*, which Wu read in 1934,

> For the gymnast, the movement and the culture of the body are an end in themselves, but for the dance they are only the means. The body itself must then be forgotten; it is only an instrument, harmonised and well

appropriated, and its movements do not express, as in gymnastics, only the movements of a body, but, through that body, they express also the sentiments and thoughts of the soul.[42]

On the one hand, Duncan suppresses the somatic aspect of dance to distance her dance from other dance genres, the attraction of which derives mainly from the display of the somatic body. On the other hand, Duncan underscores the kinetic aspect of dance and links it to the embodiment of spirituality and philosophy (that of Nietzsche in particular). Duncan employed this two-pronged strategy mainly in the 1920s to reinforce the status of her modern dance, threatened by her own visibly aging body, the "dance crazes" of popular folk dance sweeping the United States, and the efforts of contemporary critics to immobilize her into a cultural monument.[43] This strategy of Duncan, ironically, is based on the very body-mind dichotomy she had been striving to dismantle with kinesthesia, which supposedly unifies the kinetic (*kine*) and the somatic (*aesthesia*). In this version of the triangulation among body, movement, and mind/soul in Duncan's later career, the body is the vessel for the soul and the latter is assigned a "higher" value than the former, and the body is also the carrier of movement; a corollary follows: to lift the status of dance, movement (the kinetic), *not* the body (the somatic), must be heightened to a position as "high" as the soul, so that movement itself could come to express the soul.[44] In some sense, for the aging Duncan, the essence of modern dance was not so much to free up the body and unite it with the mind as the mind freeing itself from the mortal body by sublimating the body into the transcendental movement of dance, despite the fact that Duncan's later choreographies became less "kinetic" and more "sculptural."[45]

The transnational development of the central European school of modern dance in Japan followed a similar path of heightening the status of the kinetic relative to that of the somatic. For example, in 1935, Eguchi proposed and promoted the concept of "object dance"—dance without a dancer, which pushed Duncan's two-faceted strategy to an extreme. The underlying logic is twofold. First, since the "essence" of dance is movement, and the body is only a "carrier" of movement, the body, in principle, can be replaced with other "objects." Second, since kinesthesia can be easily generalized as the sensation of movement, not just bodily movement, what can be conveyed by the movement of the body, in theory, can be at least partly conveyed by the movement of other objects. Based on this rationale, in fall 1935, Eguchi choreographed the "object dance," in which the mechanically driven movements of various inter-linked geometric shapes—such as triangles, rectangles, and ovals—were designed to substitute for the human body to express different "characters" and "emotions."[46]

Wu, however, did not follow this radical path of his mentor. Instead, he chose a path closer to, yet still different from, that of Duncan, a path that both suppresses and relies on the somatic body. In 1940 Guilin, southern China, Wu published an article in the journal *New Chinese Theater* (*Xin Zhongguo xiju* 新中國戲劇), entitled "A talk on the art of dance" (*Wuyong yishu jianghua* 舞踊藝術講話, hereafter, the "dance talk").[47] This article may be seen as a manifesto of establishing modern dance in particular, and artistic dance in general, as a legitimate and independent art in China. In the article, Wu defines (1) what can be called an "artistic dance" and what cannot, (2) the nature and elements of dance, (3) its relationship with sibling arts, and (4) the "natural law" of bodily movement. While most of the contents are directly inherited from Eguchi's teachings, of particular interest here is Wu's own interpretation of the "artistic dance" and its relationship with sibling arts. Underlying these issues, as it turns out, is the fraught relationship between the kinetic and somatic aspects of dance.

The article begins with a translingual struggle centering on the proper naming of dance in Chinese. The word "dance" in modern Chinese is *wudao* 舞蹈, a combination of two characters *wu* (to wave with hands) and *dao* (to stomp), while the Japanese word for "dance" is *buyō* 舞踊 (*wuyong*, in Chinese), consisting of two *kanji* characters, *wu* and *yong* (to jump). No later than the 1910s, the Japanese word *wuyong* traveled to China and gradually became interchangeable with the Chinese word *wudao*, though *wudao* was still used more frequently.[48] However, in the late 1930s, after Wu returned to China, he started to promote the use of *wuyong* exclusively for "artistic dance" (including his modern dance), which he translated into English as a gerund "dancing." In contrast, the Chinese *wudao*, which Wu translated into the noun "dance," was relegated to encompassing various ethnic and folk dances, dances passed down from ancient rituals, cabaret dances, and dances for the purpose of *tiyu* 體育 (physical education).[49]

One reason for Wu to redefine *wuyong* and *wudao* is that he wanted to use the Japanese *wuyong* to signify the origin of modern dance as a serious new art he learned from Japan, so that people could easily distinguish it from *wudao*, which, at that time, was widely associated with various dances as "low arts" or even "anti-arts." Wu's English translation of *wuyong* and *wudao* into "dancing" and "dance," respectively, is informing: by juxtaposing the Japanese loan word and the indigenous Chinese word and then translating both into English, Wu capitalizes on the unequal relationship among the three languages—Chinese at the bottom, Japanese in the middle, and English at the top being the ultimate semantic arbiter—to establish a hierarchy of various dances with his modern dance at the top.

The difference between "dance" and "dancing" in the English translations reveals Wu's preference between the somatic and kinetic aspects of dance. At first glance, it would seem better to choose the noun "dance" for *wuyong*, as "dance" is more appropriate for naming an independent art. However, Wu chose the gerund "dancing" instead, by which he highlighted the kinetic aspect of his modern dance. To differentiate from various ethnic and folk dances, cabaret dance, and *tiyu* dance, which had rigidified into "dances" (*wudao*) that function through displaying or exercising the somatic body, Wu attempted to depict his new dance as the vital dynamic "dancing" (*wuyong*) that is in constant emergence, capable of continually innovating. In this sense, the distinction Wu made between *wuyong* and *wudao* parallels that made by Duncan between "dancing" and "dances." As Mark Franko observes, Duncan's discourse on the poetics of her modern dance weaves through two poles: the self-expressive theme that "highlights the activity of *dancing* and its effect on the public" and the fetishistic theme that calls attention to the materiality of movement "in the making of *dances*."[50]

Moreover, these linguistic choices of Wu should also be understood in light of the situation of modern dance as a "latecomer": by the time Wu introduced modern dance to China, its sibling arts had taken root and exerted considerable influence in major cities.[51] As a result, Wu on the one hand had to extend the influence of his modern dance with the help of other new arts by positioning dance as a kinetic technique useful to those arts, and on the other hand had to differentiate it from those arts to claim its own independence. This dilemma can be best illustrated by the relation between Wu's new dance and spoken drama.

The debut of Wu's choreography in Shanghai was several dance episodes inserted into the 1935 leftist spoken drama *Nala* 娜拉 (Nora), a Chinese version of Henrik Ibsen's *A Doll's House*, and the 1935 "rightist" musical drama (*yue ju* 樂劇) *Xishi* 西施, which adapted the tale of the famous ancient beauty Xishi into patriotic propaganda—a self-sacrificing girl saving the country by using her sexuality.[52] Interestingly, while a fierce "battle" between the creators and advocates of these two plays was raging in China's major print media, Wu somehow managed to keep a certain distance from this vortex of left-or-right polemics.[53] It seems that by maintaining a low profile and using the advantageous position of being the only choreographer in Shanghai's theatrical circle, Wu managed to avoid choosing sides and find as many allies as possible for his dance.

By this point, Wu and his modern dance had become deeply embedded in the dense network of the other modern arts, especially theater, in terms of resources, personal connections, and performance practices and institutions. For example, for the dance episodes choreographed for the musical drama *Xishi*, Wu coined a specific term—*ju de wuyong* 劇的舞踊 (theater dance), signifying the auxiliary status of dance in relation to theater.[54] Later, during the war, Wu's own living expenses, travels, and public performances were largely supported by theater practitioners. To promote his modern dance, Wu's strategy was to, in his own words, "popularize dance" so as to further "establish connections with the organizations of theater."[55] For quite a long time, most of Wu's students had been theater and film actors who believed receiving some dance training would improve their performances on the stage and the silver screen. Such a situation continued right into the early 1940s.[56]

This "embedded" status of Wu's dance is evident in a passage in the "dance talk": "Nowadays, what the practitioners of stage need urgently is dancing, especially the practitioners of theater, who everywhere feel the need to learn it right now, because it provides the stage-theater actors the necessary on-stage body conditions in terms of rhythm, expression, and composition."[57] In another earlier article, framed in an explicitly evolutionary and developmental linear narrative, Wu places the modern dance training method at the highest "scientific" end of a millennia-long "natural history" of the bodily-movement training method for *all* "stage arts" (not just dance), from the rituals of pre-history primitive tribes, to ancient Greek theater, to ballet, to Duncan's dance, and finally to Laban and Wigman's "natural law" of bodily movement, in the West, and from the "old" operatic plays to the new spoken dramas, in China.[58] Clearly, Wu advertised his dance as a useful bodily "technique" for the other performance arts—similar to the role of *shenduan* 身段 (body contours) in Peking opera, except that Wu's dance is supposed to be more natural, scientific, progressive, and advanced. This is another reason for Wu to translate *wuyong* into "dancing," a useful kinetic "technique," rather than "dance," an independent genre. (By the late 1940s and early 1950s, dance had largely succeeded in obtaining a legitimate and autonomous role in

China. As a result, the loan word *wuyong* for "dancing" had been gradually replaced by the Chinese word *wudao* for "dance.")

This strategy helped modern dance to make its initial presence in the artistic arena in China, survive its most vulnerable infancy, and establish its legitimacy. Wu's talks and training lessons on the "natural law" of bodily movement became very popular among practitioners and organizations of performing arts (especially theater) along his traveling routes around the country during the war. One of Wu's talks given in the city of Changsha in August 1941 attracted an audience of more than three thousand, and they "had very huge effects."[59] However, the strategy also hindered the further development of modern dance into an autonomous art. Although Wu opened his own dance school/institute as early as 1932 and held his first public dance concert in 1935, his role was something akin to a professional choreographer and dance instructor working within the theater, rather than an independent dance artist.[60] Wu's dance amounted to kinetic techniques in the service of more developed performance arts and not an autonomous artistic genre. In an attempt to solve this problem, he observes in the "dance talk":

> In the domain of dance . . . what is of primacy is [to let] the somatic body [become something] like a good conductor of electricity, and at the same time, [to let] the somatic body to paint the picture, play the music, and do the literature. The somatic body of the *wuyong* master must first achieve the conditions of being capable of all these. As long as this requirement is satisfied, [the problem] of the independence of *wuyong* is resolved as a result.[61]

The metaphor of the body as "a good conductor of electricity" easily reminds us of Isadora Duncan's likening the dancer's body to a well-tuned musical instrument, both of which privileges the kinetic over the somatic. For Wu, and the aging Duncan as well, the somatic body in dance is largely a "tool," a means to an end, a carrier of movement. However, unlike the case of Duncan where the body should be "forgotten" in dance, or the more extreme case of Eguchi's "object dance" where the body is annihilated, Wu, in this statement, still keeps a firm place for and even confers some degree of agency on the somatic body. This is because the body, as the unique medium of dance, is the basis for Wu to build up the independence of dance. Before being able to claim its independence, the new dance had to first establish its legitimacy as a serious genre by proving to its sibling arts that it is capable of doing the jobs typically done by literature, music, and painting. Then, when it comes to the issue of independence, Wu had to rely on the otherwise suppressed somatic body to differentiate his new dance from the other art forms. That is, in Wu's discursive strategy, the somatic body needs to be at the same time downplayed for legitimacy and preserved for independence. If for Duncan, as Ann Daly observes, the status of dance as art in the West rested on the possibility of literature, music, and paintings being "done into [the bodily] dance," in Wu's case, that phrase should perhaps be subtly altered to "done into [the dancing] body."[62]

In sum, although the uneasy relation between the kinetic and the somatic in modern dance was not unique to China (as in the cases of Duncan and Eguchi), the particular position of dance in China being a "latecomer" embedded in the network of sibling modernist arts had led Wu to employ a strategy different from those of his foreign mentors. This new strategy of Wu to establish the legitimacy and independence of modern dance in China is what I am calling "reverse integration." The following section elaborates on another important reason for Wu to choose the approach of reverse integration and illustrate this strategy and the associated merits and problems by "close-reading" some of Wu's representative works.

Between Dance and Narrative

The "postliterate" modern dance, starting from the early Duncan, tended to avoid employing recognizable narrative structure, in order to distinguish itself from the narrative-framed Romantic ballet in particular and language- and text-based paradigms in general.[63] Moreover, Wigman's development in Germany further "peeled" musical accompaniment off modern dance to enhance its "purity" and independence (often only simple percussion instruments were allowed).[64] Eguchi followed a similar path of minimizing the traces of literature and music in his modern dance. For example, his "object dance" was designed to express "pure" movements, without any narrative framework. As early as 1930, even before meeting Wigman, Eguchi started to experiment with the possibility of a kind of dance without music, because he believed that music, especially masterpieces, places serious constraints on both the content and the spatio-temporal structure of dance and thus hinders the full realization of its expressive and representational power and creativity.[65] Influenced by these modernist ideas, Wu also experimented with nonnarrative dance and dance without music in a few of his earliest works composed in Japan. For example, in 1933, Wu choreographed a dance work *Perpetual Motion* (*Wu jingzhi de dong* 無靜止的動), which has no trace of narrative and is accompanied only by percussion, to express the idea that motion is absolute in the universe.[66]

However, Wu eventually chose a different path for his version of modern dance: he vigorously promoted the idea that dance should be "an independent yet integrative art," and realized in the late 1930s that this was crucial to the development of dance in China.[67] In his words, the body of the dancer should be fully able to "paint the picture, play the music, and do the literature." This is a belief Wu continued to hold for the rest of his life, even after his dance achieved legitimacy and independence.[68] Thus, this is not an expedient, but a lifelong tenet for Wu. Then why did Wu forsake this modernist experimentation and seemingly turn "backward" to emphasize integration in dance?

The answer has to do with the mismatch between modern dance as a "postliterate" art that resists incorporation into mass media and the national imperatives of enlightenment and mobilization that are hard to fully realize without language, narrative, and mass media. The imperative requires that every art reach, and be understood and welcomed by an audience as large as possible in order to maximize its utility as a means of propaganda and mobilization during the national crisis. This dilemma of popularization Wu faced is evidenced by a critical article on one of Wu's dance performances held in Shanghai in 1939, two years after the outbreak of the Sino-Japanese War. The leftist critic comments that "[Wu's dance] should strive to become popularized, in order to facilitate the intuitive reception by the masses . . . most of the works in this concert were as light-hearted as poems and proses, but [their] meanings were very abstruse. Thus, many spectators with weaker comprehension treated it as esoteric or strange." The critic further suggests that Wu purge any remaining traces of "bourgeois aestheticism," which is "crucial to the prospect and development of Mr. Wu's dance in the future."[69] Wu's integrative dance is a calculated response to such criticism and a logical outgrowth of the utilitarian cultural paradigm of the war period. As can be imagined, it would have been hard for a "pure" dance, such as *Perpetual Motion*, to win any sizable audience in 1930s China.[70]

It is noteworthy that Wu's strategy of "reverse integration" in the 1930s should not be seen as an isolated local "mutation" of modern dance. At about the same time, modern dance in the United States was experiencing a similar "leftist turn" to reach the proletarian class.[71] Mary Wigman's German modern dance too was facing pressure to appeal to the masses, although the pressure came from a different ideological direction—fascism.[72] Also, the later phase of Duncan's dance choreography underwent a transition from "pure dance" or "musical dance" as high art to a "dramatic mode" of dancing, which Duncan cast as "an art of the people."[73] Similarly, Martha Graham in the 1940s started to incorporate literary themes, narrative structures, and memetic gestures into her previous "esoteric" style of the 1930s, as a means to express American nationalism during WWII.[74] As Susan Manning argues, in general, "the kinesthesia and representational frames of early modern dance often worked at cross-purposes. Or perhaps more accurately, the juxtaposition of individualized kinesthetic subjectivity and generalized representational type created a dynamic tension underlying the form of early modern dance, a tension that grounded the paradoxical social function of the form."[75] Yet mentioning these transnational connections in the dance world is not meant to discount the local particularities "modulating" the global connections. For example, in China, Wu had to deal with the dual pressures of establishing dance as an independent serious art and transforming it into an effective tool for mass mobilization in a total war *at the same time*. In contrast, its Western and Japanese counterparts at first mainly faced the first pressure and then the second one later. This suggests, in China, the frictions and tensions between different goals and momentums of modern dance— which characterized the modern dance movements around the globe from the 1920s through the 1940s—had become more intense, and the dynamics thereof followed different pathways.

In fact, the issue of transmedial integration was not unique to dance. Rather, dance should be viewed as embedded in the greater cultural field of performance arts, which in general had been experiencing a turn toward transmedial integration.[76] For example, the new genre of musical drama (*yue ju*), represented by *Xishi*, can be seen as the transformation of spoken drama (*hua ju*) to an integrative genre incorporating music and dance back into theater, because the "tepid and quiet" (*lengdan qingjing* 冷淡清淨) spoken drama had not been attractive enough for Chinese audiences who were used to "boisterousness" (*re'nao* 熱鬧) in theatrical performance.[77] Similarly, in the case of music, the Russian Jewish diasporic composer Aaron Avshalomov (1894–1965), who mentored Nie Er 聶耳 (1912–1935, a leading Chinese composer) and was the first to orchestrate Nie's famous song "March of the volunteers" (*Yiyongjun jinxingqu* 義勇軍進行曲), experienced a transition in his creative trajectory from symphony, opera, dance drama, to the first influential musical (*yinyue ju* 音樂劇) *Mengjiang nü* 孟姜女 (with the English title *The Great Wall*, 1945).[78] Starting from symphony, Avshalomov's career ended with the integrative genre of musical in the early 1940s. The converging paths of *yue ju* (from theater) and *yinyue ju* (from music) suggest that integrating different performance art forms was an effective approach in an age of mass enlightenment and mobilization.[79] It is even more so for the "postliterate" modern dance, which had virtually no audience in China at that time.

It was in this cultural environment that Wu chose the strategy of reverse integration, although marks of it had been evident since Wu's early choreographies. Most of these works employ both a coherent narrative structure and a framing musical piece, which are recorded in Wu's written descriptions. Interestingly, most of the descriptions focus on the narrative and accompanying music, whereas the dance movements themselves are seldom mentioned.[80] Even after taking into account the difficulty of recording dance movements with words, the attention focused on narrative and music alone indicates their importance in Wu's appraisal of his own dance works.

Wu's early works are filled with gloom, sorrow, pain, and fear. They convey the despair and anxiety of individuals in a variety of roles: a desperate puppet emperor; a distressed youth who dies in front of a sculpture of a god without having any news of his lover; a young man in a long, black gown walking in a funeral procession; or a haggard man who dies of poverty and illness by the Huangpu River. With no trace of sunshine, happiness, or joy, these works "kinestheticize" dark emotions within well-developed narrative frameworks, and often at the same time kinestheticize their accompanying famous musical pieces, such as Chopin's "Funeral March" and "Nocturne" and Kreisler's "Love's Sorrow."[81]

However, the process of reverse integration was not without friction. For instance, Wu's integration of narrative is at odds with the ideology of modern dance, which fundamentally mistrusts language-based paradigms. Also, as Eguchi argues, the reliance of dance on music (especially the masterpieces) is likely to discredit the ingenuity and creativity of the choreographer. The tension between integrating music into dance and maintaining the independence of dance (from music) is manifest in Wu's effort in the early 1940s to distinguish between *changge biaoyan* 唱歌表演 (singing-performance) and *changge wudao* 唱歌舞蹈 (singing-dance). According to Wu, in "singing-performance," dance "has no independence, because without singing, [dance] movement alone cannot express its content." In contrast, in "singing-dance," "singing and dance are mutually independent and [each] can exist without the other . . . This is because dance is (simply put) an art of move-ment. This artistic movement, which has its own reasonable organization, can exist alone before the audience."[82] Clearly, for Wu, reverse integration was not about "alchemizing" other artistic genres into dance as an organic whole, such as in Wilhelm Richard Wagner's famous German Romanticism-inspired concept of the *Gesamtkunstwerk* (total work of art), in which all the other arts are synthesized as the integral yet subsidiary parts of drama, or in Duncan's conception, formed later in her career, of the "chorus," a kind of "total" theater that unites music, drama (or poetry), and dance.[83] Rather, it was more about striking a delicate balance between the integration and inde-pendence of different artistic mediums, a point further demonstrated in the next section.

It is because of these subtleties that I refrain from using such terms as intermedial "hybridity" or cross-genre "fertilization."[84] While these biology-derived terms imply a holistic "offspring" in which the "parental traits" can no longer function independently or be separated meaningfully, I am more struck by and interested in the tension between the integration and indepen-dence among these "traits."

An analysis of three of Wu's early works illustrates Wu's strategy of reverse integration and its problems. The three representative works are selected in such a way that the first two, which appear in this section, mainly integrate the elements of narrative (with music in the form of simple percussion), while the third mainly incorporates music (with no fully developed narrative other than a sketchy one implied in the accompanying music), which appears in the next section.

Kuilei 傀儡 (The Puppet)

In 1933, Wu choreographed his first solo, *The Puppet*, in Tokyo, after two years of study with Takada.[85] In 1936, Wu performed this work at the Hibiya Auditorium, where "there were no empty seats," as an independent item in a public concert produced by Takada.[86] This was the first known work of modern dance ever choreographed and performed by a Chinese artist for a Japanese audience, at a time when the Japanese Imperial Army had oc-cupied Manchuria and was at the doorstep of the North China Plain.[87] By performing this dance, Wu intended to convey a political message to the audience about his attitude toward the looming invasion.

The dance employs a double mimesis by combining both mechanical and animal movements.[88] The inspiration for the choreography comes from marionette, and the costume and makeup take the shape of a dog. The combined image of a marionette and a dog is intended to satire Puyi 溥仪 (1906–1967), the emperor of Manchuria, a "puppet" controlled by Japan. Wu uses different dog gestures and movements—such as groveling, crawling, and waging—to mock the subservient and cowardly emperor, but the movements are by no means imitation of a living dog. Instead, they are mechanical and stiff, enhancing the satirical effect by emphasizing that the actions and fate of the dog are controlled by strings in the hands of his unseen master—the Japanese colonizer. It ends with the abrupt death of the dog when the puppet strings suddenly snap. As shown in a photograph of this work, Wu crouches in a twisted shape; his deathly white face features wide-open eyes and his slender arms are half hidden by the costume (figure 2.2).

The whole dance is framed within a clear narrative structure. The dog always follows its master. Sometimes it wags its tail to make sycophantic gestures; sometimes it lies down on the ground and plays tricks to regale its master. Every now and then it watches the master, guessing at his intentions. Suddenly, it senses the angry expression on the master's face. It spots the master's enemies and quickly puts on a hideous face, barking at them. But the enemies are not easily frightened, so it opens its big mouth, exposes its sharp teeth, raises its claws, and then jumps on them. The master praises its actions, which seems to make it feel happy and complacent. Just when it turns with a wagging tail to the master, as if expecting to be petted, the strings are abruptly cut; the dog collapses on the ground, like a corpse.[89] Clearly, this dance has a complete narrative structure—from exposition, introduction of conflict, rising action, and climax, to falling action and resolution.

Wei Bu, who designed the costume and makeup, praises this performance as Wu's attempt to compete with Japanese dancers through both choreography and the political message of anti-Japanese imperialism. Wei interprets the dance as "handing out political pamphlets in the capital of Imperial Japan with big characters on them stating, 'China is against Japanese invasion! Chinese people will fight against Japan!'"[90] However, Wei's shouting out "big characters" on an imagined "pamphlet" actually reflects an anxiety surrounding The Puppet: although it presents a well-developed narrative structure and incorporates pantomime movements, it cannot convey its

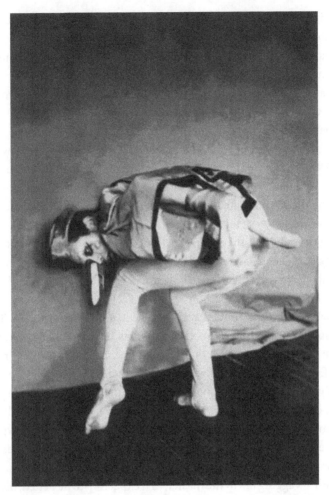

Figure 2.2   Wu Xiaobang performing *Kuilei* (The Puppet), Tokyo, 1936. Image courtesy of the China Dancers Association.

intended meaning without the addition of words. In not directly pointing to Japan, the dance is generalized and the "puppet" can refer to any groveling, sycophantic person. Of course, it is likely that Wu deliberately created this ambiguity for self-protection (he also used his Japanese name, Yamada Urarakai 山田麗介, in this performance), but the experience of *The Puppet* perhaps suggested to him that for modern dance to become an effective "weapon" of political struggle and mobilization in China, it would be necessary to rely on unambiguous narrative, and even language, to convey a precise political message.[91]

However, if modern dance was a "postliterate" reaction against the hegemony of language and words, what happens when you bring the repressed back? Does the use of language and narrative in modern dance subvert the primacy of bodily movement?[92] In fact, Wu may have been quite aware of this issue and addressed it in a self-mocking way in his dance *Strange Dream* (1937).

Qi meng 奇夢 (Strange Dream)

Strange Dream was one of the first dance works Wu choreographed in China after studying central European modern dance with Eguchi.[93] It can be seen as a summary of and self-reflection on his early life experiences of revolution, mobilization, and modern dance practices. *Strange Dream* was performed by Lü Ji 呂吉, a student of Wu, in 1937 Shanghai, before the outbreak of the Second Sino-Japanese War (1937–1945) (figure 2.3).[94] The dancer, in ordinary clothes and barefoot, plays the role of a young revolutionary who has a strange dream one night, in which he becomes a giant ticking clock. His two arms serve as the two hands of the clock, moving in a mechanical manner; lighting, and the shadows it cast, create a dark and uncanny ambience onstage.

This clock dream can be seen as an outer dream that further contains two inner dreams. In the first inner dream, at midnight, the "clock" is shocked by sudden gunshots and runs out into the street, where he witnesses enemies shooting down ordinary people. Angered, he rushes toward them, finally capturing their weapons. Extremely satisfied with his victory, he goes back to the outer dream being the ticking clock, allowing time to move forward; he sees himself as a hero who saved his nation and people. The second inner dream takes place at 3:00 a.m. The revolutionary suddenly stops being a clock, steps down from the circular stage, and, with a pistol in his hand, proudly enters a giant mansion; he waves to a large audience and then gives a political speech (performed through exaggerated bodily gestures and movements). Just when he reaches a state of fanaticism and feels extremely proud and smug, a bullet pierces his body. "Death" wakens the young revolutionary, and he realizes that it was all just a strange dream (figure 2.4).[95]

Several meaningful elements are interwoven into a well-defined narrative structure: dream, revolution, violence, speech, and death. With its layers of symbolism and embodied experiences, the narrative invites a psychoanalytic

Figure 2.3 Lü Ji performing *Qi meng* (Strange Dream), Shanghai, 1937. Image courtesy of the China Dancers Association.

interpretation. The ticking clock not only serves the structural function of dividing the narrative into two parts (two inner dreams) and signifies the dream theme of the dance, but also functions as a tool to "hypnotize" the audience, inviting them to join the dream with the dancer. Although the dreams represent the repressed unconscious, this unconscious is given a material form, or embodied, by the dance movement. Such a correspondence between the embodying movement of dance and the embodied unconscious is manifest in the fantastically seamless transformation of the dancer's

Figure 2.4 Lü Ji performing *Qi meng* (Strange Dream), Shanghai, 1937. Image courtesy of the China Dancers Association.

body back and forth between the ticking clock and the human character in the dream.

The first inner dream of the fight scene can be interpreted as the repressed memory of Wu's own war experiences during the Great Revolution.[96] In spring 1926, the twenty-year-old Wu was still a cadet studying at the Central Military and Political Academy in Wuhan. Wu and his fellow cadets were ordered by the left-leaning Republican government in Wuhan to join in a military campaign to repel attacks from troops allied with the rightist Republican government in Nanjing. Although the situation was nerve-racking for Wu and his detachment, they never had to engage enemy soldiers—they only heard distant gun shots and received friendly fire from other units. In the end, the people welcomed them home as war heroes. What ensued was the bloody "Internal Purge" by the rightist Nationalists starting from April 1927, which ended Wu's short military career.[97] This first dream can be read as a virtual realization, with a tone of self-mockery, of Wu's unfulfilled dream of becoming a revolutionary commander and war hero, a dream that highlights the blind, impetuous, and absurd aspects of his experiences of revolution and war—just like the impulsive young revolutionary in the dance who dreams that he becomes a hero by recklessly charging with bare hands toward heavily armed enemies.

Of particular interest is the speech scene in the second inner dream that seems to question the effectiveness of language in political propaganda and mass mobilization. Wu's doubts about the efficacy of language and words may also be rooted in his early life experiences. When Wu was studying at the Central Military and Political Academy, he once fainted and collapsed onto the training ground during a "tiring" political speech given by the provost, Zhang Zhizhong 張治中 (1890–1969), the famous Nationalist general.[98] After his failed military career, Wu returned to his hometown in rural Jiangsu and taught Chinese history at a middle school for about a year. He wrote his own history textbook and enthusiastically tried to enlighten his poorly educated students and instill the ideas of revolution in them. His approach, however, was not very effective: only a few students understood his lessons.[99] Wu's experiences with tiring political speeches and his failure in political pedagogy may partly explain why he turned to the world of wordless, kinesthetic modern dance.

How, then, does Wu deal with the contradiction between the principle of integration and the mistrust of language and narrative inherent in the ideology of modern dance? He seems to play around with this ambivalence, allowing for multiple interpretations of the second dream in the dance. A "literal" interpretation is that the bodily dance movement *represents* the verbal language of the speech, and thus the death of the character is caused *solely* by the speech. This reading, which is somewhat at odds with the integration principle, implies a one-sided critique of the inefficacy of language in political propaganda. An alternative reading is that the dance movement is driven and possessed, from within, by the swelling desire to speak, a desire that is silenced and repressed by the kinesthesia of modern dance. Such a reading places kinesthesia and language into a fraught dialectical relationship: the death of the character is thus not just caused by the speech; rather, it is more a result of the frenzy and hysteria caused by the struggle between the repressing bodily movement and the repressed language/speech fighting back.

The death ending of the dream can be easily linked to the "death drive," which, usually set in motion by traumatic events (such as war experiences), refers to the human instinct to return to a forever-lost "inanimate state" that death seems to offer. Interestingly, death does not come to the dreamer in the battle scene, where one might expect it, but in the speech scene. As the dance suggests, the mistrust and repression of language and speech by kinesthesia, which signifies the birth of modern dance, may be seen as a "traumatic" event, and the disturbance and struggle the second traumatic event generates—the return of the repressed language/speech—finally trigger the death drive. In the end, *both* the dancing body and speech are "killed" in the dream, not just the latter. In this sense, this "strange dream" becomes an allegory about the problems inherent in both "traumatic" events—the removal of narrative from modern dance and Wu's effort to bring it back.

Between Kinesthesia and Music

Although Wu may have been well aware of these problematics, as suggested by the prewar *Strange Dream*, he stuck firmly to the principle of integration, especially after the outbreak of the all-out war in 1937. In this respect, Wu was following the cultural utilitarianism commonly promoted in the day, because winning audiences, which was hard enough in times of peace, especially for a "latecomer" art form such as modern dance, became an even greater concern in a time of national crisis.

In fact, Western-style new music in 1930s China faced a dilemma similar to, yet still different from, that of Wu's modern dance—the struggle between maintaining its status as a serious art and embracing popularization. This dilemma is evident in one of the most representative figures of popular music in modern China—Chen Gexin 陳歌辛 (1914–1961), known as *ge xian* 歌仙 (god of songs), a term that placed him on a par with Li Jinhui 黎錦暉 (1891–1967), who was known as *ge wang* 歌王 (king of songs). Chen, who had trained in Western music, was a very good friend of Wu and composed musical accompaniment for many of Wu's dance works, including the 1935 musical drama *Xishi*.

Interestingly, instead of promoting his music in *Xishi*, as the other collaborators did (for their respective contributions) in a group of newspaper articles publicizing the drama, Chen wrote in a cynical, self-mocking tone about the compromises he had made to compose "popular music" for the play: "All the songs in *Xishi* were composed in the popular style. No matter how people praise them, I know the position they deserve: the expressionist [self] and the popular [self] . . . are separated by a distance of thousands of miles—there can be no comparison between them at all! Such a comparison would make the latter self so embarrassed that [it] couldn't find any place [to hide] . . . but in the process of striving to gain audience, we made compromises at a dear cost, in order to become popularized . . . Yet compromise should have a limit."[100]

This is not just Chen's personal stance on this matter; it represents a resistance to popularization that could be found in some segments of the arts circle before the war—as Chen remarks at the beginning of his article, "there are 'uncompromising' critics in the world, who criticize others rather harshly; I, Chen Gexin, would be unlikely to escape [their criticism]. Therefore I am 'taking a bow' in advance, giving [the critics] a heads-up . . . As for music composition, I am sympathetic toward the modernist school, so my own [composition] inevitably has that propensity."[101] Obviously, this article is Chen's preemptive defense against potential criticisms of his "popular songs" in *Xishi* by clarifying in advance his "genuine" expressionist/modernist belief and justifying his composition of popular music as an expedient "necessary evil."

By contrast, in Wu's article, which appears just before Chen's, he does not have the "luxury" of taking a condescending attitude toward the "popularized" dance in *Xishi* (to popularize his dance, Wu "made great effort to remove many difficult techniques").[102] Instead, Wu tries to establish dance as a serious art, as seen in the opening paragraph of the article: "The more civilized a nation is, the more serious the respect received by arts is, because artists have transcendent goals, by means of sub-genres as literature, theater, painting, sculpture, music, and dance, to represent the ideals they strive for."[103] It is clear that the situation of Wu's modern dance differed from that of the new music: whereas the former was under the dual pressures of establishing itself as a serious art and pursuing popularization *at the same time*, the latter had, to a considerable extent, already achieved the status as a modernist high art in the Chinese intellectual and artistic community.

Regardless of these tensions, the Shanghai-based leftist musicians of the 1930s relied, as Andrew Jones argues, on the capacity of music to "straddle different media (gramophone records, wireless broadcasting, sound cinema) and places of performance" (including concert halls, dance halls, stadium rallies, schools, streets, and factories) to effectively expand the influence of "mass music" in the cause of political mobilization and national salvation.[104] Therefore, integrating popularized new music (or mass music) was a reasonable strategy for Wu to moderate the two more or less conflicting goals of modern dance. The best evidence of the effectiveness of this strategy is perhaps his dance *March of the Volunteers*, based on and sharing the same title with the famous song, which first appeared in the 1935 leftist movie *Fengyun ernü* 風雲兒女 (Children of the storm) and had become widely popular by 1937.[105]

However, before proceeding to an analysis of this dance, it is worth noting that the integration of new music into modern dance was not smooth; the composers of new music, a genre that by this time had achieved a certain status in cultural circles and beyond, were reluctant to have their music play an auxiliary role in dance and in the process lose its independence. This tension is best demonstrated in an article by Chen Gexin on the music he composed for Wu's 1939 dance drama *Poppy Flower* (*Yingsu hua* 罂粟花).[106] In this article, Chen first utters his dissatisfaction with the music he composed for Wu's previous dance works, in which music is only an "appendage." Chen then expresses his fondness for his music for *Poppy Flower*, because "this time, music, as did dance, managed to obtain the status it deserves on the stage. While dance is drama and singing is speech, music is depiction (miaoxie 描寫)."[107] Chen is striving to maintain a relatively independent status for his music in Wu's dance. This kind of subtle power struggle among different artistic genres (and artists) is similarly reflected in the distinction, mentioned earlier, that Wu makes between singing-performance and singing-dance, through which he attempted to maintain in his strategy of reverse integration a degree of mutual independence between different artistic mediums.

March of the Volunteers

Although both *The Puppet* and *Strange Dream*, among other early prewar works by Wu, touch on issues of national crisis, war, and mobilization, they are mainly idiosyncratic expressions of Wu's life experiences, which may explain why they did not resonate particularly well with urban audiences in Shanghai. It also suggests that Wu had not yet found the right "frequency" on which to communicate with a more general Chinese audience and to further connect and fuse his individual experiences with those of the collective through kinesthesia. That "frequency," however, came to Wu ready-made in "March of the Volunteers," with its tune by Nie Er, lyrics by Tian Han, and orchestration by Avshalomov, which later became the national anthem of the People's Republic of China. Wu must have known this song well, but it was not until the fall of 1937 that he recognized a frequency in its familiar tune.

After the Second Sino-Japanese War broke out in the fall of 1937, Wu joined the Forth Branch of the Anti-Japanese National Salvation Performing and Theatrical Troupes, which toured inland cities, towns, and rural areas, using performing arts—mainly spoken drama and singing—to mobilize

Figure 2.5 The "Forth Branch" of the Anti-Japanese National Salvation Performing and Theatric Troupes, 1937. Wu is the second one from the left in the last row. Image courtesy of the China Dancers Association.

people to join the war effort (figure 2.5); among the more than forty artists, Wu was the only dancer.[108] One night during a performance rally in Wuxi, Jiangsu, Wu decided to choreograph a dance based on "March of the Volunteers," as he discovered that "not just students, but also workers and peasants knew how to sing it."[109] Facilitated by the powerful mass media and the "mass-singing rallies" in streets and factories, leftist mass music movement, and "March of the Volunteers" in particular, paved the way for Wu's dance by creating a potential national audience far larger and more socially and economically diverse than that in Shanghai.[110]

It took Wu only forty minutes to choreograph *March of the Volunteers*.[111] This alacrity can be partly explained by the extemporaneous nature of the performance, but it was more because the structure, theme, and codes of the dance were largely predetermined by the song, its lyrics and the plot of the film in which it first appeared. The major task for Wu was to use dance movement to visualize, or more precisely, to kinestheticize the contents of the lyrics line by line. For example, Wu uses three repetitions of the movement "crouching and straightening up" to embody the line "Arise! Arise! Arise" in an almost literal manner. Some of the moves were appropriated from martial arts, such as a jump in which both legs are folded up under the dancer's rear (figure 2.6), and from military exercises, such as the goose step; others were drawn from the coded gestures of anti-Japanese soldiers that figured prominently in the woodcut prints widely circulated through the print media at the time.[112] A "costume" used in the dance was real clothing borrowed directly from an old peasant watching the performance. The reception of the dance among the audience was "unexpectedly" enthusiastic, evidenced by their "cheering and applause."[113]

Figure 2.6 Wu Xiaobang performing *Yiyongjun jinxingqu* (March of the volunteers), 1937. Image courtesy of the China Dancers Association.

The success of the "unmediated bodily communication" through kinesthesia in this dance was predicated on Wu's careful selection of those bodily codes that could evoke in the audience shared experiences already formed and shaped by the mass media (such as film, gramophone records, radio broadcasting, woodcuts, newspapers and magazines) and mass-singing rallies. The song "March of the Volunteers" alone, which was sung by the troupe's chorus to accompany the dance, would have been sufficient to rouse such a shared sentiment. Ultimately, in China, the "postliterate" modern dance had to "fall back," at least in part, on the mass media and language to conduct mass mobilization.

Encouraged by the success of *March of the Volunteers*, Wu choreographed a series of dance works using well known anti-Japanese songs written by leftist musicians: *Dadao wu* 大刀舞 (Machete dance, 1937), inspired by the song *Dadao jinxingqu* 大刀進行曲 (March of the machetes, 1939) by Mai Xin 麥新; *Youjidui zhi ge* 游擊隊之歌 (Song of the guerillas, 1938) based on the song with the same title, by He Luting 賀綠汀; *Liuwang sanbuqu* 流亡三部曲 (The trilogy of exile, 1937) corresponding to the three songs *Songhua jiang shang* 松花江上 (On the Songhua River, 1936), by Zhang Hanhui 張寒輝; and *Liuwang* 流亡 (Exile) and *Shang qianxian* 上前綫 (To the front), by Liu Xue'an 劉雪庵. These dance works stirred up strong emotional responses from audiences during the Fourth Branch troupe's tour and during Wu's traveling performances later in the war. In his memoir, he mentions that these dances "were welcomed by the masses in the same way as spoken dramas were," and that sometimes the spectators spontaneously sang the songs to accompany the performances.[114] Wu's comments on the effect of his dances on audiences are corroborated by the memoirs of some spectators.[115] The success of these dance works must be ascribed, at least in part, to the success of leftist mass music.

Nevertheless, Wu's dance added something important and new to the effect of leftist mass music: this music could mobilize "the masses into a collective body singing in unison for national salvation," either through the imaginary created by its presence in film or through the collectivity formed by mass-singing rallies.[116] However, this "collective body singing in unison" was inadequate in a total war, which required not just singing, but flesh-and-blood, life-or-death, and armed-to-teeth combat. That is, there remained a gap between the collective body with a *will* to fight and the collective body ready for the *action* of fighting: Wu's dance through kinesthesia could bridge this gap.

To achieve this goal, an obvious obstacle had to be overcome—Wu's smooth, white skin, slim build, and near-sighted eyes, which could easily remind the proletarian and peasant audience of his bourgeois class origin. How could a bourgeois body legitimately represent the bodies of the proletariat and the peasantry? Wu no doubt borrowed clothes from the old peasant when performing *March of Volunteers* to appear more authentic. Shrouded in real peasant clothing, Wu's former bourgeois body symbolically dies and is resurrected as a new body of the oppressed classes. In so doing, Wu directs the attention of the audience away from the physical features of his body and focuses it on his dance movement—that is, emphasizing the kinetic over the somatic in dance.

Although the class "birthmark" on the body is hard to erase and can be only temporarily masked, dance movements, in principle, are more able to penetrate the class barrier through kinesthesia. If the "natural law" of bodily movement is truly natural, it should be natural to students, peasants, workers, and soldiers alike. The simple bodily movement of "crouching and straightening up," for example, even when performed by a bourgeois intellectual, can deliver a sense of transition from an oppressed and restricted bodily state to an active and empowered one; such a movement can be understood and re-experienced by members of an audience, regardless of their class origins.

More important, the purpose of these dance works was not just to generate physical and psychological responses in the audience by performing bodily movements familiar to them. Rather, justified by the war and the nation's need for vengeance, the dances instilled in the audience a new militant culture of bodily movement through kinesthesia, which inevitably involved systemized, although aestheticized, violence. For instance, the movements of "hacking toward the devils' heads with machetes," firing with rifles, throwing grenades, and stabbing with bayonets figure saliently in these dances.

The kinesthesia these violent dance movements project in some sense transforms the audience from pure spectators sitting or standing offstage into participants who can virtually experience those same violent movements together with the dancer onstage. Through this empathetic experience, the bodily movements of one person may generate a simulated bodily experience similar to the original one, within the sensory and cognitive systems of the spectators, in such a way that they feel as if or imagine they are performing those same movements.[117] Such a performative kinesthetic process provides a possibility, through the sensory and the imaginary, for turning the static "collective body" with a will to fight into an active one ready for fighting.[118]

Although no record exists about the exact bodily responses of the audience, Wu's dances seem to have had at least some kinesthetic effect on spectators; Wu uses the word *feiteng* 沸騰 (boiling), an adjective full of motion, to describe the fanatic state of the audience watching his *Machete Dance*.[119] In the end, Wu's unfulfilled dream of being a revolutionary commander is realized onstage.

However, the effectiveness of kinesthesia is by no means unconditional. This has already been demonstrated by the "maladaptation" of modern dance, which Wu learned from Japan, in the vastly different sociocultural environment of Shanghai. Likewise, the kinesthetic effect of Wu's mass-mobilizing dances on spectators seems to vary across regions (rural, urban) and composition of audience (peasants, workers, soldiers). Wu uses various words, such as "welcomed," "cheers and applause," and "boiling," to describe different audiences' reactions to his live performances.[120] Unsurprisingly, the most positive response these dances evoked was from the military.

In spring 1938, Wu performed *March of the Volunteers* at the headquarters of the Communist-controlled New Fourth Army. During the performance, the excited soldiers spontaneously stood up, clapped their hands to the rhythm, sang the song, and urged Wu to perform the dance again and again—in the end, Wu performed five times.[121] This "unforgettable" experience suggests that the bodies of soldiers, trained in a homogeneous military "kinesthetic culture," were well tuned to Wu's mass-mobilizing dances with military themes. This was perhaps a both exciting and disturbing discovery for Wu: exciting because it indicated a great opportunity to extend the influence of his dance and establish it as a legitimate and useful art in China by associating it with the military; disturbing because it suggested the potential danger of his dance's being permanently ensnared by the military and overwhelmed by the themes of violence and war.

Although Wu did not publicly express this concern, it may be inferred from the two parallel paths he chose to follow in the decade to come. Along one path, he continued to cooperate with the Communist-controlled armies

Figure 2.7 Wu Xiaobang directing the rehearsal of the *Jinjun Wu* (Dance of the Strategic Offense), Dongbei minzhu lianhe zhengzhibu xuanchuandui (The Propaganda Group of the Northeast United Democratic Political Division), 1948. Image courtesy of the China Dancers Association.

to choreograph mobilizing dances with military themes. The culmination of this path is his 1947 group dance *Jinjun wu* 進軍舞 (Dance of the strategic offense, figure 2.7), which represents the training and battles of the infantry, cavalry, and artillery.[122] While the previous mass-mobilizing dances were largely built on the already successful "mass music," this dance can be seen as a more typical case of "reverse integration," because its narrative and accompanying music were composed particularly to fit this dance. *Dance of the Strategic Offense*, choreographed in Harbin at the turning point of the Second Civil War (1946–1949) between the Communists and Nationalists, was performed almost ritualistically before soldiers were sent to battlefield and during victory celebrations.[123] Within a year and a half after its debut, more than twenty performance troupes, and more than two hundred performers in total, had come to Wu to learn the dance.[124] Accompanying the sweeping victories of the People's Liberation Army, this dance traveled across China from the northernmost city of Harbin to the southernmost Hainan Island.[125]

Along the second path, Wu choreographed many works having little to do with the national cause. The themes of these works include, to name a few: the sorrow of love, the innocent wish of a young girl, pure friendship, the confusion of a poet, the struggle between a young monk's mundane desires and his religious faith, a playful little girl, an ordinary man struggling within layers of webs set up by everyday life, nostalgia, the happiness of two lovers, and autumn melancholy.[126] These dance works cannot be interpreted, as some of Wu's contemporary critics suggest they should, as mere residuals of Wu's pre-war modern dance endeavor, because of their sheer number (accounting for almost half of the works Wu choreographed between 1937 and 1944) and the fact that he created them incessantly throughout the war.[127] Rather, the bifurcating paths seem to reflect a tension between the dual goals of modern dance in China—to establish itself as something of general significance in the cause of national salvation and as an independent high art.

3

Dancing Reclusion in the Great Leap Forward

Conflicting Utopias and Wu Xiaobang's "Classical New Dance"

I have always insisted that dance should innovate and reject rigidification and formulization. Every time I see people who have made breakthroughs and innovations, I regard them as my kindred spirits. Therefore, those who revere the traditions of classical and national dances have treated me as a heretic and kept a far distance from me . . . Seeing them isolating Tianma [Wu's dance studio], my heart was afflicted with struggles—to hold on or to give up?

—Wu Xiaobang, "The Confession of an Enlightener of New Dance"

Modern dance never produces fixed movements and gestures. There is no fixed structure in modern dance works . . . Thus, it is definitely impossible to pass down any single modern dance movement and gesture to the next generation, which means modern dance has no element that can make it join in the camp of classical dance . . . modern dance is a different form in stark opposition to classical dance.

—Eguchi Takaya, Wu Xiaobang's Japanese dance teacher

Imagine our bird's-eye view is hovering above Beijing in the late 1950s. To locate the nucleus of the Chinese dance world at that time, our sight would glide to the capital's southern area and zoom in to focus on two newly built, adjacent, grand Soviet Russian–style buildings next to the tranquil Park of the Joyfulness Pavilion (*Taoran ting gongyuan* 陶然亭公園).[1] This was the recently founded Beijing Dance School (*Beijing wudao xuexiao* 北京舞蹈學校), predecessor of the Beijing Dance Academy, the first and most renowned

When Words Are Inadequate. Nan Ma, Oxford University Press. © Oxford University Press 2023.
DOI: 10.1093/oso/9780197575307.003.0004

dedicated dance educational institution in the People's Republic of China (1949–).[2] By 1958, the four-story buildings had already boasted eighteen spacious studio rooms covered by wooden dance floors, eight classrooms for cultural courses, and one makeup room, all of which were equipped with heating systems, a rare feature in 1950s Beijing. Headed by Dai Ailian 戴愛蓮 (1916–2006, see chapter 4) as the president and Chen Jingqing 陳錦清 (1921–1991) the vice president, the school launched seven teaching and research programs staffed by forty-three faculty members, including foreign instructors (especially Soviet ballet and folk dance teachers), and developed a comprehensive curriculum consisting of Chinese classical dance (*Zhongguo gudianwu* 中國古典舞), Chinese folk dance (*Zhongguo minjianwu* 中國民間舞), ballet, foreign folk dance, choreography, piano, Chinese music, and other cultural courses. Beijing Dance School trained the best Chinese dancers throughout the 1950s to bolster the institutional system of dance for the new socialist regime. The school was also prolific in stage production—forty-nine dance works, foreign- or Chinese-themed, were choreographed within the first three years following its establishment.[3]

Although the Beijing Dance School, with its central and official status, cast bright lights on the dance stages of socialist China in the 1950s and 1960s, the focal point of this chapter passes over those two grand buildings and lands in an almost hidden alley in Beijing. In 1958, a two-quarter Chinese quadrangle (*siheyuan* 四合院) in the East Fourth Second Alley, about two miles northeast of the Beijing Dance School, was being remodeled, which would become the base of Wu Xiaobang's Heavenly Horse Dance Studio (*Wu Xiaobang Tianma wudao gongzuoshi* 吳曉邦天馬舞蹈工作室, 1957–1964, hereafter Tianma for short; figure 3.1). The back quarter of the compound consisted of two rooms as residence for Wu's family, three small studio rooms, and a large one (around 1,100 square feet) converted by covering the courtyard with a wooden dance floor and roof shading. The front quarter—with newly planted trees, Chinese enkianthus and chrysanthemums, a fish tank, and a pair of budgerigars—accommodated two groups of people that could not be more different: about a dozen Tianma students, boys and girls in their late teens or early twenties, who were "always energetic and lively," and the much quieter and spiritual musicians who were Daoist priests invited by Wu to join Tianma from the Temple of Mystery (*Xuanmiao guan* 玄妙觀) in Suzhou, Wu's hometown.[4] While always keeping a certain distance from each other, the Daoist musicians and the young dancers lived in an odd harmony in the same quarter.[5]

Figure 3.1 Wu Xiaobang (middle, second row) and students at the Tianma Dance Studio, 1956–1960. Image courtesy of the China Dancers Association.

The spatial configuration depicted above—a hidden Chinese quadrangle vis-à-vis two imposing Soviet-style buildings, and young dancers living alongside old priests—epitomizes the curious case of Tianma. In the late 1950s, a low-key, single-artist-centered endeavor stood in an uneasy relation with the large-scale collectivization and socialist transformation sweeping across the country, including the artistic field, and created an unusual combination of the new and the old, the foreign and the indigenous, youthful exuberance and intellectual pensiveness, secular politics and introspective spirituality.

The Curious Case of Tianma

Stated in an announcement in 1956, right before the founding of Tianma, Wu's goal for the studio was to let it grow "from small to big, gradually become corporatized, and hopefully turn into an economically self-sufficient artistic troupe within a certain period of time. When performing, its name will be changed to Tianma Dance Art Troupe."[6] According to Wu's blueprint, Tianma would become not only a financially independent, market-oriented dance company, which resembles its Western counterparts, but also a graduate-level educational institution and an advanced research institute for dance.[7] Economically speaking, this "market enterprise" of Wu seems especially remarkable during a time when it was declared that the Socialist Transformation (1953–1956) and the groundwork for planned economy had been completed nationwide. Politically speaking, Tianma's birth was facilitated by the *Shuang bai fangzhen* 雙百方針 (Double hundred policy: "Let a hundred flowers bloom and a hundred schools of thought contend"), a major short "liberal" interlude (1956–1957) in the cultural and intellectual realm between waves of political purges and censorship.[8] Yet what makes Tianma politically unique is that it was the first and, to the best of the author's knowledge, the only central-government-sponsored art studio for an individual expert-artist in socialist China—the Ministry of Culture was Tianma's direct supervisor—which was a rare and bold experiment for both the artist and the state.[9]

As suggested by its name, Tianma, "the heavenly horse," signifies the ambition of Wu (who was born in the year of horse in Chinese zodiac) to spread his wings of creativity and soar into the heavens of artistic and economic freedom. Unsurprisingly, this endeavor had been in a strained relationship with the socialist state, because the "heavenly horse" was ultimately foaled, fed, and harnessed by the state. What might be unexpected, however, is that Tianma lived for almost six years (with an interruption of over a year from 1961 to 1962), which went far beyond the Double Hundred period and survived several unfavorable political movements; Wu not only managed to turn a considerable profit from 121 concerts during five national tours, which attracted more than 166,000 audience in total, but also was able to put most of his artistic, organizational, and pedagogical visions into practice.[10] Unlike his Western counterparts as represented by American modern dancers who, since the mid-1940s, had been striving to balance the independence of modern dance against the penetration of both the market and politics while at the same time benefiting from the financial and institutional supports provided by both, it seems that Wu, in the late 1950s, experimented with a different strategy to introduce some kind of check and balance among the trio of art, market, and politics.[11] Wu intended to bring (limited) market force back into the performance industry to counterbalance the predominant influence of the state and its political ideology, so that he could maintain a certain degree of independence for his art between the two forces. Yet, as shown later in this chapter, the relationships among Wu's dance, the market, and politics had always been strained ones.

In the secluded Beijing quadrangle, Wu, who had been a student of modern dance and promoter of the "new dance" (see chapter 2), looked back to the past to create what he called the "classical new dance" (*gudian xin wu* 古典新舞).[12] Because his new dance had quickly fallen out of political favor since the 1951 *wenyi zhengfeng* 文藝整風 (Rectification Campaign in the literary and artistic realm) due to its underlying "bourgeois ideology," Wu had to hide his new dance in the disguise of "classical dance" to continue his modernist endeavor, which became the paradoxical "classical new dance."[13] This conflation of the classical and the modern in name should not be surprising— Isadora Duncan once established the legitimacy of early modern dance by associating her dance with ancient Greek culture (see chapter 1). Due to the genre's ephemerality, dances alleged to be "ancient" became an "empty signifier," which can be conveniently filled by the modernist dancer with different meanings, and thus "antimodern-classicism" had paradoxically become an important facet of early dance modernism.[14]

Nevertheless, Tianma constitutes an interesting case. On the one hand, a privileged leading artist with authority of expertise subjected himself, in large part sincerely, to the socialist state; Wu had been a member of the Chinese Communist Party (CCP) since 1949 and president of the Chinese Dance Art Research Association (*Zhongguo wudao yishu yanjiu hui* 中國舞蹈藝術研究會, hereafter, Dance Research Association for short)—the official national organization of dancer-choreographers—since 1954. On the other hand, by exploiting the ambiguities and inconsistencies in state policies and carefully treading through the interstices in ideological discourses, Wu succeeded, for quite some time, in directing state-controlled resources to openly advance his artistic pursuit that diverged from and even ran against the dominant ideology during a time of strict censorship. Therefore, the case of Tianma highlights the complexity of the artist-state relationship in late 1950s socialist China: the state's control over artistic production, restrictive as it was, turned out to be more porous than commonly believed, and the state was even willing to selectively grant considerable flexibility to a trusted artist for creative exploration and experimentation.

It is noteworthy that Wu's modernist "maneuvering" under constraints of the socialist state concurred with what Jens Giersdorf called the "resistive and oppositional" strategies adopted by Wu's counterparts in other countries of the socialist bloc during the Cold War.[15] For example, some East German dancer-choreographers of, or influenced by, *Ausdruckstanz* (expressionist dance)—a major source of Wu's new dance (see chapter 2)—managed to either keep the genre alive as an independent system or integrate its elements into the officially sanctioned Soviet "revolutionary ballet" in a regime that repressed *Ausdruckstanz* on the ground of its excessive individualism and formalism (a socialist code word for modernism).[16] In the Soviet Union, some ballet choreographers with a modernist bent also succeeded in pursuing their own artistic approaches that countered the prevailing Soviet "revolutionary" aesthetics.[17] These paralleling modernist developments in various dance genres in socialist regimes were not pure coincidences; rather, they reflected dance's general significance "as a form of resistance due to its censorship-evading capacity and its ability to communicate multiple meanings that went beyond—and that contradicted—spoken language."[18]

Despite this parallelism resulting from dance's non-linguistic nature, Wu faced unique political conditions in China. Whereas the ideological hegemony his foreign "kindred spirits" worked to subvert was "socialist realism," Wu's major target was the political-artistic imperative of creating the "national dance form" (*wudao de minzu xinshi* 舞蹈的民族形式), which sought to establish codified dance forms that can represent the national identity of the newly founded socialist China.[19] Moreover, Wu's Tianma project bore the brunt of the Anti-Rightist Campaign (1957–1958)—which aimed to purge "bourgeois intellectuals" who were alleged to be against or have reservations about the one-party system and collectivization—and the Great Leap Forward Movement (1958–1960), a radical national economic and political campaign directed at realizing the communist utopia at a dazzling pace.

Under these circumstances, Wu adopted a two-pronged strategy to negotiate a certain degree of artistic freedom within ideological and institutional constraints. Specifically, Wu used his classical new dance to achieve two sub-goals: first, to subvert the official imperative of creating the "national dance form" by refusing any codification of choreographic vocabulary and by stressing the modernist need for constant innovation in dance movement, and yet to preserve the identifiability of "Chinese national characteristics" in his dance by highlighting the abstract "classical ethos/spirit" (*gudian jingshen* 古典精神); second, to systematically construct—through not just choreography but also an organizational regime of teaching, learning, research, and everyday life—an individual-based, spiritual utopia with a reclusive spatiality and slow temporality to resist the collectivist, labor-centered communist utopia with an all-encompassing spatiality and ever-accelerating temporality (which culminated in the Great Leap). That is, Wu elevated *spirituality* in his discourse and practice of classical new dance to counter both the national *form* and the socialist physical *labor*. Elevating spirituality was nothing new in the history of modern dance: Duncan, drawing from late nineteenth-century discourses in physical culture (e.g., Delsartism), science (e.g., Ernest Haeckel's evolution theory), and philosophy (e.g., Nietzsche), cast the body as expression of the soul and thus "transformed her dancing into a means of prayer and effectively consecrated the art form" as high art.[20] However, as shown later, unlike Duncan, who ultimately strived to achieve the unity of body, mind, and soul, for Wu's classical new dance, the heightening of spirituality—as a subversive and resistive strategy in this case—unexpectedly caused a fundamental split between the mind and the body, the spiritual and the material.

"Subversion" and "resistance" here should not be simply understood as the artist's direct confrontation against the state. Rather, it was a subtle, yet decisive strategy of the artist to push the envelope, from within, of the ideological control of the state, of which he was a loyal subject but nevertheless pursued an unsanctioned agenda by following *and* exploiting the rules of the game and by constantly "nudging" policy boundaries to test and negotiate the limits. Accordingly, the utopia of reclusion in Wu's choreographies does not correspond to the modernist idea of "artistic autonomy," which suggests that the artist's creative activities "do not depend on or necessarily reflect extra-aesthetic processes (e.g. economic, cultural or political processes)."[21] Instead, Wu's "classical new dance" is every bit as political as it is artistic, despite its apolitical appearance; it can be seen as both political commentaries/interventions and artistic "world-building." This strategy of Wu, along with the reclusive utopia he constructed, was conflicted in nature. Moreover, this conflictedness was not just a "trauma" resulting from political struggles but also had roots in the intrinsic problems of modernism in dance and in the split modern subject.

To demonstrate these, the rest of the chapter first teases out Wu's modernist strategy to theoretically subvert the "classical dance form"—a major representative of the "national dance form" being developed by the Beijing Dance School since the mid-1950s. It then examines the innovations and controversies of Wu's organizational and pedagogical practices at Tianma that brought his vision for classical new dance into reality. It next shows how Wu, in his choreographies, appropriated the ideal of "reclusion"—which has a long, prominent history in the Chinese intellectual tradition—to create an individualistic utopia as an intellectual enclave within and against the collective communist utopia that fueled the fanatic Great Leap. To demonstrate Wu's strategy and its conflicted nature, close analyses of two representative works of his classical new dance are offered. The chapter ends with Wu's last choreography and Tianma's downfall.

A Modernist Critique of the "National Form" and "Invented Tradition"

In the mid-1950s, the Beijing Dance School began to invent the "classical (Chinese) dance" (Zhongguo gudian wu 中國古典舞) by mainly adapting the dance (or dance-like) codes integrated in the Chinese *xiqu* 戲曲 (theater, such as Peking opera), and to build a corresponding training system by combining the regimes of both Soviet Russian ballet and the Chinese *xiqu*.[22] This project sprang from the political imperative of searching for the "national forms" in all major arts demanded by the CCP, which can be traced back to Mao Zedong's 1942 "Talk at the Yan'an Forum on Literature and Art" (and beyond to the late 1930s). The "classical form" is an important constituent of the "national form," as evidenced by Mao's famous dictum *gu wei jin yong, yang wei zhong yong* 古為今用, 洋爲中用 (Make the past serve the present and the foreign serve the Chinese).[23]

Emily Wilcox has interpreted this process by critically extending the framework of "invented tradition."[24] This term is first developed by Eric Hobsbawm and Terrence Ranger to refer to those "spurious" traditions that are claimed to be old and authentic but actually new in origin and even invented.[25] Joshua Goldstein, by studying the formation of Peking opera in the colonial context, further argues that the participants involved in the invention did not intend to conceal, but instead were quite explicit about their intention and action of inventing, as a conscious means to form a competitive cultural identity for the cause of nation-building against the pressure imposed by Western (or Westernizing) cultural hegemony.[26] Wilcox's critical application of the invented-tradition framework to the case of "classical dance" is similar to that of Goldstein, but she changes the original context of colonial modernity to that of the socialist era and further develops a new concept—"dynamic inheritance," which emphasizes that "cultural traditions inherently change and that they thus require continual innovation to maintain relevance to the contemporary world."[27]

However, the framework of invented tradition and its variants are inadequate to explain some important aspects of the national form project. There were several motivations driving this lasting cultural-political project. First, in the late 1930s, Mao was keenly aware of the fact that in order to efficiently mobilize and organize the masses (mainly peasants and workers) to win the wars and speed up the revolution, abstract political ideas—such as nationalism, and Marxism-Leninism and its analytical methods—must be presented in literary and artistic forms familiar, intelligible, and appealing to the masses, that is, the national forms.[28] This idea is often expressed as "use the old bottle to hold the new wine" (*jiu ping zhuang xin jiu* 舊瓶裝新酒); or in Mao's words, "as for the literary-artistic forms of the past, we do not refuse to make use of them. However, as long as these old forms come to our hands, being transformed and added with new contents, they turn into things that are revolutionary and serve the people."[29] Second, to achieve this goal, the CCP used this cultural campaign as a means to control the cultural producers (intellectuals and artists), many of whom had bourgeois and Western leaning attitudes, and to transform them and their works into a productive yet submissive part—or "cogs and screws," in Lenin's words, quoted by Mao in his "Yan'an Talk"—of the gigantic revolutionary machine.[30] At last, after the founding of the People's Republic, the young socialist state needed some distinctly Chinese forms in the artistic realm to create an unprecedented, unified national culture as a means to further the domestic sociopolitical transformations and, on the international stage, to present the national image and pride of China, signal China's status in the socialist bloc, and articulate its stance against Western capitalist-imperialist ideology and culture during the Cold War.[31]

While the concepts of invented tradition and dynamic inheritance largely concern the first motivation (nation-building and revolution) and the last one (identity, nationalism, and anti-colonialism at both the domestic and international levels), they say little about the second point, which, in the Althusserian sense, concerns interpellation and subjection/subjectivation.[32] It is on this latter dimension that resistance took place. For the bourgeois-leaning intellectuals and artists, the utilitarian campaign of inventing the national forms may be both enabling and disabling. It was enabling because it provided an effective way for them to greatly extend the influence of their arts among the masses in the sublime cause of revolution, nation-building, socio-cultural transformation, and even on the international stage.[33] This was especially appealing to the fledging art of dance, which had limited influence compared with the other more well-established arts (see chapter 2). However, this "popularization" (dazhonghua 大眾化) was achieved at the cost of intellectuals and artists losing their relative independence—a status that could afford them the right to criticize the Party, the state, and the social reality. Therefore, it is unsurprising that the discourse on the national form became one of the major battlefields where struggles occurred.[34] At stake was the subjecthood of intellectuals and artists—whether or how to answer the call of creating the national form determines whether or how to subject themselves to (and be subjectivated by) the interpellation of the CCP.[35]

The most famous dissident was perhaps Hu Feng 胡風 (1902–1985), a high-profile writer and literary and art theorist who was condemned by the Party and Mao as an "anti-revolutionary" due to his open opposition of the CCP's cultural policies and the underlying theories.[36] Hu insisted that the national form should be defined by the Westernized new literary and artistic forms developed since the May Fourth Era (mid-1910s to early 1920s), rather than by traditional/classical or folk forms.[37] Wu shared similar May Fourth sentiments with Hu on this matter. As late as in 1957, two years after the shockwave of the nationwide, systematic criticism of Hu's literary and art theory reached the discursive field of dance, Wu still publicly claimed that "after the May Fourth, the dance formed by adapting European culture to the particular circumstances of China is also [part of] tradition" and denying this is to "cut off tradition."[38] Differing from Hu, however, Wu adopted a more circuitous strategy of subverting the national form in the case of classical dance to achieve a theoretical goal in some sense even more radical than that of Hu's. The ultimate goal of Wu was to object in his choreography any systemized dance codes (as an example, the codified system of ballet vocabulary), which is the prerequisite for any dance to be qualified as a coherent dance *form*, be it national, classical, or folk. That is, Wu aimed to reject all together the stability and coherency of codified forms—the very premise underlying the discourse on the national form. Such a modernist pursuit— inherited from the central European modern dance school through Wu's Japanese teacher Eguchi Takaya (see chapter 2)—was fundamentally subversive in China's socialist context, since the national form in the making was a formal "bridle" that would harness artists and their artistic creation to serve the revolutionary machine.[39]

To achieve this ambitious and risky goal to deconstruct the national dance project, Wu employs a threefold strategy, which is strikingly similar to, yet goes beyond, the critical logic of the invented-tradition framework. First, he criticizes the formal sources of the classical dance being developed by the Beijing Dance School—the *xiqu* tradition originating in late imperial China—being not "authentic" and representative enough. After all, the dance-like movement integrated in *xiqu* is only integrated to theater, far from a well-established independent art. Moreover, Peking opera as the "national drama," a major basis for building the classical dance, is itself an "invented tradition" with a history not much longer than that of the May Fourth "new culture."[40] Therefore, Wu on the one hand relativizes *xiqu* as only one of many dance traditions, including, paradoxically, the May Fourth "tradition" of his new dance.[41] On the other hand, Wu observes that more "authentic" traditional dance forms do exist, which remain largely intact in the form of religious ritual dance, such as *Yi wu* 佾舞 (Rank dance, the Confucian ritual dance performed in the memorial ceremony for Confucius), *Nuo wu* 儺舞 (Exorcism dance, a kind of Shamanic ritual dance), and various Daoist and Buddhist ritual dances, preserved by generations of clergy in temples.[42] In Wu's view, these living ancient dances are the more "genuine" tradition, and thus the Beijing Dance School's strategy of constructing the classic dance, which "particularly emphasizes the *xiqu* tradition," is in fact "denying the preserved dance [traditions] of the ancient times."[43]

Second, Wu argues that these more "authentic" traditional dance forms should be first "excavated" and preserved for their historical and anthropological values and should not be hastily appropriated as the basis for constructing the classical dance. For example, when directing a two-year (1955–1957) nationwide field research as President of the Chinese Dance Art Research Association, Wu found that many of the Shamans who knew the *Nuo* dance had changed their profession to performers of theater during the Socialist Transformation. In order to save the fast-disappearing ancient dances like *Nuo*, Wu proposes that "dancers had better not destructively change them at first, [but instead] let them remain what they are and cherish these materials like discovered historic artifacts."[44] By adopting this preservationist view of dance traditions, Wu aims to undermine the authenticity of the classical dance form in the making, which espouses the logic of dynamic inheritance.

As the last step of his strategy, Wu argues that what the classical dance should and could grasp is not any invented classical dance form, whose authenticity is inherently problematic, but rather the general "classical ethos." At first glance, the "classical ethos" seems even more abstract and elusive than the classical form. However, it could more easily evoke consensual sentiments among Chinese people (at least among intellectuals), because the classical ethos—aesthetics, attitudes, beliefs, virtues, and so on—is supposed to be passed down across generations through, among others, the written classics of history, literature, philosophy, and artistic artifacts. In this sense, the classical ethos, however defined, is more lasting and "authentic" than any ephemeral dance form claimed to be "classical." In Wu's own words, "the classical is by no means just a category of temporality or times, and the classical ethos . . . is by no means just something that belongs to a specific time either; in modern life continues the classical ethos."[45] Therefore, by shifting the focus from the classical form to the more abstract, and thus more elastic, "classical ethos" that supposedly transcends the temporal division between the traditional and the modern, Wu intended to free dance choreography and training from the restriction of any "classical" formal codification, and thus to preserve the possibility of employing modern dance philosophy and methods in his classical new dance.[46] In Wu's view, as long as centering on the classical ethos, dance form should *not* be limited to the classical codes based on *xiqu*—"the techniques [of choreography] can be diverse . . . such as those of symbolism and Romanticism," and expressionism, naturalism, futurism, and mysticism should be "all integrated together, being eclectic, so that [choreography] can be successful."[47]

This is exactly where Wu goes beyond the logic of invented tradition and the discourse on the national form. Wu's classical new dance was a modernist critique of both: for him, the incessant innovation of dance movement, free from systematic codification, should be an imperative for choreography (i.e., innovation *against* codification).[48] This view differs from that of dynamic inheritance as well: although the latter too emphasizes that constant innovation is intrinsic to dance traditions and thus also advocates an elastic interpretation of traditions, it ultimately aims at creating certain codified, if evolving, dance forms (i.e., innovation *for* codification). To be clear, despite Wu's consistent emphasis on innovation, he did not at all object borrowing dance moves or gestures from existing forms or styles; neither did he oppose, for any dancer, forming a relatively stable style of choreography, which entails repetition of certain elements, such as dance moves, patterns, and structures, across different dance works—Wu himself did all those things in his teaching and choreographing. Rather, his eclectic attitude towards choreographic techniques was intended to reject any dominant system of dance codes, including any codified "tradition."

In contrast to Hu Feng, who, while admitting the necessity of the national form, antagonized the May Fourth "new culture" against "tradition" in the struggle of defining the national form, Wu worked within the logic of tradition to subvert the national form. In Wu's view, "tradition" (the old) was *not* the most dangerous enemy of the May Fourth legacy (the new), because what counts as tradition is always malleable and subject to (re)interpretation—his new dance did find cover in "tradition" as the classical new dance. Instead, what was more threatening to his new dance was the national form in the making, which, whether classical or modern, would become a formal bridle once it took shape. Any codified dance form is, in the words of Wu's Japanese teacher Eguchi, "in stark opposition" to the ideology of (central European) modern dance based on the "natural law" of bodily movement, which denies formal codes as the building blocks and organizing principles of choreography and, instead, taps directly into the infinite movement possibilities derived from the Labanian spatial and movement theories and Mary Wigman's choreographic method of *Gestalt im Raum*, or shape in space (see also chapter 2).[49] Wu's Tianma and classical new dance were a circuitous effort to break free from the bridle of the national form—ultimately, it is the codified *form*, instead of *content*, that was the main enemy of his modernist ideal. As Wu put it publicly in 1957, "all human creation and research need freedom, but freedom can never be gained without effort; freedom depends on us reaching our hands to society and nature to fight without stop."[50]

A Hermit Hiding in the City: Tianma's Organizational and Pedagogical Innovations

Wu's practical goal was less radical, though no less ambitious, than his theoretical one. He did not intend to, and could not, replace the classical dance (and the national dance forms in general) with his classical new dance; his aggressive gesture toward the former was more of a defensive strategy for the latter. Wu had been marginalized in the practices of dance choreography, performance, and education, especially after he turned down the state's generous offer of the position as the first president of the Beijing Dance School, which was Wu's gesture of protest toward the higher authority's decision to impose Soviet Russian ballet (and the Chinese *xiqu*) as the primary training system of the school.[51] By 1957, Wu himself had been off the stage for more than a decade and had not choreographed any dance work for seven years.[52] Thus, Wu's practical goal was limited to carving out a plot in the socialist artistic field for his classical new dance—a haven for his modernist ideas—as a "unique flower among hundreds."

Nevertheless, Wu did have some advantages on his side. Although Wu had been practically excluded from the stage of dance choreography and performance since 1950, he had managed to maintain his central position in the discursive field of dance by transforming his identity from a dancer-choreographer to a dance scholar and academic authority. Throughout the 1950s, Wu was the only major dancer who ever systematically wrote on virtually all areas of dance as a discipline, including dance historiography, theory, choreography, and pedagogy. He also conducted extensive field research at the national level: Wu first studied ethnic dances of the borderlands from 1952 to 1954 as the director of the Ethnic Minority Cultural Work Group, and then studied folk dances and religious dances in South and East China from 1955 to 1957.[53] Moreover, as president of the Dance Research Association, Wu established the key discursive device—the major academic and professional dance journals—and thus his authority in the discursive field of dance.[54]

Therefore, before the founding of Tianma, the core of the Chinese academic dance world in the 1950s can be roughly divided into two specialized camps, as symbolized by the geography depicted at the beginning of the chapter. The first is represented by the dance practitioners at the Beijing Dance School, backed up by Soviet experts, who dominated the realm of practice, including dance choreography, performance, and education. The second camp was headed by Wu Xiaobang, with the institutional support of the Dance Research Association, specialized mainly in academic research, including dance history, anthropology, theory, and criticism.[55] The two camps cooperated and competed, maintaining a delicate balance of power between practice and discourse in the field of dance.[56]

Wu, as a dancer-choreographer, was not content with being left out from the practical realm and made persistent effort to put his artistic vision into practice, which culminated in the birth of Tianma. The nature of Tianma was, in Wu's words, a cutting-edge "scientific experimental lab," through which Wu intended to create a distinct organizational form integrating dance research, education, choreography, and commercial performance.[57] That is, Tianma was not just a small dance studio; it contained the functions of a dance educational institution, a dance company, and a high-level research institute that, according to Wu's blueprint, would eventually become qualified for training graduate students.[58] In some sense, Wu attempted to combine flexibly in Tianma the characteristics of the model of academic institution and that of apprenticeship. This approach of organizational innovation was so ahead of time that it would not be picked up again by the *xiqu* education until the new millennium.[59] Therefore, it is unsurprising that Tianma had been highly controversial since its birth, because it not only represented a heretical school of artistic thoughts, but also constituted a novel organizational alternative to the Soviet model of academic institutions that had prevailed in China. The balance of power had been upset.[60]

Wu was aware of the political risks and meticulously guarded Tianma from making imprudent mistakes, which would potentially draw political attacks. Tianma to Wu, in his own words, was like "a precious son [he] had at an old age" (when Tianma was founded Wu was already fifty-four). Starting from 1956, Wu cut down his publications to minimum to keep a low profile in the turbulent times.[61] Tianma itself, as symbolized by the walled *siheyuan*, had literally lived a hermit life. Students of Tianma could leave the studio only on Saturday and must return by Sunday night, and were not allowed to develop romantic relationship, get married, or be involved in any "unhealthy social activities," both inside and outside Tianma. Wu consistently turned down high officials who requested the female students to be dance partners in important balls, and film companies that invited the Tianma students to shoot dance scenes.[62] Ironically, Wu, who himself grew up wandering freely in the boisterous urban cultures of Suzhou, Shanghai, and Tokyo and pursued the liberating art of modern dance, had to force his young students to live an ascetic life under political pressure. Nevertheless, in the eyes of the Tianma students, Wu's care for them "seems to surpass that for his own children," and Wu "held as abhorrent the humiliation or physical punishment inflicted upon students by the Soviet experts and the education of apprenticeship in Old China."[63]

The training methodology and philosophy of Tianma were also innovative, which used the central European modern dance system of "natural bodily movement" and dance composition to synthesize elements of other training traditions (figure 3.2). A typical day of the Tianma students begins at 8:00 a.m. with a one-and-a-half-hour "basic training" class, which includes the teaching of the natural bodily movement, reformed ballet basics, Chinese martial arts, and *tanzi gong* 毯子功 (literally, skills on carpet, the method of

Figure 3.2 Wu Xiaobang teaching students at the Tianma Dance Studio, ca. 1957. Image courtesy of the China Dancers Association.

physical skill training used in the *xiqu* tradition). The second class focuses on developing the students' creativity and imagination necessary for choreography. Students are required to creatively use different rhythms of breath and movement to express various emotions (such as happiness, sadness, regret, and disgust), to represent daily bodily movements (walking, fording a river, plucking flowers, and riding a bike), and to interpret all kinds of people and animals (normal or abnormal). The afternoon is usually devoted to choreographing and rehearsing dance works for public performance, practicing Chinese musical instruments and folk songs, and cultural courses on literature and arts (including history of Chinese dance, music, and literature).[64]

Wu's eclectic training system of classical new dance differed fundamentally from that of the classical dance in the Beijing Dance School in several important aspects, though the two shared some sources. First, the tenet of natural bodily movement was the master principle, based on which the ingredients of other systems were carefully selected, reformed, and integrated. For example, there were no barre or mirror utilized in Tianma's training courses (including the course focused on ballet basics)—a modern dance tradition Wu inherited from his Japanese teachers Takada Seiko and Eguchi Takaya (see chapter 2), because Wu believed those tools are for the trainees to correct their postures and movements according to the "affected" standard of beauty imposed from without, rather than to understand and master the "natural law" of bodily movement from within.[65]

Second, learning the techniques of ballet, *xiqu*, and martial arts was only for the purpose of cultivating the necessary bodily skills, but not for achieving formalistic exactitude of coded movement or physical virtuosity. In fact, Wu made great effort to ensure that his students do not fall into the "traps" of these codified formal systems—the dictum recalled most frequently by Wu's students later in their life is: "Learn, then must forget," because Wu maintained that "only after forgetting what has been learned [as codified forms] can one truly enter the realm of creation [based on the natural law]."[66] In the eyes of Wu's critics from the classical dance camp, Wu's "using" the Chinese dance tradition (as represented by *xiqu*), or any other tradition, is offensively "insincere" and "nihilistic."[67] Yet this is exactly how Wu deconstructs the classical dance form in the making.

Third, while Wu may be "nihilistic" about the "classical form" in his training methodology, he seems to be serious about the "classical ethos." When the Tianma troupe toured the country, the places Wu led his students to visit the most were temples, as he believed that these religious institutions "preserve the essence of Chinese culture"[68] and "if we do not immerse ourselves in the history of Daoism, Confucianism, and Buddhism, we cannot reach the depths of the thoughts of the Chinese society."[69] That is, Wu strove to replace the formal with the spiritual in defining the "classical" or "tradition." If Wu's "nihilistic" deconstruction of the classical form was to break the "old bottle," then his emphasis on the "classical ethos" was to bring back the "old wine." Wu's strategy was thus in diagonal opposition to the imperative of "preserving the old bottle while filling it with new wine."

Wu's sincerity toward the classical ethos, however, should not be taken too seriously either. The reason why Wu brought back the classical ethos in the first place was: only by encroaching on the monopoly of the classical form in defining the "classical" and "traditional" could he carve out a space to preserve his "new bottle" of new dance, and together with it, his version of the "new wine"—the underlying modernist ideas. In the early 1980s, after the advent of the Reform era, Wu could finally utter his complaint about the dominant status of "classical themes" in Chinese dance choreography and advocate the necessity of "strengthening the modern consciousness."[70]

"Reclusion" in the Great Leap Forward: Utopia against Utopia

In 1958, Mao and his comrades launched the Great Leap Forward Movement, in the hope of quickly transforming the underdeveloped Chinese economy into an industrialized communist one that could compete against both Western capitalist countries and the Soviet Union. This movement was spurred by an inflated sense of optimism and urgency among the CCP leadership—especially Mao himself—brewing from the relatively smooth Socialist Transformation and the completion of the First Five-Year Plan (1953–1957) in the economic sector, the international reputation gained by playing an important leadership role in handling the 1956 Polish and Hungarian Crises within the socialist bloc, and the "victory" of the Anti-Rightist Campaign in the domestic political and ideological realm.[71] The campaign, with the slogans of "surpassing Britain and catching up with the United States" and "racing into Communism," originally aimed to build the Communist utopia within an extremely short period, but instead resulted in one of the greatest famines in modern Chinese history.[72] The whole nation was swirled into this forward-looking, frenetic-paced movement. This also impacted the artistic field, which, together with mass media, was fired up to mobilize the masses into this utopian campaign.

With the acceleration of the socialist construction, the art institutions, like all "work units," developed production plans. Painters found themselves being required to create a large number of works within a short period to promote the campaign, including works of immense scale. The artists of the Central Academy of Fine Arts, for example, completed 138 murals before they went to labor in the countryside.[73] Literary works, especially poems, were collected and produced in unprecedented quantities, "like wheat and steel." In the musical field, just in early 1958, several million pieces were collected in Shanghai alone, of which two thousand were published.[74] The agitprop dances, produced and performed by worker-peasant-soldier amateur artists under the slogan of "More, Faster, Better, and Cheaper," also emerged on the stage.[75] As the scholar Jie Li observes—based on her study of photography in the Great Leap—"the people used not only painting and poetry, photography and film, but also the fields and their laboring bodies as media to express, realize, and constitute utopian images."[76] Those dances of the masses are not only the quintessential embodiment of what Li calls the masses being turned into media, but also collective, corporeal blueprints for the social organization of the communist utopia.

Against this backdrop, Tianma's eleven or so works of classical new dance would seem out of place.[77] The unifying themes of these dances are *yu* 漁 (fishing), *qiao* 樵 (woodcutting), *geng* 耕 (farming), and *du* 讀 (reading), which, in Wu's view, characterize the traditional Chinese way of living.[78] At first glance, these themes represent different kinds of physical (and mental) labor, and do not seem incompatible with the gist of the Great Leap. However, the particular classical ethos underlying these labor themes, as admitted by Wu later in his life, is the millennia-old Chinese intellectual ideal of "reclusion," which may be characterized by material simplicity, individual self-sufficiency, meditative calmness, artistic leisure, disinterested poise, enjoyment of nature, and the condescendingly critical yet detached stance against the mundane (political) world.[79] Thus, the intellectualized and spiritualized images of hermit-fisherman, woodcutter, and farmer in the Tianma dances—accompanied by characteristically slow-paced and spiritual Chinese classical music—became the antithesis of the communized/ collectivized farmers and workers who razed enormous forests and reported fictional unit agricultural yields and steel outputs of astronomical quantities.[80] If Tianma's reclusive life offstage was a low-key defensive strategy, its dance works onstage representing the "backward-looking" images of reclusion would seem a blatant mockery of the national leap-forward frenzy.[81]

Putting the images of reclusion onstage in the historical context of the late 1950s was by no means Wu's nostalgic response to the fast disappearing "traditional way of living." Rather, Wu, as an urban intellectual-artist who claimed to belong with the May Fourth generation, appropriated "reclusion" to make a political stance. The critical strength of the imagery of reclusion rests on the fact that reclusion, as an intellectual ideal, provided the exact economic, aesthetic, and ideological opposite of the socialist-communist model that, despite intermittent setbacks and oscillations, had been quickly expanding its grip on the country.

In the economic realm, the Socialist Transformation (1953–1956) managed to collectivize or nationalize the majority of agriculture, handcraft industry, and capitalist industry and commerce in merely three years. For example, in the agricultural sector, millions of peasants handed over the land plots just assigned to them during the Land Reform (1950–1953) to the Agricultural Producers' Cooperatives, which aimed to collectivize agrarian production.[82] Such a process culminated in the even larger social organization of People's Communes mushrooming during the Great Leap, which became a "trinity" of political-military governance, economic production-consumption, and everyday life—as summarized by Mao's own words: "People's Commune is a good name; [it] includes industry, agriculture, commerce, education, and the military. Its characteristics are, first, big, and second, public."[83] These collectivizing movements on a national scale not only aimed to restructure the millennia-old family-based natural economy, but also encroached on private life itself. The commune system sought to abolish private property, dismantle borders of kinship-based "natural villages," and bring down family structures, assisted by the expansion of collective daycares and nursing homes, the establishment of the public dining halls, and the prohibition of cooking at home.[84] The rural workforce was largely militarized, as epitomized by the slogan: "Organization militarized, operation combatized, and everyday life collectivized" (*zuzhi junshihua, xingdong zhandouhua, shenghuo jitihua* 組織軍事化, 行動戰鬥化, 生活集體化).[85]

Similar processes also took place in the intellectual and artistic realm. Following the Soviet model, almost all intellectuals, writers, and artists were organized into various academic or professional institutions or associations led directly by Party cadres and governmental bureaus.[86] Organizations like these greatly facilitated the CCP's political control over intellectuals and artists, as manifested in the Anti-Rightist Campaign preceding the Great Leap, during which about 400,000 to 700,000 people, mostly intellectuals, were singled out as "Rightists" to meet the quota of five percent assigned to each "work unit," deprived of their positions and forced to perform physical labor in the countryside or factories—the so called "labor reform."[87] This process further developed into anti-intellectualism and the general deterioration of intellectuals' social status during the Great Leap.[88]

Against this weltering tide of drastic social changes, the imagery of reclusion represents a diagonally opposite model. Instead of large-scale collectivization of production and consumption, reclusion promotes the ideal of self-sufficient, individual-based "natural economy." Unlike the aggressive socialist-communist construction that emphasizes the superiority of human power over nature and thus destructively transforms nature,

reclusion stresses the harmonious equilibrium between humans and nature. In contrast to the debasement of intellectual labor as something to be
"reformed" through physical labor, reclusion spiritualizes physical labor as
an intellectual means to achieve higher consciousness. Different from the
collectivizing processes which intrude into private life, reclusion holds the
ground of private life against the encroachment of the public. While the new
socialist regime interpellates intellectuals with a dominant ideology and
transforms them into "cogs and screws" in the revolutionary machine, reclusion defends the independent status of intellectuals, which enables them to
treat "criticizing the government" as a right they can either defiantly claim or
condescendingly forsake, rather than a "responsibility" that can be imposed
upon or taken away from them by certain authorities. It is because of this critical strength (yet with an apolitical appearance) of the imagery of reclusion
that Wu appropriated it in his classical new dance to kinesthetically construct
an individualistic utopia with a reclusive spatiality and timeless temporality
to resist the collective communist utopia with an all-encompassing spatiality
and ever-accelerating temporality.

However, Wu's resistance was not a head-on confrontation against the
state. Just like he did not choose to openly pit his new dance against the classical dance but instead found cover within it for self-protection, Wu con-
cealed, though perhaps only thinly, the imagery of reclusion in the disguise
of mundane labor. Ultimately, Wu himself was a CCP member subject to the
Party's rule. Thus, Wu's strategy was conflicted in nature.[89] To demonstrate
the contradictions inherent in Wu's classical new dance, the rest of this section provides close analysis of two representative dance works of Wu.

Si fan 思凡 (Longing for the Mundane): Faith vs. Desire

A graduate student of Wu's once recalled a scene from one of the last public
performances of Tianma right before its downfall in 1960:

> Three nights in a roll, when Teacher Wu finished his performance of *Si fan*
> and went to the front of the stage to answer the curtain call, barefoot, with
> his face covered by sweat, ten fingers put together devoutly, we watched
> with excitement, and grief as well. We vaguely felt that his salutation was
> bidding farewell—the beams of stage lights shooting on his body would
> probably soon turn dim . . .[90]

The location of the performance was the famous *Lanxin daxiyuan* 蘭心 大戲院 (Lyceum Theater) in Shanghai, a luxurious legacy reminiscent of the city's colonial cosmopolitan past complicated with both glory and disgrace. It was also at this same theater that, back in the 1930s, Wu held some of his earliest modern dance concerts. Now here again, thirty years later, Wu, at the age of fifty-five, was unwillingly approaching the end of his career as a professional dancer-choreographer. Despite the turbulent decades that had passed by, some of Wu's old audience of the 1930s—many were his friends working in theater, film, literature, music, and the fine arts—regathered in the theater to support and celebrate Wu's performance, which turned out to be the final high point of his dancing career.[91]

The last dance of the concert was *Si fan*, which, with the image of Wu as a Buddhist monk putting his two palms together, had left a lasting impression among the audiences of 1960. This dance shared the same title, theme, and similar storyline with the well-known, centuries-old *kunqu* 昆曲 (Kun opera) work.[92] Mei Lanfang 梅蘭芳 (1894–1961), master of Peking opera (who contributed to some of the choreographies by the Denishawn dancers, pioneers of American modern dance), also once studied and performed this *kunqu* drama in the early Republic era.[93] He learned and further developed many elegant, expressive dance moves from *Si fan*, the experience of which was instrumental in Mei's perfecting his Peking opera performance.[94]

It is noteworthy that Wu's *Si fan* was not part of his Tianma works of the late 1950s, but choreographed eighteen years earlier in 1942 Qujiang 曲 江, Guangdong province. It was one of Wu's earliest few classical-themed solos, and Wu regarded it as among a group of his representative new-dance works that helped him establish "an unshakable confidence in the art of modern dance."[95] By including the new-dance *Si fan*, created fifteen years earlier, as the last item closing his concert of classical new dance, Wu seems to suggest the direct lineage between the two—letting it end at where it all began. Therefore, a close analysis of *Si fan* may reveal some common themes and problems that had persisted through the fifteen years in-between that crosses the 1949 divide of the republican and socialist eras in the standard historical periodization. Then, why did Wu—who strove to distinguish his "new dance" from the "old dance" integrated in *xiqu* and, later, his "classical new dance" from the *xiqu*-based "classical dance"— borrow the theme of a famous *xiqu* work in composing a new-dance work, which he retrospectively saw as the origin of his classical new dance?

Figure 3.3 Mei Lanfang rehearsing *Si fan* (Longing for the Mundane), ca. 1916. Image courtesy of the Mei Lanfang Memorial Library.

In fact, Wu was not the first choreographer who adapted *Si fan* into new dance. In the early 1920s, Fujikage Shizue 藤蔭靜枝 (1880–1966), a female pioneer of Japan's new dance movement, choreographed a Kabuki-based, new-dance work with the same title *Shi han*.[96] Kujikage's choreography was based on the "snapshots" and story outline of Mei's *kunqu Si fan*, which were sketched, painted, recorded, and brought back to Japan by Fukuchi Nobuyo 福地信世 (1887–1934), a Japanese geologist, theater-lover, and a mutual friend of Mei and Fujikage.[97] Fujikage's Kabuki adaptation became a big success after its premiere in 1921—it has been regarded as a "much-awaited" breakthrough for new dance in Japan's *Shin buyō undō* 新舞踊運動 (the new dance movement).[98] Considering Wu's experience of studying dance in Japan in the late 1920s, he might have also known about, if not watched, this Kabuki version of *Si fan*.[99]

Figure 3.4 Fujikage Shizue (right) performing *Shi han*, Tokyo, 1921. Image courtesy of the Tsubouchi Memorial Theatre Museum, Waseda University.

From Mei's *kunqu* rendition (figure 3.3) to Fujikage's Kabuki version (figure 3.4) and to Wu Xiaobang's new dance (figure 3.5), *Si fan* (or *Shi han*), follows a similar plot, staging a secluded, obsessive longing for the mundane (the desire for love or sexual pleasure).[100] The popularity of the *Si fan* theme for dance adaptation in early twentieth-century East Asia suggests there was something "modern" and representative about this centuries-old drama that attracted the modern choreographers.[101] As Wu explained in the 1950s, "this is a theme about the sharp conflict between *shen* [神 (divinity, faith)] and *yu* [欲 (desire)], which had been widely employed by many great artists since the European Renaissance."[102] It seems that Wu was not interested so much in the play's "Chineseness" or "traditionalness" as in its dramatic theme that can afford a May-Fourth-style new interpretation of "universal modernity"—understanding this ideological starting point of Wu's *Si fan* is important to further examining his classical new dance fifteen years later.

The original Kun opera tells a story of a young girl named Zhao Sekong 趙色空 (meaning "physicality is emptiness"), who was forced by her parents to

Figure 3.5 (a) (b) (c) (d) Wu Xiaobang performing *Si fan*, 1942. Images courtesy of the China Dancers Association.

become a Buddhist nun when she was a child, as a sacrifice for the parents' redemption. Her life in a convent secluded in the mountain goes by peacefully until she turns sixteen. Thereafter, her mood and emotion change, as she desires mundane life and sexual pleasure, which conflict with her religious education. The conflict is resolved as Zhao finally runs out of the temple and down the mountain to pursue her mundane happiness. The performance takes the form of a soliloquy, often featuring a long uninterrupted dance solo of the heroine (typically performed by a male actor who specializes in female roles), accompanied by her *nianbai* 念白 (the spoken part of the drama). The actor needs to be able to express the mixed subtle feelings of melancholy and longing, balanced by the free and delightful mood of a sixteen-year-old girl and her various sensorial and psychological responses to the world outside the convent.[103]

This narrative of *Si fan* is a variant of the typical classical literary theme of *si chun* 思春 (literally, longing for spring), in which a beautiful teenage girl reaching her puberty rebels against the Confucian patriarchal authority to pursue romantic love. Yet in *Si fan*, the mundane fatherly figure is replaced with a more abstract and symbolic one of faith. It is probably this sharper contrast between concrete physicality and abstract spirituality expressed through a single character's soliloquy—as implied by the heroine's name "physicality is emptiness"—that makes the *Si fan* story seem so "modern" and attractive to the modern choreographers in early twentieth century East Asia, who often found themselves struggling to balance the sensual body and abstract ideals in exploring the conditions of modern subjecthood through choreography.

In Wu's *Si fan*, the stage set features a red wall topped by glazed tiles separating the monastery interior from the outside world, a spatial symbolization of the character's internal conflict. Beyond the wall one can see the top of a willow with crooked branches and a distant mountain peak, which transform the stage into a secluded space.

Accompanied by Huang Youdi 黃友棣 (1912–2010)'s violin solo *Dusk on the Dinghu Mountain* (a Chinese-styled piece composed according to the principles of Western classical music), the dance begins with Wu, as a barefooted young Buddhist monk, sitting cross-legged on a cattail hassock. The monk, in a gray-and-black Kasaya with a string of prayer beads hanging around his neck, is chanting scriptures piously with his eyes closed. The monk's palms are put together in a praying gesture, which becomes a persisting motif throughout the whole dance. This rigid gesture—which greatly restrains the freedom of movement of the arms, hands, fingers, and the upper torso—symbolizes the constant self-discipline of religious spirituality.[104]

As time goes by, more and more tourists, supposedly young men and women, pass by the monastery. Their voices disturb the internal tranquility of the monk. He gradually loses his composure and leans his head slightly and slowly to each side, listening attentively to the sounds of the mundane world. The monk cannot help but stand up and, attracted by the voices outside, walks slowly toward the red wall while still praying toward the Buddhist altar. The subsequent dance movements then unfold in the push and pull between these two opposite directions, kinestheticizing the character's internal struggle. At first, the wavering of faith is visualized by small movements of body parts, such as a quivering motion of a raised ankle. As the outsiders get closer and their voices louder, the monk's internal conflict intensifies, represented by bigger movements such as stretching his body and raising his head to peek beyond the wall. The brewing tension culminates in a sweeping action of "scratching his head with his right hand." This breaks the motif of the "two palms put together," suggesting the monk's frustration and failure to conceal his inner struggle. After the climax, as the tourists wander away and their voices fall to distant whispers, the monk gradually gathers his mind, puts his two palms back together, and resumes chanting scriptures against the ringing of the temple bell to express his repentance.[105]

Although Wu borrowed the theme and story from the *kunqu* version, he denied any direct connection between this new dance choreography and the bodily codes of the "old" drama. Mei Lanfang's rendition of *Si fan* anchors its meaning on the *nianbai* and the lyrics of arias, while the dance-like movements and gestures visualize the textual content in a literal manner.[106] Wu's choreography, without any assistance from language, instead centers on the monk's conflicting bodily reactions to the acoustic stimuli inside and outside the temple wall (for instance, the ringing of the temple bell and the voices of the tourists).

Two other major differences distinguish Wu's *Si fan* from Mei's. First, Wu changed the character of the teenage nun to a young monk. In the Chinese context, this was especially important because it also abandoned the tradition of cross-gender performance used in Mei's version. Following the ideology of the May Fourth movement, Wu criticized cross-gender performance in China's "old drama" as a form of "backward feudalistic oppression" of the body that was contradictory to the modern-dance principle of "natural" bodily movement.[107] Although men dominated theatrical performance, in 1940s China dance was still widely deemed a profession for women, and being a male dancer was highly scandalous. Wu himself was often sneered at and criticized.[108] In this context, Wu chose to align the binary gender roles of the dancer and the character in his choreography and denounced cross-gender performance.[109] This attitude is reflected too in Wu's choreography: after hearing the voices of young women outside the temple, the monk walks several steps forward with an awkwardly feminine gait, mocking the gender-crossing performance in the *xiqu* tradition.[110]

The second difference is the seemingly conservative ending of Wu's version: he changed the original ending of the nun escaping from the convent and pursuing her mundane happiness to an opposite one of the monk staying in the monastery and repenting to Buddha of his wavering of faith. It seems that, unexpectedly, Wu chose a more suppressive ending over the more liberating one. To understand this paradoxical choice of Wu, one needs to consider the status of dance in relation to *xiqu* in early twentieth-century China.

The rise of *xiqu* as a performance art since the late imperial era can be generally seen as a continuous process of competition, mutual appropriation, and symbiosis between literature, originally a privilege of the literati, and urban popular culture, which relies more on the various senses of the body as complements to the textual and the verbal. Since the 1910s, chasing the demands of the mass-mediated cultural market, Peking opera increasingly appealed to female sensuality and visuality. As a result, the role type *dan* 旦 (female role) gradually replaced the previous centrality of the *sheng* 生 (male role) actors in Peking opera, as represented by Mei's rise to fame as a top *dan* actor.[111] By the 1930s, Peking opera had largely succeeded in striking a balance between *ya* 雅 (the refined) and *su* 俗 (the popular), as manifested in its status being elevated to the "national drama" embraced by all political factions.[112]

However, dance was still struggling at the *su* and sensual end of the spectrum. In early twentieth-century China, dance was almost entirely identified as a low art, or even anti-art, that relied on sensuality to serve the purpose of entertainment. It was seen as devoid of intellectual content and often associated with debauchery.[113] As Wu remarked in 1941 (one year before he choreographed *Si fan*), dance had been "the commodity in the hands of merchants selling laughter, the martial arts of peddling kung fu performers, or interludes for [the performance of] magicians on stage," where the phrase "selling laughter" connotes prostitution in Chinese.[114] Even as late as in the 1980s, Wu still complained that, in Chinese dance institutions, the narrow focus of ballet and classical dance training on bodily techniques had fed into the common misperception of professional dancers being "physically advanced yet intellectually retarded."[115] Therefore, Wu's new ending may be interpreted as his attempt to elevate faith and intellectuality to counterbalance desires and sensuality, implying Wu's fear of his new dance being associated excessively with the latter.

However, such a "victory" of faith and rationality incurs a heavy cost. According to the script of the dance, after his agonizing conflict, though still chanting scriptures, the monk's mind "cannot return to the realm of Buddha anymore. He opens both arms, looks up to the heavens, questioning and imploring, and eventually collapses onto the cattail hassock."[116] This trauma seems to suggest Wu's concern that the unity of the mind and the body, spirituality and corporeality—which modern dance had been striving to achieve since the time of Duncan—was ultimately a utopia in the age of mass popular culture, in which the dancing body was irreversibly objectified and commodified.

The ending of Wu's *Si fan* may also reveal the ambivalent attitude of Wu, as an independent artist, toward the relationship between art and politics. As discussed in chapter 2, Wu, on the one hand, believed that his new dance must engage in the greater cause of mass mobilization and national salvation to establish its legitimacy in China. During the four years following the outbreak of the Second Sino-Japanese War in 1937, Wu joined forces with other leftist artists in the war effort by touring South China, choreographing and performing many dance works with mobilizing themes. On the other hand, however, Wu also wanted to maintain some degree of independence for his art and focus more on the "artisticity" (in Wu's words, *yishu xing* 藝術性) of dance, and thus often refrained from full political engagement.[117] In July 1942, at the height of the Pacific War and right after Mao's "Yan'an Talk," Wu postponed his plan to go to the Communist-controlled Yan'an, but instead accepted the invitation to teach dance at the Nationalist-run Qujiang Provincial School of Specialized Arts (*Qujiang shengli yishu zhuanke xuexiao* 曲江省立藝術專科學校) in Guangdong, because the school offered him better teaching and practicing facilities and a more liberal environment for developing both the pedagogy and choreography for his new dance.[118] To some extent, Wu's entire career can be characterized as this pattern of periodic oscillation between the two states—one more politically engaged and the other more withdrawing.

It is in Qujiang that Wu conceived *Si fan*. There, Wu lived a semi-reclusive life for one year, which for him was the most productive period of his dancing career.[119] Wu's choreographing and teaching practices in Qujiang also became an important basis for his Tianma Studio later. The residence of Wu's family in Qujiang was an isolated, brand-new, single-family house located on a terrace carved out on a mountain in the suburb. The chancellor of the school selected this location in person and authorized the construction of this new house particularly for the Wu family to filter out the various distractions of the wartime chaos. The house was surrounded by a thick forest of pines, from which one "can watch sunrise in the morning and listen to the howling of the pine waves at night."[120] This secluded environment provided direct inspirations for Wu's *Si fan*.[121] Wu may even, to a large extent, identify himself with the monk in the isolated temple—Wu was often likened to a lonesome monk "preaching" the art of new dance—struggling between the "faith" of his lofty and lonely artistic pursuit and the "desire" of engaging in the down-to-earth politics in the mundane world outside the ivory tower.[122] Thus, Wu's ending of *Si fan* may also be interpreted as his strenuous balancing between the independence of his art as interiority and the outside political world.

As shown below, these tensions reflected in *Si fan* between the mind and the body, the spiritual and the physical, art and politics, along with the theme of reclusion, were all carried over to Tianma in the socialist era, though in different manifestations. Therefore, Wu himself regarded *Si fan* as integral to the development of his classical new dance in the 1950s and included it in the repertoire of Tianma.

Yüfu le 漁夫樂 (The Joy of an Old Fisherman): Conflicted Consciousness in Utopia

If the fissure between intellectuality and physicality, as represented in Wu's 1942 *Si fan*, is ultimately an outcome of the commodification and objectification of the body by the semi-colonial capitalist economy, the newly established People's Republic seemed to have dramatically eradicated the root of such a fissure within a few years through various campaigns of socialist transformation. Ironically, however, this fissure stubbornly re-emerged in a different form. The late 1950s witnessed the fast decline of the social status of intellectuals in a general tide of anti-intellectualism and the rise into primacy of manual labor—in the name of abolishing the differences between intellectual work and manual work, between the professional and amateur—which culminated in the Great Leap.[123] The body was redeemed from being an objectified commodity only to be re-objectified as the source of labor fueling the construction of the communist utopia.

As a result, many dances, which mimicked the physical labor of farmers and workers involved in daily production, were created and performed by amateur or semi-professional dance troupes associated with local "work units."[124] This new development, however, should not be simply romanticized as a democratizing or equalizing process from the bottom up. All these dance troupes and their artistic creations, just like other amateur artistic organizations, were under the direct leadership of the same Party cadres running the parental "work units," and thus being part of the revolutionary machine that was cranked up to exalt and spur the passion and productivity of the masses in the Great Leap.[125]

After watching a large-scale performance of the "dances of the masses" in 1959, Wu, who had been concerned about the distinction of professional dancers being eclipsed by the rising amateurs, questioned the validity of calling the onstage mimicking of physical labor "the art of dance."[126] He complained that the audience could not understand the highly specialized production procedures but only felt a huge kinesthetic burden—the "workers" onstage "seem to be so oppressed by the production processes and machinery that they could hardly breathe."[127] Other dance critics similarly commented that many of those dances "simply and purely represent production processes and technical operations" in a repetitive, tedious, and dull manner, without revealing "the spirit of people in labor," and that "one can see [in the dances] only machines, not people, only procedures of operation, not activities of characters."[128]

It is worthwhile to briefly compare these "labor dances" with the American counterpart in the so-called radical decade of the 1930s. Facing the dire situation of labor during the Great Depression, American modern dancers took a "leftist turn" in joining the "proletarian avant-garde" to explore the formal ties between dance and labor.[129] Mark Franko argues that these labor-related choreographies "made it possible to see in dance a laboring body abstracted from representation . . . and hence also a body abstracted from skill . . . as well as from production" and thus constituted an "alternative modernism" in dance.[130] By contrast, in the Chinese case, it was exactly the extra-realistic representation in dance of detailed production skills and processes, "devoid of intellectual content" (and thus of abstraction), that stimulated the critics' dangerously subversive kinesthetic responses mentioned above, which imply that the body in socialist labor is no less alienating than that commodified by the capitalist industry of the past.[131]

Although the inner struggle between spirituality and physicality in Wu's 1942 *Si fan* is agonizing, it provides at least an illusion of agency for the monk (or the artist) in the form of a voluntary choice between two comparable options. The sensual body being objectified, for better or worse, still constitutes an option no less attractive to the artist than spirituality (the existence of two comparable options is the premise for internal conflict). Under the new socialist regime, however, the "labor-ized" body, together with the dominant ideology, became perhaps so pervasive and intrusive for the artist that it further limited the scope of voluntary choice and, thus, precluded the possibility of foregrounding any unresolved *internal* conflict. A corollary follows that if there was still conflict at all, it must have taken a more "externalized" form in choreography.

The manifestation of this "externalization" of conflict in the classical-new-dance works of Tianma is, paradoxically, their conflict-less "happy endings." In contrast to Wu's early new-dance works in the 1930s and early 1940s, which typically end with an impasse resulting from the intense inner struggle of the character, there is little conflict in his Tianma works, and even that minimum struggle is usually resolved in a characteristically idyllic ending. These happy endings were not simply Wu's praise, sincere or not, of the socialist regime (to be sure, they did have such a function at the surface, just like some of Tianma's more obviously eulogizing works). Rather, the attenuation of internal conflicts is the result of Wu's fuller embrace of spirituality (or artisticity) and further expulsion of physicality (or politics) in his choreography by appropriating the intellectual ideal of reclusion.

In Tianma's classical new dance, the various images of reclusion are in fact much more aggressive than their idyllic appearances, such as an old drunken fisherman dozing by the river, an old farmer appreciating and taking care of his chrysanthemum flowers in the garden (alluding to Tao Qian 陶潛, the iconic fourth- and fifth-century hermit poet), a young woodcutter dancing to the music piece *Yangchun baixue* 陽春白雪 (Bright spring and white snow, which idiomatically denotes highbrow art and culture), and a young shepherd reading books and falling asleep in the meadow.[132] Wu intended to use these images of "intellectualized" laborers to "de-labor-ize" the physical body—or in Franko's modernist terms, to abstract the body in labor from skills and production—occupy the interiority with spirituality (or artisticity), and expel physicality (or politics) into the margin as exteriority. By pushing the frontier of the conflict "outward," Wu was trying to defend in his choreography the relative intellectual independence of artists. Ironically, in the case of Wu's Tianma choreographies, the art of dance, which relies fundamentally on the somatic body, had to downplay its own physicality—an irony of which Wu, as shown below, may be quite aware. Therefore, the happy endings in Wu's Tianma works are symptomatic of the exacerbation, instead of resolution, of the conflicted consciousness inherited from his earlier works, as represented by *Si fan*.

If the pre-Tianma *Si fan* initiates the struggle between spirituality (or artisticity) and physicality (or politics) as an internal conflict, then *Yüfu le*, the first Tianma solo both choreographed and performed by Wu, represents the continuous expansion of spirituality, as the interior, against physicality, as the exterior. In *Yüfu le*, while the spiritual has been elevated and expanded into dominance, the physical, as the repressed, stubbornly reemerges onstage as the dreamy unconscious, challenging the spiritual.

Yüfu le was first performed by Wu in a public dance concert of Tianma in Chongqing on June 12, 1957.[133] This was the first public concert of Tianma and Wu's first stage performance in the socialist era. The concert was held at the People's Auditorium of Chongqing, which could accommodate an audience size of four thousand, and went on for three nights. Aging had taken a toll on Wu. After each performance, the fifty-two-year-old dancer "felt extremely exhausted, just like having fallen severely ill."[134] Nevertheless, Wu managed to perform the dance works with great passion.

Different from *Si fan*, the stage setup of *Yüfu le* is minimalistic—just a tree stump and a plain backdrop with a brighter upper part and a darker lower part (figure 3.6a). Also, in contrast to *Si fan*, there is no physical feature separating the stage space in *Yüfu le*. Wu appears on the stage as an old fisherman with a red face, an alcoholic nose, and a long white beard (all are painted on or attached to a mask). The old man wears a wide bamboo rain hat, and around his waist hang a creel, a bottle gourd filled with wine, and a fishing rod (figure 3.6b).[135] This image of Wu is so representative of the numerous renditions of the old hermit-fisherman in Chinese literature and paintings that his very appearance on the stage might trigger the imagination of the educated audience to automatically add all the relevant landscape features to the space, such as the flowing river, the fishing boat, the serene mountains, the whispering forest, and the hazy mist. Assisted by the

Figure 3.6 (a) (b) Wu Xiaobang performing *Yüfu le*, 1957. Images courtesy of the China Dancers Association.

slow-paced Daoist ritual music *Zuixian xi* 醉仙喜 (The happiness of a drunk deity), Wu uses this visual allusion to reclusion to fill up the vast imaginary space with spirituality.

According to the dance script, the old fisherman rows a wooden boat (no prop boat on the stage) toward the riverbank, smiling. Once getting off the boat, he habitually puts down all the items hanging around his waist, sits down on the tree stump, and begins his preparation. While looking around and enjoying the scenery, he baits the hook and then tosses it into the river in a relaxed manner. After securing the fishing rod below a willow, he opens the bottle gourd, takes a good smell at it, and then starts drinking while fishing and enjoying the view with great satisfaction, leisure, and intoxication. According to a brief introduction to the dance printed on the playbill of the concert, the fisherman "always gets drunk when drinking."[136] Bathed in the warm sun, the alcoholic old fisherman soon gets tipsy and gradually falls asleep.[137]

The stage light dims down at this point. When the stage lights up again, Wu reappears on the stage as a dapper handsome young man carrying a Chinese folding fan—this is the fisherman in his youth being dreamed about by the old self. His graceful manner and costume invoke the classical literary and theatrical image of the young (Confucian) scholar-talent (figure 3.7). Whereas the first scene is characterized by slow and minimal activity, the dance movement of this second scene is much faster and more active. The young man, who has been greatly pleased and energized by the beautiful scenery, suddenly gets attracted by a pretty butterfly. The whole scene then unfolds through a series of playful moves of the young man chasing and attempting to catch the butterfly (figure 3.8).[138] The butterfly is substituted for the structural role of the beauty in the traditional beauty-and-the-talent literary theme; therefore, Wu's adaptation of this classical theme in the dream scene can be seen as a manifestation of the repressed romance, sensuality, youthful freedom, mundane happiness, and physical energy.

Moreover, the butterfly in the dream may also be understood as an allusion to the famous "butterfly paradox" brought up by the Taoist philosopher Zhuang Zhou 莊周 (or Zhuangzi) (ca. 369 BC–ca. 286 BC).[139] In this dance, the young man, in his final attempt to capture the butterfly, trips on an exposed tree root and then falls onto the ground. The stage light turns dim again. After the stage re-lights up, Wu turns back to be the old fisherman dozing on the tree stump, who is then suddenly woken up by the fall happening in the dream. Just like Zhuangzi, the fisherman is confused for a

Figure 3.7 Wu Xiaobang as a young scholar in *Yüfu le*, 1957. Image courtesy of the China Dancers Association.

moment, looking around, at a loss.[140] He cannot tell which self is more real, the sober and active young Confucian scholar in the dream or the drunken and debilitated Taoist old fisherman in reality.

It is in this specific moment that Wu shocks the Confucian social and physical determinacy of the beauty-and-the-talent theme into Taoist epistemological skepticism, questioning the possibility of any definite identity and knowledge of the subject. As a result, the repressed no longer exists as a mere specter in the dream but intrudes into "reality" in flesh and blood. Ultimately, the young man on the stage is no less real, or in some sense even more real, than the old fisherman—it is the latter who wears a mask. This understanding seems to be shared by the renowned painter Ye Qianyu 葉淺予 (1907–1995), a good friend of Wu, as demonstrated by his sketches of a 1957 performance of *Yüfu le* (figure 3.8): while the "snapshots" of the dancing young scholar in the dream occupy most of

Figure 3.8 Sketches of Wu Xiaobang performing *Yúfu le*, by Ye Qianyu 葉淺予, ca. 1957. Image courtesy of Ye Mingming.

the space, there is only a single, small image of the drunken old fisherman at the bottom. This interpretation is also consistent with the well-known Chinese idiom to which the image of the drunk old man may allude: "the ulterior motive of the drunk old man does not lie in the wine" (*zui wen zhi yi bu zai jiu* 醉翁之意不在酒).

However, since any unresolved internal conflict is no longer a viable option, the dance could not end here in a psychological impasse as in many of Wu's previous new-dance works. The old fisherman finally realizes that he just had a dream, and "smiles while shaking his head."[141] Reminded by the setting sun, the fisherman stands up, goes to check his fishing pole, and happily found that there has been a big fish on the hook. He squats down, strenuously pulls up the pole, and catches the fish with great effort. The butterfly lost in the dream seems to have turned into the fish caught in reality—another allusion to Taoist dialectics.[142] He then puts the fish into the creel, fetches the bottle gourd, unmoors the boat, and gets aboard. With the fish he caught, together with the dream itself, the fisherman disappears from the stage.[143]

The reception of *Yüfu le* among the audiences seems sharply divided. While some intellectuals and artists "felt much moved" and highly praised its "thoughtfulness," other common audience commented that "it is hard to understand what it tries to express."[144] Such contrasted reactions among the audience need to be explained in light of both the split imagery of *yüfu* (fisherman) in the Chinese literary tradition and the particular historical context of the performance in mid-June 1957.

In Chinese literary history, the image of the fisherman is charged with disparate and contradictory cultural connotations. In addition to the theme of reclusion that is exclusively associated with intellectuals and elite literati, the fisherman is also a symbol for rebellion of the underclass in popular culture. For example, many of the grass-root rebel leaders in the widely-circulated vernacular novel *Shuihu zhuan* 水滸傳 (Water margin) come from the fisherman class, who had become a cultural icon since the late imperial era and was also later popularized by the *xiqu* media, such as the Peking opera *Dayu shajia* 打漁殺家 (Fishing and murder). In the orthodox Marxist historical-materialist interpretation, the water margin heroes are further regarded as a symbol for the spontaneous class struggle initiated by the oppressed underclass against the feudalistic landlord ruling class, which includes literati scholar-officials. Therefore, the image of the fisherman is troubled with the reclusion/rebellion and intellectual/physical splits, which had been reflected in its bifurcating reception among the audiences. It is unsurprising that the common audience, who mainly came from the under-educated working class and were mostly familiar with the image of the fishermen as grass-root action heroes (and Wu's previous revolutionary new-dance works such as the *March of the Volunteers*, see chapter 2), were perplexed by Wu's elitist "bourgeois interpretation" of the fisherman as a Taoist hermit.[145]

In contrast to the reactions of common audience, intellectuals and artists seem to be more able to appreciate *Yüfu le*.[146] Many of those who praised Wu's choreography in this performance would soon be classified as "Rightists" in a few weeks or months.[147] This Chongqing concert of Wu in mid-June of 1957 was accidentally held at a historical juncture. Just a few days earlier, on June 8, Mao published an editorial at *Renming ribao* 人民日報 (The People's Daily, mouthpiece of the CCP) titled "Zhe shi weishenme?" 這是爲什麽 (Why is this?), which officially marks the onset of the Anti-Rightist Movement and the de facto reversal of the Double Hundred policy.[148]

A few months earlier, during the Party Rectification Campaign accompanying the Double Hundred policy, Mao overestimated the loyalty of intellectuals and encouraged them to criticize the malpractices of low-level Party officials without challenging the whole system, which is called *Da ming da fang* 大鳴大放 (Airing views freely and loudly).[149] However, many intellectuals—who had endured waves of the so-called "Thought Reform Campaigns" and political purges that aimed to suppress the West-leaning, May Fourth liberal spirit and to indoctrinate Marxism-Leninism—crossed the line and uttered their dissatisfactions by going as far as attacking the one-party system of the CCP. What is more ironic is that young college students, who were brought up and educated in the "new society," became a major radical force in this liberal movement—they saw themselves as successors of the May Fourth generation and the Chinese counterpart of those dissidents in the post-Stalin Soviet Union and East European countries. Mao was so disillusioned in intellectuals and unsettled by a feeling of betrayal that he quickly reversed the *Da ming da fang* into the Anti-Rightist Campaign in early June, 1957.[150]

Wu was sympathetic toward this liberal endeavor of intellectuals and students; he had always identified himself as a member of the May Fourth generation. The image of the young talent in *Yüfu le* freely chasing the butterfly in the dream of the old fisherman is reminiscent of his liberal, "bourgeois" youth that, in Wu's own words, "had been suppressed by waves of 'leftist' literary and artistic thoughts."[151] However, constrained by his Party membership and leadership in the dance field, Wu was impossible to stand openly by the side of the "rightist" intellectuals and students. Nevertheless, in a conflicted manner, Wu would continue to use his classical new dance, as represented by *Yüfu le*, to construct a timeless, reclusive spiritual utopia for himself, his Tianma students, and the "rightist" intellectuals against the Anti-Rightist purge and, a few months later, against the utopia of the frenetic Great Leap. This was perhaps the "ulterior motive" of Wu as the "drunk old man."

The political significance of Tianma's classical new dance in this historical moment was well understood by some of the liberal intellectuals.[152] The cover picture of the playbill of the Chongqing concert was designed by Wang Zimei 汪子美 (1913–2002), an established caricaturist who, in a few months, would be wrongly condemned as an "extreme-rightist."[153] The picture has a white upper part and a dark green bottom part, which represent the sky and earth, respectively. A strange yet beautiful flower stretches out from the dirt, reaching toward the sky. What is noteworthy is its crooked stem in the earth, which suggests that the small plant had struggled against great pressure before it reached the surface. This flower symbolizes the courage, struggle, and accomplishment of Wu and his Tianma against the unfavorable political climate. Although the "heavenly horse" would continue to live for five more years, its "fate," with hindsight, had been sealed in its very first public performance in 1957 Chongqing, tied up with the tragedy of its "Rightist" friends, or even much earlier, in the traumatic internal conflict of the split modern subject in the 1942 *Si fan*.

The Suicidal Hermit-Assassin: *Guangling san* 廣陵散 (Song of Guangling) and Tianma's Downfall

The conflicted nature beneath the peaceful surface of reclusion finally break out as radical, self-mutilating violence in the last dance work of Tianma (and of Wu), *Guangling san*, which was choreographed in 1960 but never performed publicly.[154] *Guangling san* culminates the expansion of the spiritual as interiority to expel the physical as exteriority in Tianma choreographies (a process beginning with the pre-Tianma *Si fan*), which causes the final burst of the "balloon" and thus the self-annihilation of both the interior and the exterior.

The music accompanying the dance is the well-known ancient *guqin* 古琴 (Chinese zither) piece with the same title, which is associated with two legendary deaths. The first is the death of Ji Kang 嵇康 (ca. 223–ca. 263), one of the most exalted iconic, and iconoclastic, Taoist hermits in Chinese history. It is said that *Guangling san* was the last piece Ji played calmly on the execution ground right before his unjust death, with his final sigh: "*Guangling san* will be lost forever from now on!"[155] The second is the death of the well-known Warring-States assassin Nie Zheng 聶政 (?–397 BC). The whole *guqin* piece of *Guangling san* is said to be a musical interpretation of the heroic deed of Nie.[156] After accomplishing his mission of assassinating a powerful ruler, Nie committed suicide before he got caught; moreover, in order not to implicate his family and friends, Nie first made his body unidentifiable by using a dagger to disfigure his face, carve out his eyes, cut open his abdomen, and let the intestines flow out.[157] Wu's *Guangling san* is a direct adaptation of this bloody story of Nie.

Although Wu did not literally act out this scene of gore in his choreography (he used a mask of disfigured face to represent the self-mutilating theme), the aggressiveness of the conflicted consciousness behind the tranquil façade of reclusion is betrayed in a most violent and unexpected manner. Sensing the

impending demise of Tianma, Wu carried out his final revenge in the hermit/
assassin dual-themed *Guangling san*: he on the one hand alluded to the death
of Ji Kang the hermit, to mourn Tianma, the "precious son" he was about to
lose at an old age; on the other hand, by choreographing the story of Nie the
assassin, he turned the spiritual theme of reclusion into a physical act of sui-
cidal assassination, which results in the final destruction of both the spiritual
and the physical through self-mutilation. In the end, between the peaceful
hermit and the violent assassin is only a paper-thin mask, with the two split
identities becoming one and none under the death drive.

Starting from January, 1960, groups of articles that systematically criticize
Wu and Tianma appeared in nine of the twelve monthly issues of *Wudao*
(dance), the official journal of the Dance Research Association and the single
most influential professional periodical in China's dance field.[158] The attacks
of Wu were leveled at four major target points: Wu's bourgeois liberal leaning
and reluctance to accept socialist-communist thought reform, as reflected in
his words and choreographies; his emphasis on artisticity (or poetics, *shiyi*
詩意) over contemporary political imperatives in both the form and content of Tianma's dance works; Wu's "nihilist" and yet "uncritical" attitudes
toward tradition; and his condescending, elitist-professionalist inclination
that had distanced him from amateurs of the masses in the Great Leap.[159]
On top of these published criticisms, the political pressure Wu and Tianma
had been facing since 1958 peaked during The Third National Conference
of Representatives of the Chinese Dance Art Research Association held in
Beijing from July to August, 1960. In the meetings, Wu, who was then the
president of the association, were reproached by representatives from all
over the country.[160] Even the few sympathizers of Wu were quickly silenced
under enormous collective pressure and the initial debate soon turned into a
one-sided tirade (see epilogue).

As recalled vividly by one of Wu's former students, in the final days of
Tianma, the only option left for Wu and his students was "waiting" in depression for the death sentence of the "heavenly horse." Wu was the one that
changed the most: he, now with unshaven face, could often be seen sitting
alone under the roofing of the courtyard-turned, big empty dance studio,
reading a very thick book—the epic poem *Don Juan* by Lord Byron—against
the sunlight sifting through the shade and, occasionally, with a cigarette between his fingers.[161] Soon Tianma was officially disbanded by the Ministry
of Culture at the end of 1960, and most of Wu's students went to Tianma's
"archrival," the Beijing Dance School. Wu, in the name of treating some

medical condition, retreated to his hometown Suzhou into deeper reclusion, carrying with him the book *Don Juan* and, together with it, the Romantic literary and artistic thoughts—as represented by its famous poet author—that had greatly influenced Wu in his bourgeois youth. Although the resilient Wu managed to partially reopen Tianma in 1962, where he could resume its minimum educational function to advise three former Tianma students (this time, as graduate students) until its permanent shutdown in the summer of 1964, the prime of Tianma ended in 1960.[162] Wu would have to endure almost another two decades, including the even more turbulent Cultural Revolution (1966–1976), until he could rerise as a central figure in China's dance world in 1979—this time, at the age of seventy-three, as the elected president of the newly renamed Chinese Dancers' Association (the former Dance Research Association).[163]

I conclude this chapter with a "confession" made by Wu in the early 1990s, which is included in his autobiography as the prologue. From it one can still discern the historical residual of Wu's conflictedness:

> I wish very much that I could see this book [Wu's autobiography] as Rousseau writing the *Les Confessions* . . . [Yet] I am a CCP member, so I have my own standards for confession . . . During the decades of social change and revolution I have experienced, the winds and rains of history, just like sweeping fallen leaves, had swirled the people of our time into different movements and trends of thought. So had revolution—it had blown some people together, but may have also blown some apart. Even though there were certain people who had not been drawn into a particular whirlpool, living a seemingly peaceful life, but in their heart, it may have not been completely satisfying. This is the characteristic of the time I had lived in, the truth of those turbulent years. I am just part of that truth.[164]

In this confession, Wu foregrounds the dominant political forces that had been ruthlessly shaping the fates of people by depicting the latter as passive and lifeless "fallen leaves" drifting randomly in the "winds and rains of history." However, what is hidden between the lines is the other side of the story highlighted in this chapter—the agency and effort of certain artists, as represented by Wu, to persistently negotiate, nudge, and test the limits of ideological control, thereby exposing the cracks and interstices beneath its seemingly monolithic surface. In some sense, the fate of the reclusive Tianma, and Wu himself in this period, paradoxically resonates with the highly sociable Don Juan in the literary figure's duality. On the one hand, like Mozart's classical operatic rendition of Don Giovanni, who—as a relentless and unrepentant womanizer driven by the death drive—compulsively "jumps" (in a quite choreographic and kinesthetic sense) from one woman to another only to defer his inevitable fall into hell, Wu, increasingly seen as an unapologetic "bourgeois" heretic in China's dance world and thus facing great pressure, had to jump desperately from one choreography to another and from one performance to another, in the hope of proving Tianma's worthiness and living out the most of its potential before its anticipated death.[165] On the other hand, also like Lord Byron's unconventional rendition of Don Juan as a charming, romantic, naïve, and brave young man who is susceptible to various seductions and the vicissitudes on the grand stage of politics but nevertheless soldiers on, Wu's Tianma, even though inescapably sucked into the political whirlpools of the time one by one, kept trudging ahead until meeting its end.

4

Writing Dance

Dai Ailian, Labanotation, and the Multi-Diasporic "Root" of Modern Chinese Ethnic Dance

As the musician needs to record the precise and minute details of his composition to insure correct performance of his score, so the choreographer needs a notation capable of equal accuracy.

—George Balanchine, "Preface" to *Labanotation*

I have always stressed the point that the endeavour to describe the movements of a dance in special symbols has one main purpose. That is the creation of a literature of movement and dance.

—Rudolf von Laban, "Foreword" to *Labanotation*

One evening in July 1945, a month before the final surrender of the Japanese Empire in the Second World War, a twenty-nine-year-old young man was trudging alone on the rough and unfamiliar terrains of the remote mountains in Wenchuan 汶川, a county located in the northern section of the Hengduan 横断 mountain ranges separating the Tibetan Plateau to the west and the Sichuan Basin to the east, about 90 miles northwest of Chengdu— the provincial capital of Sichuan in southwest China. Exhausted and lost, the young man was weighed down by an overwhelming sense of loneliness, as the night gradually fell into the endless, lifeless, and unbearably soundless mountains surrounding him. Just when he became desperate, a cat flashed past him. Realizing that a domestic cat cannot run far from a human settlement, he gathered his last strength to chase the cat. Following the feline over a ridge and into a valley, the man was astonished by the spectacular view unfolding in front of him: a group of obelisk-shaped stone forts towered like a forest, even dwarfing the mountains in the background. Awed by the architectural and natural spectacle, the man felt like he was entering a "mythical

When Words Are Inadequate. Nan Ma, Oxford University Press. © Oxford University Press 2023.
DOI: 10.1093/oso/9780197575307.003.0005

world." It was the Jiashan Settlement 佳山寨 of the Qiang 羌 people, the first destination of his trek.[1]

This young man was Peng Song 彭松 (1916–2016), who was first trained in Western theater, opera, and music, started to learn modern dance five years earlier with Wu Xiaobang, and would become a prominent choreographer and dance historian later in his life.[2] Peng's task at the Jiashan Settlement was to learn the dance of the Qiang people. This marked one of the beginnings of Han-Chinese dancers' study, collection, and adaptation of ethnic minority dances, which would become part of a much larger and enduring project of transforming ethnic dances into a modern "Chinese" dance genre.[3] During his stay, Peng learned Qiang songs and dances from the *duangong* 端公, or shamans, the local spiritual and intellectual leaders whose responsibilities included exorcism, healing, preserving, telling, and interpreting local "histories" or "myths."[4]

Peng recorded one such mythic history of the Qiang people he heard from the village chief who could speak Mandarin.[5] According to the chief, long ago, before the Qiang people migrated to this area from somewhere far away, they had their own written language. There were two ancient warring nations: *Gula* 古拉 (the ancestors of the Qiang people) and *Zila* 子拉 (supposedly "China").[6] Gula was utterly defeated in the war and forced to migrate in a nomadic way, along with herds of goats.[7] At first, they carried with them their religious scriptures—words written on tree leaves. However, at one point the goats became hungry and ate all the scriptures, and the Qiang lost their written language forever. After they settled down later, they killed the goats and used the skins to make drums. Now, only when the shaman strikes the goat-skin drum and dances to it can he recall the words of the lost scriptures. The songs and dances Peng learned from the shaman were part of this religious ritual to invoke the lost scriptures for exorcizing ghosts.

Peng journeyed on westward, deeper into the mountains. About 35 miles west of Wenchuan, he arrived in the Lifan 理番 county, the land of the Jiarong 嘉戎 people (now classified as a branch of the Tibetan but sharing many cultural similarities with the Qiang).[8] Resting in a hay-made hut-like inn, Peng was invited by the owner, a Han-Chinese, to attend a Jiarong wedding. The wedding room was simple and crude, but the bride had "astonishing beauty."[9] The inn owner told Peng that the bride was a slave owned by a local Jiarong chieftain but refused the latter's sexual request. As a punishment, the angered master decided to wed the pretty slave girl to an "extremely ugly man." Despite the cruel story of slavery, the wedding turned out to be a Dionysian event thoroughly enjoyed by the local Jiarong guests. After the ceremony, the guests, both men and women, started to sing, dance, and drink.

This was the first time Peng ever saw the Jiarong *guozhuang* 鍋莊 dance. According to Peng's detailed account, all the Jiarong guests were in full ceremonial costumes, and the women's dresses, in Peng's view, were similar to the Han style of ancient times. The people stood next to each other in a single line forming a semi-circle, holding the neighbors' hands or shoulders. Men and women started to sing in turns to the opposite gender group, slow at first, with hands swaying and feet tapping to the rhythm. The singing gradually became stronger, faster, and more exciting; so did the dancing. The dancers began to stamp their feet, squat and then straighten up, and swirl at a dazzling speed. They occasionally broke out of the formation to rest and gather around a jug of sweet rice wine placed on the ground. Each used a long thin bamboo straw to drink the wine, which further heightened the crowd's mood for singing and dancing. The party lasted deep into the night. Peng learned this *guozhuang* dance of the Jiarong.[10]

In late August, after the news of Japan's surrender finally reached the remote mountains, Peng embarked on his journey home. When he reached the border between the lands of the minorities and Han-controlled regions, Peng was stopped by some Nationalist soldiers guarding the passage. The soldiers rudely searched Peng's body and luggage for money and crude opium. In the eyes of the "greedy" soldiers, any Han entering and returning from the lands of the "barbarians" must be either a regular merchant or an opium trader that smuggles opium from British India to inland China—a trans-Himalayan trading route that had connected the British empire, Tibet, and China proper for over a century.[11] Either case, the traveler would be a lucrative source of extra-income for the Nationalist soldiers. Yet they were disappointed this time, as a Han going to the "barbarian" lands to collect dances was something they "had never heard of."[12]

The account above is based on a travelogue written by Peng two years after his 1945 journey in West Sichuan and published as an article in the *Xinmin bao* 新民報, a newspaper that had a wide readership in China's major metropolises and adopted an independent political stance often critical of the Nationalist government.[13]

Yet, Peng's 1945 summer fieldwork was only part of a much larger and more enduring project of collecting ethnic-minority dances in China's borderlands and creating modern Chinese ethnic dance, which would become one of the mainstream dance genres—on equal footing with Chinese classical dance and, by some measure, more widespread and popular than ballet and modern dance—in the People's Republic of China (1949–).[14] This larger project was pioneered by Dai Ailian 戴愛蓮 (aka, Eileen Isaac or Tai Ai-lien, 1916–2006), the main dancer-choreographer under study in this chapter. It was Dai that had taught Peng modern dance and ballet for one year by 1945 (after Peng's study with Wu Xiaobang) and decided to send Peng to collect ethnic dances in the Qiang and Jiarong regions.[15]

Dai, known as the "mother of modern Chinese dance," was a monumental figure in the dance history of modern China. Born into a wealthy third-generation Cantonese immigrant family in Trinidad, Dai was a subject of the British empire. She moved from the marginal island to London at age fourteen to receive ballet training, where she later also studied the central European school of modern dance. Dai went to Hong Kong in 1940 and mainland China in 1941 at the height of the Second World War, and eventually became a citizen of the socialist state. She was the first president of the prestigious Beijing Dance School (predecessor to the Beijing Dance Academy), co-founder and director of the National Ballet of China, and the first president of the Chinese Dancers' Association. Dai was the only dancer that had attained a status on a par with Wu Xiaobang in the dance history of modern China and, in fact, Dai's international influence surpassed Wu's due to her overseas background and connections.[16]

Dai was the first professional dancer that had devotedly collected ethnic minority dances in China's southwestern borderlands and further adapted and performed them on stage as theatrical dance in the mid-1940s. As early as in 1941, when she passed the *Dayao shan* 大瑤山 (the Great Yao mountain) in Guangxi province, she saw a drum dance from the Yao 瑤 people and then created a dance work inspired by it.[17] In late 1945, shortly after Peng's return, Dai went to Kangding 康定 (about 200 miles southwest of Chengdu), then the provincial capital of Xikang 西康 (now part of Sichuan), to collect ethnic dances.[18] She played a vital role in inspiring the borderland dance movement in the late 1940s, the basis for institutionalizing ethnic folk dance as a major academic and professional discipline and genre in the Chinese dance world in the 1950s.[19] Dai's life-long passion for ethnic dance is manifest in her own words: "While ballet is my work, ethnic dance is my love."[20] Clearly, Dai assigned a higher emotional value to the "native" ethnic dance over ballet.

In Chinese historiography, Dai's life and career are cast into the narrative of *hua qiao* 華僑 (overseas Chinese sojourners) returning home (or *gui qiao*

歸僑, returned overseas sojourners), the Chinese analogy to the teleological connotation of diaspora.[21] Both *hua qiao* and diaspora presume the dominant gravity of an ancestral land, real or imagined, as the nostalgic anchor of cultural identity, with the exilic existence seen as unrooted, unfulfilling, and temporary.[22] This narrative of returned *hua qiao* stresses the predestined triumphant end of homecoming.[23] By employing such a linear narrative predicated on a "Chinese identity" consistent across space and time, the complex diasporic experiences of Dai are reduced and subsumed into the master discourse of Chinese nationalism. A direct consequence is that the historical account of Dai's definitive contribution to the creation of modern Chinese ethnic dance has become a nationalist and nativist one, and Dai's passion for ethnic dance has been interpreted mainly as her patriotic sentiment realized by root-searching via dance.[24]

Emily Wilcox challenges this Sinocentric narrative by arguing that Dai's "Sinophone epistemology" formed by her *hua qiao* experiences enabled her to engage in what Shu-Mei Shih calls the "multiply-angulated critique" in her early choreography of Chinese ethnic dance (along with modern dance) to embody a kind of Chinese identity "that is highly local and yet transcends any singular identities or affiliations."[25]

This chapter further expands and complicates the understanding of the origin of modern Chinese ethnic dance by situating it in relation to Dai's—what I call—*multi-diasporic* experiences happening within a larger geographic background of intercultural exchanges, which were in turn facilitated and conditioned by a long-existing global colonial network both mobilized and undermined by the Second World War. Specifically, the rest of the chapter first goes back to Peng's travelogue and leverages it to contextualize the genesis of modern Chinese ethnic dance around four major themes that interweave throughout the chapter. The second section then reframes Dai's diasporic experiences of "homecoming" into an alternative one of multiple, sequential diaspora; that is, Dai's "homecoming" process may also be seen as a kind of diaspora upon diaspora, characterized by overlapping mismatches, misidentifications, and misalignments.[26] Section three situates Dai's early experiments on ethnic dances within the wartime ethnopolitics in and beyond China's southwestern borderlands; discusses how Dai presented and performed China's ethnic dances as Oriental dance in 1947 New York in relation to the "ethnologic dance" in the mid-century American scene of world dances and, conversely, how Dai conceived and promoted Oriental (Asian) dances in 1950s and 1960s socialist China as ethnic dance closely related to

China's own; and explains how Dai's multi-diasporic experiences had shaped her two-way, transnational and transcultural conceptions and practices of ethnic dance. The last section demonstrates Dai's collecting, understanding, choreographing, distributing, and performing ethnic dances were fundamentally (trans)mediated by Labanotation—a "universal" notation system for body movement developed by the central European school of modern dance. By contributing eight Tibetan dances written in Labanotation to the Dance Notation Bureau in 1947 New York, Dai, for the first time, expanded Laban's vision of building "a literature of dance" into a new one of "a world literature of dances." In the end, Dai's construction of China's ethnic dance was filtered through the theoretical and methodological lens of modern dance, and her root-searching via dance was not only a (re)rooting process, as in the traditional diasporic narrative of homecoming, but simultaneously a reversed journey of uprooting and displacing the collected and constructed Chinese ethnic dances—extracted and abstracted into labanotation—onto the international discursive stage of world dances.

Contextualizing the Genesis

In this section, to provide a historical and intellectual background for the chapter, I return to Peng's travelogue and explicate how his recorded personal experiences exemplify four major themes of the project to create modern Chinese ethnic dances: the multiple roles of the dancer, the Nationalist-Communist rivalry in ethnopolitics, the colonial influences, and the anthropological-ethnological connections.

The Multiple Roles of the Dancer

The travelogue genre, the content, the narrative strategy, and the publishing venue of the article reveal the multi-layered, and sometimes contradictory, identities and roles of the dancer in the process of creating modern ethnic dances. As a professional dancer, Peng sincerely admired the rich dance cultures of the ethnic minorities, learned new dance styles from them to enrich his choreography and repertoire, and took the risk of crossing ethnic and cultural boundaries by committing his modern-dance and ballet-trained body to performing ethnic dances.[27] As an amateur ethnographer conducting fieldwork, he "objectively" observed, analyzed, and recorded the alien customs of *other* peoples very different from his own dominant Han culture. As a Han traveler-explorer, he ventured into the unfamiliar and dangerous lands of the "barbarians," ferreted out exotica, and brought them back for consumption by his urban (mostly) Han compatriots through mass media. As a misrecognized "international trader-smuggler," he was symbolically embroiled into the transnational infrastructure of the world colonial network. As a socio-political commentator, he contributed to the national discourse of ethnopolitics and nation-building and offered his subtle criticism of the corrupted Nationalist ethno-policies. This multi-layer, multi-scope mode of working and (mis)identification was typical of most of the pioneers of modern ethnic dance in China.[28] As a result, it deeply complicated the construction of the new genre, the discursive power relations that defined the genre's meanings and roles in the larger social, cultural, and political context, and the reception of the dance works among different audiences.

The two stories recounted by Peng—the mythic origin of the Qiang dances and the unfortunate yet happy Jiarong wedding—shed further light on the complicated roles of the dancer and ethnic dances in the contemporaneous ethnic-cultural politics. According to the myth, the Qiang people understood themselves as the diasporic descendants of an ancient nation defeated and exiled by the superior Han-Chinese and thus lost their own written language—the symbol of advanced civilization. Music and dance exist only as an inferior substitute that mystically connects the Qiang with their lost written civilization. However, what Peng did not mention (or did not know) is that all the Qiang shamans had always been well-trained in reading and writing Chinese and thus had access to Han religious scripts, and the local Qiang religion was heavily influenced by Han Daoism: most of the scriptures chanted and danced by the shamans were derived from Daoist scriptures, not from some lost ancient texts.[29] Therefore, in the local cultural-political context, the myth of the extinct written language and the substitutive dance, to some extent, served to conceal and maintain the shamans' monopoly over the symbolic power and resources closely related to the Han culture.

Yet, from the perspective of the Han-Chinese, the mythic history of the Qiang confirmed the common belief that while the Han civilization, though highly sophisticated in writing, had long lost most of its dance tradition, the cultures of ethnic minorities, though primitive and illiterate, were rich in dance.[30] Peng's recount of the mythic history thus performs the act of *othering* by simultaneously transforming the dances of the *other* as exotica that stands for the opposite of the Han culture and affirming the superiority of the latter.[31] However, this othering that downplays the Han-Qiang cultural connections, to some degree, ran against the goal of constructing ethnic dances as a "Chinese" genre, rather than the dance of the other.

This tension is also present in Peng's account of the Jiarong wedding and dance party. Peng highlights the cruelty in the sexualized dramatic backstory of slavery, which again suggests the inferiority of the "primitive" and "barbarian" Jiarong culture relative to the Han counterpart. Yet he enthusiastically portrays the Jiarong dance-drinking party as a healthy, energetic, and liberating communal activity that, at that time, could serve as the antidote to both the repressive and rigidified Confucian morals and the imported "decadent" cabaret dance culture in the Han-Chinese metropolises. This echoes the "exoticizing and paternalistic sentiment" of the May Fourth era folklorists who had looked for inspirations from ethnic minority arts and literatures to rejuvenate the Han culture.[32] To counter-balance the exoticizing tendency, Peng points out the supposed similarities between the Qiang dress and the Han counterpart of "ancient times"—other Han scholars also made similar observations on the dresses of not just Qiang but some other ethnic groups in southwest China.[33] In so doing, Peng seems to hint at the traces of past sinicization and thus also the possibility for the future acculturation of ethnic dances into a "Chinese" (not simply Han) genre.

Despite the exoticizing and, to a lesser extent, eroticizing tendencies, it is this constant potentiality of two-way acculturation that places the origin of modern Chinese ethnic dance right beyond the explanatory framework of "internal orientalism."[34] Defined as the cultural politics that exoticizes and eroticizes ethnic minorities as the absolute other of the Han self to affirm the coherency and superiority of the Han identity, the perspective of internal Orientalism often underestimates the porosity of the boundary between the self and the other.[35] As demonstrated later, the overlapping, amalgamating, and shifting among different identities and viewpoints were the norm, rather than the exception, of the genesis of modern Chinese ethnic dance.

The Nationalist-Communist Rivalry in Ethnopolitics

This subtle tension between exoticization and acculturation should be understood in light of the discrepancies in the Communist and Nationalist ethnopolicies in the 1930s and 1940s that can be traced back to the Qing empire.[36]

In 1947, the same year as Peng published his travelogue, the Nationalist leader Jiang Jieshi 蔣介石 (1887–1975) published the revised version of his treatise *Zhongguo zhi mingyun* 中國之命運 [China's destiny], in the first section of which he systematically states his ethnopolitical vision for China. By arguing that the "five stocks"—Han, Man (Manchu), Zang (Tibetan), Hui, Meng (Mongol)—are all descendants of a single mythical ancestor, *Huangdi* 黃帝 (the Yellow Emperor), Jiang promotes a singular monogenic *Zhonghua minzu* 中華民族 (the Chinese nation-race) with Han as the nucleus that is coextensive with the sovereignty of the modern Chinese state.[37]

In contrast to Jiang's assimilationist approach to a homogenous nation-state, the Communists had been envisioning China as a unified multi-ethnic state in which the distinction of each *minzu* is recognized and respected, and all ethnicities enjoy equal footings and political representation under the umbrella identity of *Zhonghua minzu*. By 1947, the temporary alliance between the Communists and Nationalists during the Second Sino-Japanese War had already come to an end, and a full-scale civil war broke out about one year earlier between the two Parties vying for control of China. As the war escalated, the ethno-policies between the two Parties became more confrontational, and the Communists intended to use the recognitionist policies to enlist support from non-Han regions.[38] Within this context, despite its Han-centric view, Peng's travelogue seems to offer a subtle criticism of the Nationalist ethno-policies by promoting the distinct cultures and polygenic origins of ethnic minorities and exposing the Nationalist soldiers' exploitative practices and attitudes toward the non-Han regions. (Yet Peng's text does not provide any direct evidence suggesting Peng espoused the Communist ethno-policies.)

Another debate in the 1940s related to but beyond this Nationalist-Communist divide was that over the "national forms" already discussed in the previous chapter. Dance was also drawn into this debate centering on the question to what extent the Chinese national forms could be built upon the urban-based Western, yet already more-or-less indigenized, or "Westernized" artistic forms (such as Wu Xiaobang's "new dance") or rural-based "native" folk vernacular forms (such as the *xin yangge yundong* 新秧 歌運動, or the new *yangge* dance movement).[39] At first glance, the project of modern ethnic dance seems to be in line with the latter based on local folk forms. However, the extent to which the ethnic-minority (or non-Han) dances, local and folk as they were, could be called "Chinese" was itself a controversy that further complicated the national-form debate which mainly addressed the dominate Han culture. As demonstrated later, from the perspective of a typical Han spectator, the dances of the ethnic minorities may not be much less foreign than Western dances.

The Colonial Influences

The Communists and the Nationalists were not the only powerful players in China's southwestern regions of non-Han communities. Since the nineteenth century, due to the colonialization of South and Southeast Asia, imperialist powers, especially France and the British Empire, had been projecting cultural, economic, and political influences onto China's southwestern borderlands.[40] Trading routes and supporting infrastructure had been established (which led to the scene of the Nationalist soldiers' misrecognition of Peng as an international trader-smuggler). Some of the routes were further expanded and reinforced for military and logistic purposes during the Second World War as a result of the alliance among China, Britain, and the United States against Japan.[41] These developments had strengthened the cross-border connections between China's southwestern frontiers and British colonies such as Burma and India.[42]

In the academic realm, it is also colonial influences that initiated the modern study and ethnotaxonomy of non-Han communities in the southwestern borderlands and thus played an important role in the formation of modern ethnic identities in China. Since the mid-nineteenth century, Westerners—mainly French and British missionaries, explorers, military officers, and scholars—had conducted various field studies on the ethnic minorities in the southwestern frontiers.[43] For example, the Qiang ethnicity was first systematically studied by the British Protestant missionary Thomas Torrance (1871–1959) during the 1910s and 1920s in the same area as Peng conducted his fieldwork about three decades later.[44] Based on his Eurocentric misunderstanding of Qiang's religion being monotheism and the mythic history of the Qiang's migration and their lost scriptures and written language, together with other misinterpreted evidence, Torrance misidentified the Qiang as the descendants of the ancient Israelites—a mistake not uncommon among the Western missionary-scholars' studies of ethnic groups in southwest China.[45] As a result of Torrance's preaching, many Qiang accepted Torrance's claim of Qiang's Israelite origin in the 1930s and 1940s.[46] Nevertheless, the Western (mis)identification facilitated the formation of the self-identity of these ethnic groups.[47]

Another important case is the 1899–1900 field research conducted by the British military officer Henry Rodolph Davies (1865–1950) in the Yunnan province (north of Burma).[48] Davies was well trained in many Asian languages—including Persian, "Hindustani," Burmese, Pushtu (Pashto), and Chinese—which together "[c]artographically . . . traced a long crescent, originating in Afghanistan and sweeping through northern India, Burma, and the Sino-Burmese border region of southwest Yunnan," corresponding to the British colonial arch that pressed against the southwestern borderlands of the Qing Empire.[49] Requested by a British entrepreneur with support from the British authorities, Davies led an expedition to survey a possible railway route linking British India and China's Yangtze Rivier region via Yunnan, as the British and the French were competing to find shorter trade routes to China's economic center.[50] In addition to mapping in detail the geographic terrain of the region, Davies conducted linguistic analysis of the languages of many ethnic groups in Yunnan along the route of his over two-thousand-mile expedition. His linguistic approach, later called the "Davies model," according to Thomas Mullaney, would become the theoretical and methodological basis for the large-scale ethnic classification to be carried out in socialist China.

Specifically, Davies coded in a big table the pronunciations of the same set of over a hundred core everyday words in the language of each ethnic group, compared the differences and similarities in the coded pronunciations between the languages of different ethnic groups, and then estimated the "distances" between the languages. Based on these relative linguistic distances, Davies constructed a tree-like lineage of ethnic groups, with "clusters" of ethnic groups "close" to each other in terms of language.[51] He identified twenty-two such big clusters in Yunnan that would roughly correspond to the concept of *minzu* in the socialist era; half a century later, the anthropologists in socialist China adopted the Davies model (with some modifications) to eventually classify the hundreds of ethnic groups in China into fifty-six *minzu*.[52] Interestingly, as shown in this chapter, Dai later attempted to use a similar "scientific" logic based on comparison between dances of different ethnic groups written in coded signs to identify and distill shared patterns into a common Chinese dance "language." Here, dance and language formed yet another unexpected parallel in the colonial and postcolonial contexts.

The Anthropological and Ethnological Connections

The contrast between the abundant knowledge about China's ethnic minorities generated by Western agents and the ignorance of the Han-Chinese academia on this subject created a deep sense of crisis among many Chinese intellectuals and scholars in the early twentieth century.[53] Even as late as in the early 1940s, the linguist Wen You 聞宥 (1901–1985), conducting fieldwork in the Qiang region, still lamented that it was such a pity for Chinese academics that they did not know the Qiang—a people often seen in ancient Chinese writings—still existed in China.[54] Naturally, in the eyes of Han intellectuals, the Western anthropological studies of and interferences with the ethnic minorities posed a serious threat to China's national security and sovereignty because these activities were facilitated by and facilitated the West's imperialist expansion into China's southwestern borderlands. This sense of crisis stimulated Han-Chinese scholars' anthropological interests in the ethnic minorities of the frontiers and spurred the growth of anthropology and ethnology in China.[55]

As cruelly put in 1930 by Yang Chengzhi 楊成志 (1901–1991)—a founding figure of anthropology and ethnology in China who is widely regarded as the first Han-Chinese anthropologist conducting systematic fieldwork in ethnic-minority regions—the southwestern frontier was "virtually like a tame pig, trapped between a tiger and a lion, with the British and French imperialists [on one side] attacking freely the aboriginals in the borderlands . . . Compared with letting the foreigners slaughter and cook [the pig], we [the Han-Chinese, on the other side] would rather do it by ourselves."[56] In some sense, the metaphor becomes doubled because this Han-centric condescending tone toward ethnic minorities was not uncommon among the early generations of (Han-)Chinese anthropologists who ironically received systematic training in anthropology and sociology in France, Britain, and the United States—the "imperialists on the other side."[57] Although these anthropologists criticized the ignorance, arrogance, and biases of "traditional" Chinese intellectuals toward the ethnic minorities, they themselves, more or less influenced by Darwinism, often referred to the ethnic minorities variously as *yiren* 夷人, *yemanren* 野蠻人, *yeren* 野人, *fan* 番; all are derogatory appellations inherited from the imperial era that can be roughly translated as "barbarians."[58] Some of them went as far as claiming the non-Han communities to be hundreds of "small independent states" within the Chinese state, which undermined the unity of China and thus needed to be subdued and Sinicized, and proposed to use the territories and resources of the ethnic-minority regions to solve the social, economic, and political problems of China proper.[59]

Chinese anthropologists' interest in the southwestern ethnic minorities also led them closer to the scholarship produced by the French and British agents. They often first consulted the local foreign missionaries before conducting fieldwork, and some of them even crossed the border to the other side: Yang Chengzhi once went to French Indochina to collect primary and secondary sources at *École française d'Extrême-Orient* in Hanoi.[60] It is clear that the modern anthropological knowledge about the ethnic minorities in southwest China was the product of a transnational and transcultural, competitive and collaborative process happening within a (semi-)colonial context.

The origin of modern Chinese ethnic dance was closely related to the development of anthropology in China in this process. Ethnic dances, as part of the non-Han communities' everyday cultural life, had already caught the attention of some Chinese anthropologists. They treated dance as an essential part of the arts and religions of ethnic minorities.[61] The war against Japan pressed China's various resources to flow southwestward into the borderland provinces of Sichuan and Yunnan. Following this flow were academic institutions, intellectuals, scholars, and artists, including dancers.[62] The lands of the "barbarians" then became China's new military, political, and economic bases, and the geographic corridor for receiving foreign aid to support the war effort. The heightened concern for national survival, the disruption of prewar research agenda, and the proximity to ethnic-minority regions made many scholars who were not specialized in anthropology shift their research focus onto studying the ethnic minorities, which greatly boosted the production of anthropological knowledge about the borderlands and its peoples.[63] These (trans-disciplinary) anthropologists and their expertise turned out to be essential to the dancers and their project of creating modern ethnic dance, because the dancers had virtually no knowledge about the non-Han communities or academic training in doing fieldwork. Moreover, as shown later, the discourse on the new dance genre was also built largely upon the discourse of anthropology in China.

In the case of Peng, although he was alone when arriving at the Jiashan Settlement of the Qiang, the first half of his journey and the last part of his fieldwork in the Jiarong area were both guided by Li Fanggui (aka, Fang-Kuei Li) 李方桂 (1902–1987), the Michigan- and Chicago-trained world-renowned linguist who was a founding figure of linguistics in China specialized in American Indian, Sino-Tibetan, and Thai languages and would be elected the vice president of the Linguistic Society of America in several years.[64] At that time, Li was conducting fieldwork in the region with two students. Peng joined them and Li pointed Peng to the Jiashan Settlement to collect dance.[65] When Peng arrived in the Jiarong area later, Li introduced Peng to the local chieftain, whose daughter was a student of *Huaxi xiehe daxue* 華西協和大學 (West China Union University) in Chengdu—a major academic base of anthropology during the war—and knew Li very well. It is these personal supports that ensured Peng's success in collecting songs and dances in the region.[66]

Triple Diaspora: The Dancer Simultaneously Abroad and at Home

Further complicating the genesis of modern Chinese ethnic dance is the fact that Dai Ailian, who started the project, was not even a Chinese proper and could not speak or write Chinese properly. Instead of offering a comprehensive biographic summary, the goal of this section is to revise the Sinocentric narrative of Dai's Odyssean return in Chinese dance historiography by recasting some crucial aspects and moments of her life and career into what may be called multiple, sequential diaspora.[67] That is, "homecoming," relevant as it is, is just one side of Dai's story; the other side is that Dai's journey home may also be seen as a kind of diaspora upon diaspora, fraught with anxieties, mismatches, and negotiations between multiple worldviews and identities across various borders, in addition to a newly acquired sense of belonging. This diasporic current reconfirms that the rise of Chinese ethnic folk dance in the mid-1940s was not an isolated nationalist response to the particular political crises of China, but an outgrowth of the extensive global circuit of cultural, economic, and political transactions conditioned by the world colonial network that had reshaped modern China.[68] Note that by recuperating these diasporic "roots," this study by no means denies the dominant influence of nationalism on Dai's artistic practice, identity negotiation, and the general development of ethnic dance in China. Rather, it shows how the artist's personal diasporic anxiety and aspiration, as an undercurrent, rode with the nationalist mainstream (and vice versa), yet often with a vector of diverging momentums.

Diaspora I: Trinidad

Dai's grandparents (or great grandparents) from both the paternal and maternal sides migrated from Guangdong (aka Canton) in southeast China to British Trinidad, very likely as indentured laborers, sometime between 1853 and 1884, most likely in 1865.[69] This migration was, on the one hand, pushed by the population explosion in south rural China and the social upheavals caused by the Taiping Rebellion (1850–1864) and, on the other hand, pulled by a great shortage of labor in the sugar plantations in the British West Indies as the result of the abolishment of slavery in 1834.[70] The British authorities intended to introduce a "middle class" of free Chinese laborers as a social buffer between the white Europeans on the top of the colonial hierarchy and the often riotous black "ex-slaves" at the bottom, because the British widely believed that the Chinese were more hard-working, obedient, content with the status quo, and easily assimilated into the colonial system both culturally and economically.[71] In fact, many of the Chinese laborers had already been converted to Christianity before they left China, and there were many reports by Europeans that the Chinese laborers, especially women, quickly started to purchase and put on European-styled clothing upon their arrival.[72]

Beside the Chinese, (East) Indian indentured laborers were also introduced into the West Indies. Because the cultures and behaviors of the Indian workers were further away from the values upheld by the British authorities, the Chinese enjoyed a slightly higher status in the colonies; the term "coolie" was reserved for the Indian workers, rather than the Chinese.[73] That is, the British colonial hierarchy in South Asia and the Far East reproduced itself in the small island of Trinidad.

The Chinese in Trinidad moved quickly off plantations starting from the 1870s, first often as peasant food cultivators and truck gardeners, and then engaged in petty commerce, such as shopkeepers; some of them later became very successful, including the families of Dai's parents.[74] By the time Dai was born in 1916, her Christian family had become quite wealthy and respected, with some local street and buildings named after their mistransliterated "Jewish" surname "Isaac."[75] Dai received very good British-styled education, including French, Latin, music, and dance. Starting from her parents' generation, the family spoke only English (though her father still knew some Cantonese).[76] The generation of Dai had become quite "rooted" in the British Trinidad: "being Chinese" for her was only a racial label that had little to do with her cultural or national identity in connection with the ancestral land; the paternal family even forgot their original Chinese surname ("Dai" was not the original surname, but the result of a series of mis-transliterations).[77]

Although the four major races largely socialized separately, there were considerable inter-racial interactions. Dai attended elementary school with "Chinese, black, and a small number of white kids," and her family hired African servants.[78] Dai took ballet classes with White girls, upon the permission by the girls' parents.[79] Some of Dai's female relatives married Indian husbands.[80] Dai, as a child, often went to the workshop of their gold-silversmith Indian neighbor, sitting quietly in the corner and watching in amazement how he used a small furnace to work gold and silver blocks into refined jewelry "like a magician."[81] Since the 1870s, the Indian festival of Muharram ("Hosay") had become an all-inclusive festival on the island with active Chinese and African participants; so was Easter.[82] It is on those occasions that Dai was exposed to the rich music and dance cultures of the Indian and African immigrants, in addition to the tap dance influence from the nearby United States.[83]

In a couple of decades, when Dai arrived in China's southwestern borderlands neighboring India, she would probably feel uncannily "at home," finding in place a similar structure of trans-Himalayan colonial hierarchy and intercultural exchanges, only this time on a much larger geographic scale and with the Africans replaced by the borderland ethnic minorities. Dai's colonial experiences in Trinidad would provide her with a unique vantage point from which she could see in a fresh light the dances of the borderlands in relation to the dance of the Han, and the dances of India and other British/European colonies on the other side of the border, such as Burma and Indonesia.

Diaspora II: London

For Dai Ailian, her personal (instead of familial) diasporic experiences began at age fourteen in 1930 when she moved with her mother and two elder sisters to London, where she would stay for the next ten years. The reason for the moving was that Dai's father became obsessed with gambling and the family started to lose money. As a result, her mother wanted to be more financially and personally independent by learning tailoring in London, and at one point the mother decided to take her daughters with her.[84]

Life in the cosmopolitan London was both familiar and different for Dai. Due to the deteriorating family finance and the predominant white population, she enjoyed much less privilege in London than she did back in Trinidad. She continued to study ballet and later German modern dance, yet this time under the instruction of some of the "leading figures in the British dance world, including ballet dancers Anton Dolin, Marie Rambert, Margaret Craske, and Lydia Sokolova," and modern dancers Lesley Burrows-Goossens and the teachers such as Sigurd Leeder and Lisa Ullmann of the famous Jooss-Leeder Dance School at Dartington Hall; and Dai continued to be the only girl of color in the classes.[85] A certain racial hierarchy was also in place in the capital: due to her Asian look, she was often asked to play some "oriental" roles in public and commercial-entertainment dance performances, such as American Indian, Persian, Tibetan, and also Chinese, catering to the Orientalist appetite of the Western audiences.[86] Dai, being an "Oriental" with a short stature, never got into a real ballet company; in her own words, "I was the wrong height and the wrong color."[87]

However, this culturally entrenched racial stereotyping was only part of Dai's life in London. According to her oral history, Dai, being a British citizen, was able to socialize with and make much more "white" friends in London than in the semi-segregated Trinidadian society. At the (inter)personal level, it seems that Dai got along quite well with her cosmopolitan London friends.[88] These friends—teachers, neighbors, classmates, colleagues, "boyfriends," and ordinary friends—rich or poor, young or old, men or women, all offered generous helps to Dai in both her life and career and some of them would become important life-long international connections after she went to China. Dai recalled these experiences in London fondly later in her life.[89] Also, because there were very few Asians in England, whenever Dai went into the street, she could easily catch the (mostly friendly) attention of the Europeans, in a good way for Dai as a performer, although she felt a little awkward.[90]

Unexpectedly, the truly disturbing, yet subtle, racial tension at the personal level was caused by the other overseas Chinese in London. There were communities of Chinese merchants and students active in the city, and naturally the Europeans tended to see Dai as one of the Chinese. Sometimes because people thought she was a Chinese, they would ask her whether she can perform a Chinese dance, but Dai did not know any.[91] It is probably these moments of race-based (though friendly) misidentification that made Dai start to rethink her "Chinese" identity. For her, "being Chinese" was no longer just about race, but now a new cultural and national identity became gradually attached to it. At first, Dai struggled with and even resisted this new (mis)identification. According to Dai's recollection in 1947, because the "drawbacks in character" (dishonesty) among some of the Chinese merchants in London damaged the overall reputation of the Chinese community among the Londoners, Dai often felt ashamed about being associated with them. Only when she started to think that her ancestors, who also came from China, were honest and hardworking people did she begin to make peace.[92] That is, the dormant familial memory from "diaspora I" was activated to serve as the "glue" to bind the newly acquired cultural and national identities with the racial one during "diaspora II." However, as shown later, this binding of identities was never absolute.

For Dai, being a cultural Chinese in London was by no means easy. Again, the tension came mainly from the relationship between Dai and the Chinese, instead of the European, communities. Because Dai "despite being a Chinese, knew little about the Chinese culture, and even could not speak Chinese," whenever Dai met Chinese students studying in London, she always "envied them, feeling that they were superior," which made her "feel very awkward and embarrassed."[93] In Dai's words, "in the eyes of the students from China, I was also a 'foreigner,' so I felt a strong sense of inferiority about my identity."[94] Only after the Second Sino-Japanese War broke out in 1937, when Dai started to regularly perform China-themed dances at the fund-raising events held by the China Campaign Committee—a British organization set up with the assistance of Chinese students, intellectuals, and other members of the Chinese communities in England to support China in the war—did she finally blend herself into the Chinese communities.[95] Thus, Dai's new Chinese identity was not just formed by the colonial racial order in London—a more rigid racial hierarchy had already been in place in Trinidad. Rather, it was also the result of the triangular mutual gaze, interaction, and (mis)identification among Dai, the Europeans, and the overseas Chinese communities united under a strengthened national identity during the war.

Dai's conception of Chinese dance also took shape in this cosmopolitan environment full of intercultural exchanges in a colonial context. Dai, as a "Chinese" dancer who never saw a real Chinese dance, had been exposed to various performances of "Oriental dances" in London, such as Japanese,

Javanese, and Indian dances.[96] The fact that there was no "Chinese" dance on an equal footing with these Oriental dances on the cosmopolitan stage bothered her because dance was the major medium for Dai to negotiate between her colonial-diasporic and the newly acquired Chinese identities. As shown later, in Dai's view, the "Chinese dance" (to become) may not simply be an isolatable "national dance" vis-à-vis the Western ballet and modern dance. Rather, it also belonged with the Oriental dances as, in some sense, "ethnic dances" in a world colonial empire—a natural extension of the African and Indian dances she had been familiar with in Trinidad. This may also be likened to how Dai learned about Chinese history and its status in Asian cultures by reading English books in the British Museum Library, the ultimate symbol for the colonial knowledge of world-empire building.[97] After the Jooss-Leeder School closed, Jooss recommended Dai to work in the dance troupe of the famous Indian dancer Ram Gopal because he thought both the Chinese and the India were "Orientals." Dai did not seem to feel offended; she accepted the recommendation without strong reservation, if any.[98]

Parallel to Dai's Chinese ancestral lineage, more and more with which she began to identify herself (in Dai's words, *ren zu gui zong* 認祖歸宗, meaning recognize and return to one's ancestral lineage), Dai also placed herself within a Western lineage of dance.[99] Dai said in her oral history that she had two "grandfathers" of dance: the paternal one was Enrico Cecchetti (1850–1928), whose method of classical ballet training was inherited by Dai's London ballet teachers, and the maternal one was Rudolf von Laban (1879–1958), whose system of modern dance was carried on by the Jooss-Leeder Dance School. This Western lineage of dance education formed the theoretical and methodological point of view from which Dai would envision the "Chinese dance" or the "Chinese ethnic dance" to become, and also analyze and study "various dances around the world."[100]

Diaspora III: China

Dai's journey to China in 1940 was at once "homecoming-root-searching" and the beginning of her experiences of a new diaspora, leaving behind most of her personal connections established throughout the ten years in London, many of which would not be renewed until almost four decades later after the end of the Cultural Revolution. The declaration of war between Britain and Germany ended Dai's dance education. Holding a British passport yet funded by the Chinese Embassy to Britain, in January 1940, Dai boarded a ship from Liverpool to Hong Kong, where she had some relatives.[101] The long voyage attested the great expanse of the British empire, taking multiple stops in Egypt, Sri Lanka, and Malaya (all being British colonies), with the last section of the voyage once again tracing eastward "a long crescent" that semicircled the southern borders of China ending in Hong Kong.[102] Starting from Hong Kong, Dai would soon trace another long crescent westward along the other side of the borders from Guangdong, via Guangxi, and finally to Sichuan.[103] With views from both sides of the borders, Dai would create the "dances of the borderlands" in a couple of years that would become a national sensation.

Dai's newly acquired Chinese identity was quickly acknowledged by the press in Hong Kong. Shortly after her arrival in the spring of 1940, probably through the sources in the China Campaign Committee in London, the March 31 issue of the Hong Kong version of the mainland-based newspaper *Dagong bao* 大公報 (aka, Ta Kung Pao) published a short article, calling Dai "our country's young expert of dance, who had been sojourning in London." It comments that "her dance was highly regarded [in London]. Upon her arrival in Hong Kong, in addition to thoroughly studying the dance art of China, she also plans to create various new forms of dance steps, in the hope of expressing the new spirit of the newly rising China."[104] The next day, Dai was contacted by Song Qingling 宋慶齡 (1893–1981), the former first lady of China, who soon asked and helped Dai to hold dance concerts for the fundraising events held by the China Defense League (Song was the chair).[105] It seems that Dai's desire for identity recognition matched China's political need for Dai's dance skills and her exemplary status as *gui qiao* (returned overseas sojourner) in the mass mobilization of war. Within a year, Dai obtained a Chinese passport, establishing some kind of dual Chinese-British citizenship.[106] In addition to this convergence of interest, the fact that Dai quickly married to Ye Qianyu 葉淺予 (1907–1995), a well-connected famous Chinese painter and cartoonist, also greatly helped Dai to get accepted into the artistic and intellectual circles of China.[107] A few months later, by the time when Dai arrived in Guilin, Guangxi, she had begun to "feel very comfortable among people who look the same" as herself, mainly Ye's artist and intellectual friends and relatives.[108]

However, in this alliance between Dai's personal diasporic identity and the greater national(ist) interest, the two were not always perfectly aligned.

The tension between the two intensified after the Communists took power in 1949. As Shelly Chan points out, the reintegration of returned overseas Chinese in the socialist regime in the 1950s was a fraught process, because the state increasingly saw the "unknown foreign past" of the returnees as a sign for subversive "disobedience and immutability."[109] This was also more-or-less true in the case of Dai. On the one hand, the Communist Party bestowed many high-rank titles, positions, and honors to Dai as mentioned above. On the other hand, the Party mainly used the "outside-Party patriotic democratic returnee" identity of Dai as a facade, while the decision-making power was still in the hands of party members usually in an officially second position of an organization—a situation not unique to Dai.[110] In fact, Dai had always wanted to join the Party, but was rejected on the ground that staying outside the Party can make greater contributions to the country (her wish was only to be granted in her deathbed, fulfilling her last national duty).[111] Dai's choreographing and dancing career was de facto ended against her will after she was assigned to the prestigious, yet largely "decorative," position as president of the newly founded Beijing Dance School in 1954.[112] The Party officials' distrust in Dai continued into the late 1980s.[113]

Dai's diasporic experiences in China were far from fulfilling. After the end of the Cultural Revolution, Dai went abroad almost every year, renewing old international connections and establishing new ones.[114] In the 1990s, while sojourning in London, she once admitted to one of her previous students who also decided to live abroad that "after I grew old, I still prefer to living in England, feeling freer . . . So, for these recent years, I have always lived in England whenever possible . . . Only when I needed to attend a conference did I go back to China. I want to keep myself from politics as far away as possible . . ."[115] However, Dai decided to spend her last few years in Beijing. As another student close to Dai recalled, during a visit to Dai's home in Beijing in her last months, the student found out that "her fridge was empty" and "she had run out of meals like this for several times," while, ironically, her home was full of expensive bouquets of flowers sent by various organizations. The student further commented: "because a lonely and famous old lady like her had [lived in] very complicated environments, with a cultural background and personality different from ordinary people, it was hard [for me] to help her . . . Although she appeared strong on the outside, she was full of sorrow inside. Pains and loneliness made her sometimes want to end her own life . . ."[116] On another occasion, Dai confided to a student: "I wish my ashes could be spread into the sea [after I die], because I myself came from the other side of the sea."[117] In the end, Dai's diasporic identity falls in the middle of a triangular relationship among Trinidad, England, and China, just like the oceans between continents.

It is within the context of Dai's multiple diasporic identities and the historical and intellectual background laid out in the previous section that one needs to understand Dai's project of creating modern Chinese ethnic dance as a transnational, transcultural, and transdisciplinary one—as much as a nationalist one—under both a world colonial hierarchy and a domestic Han-centric ethnic hierarchy.

The Dance of the Borderlands and the Dance of the Orient

Shortly after Peng returned to Chengdu, on September 15, 1945, Dai, her husband Ye Qianyu, and the guide Zhuang Xueben 莊學本 (1909–1984) embarked on their over-a-month journey to Kangding, Xikang.[118] Zhuang was not an ordinary guide but had a very colorful background that turned out to be instrumental in the creation of Dai's ethnic dances. In the autobiographies of Dai and Ye, they refer to Zhuang as a "photographer"; yet Zhuang was much more than that.[119] Born in Pudong, Shanghai, Zhuang was a self-trained master photographer and half-trained anthropologist/ethnologist. From 1934 to 1945, he trekked through vast lands in Sichuan, Xikang, Gansu, Qinghai, Yunnan, and India, took over 3,000 photos and wrote hundreds of thousand words of research reports, travelogues, and diaries on more than ten different ethnic groups in China's southwestern borderlands.[120] His *Qiang rong kaocha ji* 羌戎考察記 (A record of the investigation of the Qiang and Jiarong,1936) and *Xinan yizu diaocha baogao* 西南彝族調查報告 (An investigative report on the Yi in southwest, 1941) were important works in the history of Chinese anthropology.[121] Now, Zhuang is regarded as the pioneer of visual anthropology in China.[122]

Moreover, Zhuang worked in India as a manager for the *Kang-Zang maoyi gongsi* 康藏貿易公司 (The Xikang-Tibet trade company).[123] This transnational company "was run by influential Khampa merchants, powerful local headmen, and authoritative lamas in the southwest," dealing with "various sorts of businesses in an extraordinarily large commercial network ranging from Kokonor [Qinghai] to Xikang, Tibet, and the Indian subcontinent," having headquarters in Kangding, Lhasa, and Calcutta, with "branches along the traditional Sino-Tibetan commercial routes."[124] The reason why Dai first sent out Peng alone for fieldwork was because she had to wait Zhuang to finish his jobs in India and came back to Chengdu.[125] In fact, just two years earlier, Dai's husband Ye also went to India as a war correspondent to visit the Chinese Expeditionary Force being trained by the Americans in Ramgarh, Bihar, northern India. During his travel in India, Ye became so fascinated by Indian dances that he began to paint many Indian dancing figures for years.[126] Again, the origin of modern ethnic dance became inextricably intertwined with anthropology in China and the trans-Himalaya economic and cultural connections during the war.

Zhuang's anthropological expertise and rich transnational-transcultural experiences were indispensable to Dai's travel and fieldwork in Kangding, Xikang. The founding of Xikang as a new province in 1927 was the Nationalists' attempt to strengthen their control over the troubled borders between China proper and Tibet, then a de facto independent state often in confrontation with the Chinese. Yet the Chinese rule there was largely nominal. Even in Kangding, the provincial capital, the local people did not accept the official Chinese currency, fabi 法幣, so that the Nationalist officials had to resort to bartering to subsist.[127] The Tibetans there were generally defensive and unfriendly towards the Han.[128] With the help from Zhuang, and also his Tibetan colleague and friend, Gesang Yuexi 格桑悅希—a manager of the Xikang-Tibet Trade Company—Dai and Ye smoothly conducted the fieldwork to collect songs and dances of the Tibetans.[129]

Dance as Ethnopolitics: The Plenary of Borderland Music and Dances

By combining the fieldwork of Peng in northwest Sichuan and her own in Kangding, starting from March, 1946, Dai held eighteen gala-styled concerts of "borderland music and dances" (*bianjiang yinyue wudao dahui* 邊疆音樂舞蹈大會) in Chongqing and four concerts in Shanghai within a few months, which caused huge sensations in major cities across the country.[130] This event is widely regarded as the birth of modern Chinese ethnic dance.[131] The dance styles of the *Plenary* represented the folk dances of the Yao, Miao, Yi, Uyghur, Qiang, Jiarong, Tibetan, and Han ethnicities spread across the provinces of Guangxi, Guizhou, Yunnan, Sichuan, Tibet, and Xikang.[132] Among the fourteen or so performance works, the choreographies may be classified into four categories: dances based directly on Dai and Peng's fieldwork with minimal adaptation; ethnic dances Dai learned second-handedly from other Han-Chinese; dances based on Dai's textual research and imagination; dances directly contributed and performed by ethnic minorities.[133]

Published as an introduction to the *Plenary*, there was an article attributed to Dai with the title "Fazhan zhongguo wudao de diyi bu" 發展中國舞蹈的第一步 [The first step in developing the Chinese dance], which may be seen as the manifesto of modern Chinese ethnic dance.[134] In it, Dai laid down the methodological groundwork for building a coherent Chinese dance genre: first, conduct comprehensive survey and research on all dances of all ethnicities in China, and second, "synthesize" (*zonghe* 綜合) all dance styles into a Chinese dance style. This synthetic approach seems to be closer to the Nationalist assimilationist ethno-policies, though the "Chinese dance" to become would not necessarily be a Han-centric one.[135]

The significance of both the *Plenary* and the manifesto need to be understood in light of the Nationalist ethnopolitics in the wartime international realpolitik. After the Nationalist government moved to Chongqing during the war, Jiang had been trying to reestablish control over the de facto independent "states" of Xinjiang in the northwest and Tibet in the west.[136] Although Jiang had largely succeeded in bringing Qinghai, Gansu, and Xinjiang back to the control of the central government by 1944, he made little headway toward Tibet due to strong Tibetan resistance and the involvement of British interests. Since the early 1940s, the Nationalist government had been in negotiation with the British, British-Indian, and Tibetan governments on the project of constructing an India-Tibet-China pack route to increase imports of war supplies from the Western allies, which was never carried out due to the Tibetan government's distrust in the Nationalists' motivations.[137] At that time, a Chinese could not directly enter Tibet from inland China; rather, the Chinese needed to first go to British India to obtain an entry Visa issued by the Indian government and then enter Tibet from the Indian side. That was why Zhuang Xueben chose to work in India in the first place—he wanted to enter Tibet from India (but he never managed to get a Visa to do so).[138]

Jiang's counter strategy to tackle this impasse was twofold. In the short run, he managed to gain the support of the powerful Xikang-Tibet Trade Company (for which Zhuang worked). He planned to use its dominant trade network to introduce the Chinese currency *fabi* into circulation in the Tibetan area, and together with the planned India-Tibet-China pack route, to bring Tibet economically closer to China.[139] In the long run, politically, Jiang intended to separate the Tibetan political system from the religious one, so that Han or pro-Han Tibetans would eventually be able to participate in the political affairs of Tibet.[140] Gesang Yuexi, manager of the Company and the guide for Dai and Ye in Kangding, was such a firm pro-Han Tibetan supporter of this secularization policy.[141] In 1943, the core members of the Company "were given an audience by Jiang, and on this occasion they also formally gave Jiang their full political allegiance."[142] In fact, Gesang Yuexi and his Tibetan colleagues from the Company performed one of the dances in the *Plenary*.[143] In this context, the *Plenary* may be seen as a celebration and confirmation of Jiang's reunification achievements and authority in west China, and the economic-political alliance between the Nationalists and their pro-Han ethnic-minority allies, which would set an example for all non-Han communities and the Tibetan government.

Yet, this approach should also be understood in light of Dai's diasporic experiences. Ethnic minorities were not the original destination of Dai's imagined root-searching journey via dance, as ethnically she was a Han. However, after some search and research, Dai was convinced that the Han dance tradition had been largely absorbed into Chinese theaters and the martial arts; as a result, dance, as an independent art, was lacking in the Han culture. Then, Dai learned that ethnic minority regions were rich in dance forms, which might provide the "roots of Chinese dance" Dai had been looking for.[144]

However, Dai's attempt to claim ethnic folk dances as the roots of Chinese dance turned out to be a strenuous task, since representing "Chineseness" via ethnic minority dances is clearly at odds with the mainstream Han-centric nationalism. Dai tries to address this problem in the manifesto. She points out the striking similarities between some Tibetan folk dance and Japanese classical dance forms, and then reasons that because there is no direct historical connection between Tibet and Japan, "it is simple to reach the conclusion that both the Tibetan folk dances of Xikang and those of Japan were introduced from China and remained unchanged since the Tang Dynasty. We can also bear in mind that the cultures of Japan and Tibet were profoundly influenced by the Han people, especially during the Tang Dynasty."[145] After ascribing Tibetan dances to the privileged Han dances of the Tang Dynasty, Dai further argues that, based on geographic proximity, the folk dances of the Jiarong and Yi were probably learned from the Tibetans, and the dances of the Qiang were in turn learned from the Jiarong.[146] By constructing a genealogy of ethnic dances, the Chineseness of ethnic minority dances may be justified, as they are all descendants of the "authentic" "Han" dances of the Tang Dynasty. This narrative is aligned with the Han-centric nationalist imperative.

Yet, this manifesto does not necessarily reflect Dai's own thoughts faithfully, since at that time, Dai's Chinese level was too rudimentary to write the essay.[147] In contrast to this alleged direction of the dissemination of dance forms, "Tibet ← Tang → Japan," which affirms Han-centrism, Dai, on many less public occasions, claimed a different possible directionality, "India → Tibet → Tang China → Japan," which could also explain the similarities between Tibetan and Japanese dances but clearly defies Han-centrism.[148] Moreover, Dai went further to argue that Tibetan folk dances are the representative Han folk dance forms of the Tang Dynasty; yet few Han believed her, until Dai emphasized that "Fei Xiaotong [費孝通], the number one anthropologist of China, endorses my view."[149] Wang Mingke points out that many Chinese intellectuals, anthropologists, and ethnologists had been working on a big project of constructing a coherent developmental lineage and history for the *Zhonghua minzu* across millennia, with Fei being a prominent one among them.[150] By enlisting the support of Fei, Dai's project of constructing modern Chinese ethnic dance became explicitly entwined with this grand national ethno-historical project.

There is evidence that Dai perhaps wanted to include into the manifesto the Indian influences on the dances of southwest ethnicities. In the March of 1947, an English version of the manifesto appeared in a major British dance magazine, *The Dancing Times*.[151] This suggests that Dai might have first written an English version and then had it translated into Chinese, with the English version published in England later. The published English version was shorter than the Chinese one. By comparing the two versions, it seems that the Chinese version is a rather faithful translation of the English counterpart (or the other way around). However, there is one sentence in the English version that is not included in the Chinese version. When Dai describes the "religious masked dances" of Lhasa, she observes in the English version: "Buddhism was introduced [into Tibet] directly from India and indirectly through China, so the origin of these masked dances is left for further research."[152] Perhaps because including this sentence would seem to further dilute the already problematic Chineseness in Tibetan dance, it was left out of the Chinese version. In fact, some observant viewers of the *Plenary* recognized the "Indian influence" on Tibetan dances, as one commenter points out that two of the Tibetan dances were "thoroughly of the Indian style," and that since Tibet has been "Buddhicized from top down, the dances of Lhasa are mainly dances of India."[153]

By including India into the route as a major resource of influence, Dai went beyond both Han-centric and Sinocentric nationalism. Dai's identification of the Indian influences may have also been partly inspired by the collaboration between her husband Ye and the famous painter Zhang Daqian 張大千 (1899–1983). While Dai and Ye were waiting for Zhuang in Chengdu, they lived with Zhang for over a month. By that time, Zhang had been back from the Mogao cave 莫高窟 (built mainly in the Tang dynasty) in Dunhuang, Gansu, where he stayed for three years to copy the famous frescos, which had clear ancient Indian Buddhist influences. Knowing this, Ye wanted to learn Chinese painting with Zhang. During his stay, Ye often applied the skills learned from Zhang to painting Indian dancing figures as exercises, while Zhang borrowed these Indian figures and combined them with the fresco models to paint his own Dunhuang version of Indian dances.[154] These mixed "dance forms" realized through painting may have later inspired Dai to create her famous "Tang-Indian"-styled work *Feitian* 飛天 (Apsaras) in the early 1950s, which would further develop into a distinct *Dunhuang* style of the Chinese classical dance.[155] In addition to these external stimuli, Dai's own diasporic experiences in Trinidad and London may have also helped: after all, India, Indians, and Indian dances had never been too far away from her since her childhood.

Ethnic Dance as Oriental Dance: In the United States

As demonstrated above, justifying the Chineseness of ethnic folk dances by constructing a genealogy of ethnic-minority dances poses a challenge to the mainstream Han-centric sentiments. Possibly as a means to mitigate this ethnic tension, Dai's dances are named the "borderland dances," which justifies their Chineseness by limiting them within the supposed national borders and at the same time affirms Han-centrism by emphasizing their location at the geographic margins of China. Interestingly, in Dai's article promoting her concert, there is no such term as "borderland dances"; instead, she uses the expression "the folk dance of [a certain ethnicity]."[156] However, even the qualifier "borderland" failed to isolate Dai's ethnic dances within the national borders. As shown later, in Dai's view, China's ethnic dances may belong to a larger identity—the "dances of the Orient."

Although the choreography of ethnic dances in the *Plenary* was driven mainly by nationalist and (Dai's) diaspora-related motivations, they may have also, inadvertently or not, catered to the urban (mostly) Han audiences' appetite for exotica. One viewer used adjectives like *qiangzhuang* 强壮 (strong), *julie* 劇烈 (intense), *chiluo* 赤裸 (naked), *jiankang* 健康 (healthy) to romanticize the images of dancing ethnic minorities as the exact opposite of the "parasitic" class of "weakly fat aristocrats and urbanites," capable of "wakening our primitive souls, [making us] return to the wild field like [our] ancestors, [leaving us] intoxicated in the . . . steamed smell of the earth."[157] Another viewer wrote the following passage to describe the general atmosphere of the performance: "In the colorful and dazzling light above the stage, the inner-Asian styled costumes, assisted by the active and vital melodies, oozed rhythms of primitivity. In this moment, the spectators were drawn into a hypnotic mood; lights, sounds, and colors, all firmly grasped everyone's heart, letting us feel like being in a beautiful, strange, and magnificent fairy land."[158] This description would fit almost any of the Orientalist scenes in classical ballets.

Unexpectedly, the exotic side of the borderland dances did the Communists a favor. After the *Plenary* and its performance in Shanghai in 1946, ethnic dances quickly spread among the young college students in major cities, and the Uygur dance *Qingchun zhi wu* 青春之舞 (Dance of youth) turned out to be the most popular one.[159] Dai probably did not anticipate this: she learned this dance second-handedly from a Han woman, and thus the dance was not authentic.[160] Moreover, the dances of Xinjiang occupied a relatively peripheral position in her genealogy of ethnic dances.[161] Its popularity was partly due to the huge influence of the accompanying song *Qingchun zhi ge* 青春之歌 (Song of youth) popularized by Wang Luobin 王洛賓 (1913–1996) and partly due to the signature exotic dance move—horizontally left-and-right shifting of the head without moving the other parts of the body.[162] Students often formed a circle on the playground to practice this dance move.[163] The Communists sensed an opportunity in this seemingly "harmless," and thus uncensored (by the Nationalists), student gatherings, and used it to organize the students to participate in the anti-Nationalist movement—"Anti-hunger, Anti-civil war, and Anti-persecution."[164]

The "exoticizing" potential of the "borderland dances" became further amplified on the international stage. From September 14, 1946, to October 3, 1947, Dai and Ye, among other high-profile Chinese artists, intellectuals, and scholars, visited America upon the invitation by the US state department.[165]

In New York, Dai held several concerts with her borderland dances performed alongside Javanese dances—in some sense, her old dream in London came true.[166] She was billed as a "Chinese dancer," supposedly designating her race, newly acquired citizenship, and the dance form she was to perform.[167] However, in the eyes of the American audiences, the word "Chinese," just as "Javanese," may be synonymous with "Oriental." *Yao ren zhi gu* 瑤人之 鼓 (The Yao drum dance) was one of Dai's two dances that were filmed in New York by the famous Chinese leftist film director Situ Huimin 司徒慧 敏 (1910–1987), who was sojourning in New York at that time.[168] The film, made for China Film Enterprises of America, Inc., probably had Westerners as the major targeted audience, as it, entitled "Two Chinese Dances," was screened for the New York public multiple times from late 1947 to 1954.[169] The filmed dance is a two-minutes-forty-five-second short video.[170] What is of interest here are the closeups in the film, with all other shots being medium shots. There are only three closeups. The first one is a medium-high-angle long-take closeup of the big drum on the stage, signifying the theme of the dance. The other two are almost identical, located in the second half of the video: both are eye-level-angle, one-second short-take closeups of the swirling flying skirts with the dancer's thighs revealed underneath, with an erotic connotation.

If the exotic-erotic in the film is just the product of the voyeuristic male gaze, then Dai's own attitude toward borderland dances on the international stage may be best illustrated in her English notes prepared for introducing Tibetan dances to an American audience. From June 30 to July 13, 1947, together with the famous philosopher Feng Youlan 馮友蘭 (1895–1990) and another Chinese professor, Dai went to Upper Montclair, New Jersey, 15 miles northwest of Lincoln Tunnel, to teach a two-week summer course on Chinese ethnic dances. There were fifty students, mostly American female teachers.[171] Dai's notes "Introducing Tibetan Dance" (with the byline indicating it is from the "Notes of Tai-Ai-Lien New York—1947") could be her lecturing notes for one of the classes or, also likely, written as the introduction to the eight notated Tibetan dances she gave to the Dance Notation Bureau in New York for publication:

> Tibet is a remote land with the highest altitude in the world. The people are simple and unspoiled, with a ready laugh on their faces and a childish sense of humor towards one another. As a race they are extremely handsome, healthy, broad of chest, their skins wind-beaten and sun-burned because

so much of their life is spent out of doors. Their territory, besides Tibet proper, covers [part of] Sikiang, Munan [Yunnan?] and Chinghai provinces in China, Darjeeling, India and Mongolia . . . Religion and culture stemmed from both China and India especially during the T'ang Dynasty (618–907 A.D.) . . . The [Tibetan] dance feeling is heavy instead of light and with a "down" accent. The high leather or felt boots which are held up in place by bands of woven silk or wool, do not allow for the pointed toe and this gives the appearance of the turned out feet associated with dances of the Orient. The dancers have the earthbound quality of people who are in tune with their soil rather than the airborne quality of our modern ballet.[172]

In the notes, Dai abandons the Han-centric or Sinocentric narrative entirely and adopts a slightly Orientalist one. Dai portrays the Tibetan people as an independent race with their own history and territory overlapping with modern China and India, their culture being influenced by both Tang China and India. In terms of Tibetan dances, Dai emphasizes their features "associated with dances of the Orient. The dancers have the earthbound quality of people who are in tune with their soil rather than the airborne quality of our modern ballet." In the "othering" contrast between "their soil" and "our [airborne] modern ballet," the choice of pronouns clearly caters to the "Orientalist" view of the American audience. Throughout the notes, Dai never refers to Tibetan dances as part of Chinese dances but of "dances of the Orient." That is, the "Chinese" ethnic dances became "Oriental dances" when Dai presented them on the American stage. For Dai, the ethnic dances of China's borderlands were not simply "Chinese" dances isolatable within China's national borders (however defined); rather, they pertained to the larger category of Oriental dance (as "foreign" dance in some sense), which, as a whole, stood against Western ballet and modern dance.

Dai's ethnic dance as Oriental dance also needs to be understood in relation to New York City's mid-century scene of world dances. At a high point of internationalism, the postwar US dance press and intelligentsia applauded and embraced the rise of the so-called ethnologic dance (promoted by the NYC-based dancer-choreographer La Meri), of which "Oriental dances"—such as Indian, Japanese, and Javanese dances— were important constituents.[173] Ethnologic dance, as its scholarly name suggests, emphasizes its "authenticity" and "closeness to sources" and supposedly served the ambassadorial function of introducing, interpreting, and vindicating peoples around the world to one another.[174] However, as Rebekah Kowal demonstrates, ethnologic dance's promotion of diversity was paradoxically filtered through the lens of cultural universalism, which was based primarily on the Anglo-Western experience.[175] Moreover, ethnologic dance occupied a secondary position relative to the mainstream concert dance establishments of Western ballet and modern dance, supplying exotic cultural and movement materials to facilitate the innovation and development of the mainstream genres on the one hand, and on the other hand acting as an aesthetic foil that legitimized the dominance of modernist concert dance forms by contrast.[176]

Dai's status as, literally, a cultural ambassador representing China yet with a deep international background—like La Meri who fashioned herself as an international "cultural ambassador"—fit well in this context. Dai's "authentic" New York performances of ethnic/Oriental dances based on her first-hand "ethnological" fieldwork, and her "scholarly" lectures that contrasted "our airborne modern ballet" with "their earthbound Oriental dances," served functions similar to those of ethnologic dance in mid-century New York. Indeed, one of Dai's New York performances was held at La Meri's theater of Ethnologic Dance Center at 110 East 59th Street on March 20, 1947, as part of the "Young Artists Series," three days after a staging of La Meri's own production of Swan Lake—the classical ballet translated into the Hindu Natya dance vocabulary—at the same theater.[177] Eight months after Dai left the United States, in the highly influential dance critic John Martin's New York Times discussion of the 1948 New York summer schedule for dance performances—in which "[e]ach program, as far as possible, will contain examples of classic, modern and ethnologic dance"—a large photo of Dai performing a Chinese dance figures prominently, and Dai's film "Two Chinese Dances" is included alongside other "ethnologic" dance films to be publicly screened, such as "Spanish Gypsies," "Rhythm of Africa," "Kathak Dances of India," "Sky Dancers of Papantla," and "Dance Revival in India."[178] Clearly, in the mid-century New York dance scene, Dai's ethnic/Oriental dances were subsumed into "ethnologic dance," which stood in a subtle triangular relationship with Western classical dance (ballet) and modern dance. As shown later, this transnational triangulation deeply influenced Dai's conception of "Chinese dance" on the international stage throughout her life.

Oriental Dance as Ethnic Dance: In Socialist China

Like the case of borderland ethnic dances in the 1940s, Dai's promotion of *Dongfang wu* 東方舞 (Oriental dance) in the 1950s was intertwined with both her multi-diasporic experiences and China's (inter)nationalist agenda under the Communist rule in the Cold War.[179] Dai's understanding of the "Orient" and "Oriental dances" is derived partly from the Western perception of the East and Asia related to her diasporic experiences and partly from her own root-searching research in the 1940s and early 1950s, during which she identified connections between China's ethnic dances and the dances of other Asian countries (like India). These experiences made Dai believe that Chinese dances are part of the "dances of the Orient" and thus the identity of Chinese dance needs be constructed within the larger context of "Oriental dances."[180] For Dai, the Oriental dances of Asian nations are "ethnic dances" at the pan-Asian level. Just like a Chinese needs to learn Chinese dance, in Dai's words, "an Oriental . . . needs to learn and inherit Oriental dances."[181] This became the motivation for Dai to propose to establish an "Oriental dance class" at the Beijing Dance School in 1954. Yet the school Party leaders were not interested at first, until Premier Zhou Enlai 周恩來 (1898–1976) lent his support.[182] The support from the highest rank was informed by the understanding of the utility of dance in China's cultural diplomacy that aimed to build rapport with the newly independent Asian neighbors amidst the ever-shifting Cold-War international politics.[183] That is, the Western colonial conception of the "Oriental" was in some sense transposed into the East-West divide of the Cold War.

Under the auspices of Premier Zhou, Dai designed the curriculum for the Oriental dance class. The major dance forms being taught were Indonesian, especially Balinese dances, Indian dances, and Burmese dances.[184] Note that since Dai placed great emphasis on the "authenticity" of these national dances, they cannot be simply seen as dances of the *Orientalist* style.[185] The student body of the class consisted largely of registered students of the Beijing Dance School and also some returned overseas Chinese, mainly Indonesian Chinese.[186] However, as some Chinese students held strong Sinocentric and Eurocentric views, they were reluctant to learn Oriental dances of other Asian countries, which were deemed inferior.[187] As a student of Dai recalled, "for people at that time [1954], the Soviet Union was number one. Everybody wanted to learn ballet, learn Soviet dance, foreign things like these from the West"; next to ballet in the hierarchy was Chinese classical dance.[188] Even some high-ranking official working at the Chinese embassy to Burma tried to dissuade Dai from learning Burmese dances, saying that "Burmese dances are too ugly! Looks like using the bathroom."[189] At Dai's insistence and the mandate of the Chinese government, many students carried on with the study.[190] Clearly, Dai's multi-diasporic experiences provided her with a much more open and egalitarian view of Oriental dances. This view, formed and informed by the retooled colonial idea of the Oriental, countered both the Sinocentric and Eurocentric sentiments held by many Chinese.

At some point, Dai's diasporic conception of the Oriental identity was also at odds with the utilitarian view of dance held by the Communist government. In 1962, the *Dongfang ge wu tuan* 東方歌舞團 (The Oriental song and dance ensemble) was founded on the basis of the original Oriental dance class, which was dismissed several years earlier without even informing Dai.[191] At the founding ceremony, Chen Yi 陳毅 (1901–1972), then the vice premier and minister of foreign affairs, asked Dai to further expand the repertoire from Oriental dances to include dances from African and Latin American countries.[192] Such a decision may be understood in light of the recent Sino-Soviet split—China's diplomatic priority had shifted from the East-West ideological divide to the North-South struggle between the US-Soviet dual hegemony and the Third World countries. That is, in the view of the Chinese government, the "Oriental" needed to be reoriented and expanded to signify the solidarity of the "South." However, although Dai did not openly object to the decision, she had her own reservations. In Dai's view, because including too many different dance traditions would make the ensemble lose focus, and the dances of Africa and Latin America were less relevant to her conceived Oriental identity of Asian dances, she would rather focus exclusively on Asian dances.[193] For Dai, Oriental dances (or Asian dances) are not simply "foreign" dances but close "relatives"—in cultural, geographic, and formal senses—of China's ethnic dances, that is, Oriental dances as ethnic dances.

It becomes clear that Dai's diasporic conception of the "Orient" and "Oriental dances" falls uncomfortably between the over-rigid Sinocentric and Eurocentric views of Asian dances held by many Chinese and the hyper-elastic utilitarian view of Third-World dances (or Oriental dances as the dances of the South) adopted in the Communist government's diplomatic strategy.

Writing Ethnic Dance in Labanotation: Transmediation as a Transnational Strategy

Dai's root-searching via ethnic dance and Oriental dance was not a purely bodily process. Rather, it was often mediated by Labanotation (or Kinetography Laban), a written notation system for dance and human body movement in general initiated in the 1920s by Laban—Dai's German "maternal grandfather" of dance.[194] Parallel to the Western staff music notation system, Labanotation, using its abstract symbols, can rather faithfully describe and record any dance, including its corporeal spatio-temporal subtleties and style with various levels of detail.[195] When collecting ethnic dances or Oriental dances, Dai often first "translated" and wrote down the dance in Labanotation, and then later "re-learned" the dance by reading the notation of the dance.[196] As shown in this section, the transmediation between dance and Labanotation compellingly demonstrates that Dai's project of creating modern Chinese ethnic dance was fundamentally mediated by the worldview and methodology of central European modern dance, and Dai used Labanotation as a transnational strategy to insert Chinese ethnic dance into the global field of world dances.

The basic idea of Labanotation is as follows. First, draw a staff of evenly spaced vertical lines (similar to the music staff, but the latter is horizontally placed and has a different number of lines), and write or read from bottom up. Second, each strip-shaped space between lines designates one part of the human body: from left to right in the staff, the spaces respectively represent the left arm, the upper body, the left leg (if raised in the air), the left support (if left leg on the ground), the right support (if right leg on the ground), the right leg (if in the air), the upper body, the right arm, and the head (figure 4.1). Third, the sequence of movement directions (such as forward, backward, left, or right) of each part of the body is coded as a sequence of different geometric shapes placed in the space representing that body part (analogous to a sequence of musical note). Fourth, the heights/levels of the movement (upward, downward, or horizontal) are represented by different shadings of the geometric shapes in step three (figure 4.2). Fifth, the relative length of each geometric shape signifies the relative time duration of that movement. In summary, step one provides the overall representational framework for the system (the staff); step two accounts for the anatomical structure of the human body (various body parts); steps three and four capture the spatial aspects of body

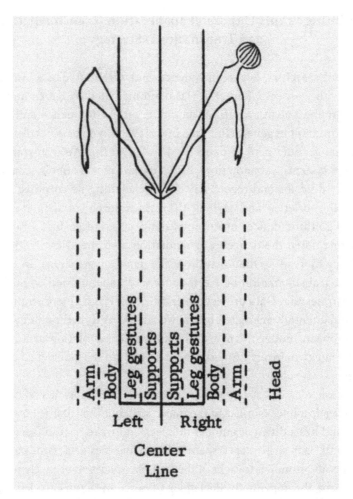

Figure 4.1 Anatomical Representation in Labanotation. Image courtesy of the Language of Dance Trust on behalf of Dr. Ann Hutchinson Guest.

movement (horizontal and vertical directionalities, respectively); step five delineates the temporal dimension (time duration of each movement).[197]

Labanotation assumes the perspective of the generalized dancer (not the viewer) as a subject negotiating his/her place in space by defining the relationship between the movements of various body parts and space-time.[198] As shown in the rest of this section, it provides a useful tool for Dai, as a diasporic subject, to negotiate her identities by finding a place for her Chinese ethnic dance in the space-time of world dances.

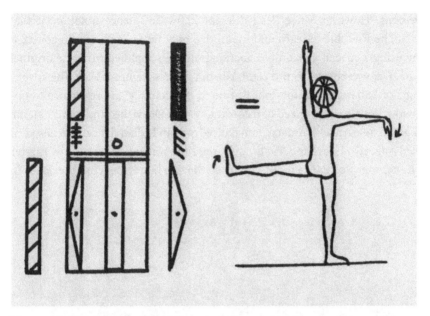

Figure 4.2 The Coding of Two Moves in Labanotation. Image courtesy of the Language of Dance Trust on behalf of Dr. Ann Hutchinson Guest.

Labanotation as a Dance Language, a Worldview, and a Choreographic Method

The invention of Labanotation fundamentally changed the "illiterate" status of dance, as suggested by the title of Laban's 1928 journal—*Schrifttanz* (Writing dance)—in which he first laid out the framework, and by Laban's ambition of creating "a literature of movement and dance."[199] In her authoritative textbook on Labanotation, Ann Hutchinson, student of Laban and classmate of Dai at the Jooss-Leeder Dance School at Dartington Hall, explicitly compares Labanotation to language with grammar, syntax, sentence, and words (including nouns, verbs, adverbs, and adjectives).[200] That is, dance now becomes subject to some sort of "scientific," "linguistic" recording and analysis, no longer being ephemeral movement that is easy to forget and opaque to human reason.

The practical advantage of Labanotation was immediately manifested in the comparison between Peng's and Dai's fieldworks in 1945, conducted within about the same length of time. In Peng's fieldwork, because he knew music notation, he recorded "many folk songs" in the Qiang and Jiarong regions. However, since Peng did not know any dance notation at that time, he was able to learn and memorize only three dances.[201] In contrast, by using a special version of Labanotation she simplified from the original one, Dai was able to record eight Tibetan dances (figure 4.3).[202] The advantage of Labanotation does not just lie in its accuracy and resistance to oblivion, but also in its speed of recording. When Dai visited India in 1954, she wanted to learn a Bharatanatyam dance from an Indian dancer. Because Dai had only two hours and she thought the time was too short to truly master the complicated dance moves, she used the two hours to record the dance in

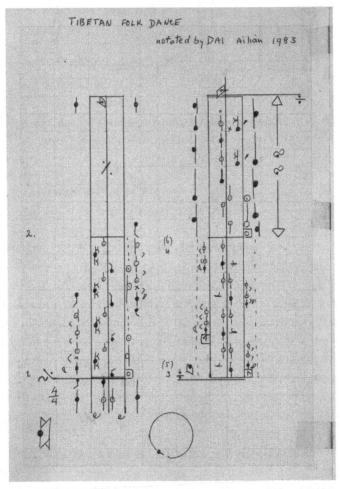

Figure 4.3 A Tibetan folk dance notated by Dai Ailian using her simplified version of Labanotation in 1983. Image courtesy of the National Ballet of China.

Labanotation, and then re-learned the dance from the notation and prac-
ticed it later during her travel. According to Dai, a couple of days later, when
she arrived at the Chinese consulate in Calcutta (or Kolkata, the city where
Zhuang Xueben worked in the 1940s), she was able to perform the dance
quite accurately and at a pace with which "many young [Indian] people at
that time cannot keep up."[203] Dai's performance impressed the famous
Indian dancer Uday Shankar (1900–1977), who commented that Dai danced
"just like an Indian girl" (note that Shankar himself had a close connection
with Dartington Hall).[204]

Due to the anatomical approach adopted in Labanotation, translating
a dance into the notation may be seen as the dancer-notator's own "dis-
membering" process, and translating the notation back into a dance as a "re-
membering" process. In the case of Dai, this suggests any ethnic or Oriental
dance mediated by Labanotation was, strictly speaking, no longer the original dance, but one that was analyzed (or dis-membered) and re-synthesized
(or re-membered) through the central European modern-dance worldview
of the human body, its movement, and its relation to space-time.

This "worldview" of dance consisted mainly of two theories about human
body movement—Choreutics (i.e., space harmony, the dance spatial counterpart to the music theory of harmony, roughly speaking) and Eukinetics (i.e.,
beautiful movement, the dance counterpart to the music theory of rhythm),
both of which Dai learned at the Jooss-Leeder Dance School at Hartington
Hall in 1939 (Wu Xiaobang also learned some version of these theories in
Tokyo in the mid-1930s).[205] This means Labanotation is not simply a note-
taking system, but embodies a whole worldview of the central European
school of modern dance. Students of Dai who learned Labanotation (or any
dance notation) often commented that the notation system provided them
with a "scientific" and "objective" perspective from which they can see any
dance in a fresh light of "reason," instead of just "feeling" and imitation
(figure 4.4).[206]

Even for dances or human body movements that were not notated, Dai
habitually analyzed those using Choreutics and Eukinetics during her observation. For example, Dai often observed everyday body movements theoretically and analytically, such as how the fishermen rowed their boats.[207] When
Dai saw dancing figures painted on antiques, she also used Laban theories
to decipher what body movements could lead to the static body gestures—a
technique crucial to some of Dai's choreographies of Chinese dance derived
from static dancing figures and fragmented movement motifs.[208]

Figure 4.4 Dai Ailian teaching Laban's spatial and movement theories in China, possibly in the 1980s. Image courtesy of the National Ballet of China.

An example for the application of this Laban-theory-based choreographic method to the composition of ethnic dances is Dai's choreographing of the duet *Feitian* (Apsaras, 1954), the predecessor of the Dunhuang-style dance, which is now typically regarded as part of the classical dance.[209] Two sources of the choreography are usually recognized: the *Chang chou wu* 長綢舞 (Long silk streamer dance) from Peking Opera and the dancing figures in Dunhuang frescos.[210] However, Dai mentioned two more sources. First, the original costume design was partly borrowed from the Indian sari. Second, the choreography was based partly on Laban's theories.[211] Although there were plenty of static dancing figures and Peking Opera–based dance moves, Dai needed to create more subtle dance vocabulary to fill the gaps of those discrete "words" and "phrases" and arrange and integrate all these disparate elements into a smooth and coherent "essay" based on certain "grammar."[212] For Dai, this "grammar" was derived partly from Laban's space-movement theories. For example, the narrative framework of the dance is: at first, two flying apsaras are far apart from each other at different heights in the sky; they see each other and try to fly closer; then, they fly and dance together at the same height; finally, they part and return to their respective original spaces and heights. A major difficulty for Dai was to use the relative movements of the two dancers on the limited two-dimensional stage to create a visual illusion of the vast expanse and various vertical levels of the three-dimensional space in which the two apsaras supposedly fly. To address this issue, Dai drew on Laban's theory of space harmony—Choreutics.[213]

Just like La Meri's promotion of "ethnologic dance" in mid-century United States was based on Anglo-Western cultural universalism, Dai's creation of ethnic dances was fundamentally mediated by Labanotation and/or informed by the space-movement theories underlying it. This "universalist," yet central European modern-dance, theoretical and methodological basis is often understated in the Chinese historiography of Dai's project of creating modern Chinese ethnic dance.

The commensurability of World Dances in Labanotation

In addition to being a dance language, a worldview, and a choreographic method, Labanotation also provides a possibility of separating dance as a work (written, without explicitly involving any particular dancer) from dance as a performance (always involving real dancers in a concrete physical environment). That is, the impersonal form of the dance becomes extracted and isolated from the specific physicality of the dancers, their personal identities and backgrounds, and the cultural context and the material environment of the performance, which cannot be achieved by filming.[214] This abstraction of dance into written symbols, of course, entails a great loss of non-form-related information. However, it is exactly this filtering-out of personal, cultural, historical, and environmental contexts that makes Labanotation into a "universal" dance language through which dances from different cultures and times become mutually commensurable and communicable in a unified symbolic form. This echoes Michel Foucault's observation of the working logic of modern sciences: "[b]y limiting and filtering the visible, structure enables it to be transcribed into language."[215] In other words, Labanotation allows the universal translation of dances around the world into symbolized objects that can be collected, purchased, exchanged, categorized, curated, and, whenever needed, recorporealized into dance performances.

Dai was probably the first dancer-notator around the world who devotedly exploited this transnational and transcultural potential of Labanotation.[216] When Dai visited the United States in 1946 and 1947, she brought with her the notations of the eight Tibetan dances she recorded in 1945 and gave copies of them to her Dartington Hall classmate Ann Hutchinson, cofounder of the Dance Notation Bureau in New York—an organization that aims to materialize Laban's vision of creating "a literature of dance" into a "library of dances."[217] Before Dai, Labanotation was mainly used to record ballet and modern dance in the West. Dai's effort of colleting ethnic dances in China and her application of Labanotation to it clearly attracted the attention of John Martin, who covered Dai in his *New York Times* column "The Dance" multiple times from 1947 to 1948. In one of those, Martin reports that the "first actual publication of a dance score for general distribution" by the Dance Notation Bureau "will be a set of authentic Tibetan notated dances by Tai Ai-Lien," who found "great need for it [Labanotation] in her collecting of folk dances in remote provinces" of the Far East, and Martin sees Dai's endeavor as integral to the Bureau's vision for dance to "amass a genuine literature, comparable to that of music."[218] By adding Tibetan dance notations to the library of dances, Dai, for the first time, provided a new vision of expanding Laban's and Martin's "literature of dance" into a "world literature of dances."

Throughout the 1980s and 1990s, together with her students, Dai continued to contribute "Chinese dances" to this "world literature" by collecting and transcribing Chinese folk dances, ancient Chinese dances, and China's ethnic-minority dances into Labanotation, compiling those into textbooks and research papers, and circulating them on the international stage (figure 4.5).[219] As spelled out in the introduction of a textbook on notated ethnic-minority dances, the purpose of the project is, in addition to transforming dance into a science and preserving dance legacies, to "communicate" with foreign dances.[220] Dai's vision of situating Chinese dance within the world literature of dances through Labanotation is perhaps best illustrated by the book series' front-cover picture designed by her ex-husband Ye Qianyu.

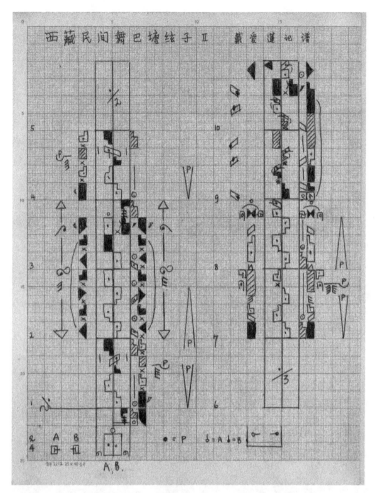

Figure 4.5 A Tibetan folk dance *Batang xianzi* notated by Dai Ailian in regular labanotation, date unknown. Image courtesy of the National Ballet of China.

Holding each other's hands, three abstract human figures, consisting of Labanotation-like geometric symbols, form a circle (figure 4.6). The three dancing figures, one in yellow, one in black, and one in white, represent the three major human races on equal footings. The dynamics of the dance is conveyed by the spatial configuration of the three figures. Hand in hand, the figures slant backward, with their feet close to each other on the ground, forming a top-like shape. The balance of the structure depends entirely on the mutual reliance among the figures and the implied swirling dance. That

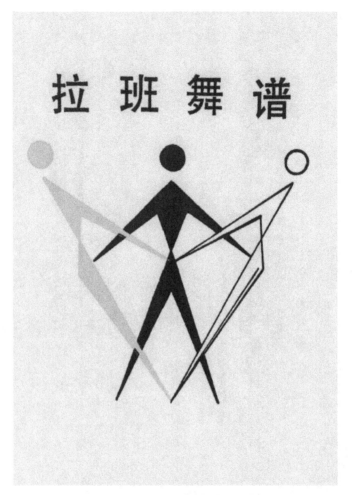

Figure 4.6 Labanotation textbook cover design by Ye Qianyu, ca. 1989. Image courtesy of Ye Mingming.

is, different human bodies and their dynamic and diverse dances can be finally united in Labanotation.

To attest the commensurability of different dances under Labanotation, Dai, together with some other dance notators, conducted experiments to prove that a dancer who understands Labanotation can dance out a dance from a totally different culture, which the dancer never saw before, by reading only the notation of the dance—just like a pianist can play out a new piece by reading the music notation.[221] For example, in the early 1980s, Dai let some American dancer-notators dance out the Tibetan tap dance notation, and some Chinese dancer-notators the American counterpart.[222] This possibility of dance as (world) literature provides an alternative to how dances are disseminated. While the typical way is that a dancer learns the dance from a certain rendition of the dance performed by another dancer through imitation and kinesthesia, the alternative is every dancer can learn from the same notation "book." A video captured a scene of Dai and her students learning an ethnic dance: it is not that the students learn the dance from Dai, but they all form a circle and dance out the dance notation on pages held in their hands.[223]

In the mythic history of the lost written language of the Qiang, the absence of written words paradoxically mystifies and reinforces the superiority of written language over the substitutive dance. In the case of Labanotation, there is also a paradox. On the one hand, to make all dances commensurable, Labanotation isolates the abstract form of dance from its complex corporeal and cultural context of performance and universalizes and reduces it into written symbols that follow the hegemonic logic of "language." On the other hand, Labanotation, like music notation, reifies and consecrates the form of dance as something fixed that can be preserved and copyrighted, so that dance, in its symbolic form, establishes its authority over and against the "manipulations" of verbal language and camera and the "whims" of dancers and performances.[224] Dai was clearly drawn to this second aspect of Labanotation: she promoted Labanotation as the tool for copyrighting dance works in China to fight against the cultural norm of "collective authorship," which, in Dai's view, violated the intellectual property right of individual choreographers.[225]

Labanotation as Scaffolding for Building the "Chinese Dance"

Despite the practical benefits of Labanotation, Dai encountered major difficulties in promoting it in China. In the 1940s, after she came to China, Dai tried to introduce Labanotation to many people, but the idea "did not catch on," and people "didn't seem to have a need for it," because during the war survival was the paramount imperative for both the artists and arts.[226] In the 1950s, after the founding of the People's Republic, Dai tried a second time. Yet she failed again, this time because the notation system was deemed too complex to be a top priority for China's dance world, which was preoccupied with building dance institutions and disciplines and developing various dance forms and choreographies.[227]

After the end of the Cultural Revolution, Dai tried a third time in the 1980s.[228] This time, the obstacles came mainly from people's doubts about some technical aspects of Labanotation. One typical resistance to Labanotation was that the wide availability of filming technologies had eliminated the need for a written notation of dance. Dai's counter argument to that was: the prevalence of audio recording devices never diminished the central importance of music notation in the field of musicology or the practices of musicians.[229] Some people thought that the West-originated Labanotation cannot faithfully record the unique and complicated movements of "Chinese" dances, and Dai proved them wrong by notating some dance moves that were believed to be un-recordable in Labanotation.[230] In addition to Dai's personal efforts, the Beijing brand of the Chinese Dancers' Association also began to develop an interest in the promotion of Labanotation. At that time, the association organized young people to dance some new type of collective folk dances, and because of the complexity involved in teaching, organizing, and coordinating these activities, they wanted to write down the dances in Labanotation.[231] With the convergence of Dai's personal aspiration and the government's interest, Labanotation finally caught on and took off in China.[232]

Dai's persistence in promoting Labanotation in China was also partly related to her diasporic identity. For Dai, a major theoretical problem of her "root-searching via dance" was: while it may make sense to see any ethnic dance in China as *a* kind of Chinese dance, it is impossible to identify any ethnic dance as *the* Chinese dance (a coherent genre identity). For example, Dai may dance a Tibetan dance, but she could not identify herself completely as a Tibetan, or the Tibetan dance as *the* Chinese dance. Yet without such identification with a coherent "Chinese" identity, Dai's root-searching could never be complete. That is why, as spelled out in her 1946 manifesto accompanying the *Plenary*, comprehensively surveying, collecting, and studying all dances in China was only "the first step for developing the Chinese dance," and the second and ultimate step would be to synthesize all these dances into the Chinese dance as a coherent genre.[233] Therefore, Dai's "synthetic" vision for the "Chinese dance" was not completely in line with the Communist Party's multiculturalist view of ethnic dances. Moreover, the development of "performing" ethnic dances in China since the mid-1950s had more or less deviated from Dai's original vision—in her view, the "rawness" of ethnic dances had been modified too much according to the aesthetics of Soviet Russian ballet, or the "balletization" of ethnic dances.[234] That is partly why Dai, in her late seventies, once again started to go to the remote settlements of ethnic minorities in Yunnan to collect "authentic" ethnic dances in the 1990s, continuing her "two-step" strategy of developing the Chinese dance in her vision. Labanotation, as it turned out, played an important role in this later project of Dai.[235]

In the July of 1990, forty-five years after Dai first recorded eight Tibetan dances in Labanotation, Dai, together with five students, went to Hong Kong to attend the Fifth Hong Kong International Dance Conference and the Second International Congress on Movement Notation, during which they presented five Labanotation papers to the international dance community.[236] In Dai's paper, titled "On '3-Step-Plus,' " she observes that the performing ethnic dance in contemporary China was "an imitation of Moisev [Moiseyev]'s Natonal Folk Dance Ensemble," uttering her dissatisfaction with the Russian influence of "character dance" in ballet on China's ethnic dance, and points out that "we cannot say the Chinese dance is a complete system."[237] Dai then shows five ethnic dance forms from five ethnic minorities of China in Labanotation. By juxtaposing the notations of the dances, Dai identifies some common step pattern shared by all five ethnic dance forms. She compares this pattern to the development of step patterns in Western ballet, arguing that it is possible to systematically classify all Chinese dance forms, both old and existing, as "the beginning of creating a scientific system of Chinese dance comparable to that of the Classical ballet."[238] In Dai's view, China had not yet formed a coherent dance system that is on a par with the major dance systems of the world, such as ballet, traditional Indian dances, and Martha Graham's modern dance.[239] Here, Dai's relational conception of the "Chinese dance" may be seen as a nationalist reorientation of the mid-century triangulation among ballet, modern dance, and ethnologic dance in the New York dance scene, of which Dai and her Chinese ethnic dances as Oriental dances were once a peripheral part.

Dai's approach of using Labanotation to classify ethnic dances in China shares striking similarities with that of Davies almost a century earlier to classify ethnic groups in China into *minzu*. Both first coded dance movement or spoken language of ethnic groups into symbols; compared and identified the common and different cultural "genes" coded in the symbols; and based on those, constructed a lineage and taxonomy of ethnic dances or languages.

However, Dai went further, as her ultimate goal was to distill the common "genes" of ethnic dances into a "complete scientific system" of Chinese dance through the scaffolding of Labanotation, a vision she never had enough time to realize.[240]

For Dai, her diasporic project of root-searching via dance was never simply about discovering certain dance roots and identifying with those. Rather, it was more about synthesizing her own Chinese dance roots out of the various notated, and thus commensurable, ethnic dance forms and, equally importantly, displacing those into the international arena of world dances, all of which become mutually communicable under the same metric system of Labanotation. At this level, Dai's synthetic approach to Chinese ethnic dance is at odds with the Chinese government's multiculturalist view of ethnic dances. Paradoxically, Dai's project of root-searching via dance was as much an uprooting and displacing process as a rooting one. In the same process, Dai, as an English-speaking dancer-scholar who received world-class ballet and modern dance training in London, also as a Third World female expert presenting dances of China to the world dance community, attains international prestige.[241] In Dai's own words, "this [attending the conference] was one of the happiest things in my life."[242] This subtle dynamic between Dai's multi-diasporic and nationalist sentiments in the 1990s is reminiscent of the complicated transnational and transcultural origin of modern Chinese ethnic dance in the mid-1940s.

Epilogue

Guo Mingda, Alwin Nikolais, and the (Anti-) American Link

The End of the New

July 31, 1960, Beijing, the group discussion sessions of the Third National Representatives' Conference of the Chinese Dance Art Research Association entered the second day. During the conference, the association was renamed as the Chinese Dance Workers Association to signal its focus shifting from academic dance research and experimentation to nationwide coordination of everyday activities of dancers and local dance organizations, a change demanded by the political imperative of "better serving workers, farmers, and soldiers" in the ongoing Great Leap Forward Campaign.[1]

In accord with the change of name, the group discussions of the conference turned out to be a coordinated attack on the president of the association, Wu Xiaobang—who identified himself more as a dance scholar, experimental choreographer, and May Fourth–styled intellectual than as a "dance worker"—and his Tianma Dance Studio (see chapter 3).[2] Ten days earlier, on July 21, the association's communication group reported to the conference leadership that "representatives from every province unanimously requested" there should be "organized discussions on Tianma, especially its controversial works."[3] In the meeting of the association's standing committee held on July 23, several core members leveled criticisms at Wu and Tianma, and Wu was pressured to make self-criticism and self-defense.[4] In the evening of July 27, Tianma was asked to perform the "controversial works" in its repertoire at the Beijing Dance School for the representatives, since many had not yet watched Tianma's works.[5] During the two days' group discussions starting on July 30, from which Wu was absent, at least over fifty representatives (counting those recorded in the meetings' minutes) from all over the country denounced Wu and Tianma.[6] Below are some selected, representative rebukes made toward Wu, which may give today's readers some

When Words Are Inadequate. Nan Ma, Oxford University Press. © Oxford University Press 2023.
DOI: 10.1093/oso/9780197575307.003.0006

idea of the enormous, collective political pressure, from both without and within Tianma, overwhelming Wu during the conference.

REPRESENTATIVE OF SHANGHAI WITH THE SURNAME BAI: "After watching Tianma's performance, I felt very uncomfortable. What kind of art directives is he [Wu] executing? It is not the directive of serving workers, farmers, and soldiers, not executing the Party's art directives; rather, it is like a protest to the Party's art directives, a counterattack launched at the Party's art directives. I was enraged after watching [the performance]. The emotions expressed in the works are those of the decadent class. [It is surprising that] there is a faction like this existing in the dance world; the Party needs to correct this thoroughly..."[7]

REPRESENTATIVE OF INNER MONGOLIA: "As early as in 1954, someone brought up his [Wu's] modernist idea ... but [that idea] was not criticized. In recent years, he did not accept [thought] reform, was further influenced by Revisionism, and thus has deviated from the Party's art directives. [He] uses dance as a weapon for the individual to express emotions ... walking down the bourgeois path of aestheticism, treating personal emotions as the source of arts, searching for artistic themes from the inner world. I heard that in 1954, he was offered the position of the president of the Beijing Dance School, but he declined, and he wanted to create his own faction, to establish a unique method of expression; he does not treat dance as a tool for serving the people ... Wu Xiaobang's world view has not been well reformed: he denies the necessity of merging the dance art with political struggle. If this continues, dance will become [something] serving bourgeois politics."[8]

ONE OF WU'S FAVORITE TIANMA STUDENTS WITH THE SURNAME ZHU: "He [Wu] does not want techniques ... To emphasize individual style, he does not allow us to learn from others. He stays away from politics; the current heated [political] movements have little to do with him. Like the Anti-American movement, everyone wanted to participate, but he asked us to rehearse [dance works]. As for thought reform, he does not keep up ... Every young performer [of Tianma] is a petty individualist ... Tianma's management style, to some extent, is patriarchal..."[9]

REPRESENTATIVE OF WORKERS WITH THE SURNAME ZHONG RESPONDING TO ZHU: "Judging from his [Wu's] works, he is dangerous. In the past, I worked in a small factory of a capitalist, who limited the workers' activities. Based on Comrade Zhu's words, [Wu] is basically like that. The comrades of Tianma should wake up, remove the shackles [imposed by Wu], and rely on the Party's leadership . . .Don't be afraid; this is what class struggle is like."[10]

REPRESENTATIVE OF HEBEI WITH THE SURNAME WANG: "The characters in Tianma's works are all young gentlemen and ladies; many reek of reactionary smell . . . When Tianma performed in Tangshan City in 1958, the workers' comments were harsh; the workers made reprimands onsite, but he [Wu] never corrected [his wrongs]. If this continues, his only fate is to end himself in front of the people."[11]

REPRESENTATIVE OF GUANGXI WITH THE SURNAME LAN: "Someone might say [Tianma's] works are neither good nor bad. I think if they offer no benefit to the proletariat, not serving the proletariat, they are bad; there is no 'in-between' work."[12]

REPRESENTATIVE OF BEIJING, DAI AILIAN (then the vice president of the Association, president of the Beijing Dance School): "As for Wu Xiaobang's artistic thoughts, because he was born into the bourgeois class, [he] definitely has bourgeois thoughts. He has not been thoroughly reformed. Modern dance is an individualistic art form, pertaining to abstractionism. In the past . . . [he] incorporated neither [Chinese] classical dance nor ballet in his pedagogy, using only the "natural law," [as if] relying on nature alone can guarantee everything . . . This [Tianma] is not flower; it is poisonous [weed] . . . Comrade Wu Xiaobang was influenced by [Isadora] Duncan. When I watched modern dance performances in America [1946–47], audiences there could not understand it either, but they all applauded loudly. This suggests that if they do not applaud, [they are] admitting their inability [to appreciate modernist art], because these audiences were all bourgeois intellectuals . . . Wu Xiaobang's works look down upon tradition. What kind of freedom is his choreography demanding? He is demanding the freedom of the bourgeoisie. In 1952, I criticized Wu seriously, but he did not accept it. Comrade Wu Xiaobang does have ambition; he took many photos, trying to prove that [China's] dance history depends mainly on him."[13]

Dai's harsh reproach toward Wu was not just a continuation of the power struggle between Dai and Wu and the two artistic camps they were backing respectively—the ballet and classical dance camp based at the Beijing Dance School and the (classical) new dance camp of Tianma (see chapter 3)—but also reflected her own predicament at that time. In fact, the four criticisms

Dai leveled at Wu—bourgeois background, individualism, modernist lineage, and American connection—could also apply, to an equal or even greater extent, to Dai, who herself had been under political pressure and just one day earlier, on July 30, also conducted self-criticism in the meeting.[14] Therefore, Dai's condemnation of Wu may be partly driven by her anxiety for self-preservation, hoping to create a distraction for her own "historical issues" in the anti-American climate of the conference.

Despite the overwhelmingly critical attitude toward Wu, a few representatives stood up and defended Wu and Tianma.[15] The debate reconstructed below from the minutes of a meeting, between a "defender" and a group of "critics," was the most sustained defense of Tianma during the conference.

THE DEFENDER: "Tianma's performance . . . had generated controversies. Some believe that Tianma's ideology is problematic, but its [formal] approach has merits. Others think Tianma is completely wrong and should be rejected entirely. I agree with the former."

CRITIC A: "You mean, in terms of choreography, the major difference between Wu and others [proponents of Chinese classical dance and ballet] lies primarily in the formal aspect, but not in the choice of fundamental [political] path. However, we believe that Wu's choreography walks down a path totally opposite to ours, having nothing in common with Chairman Mao's artistic direction."

THE DEFENDER: "Is it possible that we don't look at Tianma in terms of its political content? I think Tianma's performance has several merits. Wu's understanding of [the Chinese] tradition deserves consideration, and I think it is closer [to the real tradition than the ballet-influenced Chinese classical dance is] . . . China's tradition is based on agricultural economy, and thus has an affinity with earth, unlike Western ballet, which has a lot of jumping, as if disliking earth. If we add too much jumping [to Chinese dance], it looks awkward . . . For example, the dances of Japan, Indonesia, and India are closer to Chinese dance—quiet on the floor, not much hopping or jumping. Politically speaking, we are in line with the Soviet Union and other [Eastern European] socialist countries, but culturally speaking, we are not."

CRITIC B: "Your opinion on Tianma is different from that of the rest of us, mainly because our starting points are different. To the fundamental question whether art should reflect the current time, our answers are not the same."

THE DEFENDER: "If we approach Tianma's issues only from the perspective of politics and theme, it is easy to neglect some details . . . For example, in Western dances, the formation [of group dance] changes a lot, but in his [Wu's] works, there is less variation; there are few moves that require the splitting of legs for female dancers; their [female dancers'] steps are shorter [than in Western dances]; there is no swaying and raising of legs, no sculptural poses, which are often used in Western ballet, and no lifts . . . the dancers [in Wu's works] are more relaxed and calm, which is also our tradition. These formal features are Wu's merits."

CRITIC C: "So, do you mean there are no flaws in Wu's works?"

THE DEFENDER: "There are flaws, of course. For example, Wu's works are relatively 'flat,' lack of climax and contrasting variations, but that is also part of our tradition, unlike Westerners who tend to be more assertive and intense. But our contemporary life is clamorous, assertive and intense; that is why Wu's works look unsatisfying for today's audiences."

CRITIC D: "What you said confirms my judgment that Wu espouses Traditionalism. He addresses the modern only when he has to. And Wu's works downplay techniques . . ."

THE DEFENDER: "I heard that Wu has his own system of basic training, including martial arts, the natural law of body movement [from modern dance], etc. His basic training system differs from that of the Beijing Dance School. For the latter, everyday training uses very standard dance moves, and when it comes to choreography, they still use those rather standard moves. But in Wu's case, the dance moves used in stage choreography are quite different from those used in basic training. This suggests Wu emphasizes the holistic cultivation of artistry of dancers and choreographers."

CRITIC E: "When it comes to Wu Xiaobang's problem, you still look at the surface. That is why your argument is problematic. [Our purpose of] learning modernism and abstractionism is to use them as reference, but not to copy them. However, Wu copied and promoted them."

THE DEFENDER: "Modernism can still serve socialism. For example, if you suddenly hit the break hard on a bus, all passengers will rush forward. This is law of nature: the commonality of all movements."

CRITIC E: "[The direction of] Wu's choreography is not popularization [dazhonghua 大衆化, or appealing to and adapting for the masses], but transforming the masses [huadazhong 化大衆]. This is an issue of political stance and content, not of form. If the content is wrong, no matter how good the form is, it is of no use."

THE DEFENDER: "Politically speaking, I agree with everyone else. I just can't understand why we must reject Tianma altogether..."

CRITIC E: "Wu's fundamental problem is his wrong political direction. He hasn't accepted thought reform; we must ruthlessly fight against this kind of thought. If he does not change his direction, he will hit [the wall hard] with his head broken and blood spilled."

... The debate continued for a while...

THE DEFENDER: "I now agree with everything you say. I have changed my mind."

CRITIC F: "How do you suppose we should believe that a single afternoon's debate has changed your mind?"

THE DEFENDER: "Nowadays I don't dare to speak up liberally anymore, like what I did when I just returned from abroad."

CRITIC F: "What do you imply? Are you insinuating that the Party doesn't allow you to speak freely?"

THE DEFENDER: "..."

In the debate above, although facing a big disadvantage in number, the defender adopts a tit-for-tat strategy. While the critics stress political standards should be the commanding criteria for judging the merits of dance works, the defender suggests the artistic quality of a work can be evaluated separately from its ideological content. Whereas Dai earlier criticized Wu of his "looking down upon" the Chinese dance tradition, the defender argues that Wu's understanding and representation of tradition is more accurate, "holistic and deeper."[16] When the critics subsequently aim at Wu's "Traditionalist" approach to both content and form, the defender points out the modernist aspect of Wu's pedagogy and choreography. In response to the critics' attack of Wu's incorporating and promoting modernism, the defender insists that modernism is not incompatible with socialism, since it reflects some "universal law of nature" underlying general movement. Despite the eventual admission of defeat, the defender was obviously not at all persuaded.

It may be convenient to interpret the debate reconstructed above, and the attack on Wu and Tianma in general, as a typical demonstration of how a seemingly "democratic" process of "criticism and self-criticism"—charged with factional rivalry, personal bad blood, power jockeying, self-preservation, and often amplified by group socio-psychological dynamics—can mobilize the dominant ideology as symbolic and discursive hegemony to silence the minority voice, a phenomenon not unique to the dance circle, but quite common across the intellectual and artistic fields in 1950s and 1960s China. Yet, what this interpretation focusing on power struggle might overshadow is the underlying theoretical issue pertinent to establishing legitimacy for dance modernism in China. At the surface, the "aggressors" hold an unsurmountable advantage by framing the debate on Wu and Tianma as a head-on confrontation between two clear-cut ideologies: on one side, the Maoist proletarian political view of arts and the representative tradition-based "national dance form," and on the other, the Western bourgeois universalist-modernist view of artistic autonomy as represented by modern dance. However, at a deeper level, it is the lone defender who keeps aggressively trying to undermine this dichotomization by suggesting, through Tianma's case, the possibility that universalist modernism could be retooled and integrated with tradition, national form, and socialism—a point even Wu Xiaobang himself did not, or could not, fully articulate due to political concerns (see chapter 3). This intersection between universalism and nationalism, modernism and socialism/leftism, the modern and tradition is one of the main refrains of this book on modern dance in China.

Nevertheless, this 1960 conference ended Wu's Tianma and, along with it, his new dance (in the form of classical new dance). Although some militarized aspects of Wu's new dance (see chapter 2) were carried on by the dance troupes affiliated with the People's Liberation Army, and experiments with modernist elements would also continue throughout the 1960s and 1970s in other dance forms (such as revolutionary ballet and, as shown in chapter 4, classical dance and ethnic dance), new dance, as an independent modernist dance genre started in the mid-1930s, disappeared from the stages of socialist China.

What might be unexpected is, against the Anti-Wu and Anti-American tide in the conference, the "defender" of Tianma above was a person who had little personal connection with Wu and yet had the strongest American tie among China's first generation of professional dancer-choreographers. The name of the defender, who put up the last fight for Wu and Tianma in 1960, was Guo Mingda 郭明達 (ca. 1916–2014).

The (Anti-)American Link

In a cold December afternoon of 1955, Guo Mingda, around age forty, was sitting alone in the unheated guest meeting room of the Beijing Dance

School (then in Baijiazhuang 白家莊, where its temporary campus site was located), waiting for the school's president to come to interview him for a job position. Hours had passed, but the president did not show up.[17] Guo grew anxious because he knew something was wrong. Seven months earlier, Guo returned home from the United States after eight years of studying dance, holding great expectations for both the new socialist China and his career. Yet, he had been idling since then, because there was no free job market in the socialist regime, and he had to wait for the government to assign him to a "work unit." Unlike most other returned overseas students with degrees in science or engineering, the few like Guo who studied "unpractical" disciplines were clearly at the end of the authorities' priority list. That is why this interview was especially important to Guo; it was his first job opportunity in socialist China, and the newly founded Beijing Dance School seemed to be the perfect place for his career to take off. However, Guo sensed a fundamental mismatch: whereas the Beijing Dance School largely followed the Soviet "big brother's" model in establishing its dance educational system for ballet, Chinese classical dance, and folk dance, he studied mainly the "decadent bourgeois art" of modern dance with the "evil American imperialists."[18] "Could this be the reason for the president's absence?" Guo wondered.

Eight years earlier in the winter of 1947, Guo, with a solid background in Chinese classics and a bachelor's degree in education and a minor in sports from the National Central University in Nanjing, went to the United States to pursue graduate studies, which was sponsored by the Nationalist government.[19] Before leaving China, he tried to enrolled in one of Dai Ailian's dance classes but was rejected, because Dai accepted only female students at that time.[20] With the travel fare paid for using a whole year's family savings, Guo arrived at the University of Iowa to study dance education.[21] There, Guo took courses on folk dance, social dance, modern dance, and dance theory, and studied Margaret H'Doubler's theory and practice of dance education.[22] After earning a Master's degree in dance education, Guo continued to pursue a doctorate in dance education at New York University from 1951 to 1955, funded by the Economical Chinese Student Aid (ECA) provided by the US Department of State through an agreement negotiated between Dean Acheson, US secretary of state, and Gu Weijun 顧維鈞, Chinese ambassador to the United States representing the Nationalist government.[23] At NYU, the courses Guo took included introduction to dance, world dance history (taught by Curt Sachs), a seminar "The Dance Question" (in which well-known artists, scholars, and critics were invited to give lectures and hold

workshops), dance theory on human anatomy and physiology, dance pedagogy, and courses on modern dance techniques, especially those of Martha
Graham and Doris Humphrey (Graham's system was taught by a Japanese
student of hers, and Humphrey's by José Limón).[24]

Besides taking academic courses, Guo spent much time immersing himself in the diverse dance scenes of New York City. He often attended dance
gatherings held by (mostly eastern) European immigrant communities,
through which he learned various folk dance and music of different countries.[25] Guo also joined the Marxist "New Dance Group" affiliated with the
Workers' Union, where he took modern dance classes while using the group
as an information hub to explore other parts of the cosmopolitan dance
world.[26] Unsatisfied with the group's overemphasis on politics over artistry, two years later, Guo left and joined the dance school of Alwin Nikolais
(1910–1993) at the Henry Street Playhouse, where he stayed for about four
years and on average took twenty hours' classes every week.[27]

Nikolais, with his career taking off, paid particular attention to Guo's
training, partly because he sensed that Guo's Chinese background might be
conducive to building up his international reputation.[28] Later on, Nikolais
waived Guo's tuition and allowed him to take whatever classes he wanted.[29]
To better advise Guo, Nikolais formed a three-person study group, with the
third one being Murray Louis (1926–2016)—his leading dancer and life-
long collaborator (who would later mentor Cao Chengyuan 曹誠淵, aka,
Willy Tsao, founder and artistic director of the City Contemporary Dance
Company in Hong Kong).[30] The two advisors identified Guo's major problem
being weak in utilizing the chest and devised solutions accordingly—for example, they asked Guo to try to use his chest to "substitute for the eyes to see,
for the ears to listen" and to "use movement to think, not the brain."[31] This
idea of "movement thinking" had lasting impact on Guo's understanding
of dance and choreography. During Guo's stay in the United States, several
important works of Rudolf von Laban were published in English, including
Effort: Economy of Human Movement (1947), *Modern Educational Dance*
(1948), and *The Mastery of Movement on the Stage* (1950). After carefully
studying those books, Guo noticed that despite Nikolais' open critique of
Laban, much of his teaching derived from Laban's system. Guo confronted
his mentor with this discovery, and Nikolais' answer was "I absolutely don't
want to be limited by Laban."[32] At Nikolais' school, Guo had many chances
like this to compare and integrate Laban's theory and Nikolais' practice and
innovations.

In addition to his training at Nikolais' school, Guo studied Dalcroze eurhythmics and continued to take choreographic classes that followed Graham's and Humphrey's methods, with Graham's being taught by the composer and pianist Louis Horst, friend and mentor to Graham.[33] As a result, when Guo returned home in 1955, he became the only person in China who held a master's degree in dance (he did not obtain the doctorate, because his devotion to modern dance training distracted him from writing his dissertation) and, more importantly, had systematically studied Western folk dance, social dance, dance education, world dance history, and various American schools of modern dance and the Laban system, in both theory and practice.[34] That is why the Ministry of Culture assigned him to the Beijing Dance School, which led to the above scene of the interview without an interviewer.[35]

Guo's suspicion was right: the pro-Soviet president did not want to accept Guo due to his American background and used the absence to send a signal to Guo, hoping that he would back down. Yet, Guo stayed and waited. Late in that afternoon, right before the school was closed, four faculty members finally appeared for the interview. The interviewers mentioned nothing about modern dance, but instead asked Guo to give a demonstration of the European folk dances he learned in America. After watching his demonstration, the interviewers deemed that those folk dances were too crude and primitive, compared with Moiseyev's balletized Soviet folk dance, or "character dance." Nevertheless, the school's leadership eventually accepted Guo with reluctance, and Guo caught a cold due to the long waiting in the unheated guest meeting room.[36]

It was not easy for Guo to adapt to the new institutional environment. Whereas Nikolais' school, which had been quite well-established by the mid-1950s, had just one office and seven classrooms thanks to its economical business model, the government-sponsored, bureaucratic Beijing Dance School, with only a hundred or so enrolled students, had already had dozens of administrative divisions. Because of his "dubious" American background, the president never trusted Guo and went as far as asking someone to spy on him.[37]

In 1956, during the relatively liberal "Double Hundred Policy" period, Guo choreographed all these unpleasant experiences into a modern dance solo *The Guest Meeting Room* (*Hui ke ting* 會客廳) and performed it, along with three other modern dance works, in front of the school's faculty in an internal demonstration session.[38] In this abstract solo, there is no clear characterization of the dancer, who is in a black vest and black pants, just like an elusive shadow half-blended into the background of the "guest meeting room," which bears traces of Nikolais' aesthetics of decentralizing the dancer. This choreography, with a satirical tone, seems to embody Guo's paradoxical experience, at the Beijing Dance School, of simultaneously being an invisible man, who wants to be seen, and an outcast shadow, who is singled out, put under spotlight, and thus constantly wants to hide in the background. It turned out that this was the first and last time that Guo had a chance to choreograph and perform serious modern dance works in China; Guo soon became further marginalized at the school, because his works were seen as criticizing the socialist regime.[39]

Although Guo was de facto banned from the practice of modern dance, he continued his fight in the discursive field. In December 1956, Guo published an article in *Dance Communication*, the official journal of the Dance Research Association, with its chief editor being Wu Xiaobang, who sympathized with Guo.[40] In the article, Guo proposes to establish a new system of modern dance training and education that would be independent of and complement that of ballet, Chinese classical dance, and ethnic and folk dance being developed at the Beijing Dance School. The new system would integrate Dalcroze's Eurhythmics, Stanislavski's theory of theater and performance, Laban's movement theory and analysis, and the methodology of Euro-American modern dance, and organize all those around three core aspects of dance training—techniques, performance, and choreography.

Guo's proposal received harsh comments from critics of the classical dance camp, who believed that Guo wanted to replace the Chinese tradition with Western "imperialist universalism" embodied by modern dance, which reflected Guo's disrespect of tradition and uncritical embracement of Western bourgeois culture.[41] The critics' concern was not baseless. The eight years of Guo's studying in the United States from 1947 to 1955 coincided with the post-war period in which American modern dancers and theorists were repositioning modern dance from a historically specific genre to a universalist cultural project, with the goal to legitimize and institutionalize modern dance practices by capitalizing on the heightened public sentiments toward global unity and monies made available to cultural institutions after the war.[42] Moreover, around the time when Guo returned to China in 1955, this universalist aspiration of modern dance began to converge with the US government's Cold War strategy of promoting the genre globally as a representative of American culture in fighting the "war of ideas" against the communist bloc.[43] Since the mid-1950s, Guo's mentors—Graham, Humphrey, Limón, and Nikolais—were all more or less involved in the collaboration with the US government in this project of cultural diplomacy to showcase through modern dance on the world stage the "superiority" of the American model marketed as, paradoxically, representing "artistic autonomy."[44] As Emily Wilcox points out, the invention of the Chinese national dance forms in the 1950s, by emphasizing cultural distinctiveness, was partly a political response to this rising American universalism.[45] Guo himself in the McCarthyism-era America was a victim of this "war of ideas": when Guo left America, he was blacklisted by the US government as a "dangerous person" and banned from leaving the ship on his journey home, for his being a communist sympathizer and criticizing America's human rights situation of racism.[46]

Yet, unlike most Chinese critics of modern dance in the 1950s, who virtually "had no impression of Euro-American modern dance in their eyes and minds" but still rejected the genre altogether following the Cold War logic of containment and exclusion, Guo's proposal adopts a different strategy, which may be called the peaceful coexistence and competitive co-evolution between classical dance and modern dance.[47] In a long 1957 rejoinder, Guo further argues that his goal is to reintroduce modern dance—which he thinks is suited to create some "modern national form" connected with yet different from the "tradition-based national form" represented by classical dance—into China's dance ecosystem. Guo intends to let modern dance first compete with and stimulate the development of classical dance, and eventually reach the stage of mutual borrowing—similar to the historical dynamics between modern dance and ballet in the West.[48] As in an analogy Guo points out, "it was the introduction of foreign dance [into China] by Mr. Wu Xiaobang, Dai Ailian, etc., that triggered the discovery of borderland dances, which in turn brought about the new development of [Chinese] folk dance" (see also chapter 4).[49]

Both Wu and Guo wanted to preserve a place for some version of modern dance in socialist China. Yet, the two adopted different strategies: whereas Wu shrewdly covered his modern dance ideas under a classicist mantle in his classical new dance, Guo, who was less familiar with China's cultural politics, chose a blunter approach to claim independence of modern dance. Guo was not unaware of the risks; as he warns in the 1957 rejoinder during the Double Hundred period, "because someone believes that his direction is the most correct and his understanding the most certain, which limits his own vision, things that actually should coexist [cannot coexist]. When this partial vision is carried out in full scale, the time would come when all other kinds of valuable things are excluded," and "if hundreds and thousands of people start from one point, walk in one direction, and follow one approach, while hoping to have 'hundreds of different flowers blooming' in the artistic garden, isn't that climbing up a tree to look for fish [an idiom meaning adopting a wrong approach that cannot lead to the desired result]?"[50]

Guo's prophecy was soon fulfilled on himself. In 1958, less than two years since he joined the Beijing Dance School, Guo was classified as being "right-leaning" during the Anti-Rightist Campaign and transferred—in effect demoted and exiled—to the University of Guizhou to receive thought reform in the remote underdeveloped southwestern province, where, in Guo's words, "there is no dance department and no market [for modern dance] . . . They don't want what I have, and I don't have what they want."[51]

Nevertheless, Guo carried on his fight for modern dance, as evidenced by his vigorous defense of Wu and Tianma during the 1960 Conference discussed above. In that same conference, a certain Party official tried to persuade Guo to perform his modern dance works—just like asking Tianma to perform its controversial works—for the purpose of setting a negative example of "Revisionist arts" for "internal criticism." In such a request, Guo was urged to "listen to the Party," "bravely make self-sacrifice for revolution," and "be a target of revolution."[52] Thanks to one of Guo's senior colleagues, who admonished him of the political risks involved, Guo avoided this dangerous trap. In 1962, Guo was transferred back to Beijing, this time working for the dance theory group of the Dance Workers Association, where he had the chance to translate many English books on modern dance into Chinese, including *The Modern Dance* by John Martin, *The Art of Making Dances* by Doris Humphrey, *The Language of Dance* by Mary Wigman, *World History of Dance* by Curt Sachs, and Laban's *Effort, Modern Educational Dance*, and *The Mastery of Movement on the Stage*, all of which would have to wait until the 1980s to be published.[53]

These translated works played a non-negligible role in reviving modern dance in China after the Cultural Revolution (1966–1976), even though their influence was limited largely within a relatively small group of dancer-choreographers and dance scholars who were interested in the history, theory, and practice of Western modern dance.[54] During the Cultural Revolution, all the major dancers studied in this book were persecuted and forced to stop their dance-related work.[55] By the end of the Cultural

Revolution, even the youngest among the survivors of these first-generation pioneers had reached their sixties, and due to the lack of technical and institutional support for preserving their previous modern/new dance works and methods, those were mostly lost in history forever. On the other hand, the younger generations, who were trained in socialist China, had little exposure to modern dance. Therefore, translated works on the genre, like those by Guo, became one of the few windows through which the new generation of modern dancers and scholars in 1980s China could look into the Western modern dance world.[56] Paradoxically, modern dance, the fleeting art of abstract bodily movement, had to rely partly on words to survive the two long decades of the 1960s and 70s.

A New Beginning of the New

In October 1978, a very positive essay on Isadora Duncan's life and art appeared in *Wudao* 舞蹈 (Dance), the top professional dance journal in China, among a group of articles still bearing traces of the Cultural Revolution just two years in the past.[57] Forty-four years after Duncan's autobiography *My Life* was translated into Chinese (in 1934) and became widely popular among Chinese intellectuals and artists of the Republican era, the most iconic figure of American modern dance and modern dance in general was reintroduced into China's dance world, which was a clear political signal calling for reviving modern dance.[58] In June 1979, Guo Mingda published an article on Laban's life and career and his movement analysis in *Wudao*.[59] A mere month later, Dai Ailian attended Laban's centenary celebration in England, spoke in the eleventh conference of the International Council of Kinetography Laban (i.e., Labanotation) held in France, and visited the United States, where she also updated herself with the latest developments of American modern dance.[60] In August 1979, Wu Xiaobang, who would be elected as the president of Chinese Dancers Association (the former Dance Workers Association) in two months, published an essay titled "The Beginning of Learning Modern Dance" in *Wudao*.[61] Since then, discussions on the genre began to appear regularly in the major dance journals. During the same period, following China's opening-up and the United States's formal recognition of the People's Republic, international travels of artists and dancers and the accompanying cultural exchanges between China and the West increased significantly, and such exchanges often involved Western modern dance performances, viewings, and workshops.[62] Modern dance had made its initial comeback in China.

In practice, Guo played a major role in jumpstarting the revival of modern dance. After the Cultural Revolution, Wu, in his seventies, largely devoted himself to leadership, strategic planning, and writing in China's dance field, while Dai focused her work primarily on ballet, Labanotation, and ethnic dance. As a result, Guo became virtually the only one based in China who had received systematic Western modern dance training and was still available for directing the practice of the genre, even though he was already in his mid-sixties and had long stopped choreographing and performing.

In late 1979, seven choreographers of the army-affiliated Frontline Song and Dance Company (*Qianxian ge wu tuan* 前綫歌舞團) located in Nanjing City came to Beijing to consult Guo about innovative ways of choreographing. Since they were all trained in the same dance educational system and followed the same approach, they had no clue about how to make choreographic breakthroughs, as Guo foreboded in his 1957 rejoinder mentioned above.[63] During their initial consultation with Guo, the discussion curiously revolved around a question that was seemingly tangential (but actually pertinent to the development of modern dance in China): why did modern dance first emerge and prosper in the United States? The army choreographers' answer was that because America was an immigrant country, which had no deep cultural tradition. Guo disagreed; he held that America's cultural foundation was the European tradition, and traditional dance forms in classical ballet and opera were brought to America by immigrants. Guo instead argued that the main cause to the rise of modern dance in the United States was the existence of a "free and casual" American "working middle class" that had no fixed taste and thus were more receptive to artistic innovations.[64]

The key to understanding this debate is the "Chinese question" hidden behind the American facade: does post-revolutionary China have the necessary social, economic, and cultural conditions for developing modern dance? The army choreographers' culture-based concern seems to be that China's deeply entrenched tradition—in the dance world, represented by the dominant classical dance—might be too strong for modern dance to break through.[65] Guo's alternative, "historical materialist" answer, regardless of its academic validity, paints a more optimistic future for modern dance in China: as China's "Reform and Opening-Up" started a year earlier in 1978, the emergence of a Chinese middle class, comparable to the American counterpart, would be on the horizon, and, following Guo's logic, so would be an audience base receptive to modern dance.

Although Guo's argument above answered, in theory, the question of the socioeconomic viability of modern dance in China, it did not fully address the legitimacy concern, that is, how to justify developing modern dance—a genre widely perceived by the Chinese as an outgrowth of Western capitalist culture—in early 1980s China, where the dance circle prided itself on the socialist legacy of invented "national dance forms."[66] Guo's strategy to alleviate this concern was to challenge the East-West divide underlying the Chinese perception of the genre. As early as in 1957, Guo wrote about the "Asian influences" on early modern dance's emphasizing expression (over representation) and abstraction (over realism).[67] In the early 1980s, Guo further elaborated on the "Oriental roots" in American modern dance by pointing out the Indian yoga influences on DeniShawn's and Graham's choreography and training methods; the similarity between some modern dance principles and those of Chinese qigong 氣功 (such as "let the heart move the qi, and let qi move the body," "let intention be the primary driver [of movement]," "force should spring from the spine," and "inhaled air should sink to the abdomen"); and the more recent incorporation of Chinese Tai Chi moves into Western modern dance.[68] Today's Chinese dance scholars typically interpret these comments by Guo as his effort to fight against Eurocentrism and Americentrism in modern dance.[69] However, in the context of the early 1980s, the true target of Guo's argument was the Chinese dance world's Sinocentric tendency, which, in Guo's view, had hindered modern dance's development in China. By proving modern dance is not purely "Western" in nature, but partly "Oriental" and even "Chinese" all along, the reintroduction of the genre into China could be rendered less invasive and more acceptable.

In addition to socioeconomic viability and cultural-political legitimacy, Guo also had to address the feasibility of modern dance's breaking away from the entrenched choreographic approach that was formally based on codified national dance forms and structurally organized around the narrative-driven dance drama. Guo's proposed solution was to elevate the status of "movement thinking"—that is, thinking based on movement and kinesthesia instead of language or imagery—relative to that of "literary thinking" in choreography.[70] In Guo's view, "literary thinking" and "movement thinking" are two extremes of a choreographic continuum, with the former corresponding to pantomime-based dance drama and the latter corresponding to highly abstract dance forms. Guo maintained that Chinese choreographers tended to borrow extensively from the principles and conventions of literature and theater and, moreover, received heavy influence from the Soviet model of ballet and character dance, which led to the common belief that dance's highest developmental stage is dance drama and thus the pursuit of "literaturization" and "dramatization" in choreography.[71] For Guo, the key to reviving modern dance in China was to "de-literaturize" and "de-dramatize" dance and to install kinesthesia-oriented movement at the center of both form (to decenter codified national dance forms) and content (to decenter dramatic narrative).

In early 1980, encouraged by their initial discussion with Guo Mingda in Beijing, the Frontline Company invited Guo to Nanjing, where Guo in the 1940s embarked on his dance journey, to hold a three-week workshop on modern dance.[72] Each day, Guo spent two hours with the company on theory and another two on basic training, covering from François Delsarte to Laban. While the three-week course on the Laban-Wigman system Wu took with Eguchi Takaya in 1936 Tokyo became the basis of Wu's new dance, Guo's three-week workshop marked the revival of modern dance in practice in post-revolutionary China.[73] In the fall of 1980, the company took several dance works composed after Guo's workshop to participate in The First National Dance Competition, and one modern dance work in particular, *Hope* (*Xiwang* 希望), caused a sensation and debate in China's dance circle.[74]

Hope is the first Chinese modern dance work choreographed and performed after the Cultural Revolution. In the solo, the young muscular male dancer, almost naked (only in black shorts), danced against a plain black backdrop, accompanied by a music piece composed specifically for the dance.[75] According to the choreographer's description, the dance does not employ any narrative or assign any dramatic role to the dancer, using only abstract movement—such as breathing at different rhythms and depths, the contracting, releasing, and quivering of muscles, the curling and straightening up of fingers and feet, and various movements of the limbs and the head driven by the waving motions of the chest and the waist—to kinestheticize an emotional sequence of bodily sensations: torment, pain, struggle, confusion, fight, failure, despair, light, and finally hope.[76] This choreography, even though it incorporates some ballet vocabulary, clearly follows the "movement thinking" Guo drove home during the workshop.

The work stirred up controversy in the dance circle, and the two sides of the debate were largely drawn along the generational line. The older generations, who started their dance training in the 1940s and 1950s, were lukewarm, and some of them negatively commented that "this dance [*Hope*], at the best, is equivalent to the third-rate modern dance of 1930s America" and "isn't this something we have long criticized since the past?"[77] By contrast, the younger generation, who were trained in the 1960s and thus did not experience the systematic criticism of modern dance in the 1950s and early 1960s, were very enthused, and some opined that "This [Hope] is what dance should be like, which is worth watching, worth dancing."[78] It seems that modern dance in the early 1980s struck a rebellious chord in the young generation of Chinese dancer-choreographers, who were trained in the established system but grew dissatisfied with its increasingly rigidified approach centered around revolutionary ballet, classical dance, and ethnic folk dance.

To explicate his work, the choreographer stated that Hope is about the general struggle in the "development of human society from the primitive [stage] to the present and to future"; it is about "the humankind fighting against fate, that is: the human life's incessant search for the truth of being."[79] It seems that the choreographer adopted a universalist narrative typically associated with modern dance to counter the political rhetoric revolving around class struggle that had long dominated China's dance stage; as the choreographer explained, one of the main reasons for letting the dancer wear only shorts was to prevent the audience from identifying him with a particular social class or stratum.[80] However, despite the choreographer's universalist tone, it was not hard for the spectators to discern the historically specific subtext embodied in Hope—the affective staging of the collective traumatic experiences of the Cultural Revolution.[81]

I end my book here with Hope.[82] Up to this point, the major issues persisting throughout the development of modern dance in pre–Cultural Revolution China—the problematic relations between the new and the old, the foreign and the national, the universal and the particular, modernism and leftism/socialism, words and movement—had all resurfaced with the genre's revival in the early 1980s, yet with different manifestations. For the cosmopolitan Yu Rongling, early Western modern dance was about both "creating the new" and "reviving the old," and by leveraging this paradox, she turned the universalist logic of modern dance around into a national one to create the early court version of Chinese classical dance (chapter 1). Dai Ailian, driven by the aspirations and anxieties resulting from her multidiasporic experiences, treated modern dance as a universal, "scientific" lens and symbolic toolbox (Labanotation) to synthesize "Chinese dance" out of various ethnic dances and further displaced onto the international discursive stage the written/notated "Chinese dances," which became commensurable in the form of signs with other world dances (chapter 4).

Yet, the starkest contrast is, perhaps unexpectedly, between Wu Xiaobang and Guo Mingda, despite their tacit alliance in defending modern dance. While for Wu (chapters 2 and 3), in line with the May Fourth narrative, the legitimacy of his new dance in the 1930s derived from its "Western" modern dance origin, positioned in sharp relief to the "backward," "feudalistic" "old dance" integrated in traditional Chinese theater, for Guo, the legitimacy of modern dance in China rested exactly on the genre's incorporation of Oriental and Chinese traditions since its formative stage. Unlike Wu, who tried to expand his audience base by appealing to the wartime masses of workers, farmers, and soldiers with his left-leaning new dance in the late 1930s and, in the late 1950s, by implicitly targeting the urban literary and artistic elites with his "right-leaning" classical new dance, Guo placed his bet on the gestating Chinese middle class in the 1980s. To reinvoke here the image of the concentric Confucian poetic order spelled out in the "Introduction," whereas Wu chose a "centripetal" path to bring dance movement closer to "words" in his transmedial strategy of reversely integrating "literature"—be it in the form of general mobilizing narrative or classical literary and philosophical topoi—into kinesthesia, Guo moved in the opposite, "centrifugal" direction from "literary thinking" toward "movement thinking" along the choreographic continuum, as represented by *Hope*. These contrasts between "snapshots," fragmentary and static as they are, partly register the dramatically changing landscape of China's dance world, China itself, and China's relation to the world throughout the twentieth century, traces of which this entire book, as I hope, tries to capture and "choreograph" with a sense of dynamism—a dynamism that would continue into the twenty-first century on the world dance stage.

Notes

Introduction

1. Helene van Rossum, "Peking Friends and Family Scenes" (in the series on the films of diplomat John Van Antwerp MacMurray), September 14, 2010, in the collection of the Seeley G. Mudd Manuscript Library, Princeton University. http://blogs.princeton. edu/reelmudd/2010/09/peking-friends-and-family-scenes/.
2. Catherine Yeh, "Mei Lanfang and Modern Dance: Transcultural Innovation in Peking Opera, 1910s–1920s," in *Corporeal Politics: Dancing East Asia*, ed. Katherine Mezur and Emily Wilcox (Ann Arbor: The University of Michigan Press, 2020), 44–59, 50–54.
3. Emily Wilcox, *Revolutionary Bodies: Chinese Dance and the Socialist Legacy* (Oakland: University of California Press, 2019).
4. Joshua Goldstein, *Drama Kings: Players and Publics in the Re-creation of Peking Opera, 1870–1937* (Berkeley: University of California Press, 2007).
5. Yeh, "Mei Lanfang and Modern Dance"; See also Nancy Reynolds and Malcolm McCormick, *No Fixed Points: Dance in the Twentieth Century* (New Haven: Yale University Press, 2003), 3–10.
6. Bertolt Brecht, "Alienation Effects in Chinese Acting," in *Brecht on Theatre*, ed. and trans. John Willett (New York: Hill & Wang, 1964), 91–99.
7. This collaboration between Mei and DeniShawn would turn out to be instrumental in the sensational success of Mei's American tour five years later in 1931. See Wang Kefen 王克芬 and Long Yinpei 隆蔭培, eds., *Zhongguo jinxiandai dangdai wudao fazhanshi* 中國近現代當代舞蹈發展史 [The development history of modern and contemporary Chinese dance] (Beijing: Renmin yinyue chubanshe, 1999), 44; Mei Shaowu 梅紹武, *Wo de fuqin Mei Lanfang* 我的父親梅蘭芳 [My Father Mei Lanfang] (Tianjin: Baihua wenyi chubanshe, 2004), 184; Catherine Yeh, "Experimenting with Dance Drama: Peking Opera Modernity, Kabuki Theater Reform and the Denishawn's Tour of the Far East," *Journal of Global Theatre History* 1, no. 2 (2016): 28–37; Yeh, "Mei Lanfang and Modern Dance," 53.
8. Yu Rongling 裕容齡, "Qingmo wudaojia Yu Rongling huiyilu" 清末舞蹈家裕容齡 回憶錄 [The Memoir of Yu Rongling, A dancer of the Late Qing], *Wudao* 舞蹈, no. 2 (March 1958): 44–45.
9. Ann Daly, *Done into Dance: Isadora Duncan in America* (Bloomington: Indiana University Press, 1995), 32, 76; Carrie Preston, *Modernism's Mythic Pose: Gender, Genre, Solo Performance* (Oxford: Oxford University Press, 2011), 187.
10. Preston, *Modernism's Mythic Pose*, 147–52.

11. Mark Franko, *Choreographing Discourses: A Mark Franko Reader*, ed. Mark Franko with Alessandra Nicifero (New York: Routledge, 2019), 2; Daly, *Done into Dance*, 18, 104.

12. For the most recent collaborated project of addressing East Asian contributions to dance in general, not early modern dance in particular, see Mezur and Wilcox, eds., *Corporeal Politics*. For other "oriental" contributions to the early modern dance, see, for example, Mark Franko, *Dancing Modernism/Performing Politics* (Bloomington: Indiana University Press, 1995); Jane Desmond, "Dancing out the Difference: Cultural Imperialism and Ruth St. Denis's *Radha* of 1906," in *Moving History/Dancing Cultures: A Dance History Reader*, ed. Ann Dils and Ann Cooper Albright (Middletown: Wesleyan University Press, 2001), 256–70; Gennifer Weissenfeld, *Mavo: Japanese Artists and the Avant-Garde 1905–1931* (Berkeley: University of California Press, 2002), 233–39; Faye Yuan Kleeman, "Body (Language) across the Sea: Gender, Ethnicity, and the Embodiment of Post-/Colonial Modernity," in *Comparatizing Taiwan*, ed. Shu-mei Shih and Ping-hui Liao (London: Routledge, 2015), 217–44; Priya Srinivasan, *Sweating Saris: Indian Dance as Transnational Labor* (Philadelphia: Temple University Press, 2011); Carrie J. Preston, "Michio Ito's Shadow: Searching for the Translational in Solo Dance," in *On Stage Alone: Sololists and the Modern Dance Cannon*, ed. Claudia Gitelman and Barbara Palfy (Gainesvill: University Press of Florida, 2012), 7–30.

13. For example, see Edward Ross Dickinson, *Dancing in the Blood: Modern Dance and European Culture on the Eve of the First World War* (Cambridge: Cambridge University Press, 2017), 11–12; Gabriele Brandstetter, *Poetics of Dance: Body, Image, and Space in the Historical Avant-Gardes*, trans. Elena Polzer and Mark Franko (Oxford: Oxford University Press, 2015), 1; Susan Jones, *Literature, Modernism, and Dance* (Oxford: Oxford University Press, 2013), 30, 35. SanSan Kwan offers so far the only monograph on "Chinese" modern dance, *Kinesthetic City: Dance & Movement in Chinese Urban Spaces* (Oxford: Oxford University Press, 2013). However, her study centers on contemporary modern dance troupes and choreographies in Shanghai, Taipei, Hong Kong, and Chinatown of New York City in relation to the dynamic and distinctive urban spaces, without addressing the origin of modern dance in mainland China during the first half of the twentieth century.

14. Shu-mei Shih, *The Lure of the Modern: Writing Modernism in Semicolonial China, 1917–1937* (Berkeley: University of California Press, 2001), 11.

15. See also Rebekah Kowal, *How to Do Things with Dance: Performing Change in Postwar America* (CT: Wesleyan University Press, 2010).

16. Shu-mei Shih, *Visuality and Identity: Sinophone Articulations Across the Pacific* (Berkeley: University of California Press, 2007); Shu-Mei Shih, "Against Diaspora: The Sinophone as Places of Cultural Production," in *Global Chinese Literature: Critical Essays*, ed. Jing Tsu and David Der-wei Wang (London: Brill, 2010), 29–48.

17. Susan Stanford Friedman, *Planetary Modernisms: Provocations on Modernity Across Time* (New York: Columbia University Press, 2018), 4.

18. For the global dissemination of early modern dance, see, for example, Isa Partsch-Bergsohn, *Modern Dance in Germany and the United States: Crosscurrents and*

Influences (Switzerland: Harwood Academic Publishers, 1994); Daly, *Done into Dance*; Franko, *Dancing Modernism*; Ellen Graff, *Stepping Left: Dance and Politics in New York City, 1928–1942* (Durham: Duke University Press, 1997, 1999); Ramsay Burt, *Alien Bodies: Representations of Modernity, "Race" and Nation in Early Modern Dance* (London: Rutledge, 1998); Julia L. Foulkes, *Modern Bodies: Dance and American Modernism from Martha Graham to Alvin Ailey* (Chapel Hill: The University of North Carolina Press, 2002); Mark Franko, *The Work of Dance: Labor, Movement, and Identity in the 1930s* (Middletown: Wesleyan University Press, 2002); L. Karina and M. Kant, *Hitler's Dancers: German Modern Dance and the Third Reich* (New York: Berghahn Books, 2003); Reynolds and McCormick, *No Fixed Points*; Manning, *Modern Dance, Negro Dance*; Claudia Gitelman and Barbara Palfy, eds., *On Stage Alone: Soloists and the Modern Dance Canon* (Gainesville: University Press of Florida, 2012); Jens Richard Giersdorf, *The Body of the People: East German Dance Since 1945* (Madison: The University of Wisconsin Press, 2013); Brandstetter, *Poetics of Dance*.

19. Wilcox, *Revolutionary Bodies*, 1–32. While Wilcox argues that the heterogeneous origins and genres of Chinese dance forms work concertedly to form an inclusive and relatively coherent, though malleable, national identity of "Chinese dance," I focus more on the inherent tensions, contradictions, frictions, and fractures in Chinese dance through the lens of modern dance.

20. Sheldon Cheney, ed., *Isadora Duncan: The Art of the Dance* (New York: Helen Hackett, 1928; rprt., New York: Theatre Arts Books, 1969), passim; cited in Manning, *Modern Dance*, xx.

21. Franko, *Dancing Modernism*, xi.

22. John Martin, *The Modern Dance* (New York: A. S. Barnes, 1933; rprt., Brooklyn: Dance Horizons, 1965), 13, 19–20, 85; see also Manning, *Modern Dance, Negro Dance*, xiii, xix; Franko, *Choreographing Discourses*, 29–48.

23. See, for example, Franko, *Dancing Modernism*; Susan Manning, *Ecstasy and the Demon: The Dances of Mary Wigman* (Berkeley: University of California Press; rprt., Minneapolis: University of Minneapolis Press, 2006); Daly, *Done into Dance*; Manning, *Modern Dance*; Susan Leigh Foster, *Choreographing Empathy: Kinesthesia in Performance* (London: Routledge, 2011); Mark Franko, *Martha Graham in Love and War: The Life in the Work* (Oxford: Oxford University Press, 2012); Brandstetter, *Poetics of Dance*; Franko, *Choreographing Discourses*; Nell Andrew, *Moving Modernism: The Urge to Abstraction in Painting, Dance, Cinema* (New York: Oxford University Press, 2020).

24. Reynolds and McCormick, *No Fixed Points*, 1–32.

25. Ibid., 77–105.

26. Wilcox, *Revolutionary Bodies*, 2.

27. For challenges to this periodization in Chinese historiography from the perspective of literary history, see David Der-wei Wang, *Fin-de-Siècle Splendor: Repressed Modernities of Late Qing Fiction, 1848–1911* (Stanford: Stanford University Press, 1997); Xiaojue Wang, *Modernity with a Cold War Face: Reimagining the Nation in Chinese Literature across the 1949 Divide* (Cambridge: Harvard University Asia

Center, 2013). For a critical assessment of the definition of "Chinese dance," see Fangfei Miao, "*Revolutionary Bodies: Chinese Dance and the Socialist Legacy* by Emily Wilcox (review)," *Dance Research Journal* 51, no. 1 (April 2019): 102–5, 104.

28. Wilcox, *Revolutionary Bodies*. See also Emily Wilcox, "The Dialectics of Virtuosity: Dance in the People's Republic of China, 1949–2009" (PhD diss., University of California, Berkeley, 2011); Emily Wilcox, "Han-Tang Zhongguo Gudianwu and the Problem of Chineseness in Contemporary Chinese Dance: Sixty Years of Controversy," *Asian Theatre Journal* 29, no. 1 (2012): 206–32; Emily Wilcox, "Beyond Internal Orientalism: Dance and Nationality Discourse in the Early People's Republic of China, 1949–1954," *The Journal of Asian Studies* 75, no. 2 (May 2016): 363–86; Emily Wilcox, "Dynamic Inheritance: Representative Works and the Authoring of Tradition in Chinese Dance," in Levi Gibbs, ed. special issue "Faces of Tradition in Chinese Performing Arts," *Journal of Folklore Research* 55, no. 1 (2018): 77–112; Emily Wilcox, "The Postcolonial Blind Spot: Chinese Dance in the Era of Third World-ism, 1949–1965," *positions: asia critique* 26, no. 4 (2018): 781–815.

29. Chinese dance scholars often use the term "contemporary Chinese dance" (*xiandai Zhongguo wu* 現代中國舞) to refer to Chinese dance developed after 1949 (the founding year of the People's Republic China). However, in this book, I do not make a distinction between "modern" and "contemporary" Chinese dance, in order to emphasize the continuity, instead of rupture, in dance history across the 1949-divide between Republican China (1912–1949) and Communist China (1949–). For periodization in Chinese dance historiography, see Wang and Long, *Zhongguo jinxiandai*.

30. For the development of modern dance in post-Cultural Revolution China (1976–), see Fangfei Miao, "Dancing Cross-Cultural Misunderstandings: The American Dance Festival in China's New Era" (PhD diss., University of California, Los Angeles, 2019).

31. Dickinson, *Dancing in the Blood*, 21–26.

32. Ibid.

33. Wang and Long, *Zhongguo jinxiandai*, 14; Wilcox, *Revolutionary Bodies*, 23–32.

34. Andrew D. Field, *Shanghai's Dancing World: Cabaret Culture and Urban Politics, 1919–1954* (Hong Kong: The Chinese University of Hong Kong, 2010); Leo Ou-fan Lee, *Shanghai Modern: The Flowering of a New Urban Culture in China, 1930–1945* (Cambridge: Harvard University Press, 1999), 23–28; Daly, *Done into Dance*, 20, 159–62, 171.

35. For example, Andrew F Jones, *Yellow Music: Media Culture and Colonial Modernity in the Chinese Jazz Age* (Durham: Duke University Press, 2001); Xiaobing Tang, *Origins of the Chinese Avant-garde: The Modern Woodcut Movement* (University of California Press, 2008); Siyuan Liu, *Performing Hybridity in Colonial-Modern China* (New York: Palgrave MacMillan, 2013); Liang Luo, *The Avant-Garde and the Popular in Modern China: Tian Han and the Intersection of Performance and Politics* (Ann Arbor: University of Michigan, 2014).

36. For studies on the sibling arts, the following is a highly selected list arranged according to different art fields. *Theater*: Chen Xiaomei, *Acting the Right Part: Political Theater and Popular Drama in Contemporary China* (Honolulu: University of Hawai'i Press, 2002); Goldstein, *Drama Kings*; Liu, *Performing Hybridity in Colonial-Modern China*;

Luo, *The Avant-Garde and the Popular in Modern China*; Brian James Demare, *Mao's Cultural Army: Drama Troupes in China's Rural Revolution* (New York: Cambridge University Press, 2015); *Music:* Jones, *Yellow Music*; Barbara Mittler, *Dangerous Tunes: the Politics of Chinese Music in Hongkong, Taiwan, and the People's Republic of China since 1949* (Wiesbaden: Otto Harrassowitz, 1997); Mittler, *A Continuous Revolution*; *Literature:* Nicole Huang, *Women, War, Domesticity: Shanghai Literature and Popular Culture of the 1940s* (Leiden: Brill Academic Pub, 2005); Andrew F. Jones, *Developmental Fairy Tales: Evolutionary Thinking and Modern Chinese Culture* (Cambridge: Harvard University Press, 2011); Shih, *The Lure of the Modern* (2001); Wang, *The Sublime Figure of History*; Lydia H. Liu, *Translingual Practice: Literature, National Culture, and Translated Modernity, China, 1900–1937* (Stanford: Stanford University Press, 1995); Kirk Denton, *The Problematic of Self in Modern Chinese Literature: Hu Feng and Lu Ling* (Stanford: Stanford University Press, 1998); Xiaobing Tang, *Chinese Modern: the Heroic and the Quotidian* (Durham: Duke University Press, 2000); Richard King, *Milestones on a Golden Road, Writing for Chinese Socialism, 1945–80* (Vancouver: UBC Press, 2013); Xiaojue Wang, *Modernity with a Cold War Face: Reimagining the Nation in Chinese Literature across the 1949 Divide* (Cambridge: Harvard University Asia Center, 2013); *Film:* Zhang Zhen, *Amorous History of the Silver Screen: Shanghai Cinema, 1896–1937* (Chicago: The University of Chicago Press, 2005); Laikwan Pang, *Building a New China in Cinema: The Chinese Left-Wing Cinema Movement, 1932–1937* (Lanham: Rowman & Littlefield Publishers, Inc., 2002); Weihong Bao, *Fiery Cinema: the Emergence of an Affective Medium in China, 1915–1945* (Minneapolis: University of Minnesota Press, 2015); *Visual arts:* Tang, *Origins of the Chinese Avant-Garde*; Xiaobing Tang, *Visual Culture in Contemporary China: Paradigms and Shifts* (New York: Cambridge University Press, 2015); Julia F. Andrews, *Painters and Politics in the People's Republic of China, 1949–1979* (Berkeley: University of California Press, 1994).

37. John Martin, Introduction to the Dance (New York: Dance Horizons, 1965), 133–34; quoted in Franko, *Choreographing Discourses*, 37.

38. John Martin, *America Dancing: The Background and Personalities of the Modern Dance* (New York: Dodge, 1938), 87–88; quoted in Andrew Hewitt, *Social Choreography: Ideology as Performance in Dance and Everyday Movement* (Durham: Duke University Press, 2005), 119.

39. Brandstetter, *Poetics of Dance*, 6.

40. Ibid., 21.

41. Preston, *Modernism's Mythic Pose*, 21.

42. Brandstetter, *Poetics of Dance*, 21.

43. Susan Jones, *Literature, Modernism, and Dance* (Oxford: Oxford University Press, 2013), 7–8.

44. Andrew, *Moving Modernism*, xvi.

45. Ibid.

46. Brandstetter, *Poetics of Dance*, 21.

47. Hewitt, *Social Choreography*, 117–22.

48. Manning, *Ecstasy and the Demon*, 2; see also Daly, *Done into Dance*, 181, 215.

49. Hewitt, *Social Choreography*, 117–22.

50. Franko, *Choreographing Discourses*, 37–41.

51. Ibid., 40.

52. Translated by the author. The original Chinese text is in Guo Shaoyu 郭少虞, *Lidai wenlun xuan* 歷代文論選 [Selected works of Chinese literary theory in all dynasties] (Shanghai: Shanghai guji chubanshe, 2001), vol. 1, 63.

53. Zhu Guangqian 朱光潛, *Shi lun* 詩論 [On Poetry], in *Zhu Guangqian quan ji (di san juan)* 朱光潛全集 (第三卷) [The complete works of Zhu Guangqian] (Anhui: Anhui jiaoyu chubanshe, 1987), 13–18.

54. William H. Nienhauser Jr., *The Indiana Companion to Traditional Chinese Literature*, vol. 1 (Bloomington: Indiana University Press, 1986), 692–93.

55. Zhu, *Shi lun*, 13–18; Daly, *Done into Dance*, 145.

56. Guo, *Lidai wenlun*, 63.

57. Zhu, *Shi lun*.

58. Wang and Long, *Zhongguo jinxiandai*, 14.

59. See, for example, Ping Xin 平心, ed., *Wudao biaoyan xinlixue* 舞蹈表演心理學 [The psychology of dance performance] (Shanghai: Shanghai yinyue chubanshe, 2013), 236.

60. Ibid., emphasis added.

61. See, for example, Mark Franko, *Dance as Text: Ideologies of the Baroque Body* (revised edition) (New York: Oxford University Press, 2015).

62. For relevant discussions on the relations between dance, text, and narrative, see, for example, Ellen Goellner, *Bodies of the Text: Dance as Theory, Literature as Dance* (New Brunswick: Rutgers University Press, 1994); Amy Koritz, *Gendering Bodies/Performing Art: Dance and Literature in Early Twentieth-Century British Culture* (Ann Arbor: University of Michigan Press, 1995); Gay Morris, ed., *Moving Words: Rewriting Dance* (London: Routledge, 1996); Jane Desmond, *Meaning in Motion: New Cultural Studies of Dance* (Durham: Duke University Press, 1997); Susan Leigh Foster, *Choreography and Narrative: Ballet's Staging of Story and Desire* (Bloomington: Indiana University Press, 1998); Hewitt, *Social Choreography*; Kwan, *Kinesthetic City*; Franko, *Dance as Text*.

63. For a detailed study of the genealogy of the concept choreography, see Foster, *Choreographing Empathy*. For a summary, see Franko, *Choreographing Discourses*, 13–28; Gay Morris and Jens Giersdorf, "Introduction," in *Choreographies of 21st Century Wars*, ed. Gay Morris and Jens Giersdorf (New York: Oxford University Press, 2016), 5–12.

64. For an introduction to the theoretical issues concerning the choreography-writing relation, see Carrie Noland and Sally Ann Ness, eds., *Migrations of Gesture* (Minneapolis: University of Minneapolis Press, 2008); for a philosophical exploration of this topic, see Frédéric Pouillaude, *Unworking Choreography: The Notion of the Work in Dance*, trans. Anna Pakes (New York: Oxford University Press, 2017). See also Victoria Watts, "Dancing the Score: Dance Notation and Différence," *Dance Research: The Journal of the Society for Dance Research* 28, no. 1 (Summer 2010): 7–18.

65. Kwan, *Kinesthetic City*, 4–5.

66. Jacques Derrida, *Of Grammatology*, trans. Gayatri Spivak (Baltimore: The Johns Hopkins University Press, 1997), 9. Emphasis added.

67. Franko, *Choreographing Discourses*, 25. Italics in original.

68. Sally Ann Ness, *Body, Movement, and Culture: Kinesthetic and Visual Symbolism in a Philippine Community* (Philadelphia: University of Pennsylvania Press, 1992), 5; Sally Ann Ness, "Dancing in the Field: Notes from Memory," in *Corporealities: Dancing Knowledge, Culture and Power*, ed. Susan Leigh Foster (London: Routledge, 1996), 134; Kwan, *Kinesthetic City*, 5, 143.

69. Kwan, *Kinesthetic City*, 5.

70. Susan L. Foster, "Choreographies of Writing," performed lecture presented in the series *Susan Foster! Susan Foster!: Bodies of Work: 3 Lectures: Performed* (March 22, 2011), at the Live Arts Studio, Philadelphia Live Arts Festival & Philly Fringe, 919 N. 5th St., Philadelphia, sponsored by The Pew Center for Arts & Heritage through Dance Advance with the cooperation of the Philadelphia Live Arts Festival, https://hdl.handle.net/2333.1/3r22846r.

71. Ibid.

72. Lucia Ruprecht, *Gestural Imaginaries: Dance and Cultural Theory in the Early Twentieth Century* (New York: Oxford University Press, 2019), 25.

73. Kate Elswit, Watching Weimar Dance (New York: Oxford University Press, 2014), xxii.

74. Ibid., xxi–xxii.

75. Ruprecht, *Gestural Imaginaries*, 26, 34.

76. Brandstetter, *Poetics of Dance*, 13, Italics in original.

77. Ibid., 15–16.

Chapter 1

1. In a short autobiography hand-written by Yu Rongling in the mid-1950s, she dates her birth in 1882, which has been adopted by the official history. However, there is evidence showing that Rongling's elder sister Deling 德齡 [Princess Der Ling] was born on June 8, 1885, and Xinling 馨齡, elder brother of Rongling, was born after Deling. Moreover, the age difference between Deling and Rongling should not be greater than a few years. Therefore, a reasonable estimate of Rongling's true birth year is around 1888 or 1889. See Grant Hayter-Menzies, *Imperial Masquerade: the Legend of Princess Der Ling* (Hong Kong: Hong Kong University Press, 2008), 3, 366; Ye Zufu 葉祖孚, "Xi taihou yuqian nüguan Yu Rongling (qi)" 西太后御前女官裕容齡(七) [Yu Rongling: Lady in waiting of the West Empress Dowager (VII)], *Zongheng* 縱橫, no. 7 (1999): 50–3, 53; Yu Rongling裕容齡, "Qingmo wudaojia Yu Rongling huiyilu" 清末舞蹈家裕容齡回憶錄 [The Memoir of Yu Rongling, A dancer of the Late Qing], *Wudao* 舞蹈, no. 2 (March 1958): 44–45; Yu Deling [Princess Der Ling], *Kowtow* (New York: Dodd, Mead and Company, Inc., 1929), 271; Hayter-Menzies, *Imperial Masquerade*, 99–104.

2. Samuel N. Dorf, "Dancing Greek Antiquity in Private and Public: Isadora Duncan's Early Patronage in Paris," *Dance Research Journal* 44, no. 1 (Summer 2012): 3–27; for Duncan's bisexuality, see Ann Daly, *Done into Dance: Isadora Duncan in America* (Bloomington: Indiana University Press, 1995), 170, 249–50.

3. Daly, *Done into Dance*, 172; Hayter-Menzies, *Imperial Masquerade*, 101.

4. Yu Rongling, "Qingmo wudaojia," 45. However, the title and content of the dance work are uncertain. In her book, Chinese dance scholar Tong Yan identifies the title of the work as, in Chinese transliteration, *Aofeiliya* 奧菲利亞. However, she did not provide the source of this information. According to the transliteration, the original English title of the work seems to be *Ophelia*. In one of Duncan's earliest public performances back in the United States in 1898, there was a dance work interpreting the prominent American pianist and composer Ethelbert Nevin's *Water Scenes* (1891), which consists of five piano pieces, each with a mythological or literary allusion to a water theme. Duncan's dance was based on three of them, *Ophelia*, *Water Nymph*, and *Narcissus*. While the musical piece *Ophelia* was probably inspired by the character Ophelia in Shakespeare's *Hamlet*, Duncan's dance interpretation seems to center on the Greek mythological character Narcissus throughout the three piano pieces. Based on this and the information that Rongling at some point also performed a dance called *Shui xiannü* 水仙女 (Water nymph), the dramatic dance Yu performed in Paris in the early 1900s might be an adaptation and expansion of this earlier work of Duncan, with more roles and more discernible plot added and possibly Ophelia being the main character. If that was the case, then the role(s) Yu played could be any of Narcissus, the water nymph, or some Grecianized version of Ophelia. *Aofeiliya* might also be a mis-transliteration of Orpheus. Although this transliteration is less likely, Duncan's dance *Orpheus*, deriving from the German composer Christoph Willibald Gluck's French opera *Orphée* and evolving from 1900 to the 1920s throughout Duncan's dance career, has a more distinctively "Greek" theme and a more discernible "dramatic" structure, which better befits the description of the "Greek dramatic dance" Yu performed. If this was the case, Eurydice, wife of Orpheus, might be the role Yu danced. See Tong Yan 仝妍, *Minguo shiqi wudao yanjiu*, 1912–1949 民國時期舞蹈研究, 1912–1949 [Research on the dance of the Republican era, 1912–1949] (Beijing: Zhongyang minzu daxue chubanshe, 2013), 4–7; Daly, *Done into Dance*, 2, 148; Lida Rose McCabe, "A Maker of Imperishable Songs," *Form* 1, no. 9 (1913): 18–19, 19; Paul D. Buchanan, *American Women's Rights Movement: A Chronology of Events and Opportunities from 1600–2008* (Boston: Branden Books, 2009), 102.

5. Carrie Preston, *Modernism's Mythic Pose: Gender, Genre, Solo Performance* (Oxford: Oxford University Press, 2014), 148–49, 152; Dorf, "Dancing Greek Antiquity," 8.

6. Preston, *Modernism's Mythic Pose*, 152, 182, 185. For Duncan's contributions to and ambivalent, complicated relationship with first-wave feminism, the women's movement, and suffragism, see also Daly, *Done into Dance*, 162–64.

7. Lydia He Liu, Rebecca E Karl, and Dorothy Ko, eds., *The Birth of Chinese Feminism: Essential Texts in Transnational Theory* (New York: Columbia University Press, 2013).

8. Hayter-Menzies, *Imperial Masquerade*, 125–26, 152; Yu Rongling, *Qing gong suo ji*清 宮瑣記 [Miscellaneous records of the Qing Palace], in *Cixi yu wo* 慈禧與我 [Cixi and me], ed. Wang Shuqing 王樹卿 and Xu Che 徐徹 (Shenyang: Liaoshen shushe, 1994), 1–43.

9. Ibid.

10. Hayter-Menzies, *Imperial Masquerade*, 172.

11. Ibid., 171; Yu Deling [Princess Der Ling], *Lotos Petals* (New York: Dodd, Mead and Company, Inc., 1930), 251.

12. Yu Rongling, *Qing gong suo ji*, 11, 40–1.

13. Emily Wilcox, *Revolutionary Bodies: Chinese Dance and the Socialist Legacy* (Oakland: University of California Press, 2019), 7.

14. For the intersection of modernism and feminism in Duncan's modern dance, see Elizabeth Francis, "From Event to Monument: Modernism, Feminism, and Isadora Duncan," *American Studies* 35, no. 1 (1994): 25–45; Daly, *Done into Dance*; Preston, *Modernism's Mythic Pose*. For a theorization and introduction of early Chinese (proto-)feminism around the turn of the last century, see Liu et al., *The Birth of Chinese Feminism*.

15. See, for example, Susan Stanford Friedman, *Planetary Modernisms: Provocations on Modernity across Time* (New York: Columbia University Press, 2015).

16. Ari Larissa Heinrich and Fran Martin, "Introduction to Part I," in *Embodied Modernities: Corporeality, Representation, and Chinese Cultures*, ed. Fran Martin and Ari Larissa Heinrich (Hawai'i: University Of Hawai'i Press, 2006), 3–20.

17. Daly, *Done into Dance*, 91; Preston, *Modernism's Mythic Pose*, 5–6, 182; Elizabeth Francis, "From Event to Monument."

18. Ying Hu, *Tales of Translation: Composing the New Women in China, 1899–1918* (Stanford: Stanford University Press, 2000), 5.

19. Eric Hobsbawm, "Introduction: Inventing Tradition," in *The Invention of Tradition*, ed. Eric Hobsbawm and Terrence Ranger (Cambridge: Cambridge University Press, 1983), 7–8.

20. For example, see Hu, *Tales of Translation*; Lydia Liu, *Translingual Practice: Literature, National Culture, and Translated Modernity—China, 1900–1937* (Stanford: Stanford University Press, 1995); *The Clash of Empires: The Invention of China in Modern World Making* (Cambridge: Harvard University Press, 2004); Nanxiu Qian, Grace S. Fong, and Richard J. Smith, eds., *Different Worlds of Discourses: Transformation of Gender and Genre in Late Qing and Early Republican China* (Brill, 2008); David Der-wei Wang, *Fin-de-Siecle Splendor: Repressed Modernities of Late Qing Fiction, 1849–1911* (Stanford: Stanford University Press, 1997); Andrea Goldman, *Opera and the City: The Politics of Culture in Beijing, 1770–1900* (Stanford: Stanford University Press, 2012); Weijie Song, *Mapping Modern Beijing: Space, Emotion, Literary Topography* (Oxford: Oxford University Press, 2018).

21. See, for example, Pamela Crossley, *The Wobbling Pivot: China since 1800* (Chichester: Wiley-Blackwell, 2010); Evelyn S. Rawski, *The Last Emperors: A Social History of Qing Imperial Institutions* (Berkeley: University of California Press, 1998). This line of research belongs with what came to be known as the "new Qing history."

For discussion about this scholarship, see R. Kent Guy, "Who Were the *Manchus?*," *Journal of Asian Studies* 61, no. 1 (2002): 151–64; Joanna Waley-Cohen, "The New Qing History," *Radical History Review* 88 (2004): 193–206; and L. J. Newby, "China: Pax Manjurica," *Journal for Eighteenth Century Studies* 34, no. 4 (2011): 557–63.

22. Li Yuhang and Harriet T. Zurndorfer, "Rethinking Empress Dowager Cixi through the Production of Art," *Nan Nü* 14 (2012): 1–20; Liana Chen, "The Empress Dowager as Dramaturg: Reinventing Late-Qing Court Theatre," *Nan Nü* 14 (2012): 21–46; Li Yuhang, "Oneself as a Female Deity: Representations of Empress Dowager Cixi as Guanyin," *Nan Nü* 14 (2012): 75–118; Ying-chen Peng, "A Palace of Her Own: Empress Dowager Cixi (1835–1908) and the Reconstruction of the Wanchun Yuan," *Nan Nü* 14 (2012): 47–74; Cheng-hua Wang, "'Going Public': Portraits of the Empress Dowager Cixi, Circa 1904," *Nan Nü* 14 (2012): 119–76.

23. Song, *Mapping Modern Beijing*, 170–88.

24. Hu, *Tales of Translation*, 11.

25. See, among many others, "Sir Liang Chen's Bride: New Chinese Minister's Fiancée Boasts Boston Blood," *The Free Lance*, December 23, 1902, *Chronicling America: Historic American Newspapers*. Library of Congress. https://chronicling america.loc.gov/lccn/sn87060165/1902-12-23/ed-1/seq-4/.

26. Sir Robert Hart [the British Inspector General of Imperial Maritime Customs Service], *I. G. in Peking* (Cambridge: Belknap Press of Harvard University Press, 1976), letter 1143, quoted in Hayter-Menzies, *Imperial Masquerade*, 12.

27. For example, Rongling and her siblings all felt comfortable to dress themselves in all kinds of fancy costumes, foreign or Chinese, in public, and both Rongling and her sister Deling, fond of enacting foreign plays, once seriously thought of being a professional dancer or actress. See Hayter-Menzies, *Imperial Masquerade*, 101, 110; Yu Rongling, "Qingmo wudaojia," 45. Grace Fong, "Reconfiguring Time, Space, and Subjectivity: Lü Bicheng's Travel Writings on Mount Lu," in *Different Worlds of Discourses*, 87–114, 90.

28. "A Chinese Wedding: Distinguished Mongolian Marries a Comely French Girl," *Richmond Dispatch*, October 26, 1902, 1. *Chronicling America: Historic American Newspapers*. Library of Congress. https://chroniclingamerica.loc.gov/lccn/sn85038 614/1902-10-26/ed-1/seq-1/.

29. "A Chinese Parisian: Daughter of Chinese Minister Unique Figure in Paris Society," *Pine Bluff Daily Graphic*, January 7, 1902. *Chronicling America: Historic American Newspapers*. Library of Congress. https://chroniclingamerica.loc.gov/lccn/sn89051 168/1902-01-07/ed-1/seq-6/; Hayter-Menzies, *Imperial Masquerade*, 114.

30. "The New Chinese Minister: Expected in Washington This Week—Member of an Ancient Family and Very Wealthy," *New York Times*, March 30, 1903, 9, quoted in Anne Witchard, "Dancing Modern China," *Modernism/modernity* (The Print Plus platform) 4 (October 2019), https://doi.org/10.26597/mod.0130.

31. "French Styles the Vogue in China," *The Washington Times*, January 24, 1904, Magazine Features, 5. *Chronicling America: Historic American Newspapers*. Library of Congress. https://chroniclingamerica.loc.gov/lccn/sn84026749/1904-01-24/ed-1/ seq-27/.

32. Song, *Mapping Modern Beijing*, 170–88.

33. Hayter-Menzies, *Imperial Masquerade*, 58, 117.

34. Ibid., 119.

35. Ibid.

36. Wang Kefen 王克芬 and Long Yinpei 隆蔭培, eds., *Zhongguo jinxiandai dangdai wudao fazhanshi* 中國近現代舞蹈發展史 [The development history of modern and contemporary Chinese dance] (Beijing: Renmin yinyue chubanshe, 1999), 40–3.

37. Hayter-Menzies, *Imperial Masquerade*, 5–6; Yu Deling, *Two Years in the Forbidden City* (New York: Moffat, Yard and Company, 1911), 382; Song, *Mapping Modern Beijing*, 170–88.

38. Yu Rongling, *Qing gong suo ji*, 7, 41; Hayter-Menzies, *Imperial Masquerade*, 23–24.

39. Hayter-Menzies, *Imperial Masquerade*, xxiii, 4.

40. Ibid., 79–98.

41. Ibid., 100.

42. Ibid., 100–101; Yu Deling, *Lotos Petals*, 239.

43. Yu Deling, *Lotos Petals*, 231.

44. Ibid., 230–52.

45. Yu Rongling, "Qingmo wudaojia," 45; Yu Deling, *Lotos Petals*, 233.

46. Preston, *Modernism's Mythic Pose*, 148.

47. Daly, *Done into Dance*, 69.

48. Daly, *Done into Dance*, 124–31; Preston, *Modernism's Mythic Pose*, 5–12.

49. Yu Rongling, "Qingmo wudaojia," 44.

50. Yu Deling, *Kowtow*, 188–90; Hayter-Menzies, *Imperial Masquerade*, 11, 51.

51. Yu Deling, *Lotos Petals*, 236, quoted in Hayter-Menzies, *Imperial Masquerade*, 102.

52. Daly, *Done into Dance*, 170; Hayter-Menzies, *Imperial Masquerade*, 103; Yu Deling, *Lotos Petals*, 236–7.

53. Yu Deling, *Lotos Petals*, 234–36.

54. Ibid., 237.

55. Daly, *Done into Dance*, 81, 27–28, 42, 68.

56. Yu Deling, *Lotos Petals*, 237, quoted in Hayter-Menzies, *Imperial Masquerade*, 102.

57. Yu Rongling, "Qingmo wudaojia," 45.

58. Daly, *Done into Dance*, 80.

59. Yu Deling, *Lotos Petals*, 235–37.

60. This approach of "dance-sculptural iconography" was common among the pioneers of modern dance and performances around the turn of the century, which is called the "vitalist" paradigm—the paradoxical combination of a focus on "the dynamics of movement" and the "primarily static body imagery that was oriented along the lines of ancient sculpture." For example, Genevieve Stebbins (1857–1934) called her method "statue posing," which directly inspired Duncan. See Gabriele Brandstetter, *Poetics of Dance: Body, Image, and Space in the Historical Avant-Gardes* (Oxford: Oxford University Press, 2015), 49; Daly, *Done into Dance*, 103, 123, 125; Preston, *Modernism's Mythic Pose*, 12–20, 152–58, 169–70.

61. Yu Deling, *Lotos Petals*, 242.

62. Ibid., 240.

63. Ibid., 243.

64. Daly, *Done into Dance*, 130; Preston, *Modernism's Mythic Pose*, 99, 177–80.

65. Yu Deling, *Lotos Petals*, 240.

66. Isadora Duncan, "Beauty and Exercise," in *Art of the Dance*, ed. Sheldon Cheney (New York: Theatre Arts, 1969), 82, quoted in Preston, *Modernism's Mythic Pose*, 166.

67. Yu Deling, *Lotos Petals*, 243–34; see also Preston, *Modernism's Mythic Pose*, 157.

68. Yu Deling, *Lotos Petals*, 234, quoted in Hayter-Menzies, *Imperial Masquerade*, 102.

69. Isadora Duncan, *Der Tanz Der Zukunft* [The Dance of the Future], ed. & trans. Karl Federn (Eugen Biederici-is Leipzig, 1903).

70. Friedrich Nietzsche, *Thus Spoke Zarathustra: A Book for Everyone and No One* in *The Portable Nietzsche*, ed. Walter Kaufmann (New York, 1982), 126–27, quoted in Melissa Ragona, "Ecstasy, Primitivism, Modernity: Isadora Duncan and Mary Wigman," *American Studies* 35, no. 1 (1994): 47–62, 49. For Duncan's intellectual sources, see Daly, *Done into Dance*, 135; Preston, *Modernism's Mythic Pose*, 189. For a detailed account of the relationship among dance, evolution, materiality, and spirituality, see Daly, *Done into Dance*, 27–38, 67, 128–29, 152–53; Preston, *Modernism's Mythic Pose*, 161–62.

71. Duncan, *Der Tanz Der Zukunft*, 11, emphasis added.

72. Ibid., 14–15.

73. Francis, "From Event to Monument," 26, 29, 33; Daly, *Done into Dance*, 27, 30, 74, 109–20.

74. Angela Zito, "Bound to Be Represented: Theorizing/Fetishizing Footbinding," in *Embodied Modernities*, 21–41.

75. In fact, it seems that Duncan paid enthusiastic attention to China's (proto-)feminist cause. For example, she choreographed a dance work entitled *Long Live, the Liberation of Chinese Women* in the mid-1920s. See Wang and Long, *Zhongguo jinxiandai*, 45.

76. Zito, "Bound to Be Represented," 27; Preston, *Modernism's Mythic Pose*, 149.

77. Duncan, *Der Tanz Der Zukunft*, 12–13; Daly, *Done into Dance*, 31; Preston, *Modernism's Mythic Pose*, 165, 183.

78. Duncan, *Der Tanz Der Zukunft*, 22–23, emphasis added.

79. Ibid., 12.

80. Ibid., 18, emphasis added.

81. Ibid., 17. In some sense, this instability inherent in Duncan's philosophy of modern dance reflects a more general anxiety about constructing the nationality of America as a kind of universality that is in constant performing, unfolding, and evolving. This anxiety corresponds to the struggle of the United States, as an immigrant and assimilating nation, in its historic rise to a major global power around the turn of the century. See Andrew Hewitt, *Social Choreography: Ideology as Performance in Dance and Everyday Movement* (Durham and London: Duke University Press, 2005), 117–55. For the relationship between Haeckel's version of evolution theory and Duncan's dance philosophy, see Daly, *Done into Dance*, 98; Preston, *Modernism's Mythic Pose*, 161–62.

82. Emily Apter, "Acting Out Orientalism: Sapphic Theatricality in Turn-of-the-Century Paris," in *Performance and Cultural Politics*, ed. Elin Diamond (London: Routledge, 1996), 15–34; Michael Keevak, *Becoming Yellow: A Short History of Racial Thinking* (Princeton: Princeton University Press, 2011).

83. Yu Rongling, "Qingmo wudaojia," 45.

84. Emily Apter, "Acting Out Orientalism," 24, quoted in Dorf, "Dancing Greek Antiquity," 14.

85. Dorf, "Dancing Greek Antiquity," 14.

86. Daly, *Done into Dance*, 172–6; Preston, *Modernism's Mythic Pose*, 150.

87. Duncan, *Der Tanz Der Zukunft*, 24.

88. Ibid., 21–22.

89. Ibid., 23.

90. Ibid., 26.

91. Sterling Seagrave and Peggy Seagrave, *Dragon Lady: The Life and Legend of the Last Empress of China* (New York: Knopf, 1992); Hayter-Menzies, *Imperial Masquerade*, xxi; Yu Deling, *Two Years*, 315–16; Sarah Conger, *Letters from China* (Chicago: McClurg and Company, 1909), 247–48; Katherine Carl, *With the Empress Dowager of China* (New York: The Century Co., 1905).

92. Li and Zurndorfer, "Rethinking Empress Dowager Cixi," 6; Hayter-Menzies, *Imperial Masquerade*, 126.

93. Yu Rongling, *Qing gong suo ji*, 23–25; Yu Deling, *Two Years*, 140–44; Song, *Mapping Modern Beijing*, 170–88.

94. Jenny Huangfu Day, *Qing Travelers to the Far West: Diplomacy and the Information Order in Late Imperial China* (Cambridge: Cambridge University Press, 2018).

95. Ibid., 1–2. See also S. M. Mêng, *The Tsungli Yamen: Its Organization and Functions* (Cambridge: East Asian Research Center, 1962).

96. Day, *Qing Travelers*, 2.

97. Ibid., 2–3.

98. Ibid., 11, 154.

99. Ibid., 12–13.

100. Ibid., 15, 50–53.

101. Andrew Jones, *Developmental Fairy Tales: Evolutionary Thinking and Modern Chinese Culture* (Cambridge, MA: Harvard University Press, 2011), 5.

102. Hayter-Menzies, *Imperial Masquerade*, 147.

103. Yu Rongling, *Qing gong suo ji*, 36–37.

104. Yu Deling, *Two Years*, 24; Hayter-Menzies, *Imperial Masquerade*, 139.

105. Yu Deling, *Two Years*, 53.

106. "French Styles the Vogue in China," p. 5.

107. Yu Deling, *Two Years*, 8–9; Hayter-Menzies, *Imperial Masquerade*, 81, 125–26, 133.

108. Isaac Taylor Headland and Dr. Headland, *Court Life in China: The Capital, Its Officials and People* (New York: Fleming H. Revell Company, 1909), 105–6, quoted in Hayter-Menzies, *Imperial Masquerade*, 184.

109. Yu Deling, *Two Years*, 210 (emphasis added), quoted in Hayter-Menzies, *Imperial Masquerade*, 199.

110. Saying this does not suggest that Cixi necessarily had any direct knowledge about the scientific theory of evolution, but emphasizes the implied developmental linear temporality, which Cixi might pick up from some vernacular variants of evolutionary thinking in the "everyday discourse" discussed in Jones, *Developmental Fairy Tales*. As demonstrated by the expression "go backward," the evolutionary/developmental linear temporality had supplanted the traditional geo-cultural hierarchy of *hua yi zhi bie* 華夷之別 (the distinction between China and its peripheral).

111. Yu Deling, *Two Years*, 144; Hayter-Menzies, *Imperial Masquerade*, 189.

112. Yu Deling, *Two Years*, 53, 238; Hayter-Menzies, *Imperial Masquerade*, 146–47.

113. Yu Deling, *Two Years*, 234.

114. Yu Deling, *Two Years*, 50, 152, 188; Yu Rongling, *Qing gong suo ji*, 25.

115. Yu Deling, *Two Years*, 52–53.

116. Ibid., 356, emphasis added.

117. Yu Rongling, "Qingmo wudaojia," 45.

118. Ibid., 44; Ye Zufu 葉祖孚, "Xi taihou yuqian nüguan Yu Rongling (si)" 西太后御前女官裕容齡(四) [Yu Rongling: Lady in waiting of the West Empress Dowager (IV)], *Zongheng* 縱橫, no. 4 (1999): 34–38, 38.

119. Yu Deling, *Lotos Petals*, 232, 246; Yu Deling, *Two Years*, 102; Hayter-Menzies, *Imperial Masquerade*, 114–15, 125.

120. Hayter-Menzies, *Imperial Masquerade*, 114–15.

121. Yu Deling, *Two Years*, 101–102, quoted in Hayter-Menzies, *Imperial Masquerade*, 170.

122. Yu Deling, *Two Years*, 102–103; Hayter-Menzies, *Imperial Masquerade*, 172.

123. See, among many others, "The Dowager Being Modernized," *Arizona Republican*, July 20, 1903, 2. *Chronicling America: Historic American Newspapers*. Library of Congress. https://chroniclingamerica.loc.gov/lccn/sn84020558/1903-07-20/ed-1/seq-2/

124. Yu Deling, *Lotos Petals*, 250–51; Hayter-Menzies, *Imperial Masquerade*, 171.

125. Yu Rongling, *Qing gong suo ji*, 11. Here "Tian" refers to the secondary wife of the Chongzhen 崇禎 Emperor (Zhu Youjian 朱由檢). However, the official history only says that Tian "had many artistic talents" (*duo caiyi* 多才藝), but does not specifically mention dancing. See Zhang Tingyu 張廷玉 et al., "*Hou fei liezhuan* II" 后妃列傳第二 [The second biography of empresses and secondary imperial wives] in *Ming shi* 明史 [History of Ming] (Beijing: Zhonghua Shuju, 1974), vol. 114, 3528–46, 3545.

126. Yu Rongling, *Qing gong suo ji*, 40–41.

127. Yu Rongling, "Qingmo wudaojia," 44.

128. Yu Rongling, *Qing gong suo ji*, 8–10; Yu Deling, *Two Years*, 27–36.

129. Yu Rongling, "Qingmo wudaojia," 44.

130. Yu Deling, *Lotos Petals*, 239–40, 246–47.

131. Duncan, *Der Tanz Der Zukunft*, 22.

132. Compared with Yu Rongling's trainings in classical Japanese dance and ballet, the influence of Duncan's modern dance on Rongling's choreography should be

predominant. Yu Rongling's ballet training was only for a short term. As per Deling, the Yu sisters began their study with Duncan in either late 1900 or early 1901, which continued for more than two years (Yu Deling, *Lotos Petals*, 232, 239, *Kowtow*, 271), while according to Rongling, the study started in 1901 and lasted for two years (Yu Rongling, "Qingmo wudaojia," 45). Therefore, a reasonable estimation of the time when the Yu sisters ended their study with Duncan is sometime in late 1902. Because Rongling only began her ballet training after leaving Duncan's studio and the Yu family left France for China in early 1903 (Yu Rongling, "Qingmo wudaojia," 45; Hayter-Menzies, *Imperial Masquerade*, 123–24), the duration of Rongling's ballet training cannot be more than a year. While it is uncertain how long Rongling was trained in classical Japanese dance, it is known that the training method was imitation-based (Yu Rongling, "Qingmo wudaojia," 45), and Rongling was quite young then (around ten).

133. Immanuel C. Y. Hsu, "Late Ch'ing Foreign Relations, 1866–1905," in *The Cambridge History of China* (vol. 11), ed. John K. Fairbank and Kwang-Ching Liu (NY: Cambridge University Press, 1987), 70–141, 130–41.

134. Yu Rongling, *Qing gong suo ji*, 40–41.

135. Ibid.

136. Ibid.

137. Ibid. The picture of the "Greek dance" is from Yu, "Qingmo wudaojia," 44.

138. Note that Yu also performed a "Greek dance" in a ballet production back in Paris, which could be an "Egypto-Greek" hybrid. See Tong, *Minguo shiqi wudao*, 5. However, the dance gesture captured in the picture and the fact that Rongling was neither in ballet shoes nor en pointe both suggest that this "Greek dance" was unlikely to be a ballet.

139. Wang and Long, *Zhongguo jinxiandai*, 45.

140. Ibid.; Tian Han 田漢, "Shuo feng" 朔風 [The north wind], *Fan bao* 汎報 1, no. 1 (1927), reprinted in *Tian Han quan ji* 田漢全集 [The complete works of Tian Han] (Hebei: Huashan wenyi chubanshe, 2000), vol.13, 81–87; Alfred Westharp, "Xila shi wudao de yuanli" 希臘式舞蹈的原理 [The rationale of the Greek-style dance], *Beiyang hua bao* 北洋畫報, no. 49 (1926): 4; Pantu 叛徒, "Dengken tiaowu tuan" 登肯跳舞團 [The Duncan dance troupe], *Liang you* 良友, no. 12 (1927): 17.

141. Tian, "Shuo feng," 83, Italicized parts are written in English in the original text.

142. Ibid.

143. Ibid., 84.

144. Ibid., 84–85, Italicized parts are written in English in the original text.

145. This intersection of artistic avant-garde and political vanguard was also a persisting theme characterizing Tian's own artistic pursuit throughout his life. See Liang Luo, *The Avant-Garde and the Popular in Modern China: Tian Han and the Intersection of Performance and Politics* (Ann Arbor: University of Michigan, 2014).

146. Ellen Graff, *Stepping Left: Dance and Politics in New York City, 1928–1942* (Durham: Duke University Press, 1997), 21.

Chapter 2

1. Wu Xiaobang 吳曉邦, *Wo de wudao yishu shengya* 我的舞蹈藝術生涯 [My artistic career of dance] (Beijing: Zhongguo xiju chubanshe, 1982), reprinted in *Wu Xiaobang wudao wenji* 吳曉邦舞蹈文集 [Anthology of Wu Xiaobang on Dance], ed. Feng Shuangbai 馮霜白 and Yu Ping 余平 (Beijing: Zhongguo wenlian chubanshe, 2007), vol. 1, 1–162, 1–16.

   For readers not familiar with the history of modern China, I provide in this footnote some historical context by briefly covering relevant historical events, to fill in the temporal gap between Yu Rongling's 1904 dance concert discussed toward the end of chapter 1 and Wu Xiaobang's travels to Japan in the late 1920s and 1930s. For a more detailed conventional account, see Jonathan Spence, *The Search for Modern China* (3rd edition) (Norton & Company Ltd., 2013), 255–459.

   Both Empress Dowager Cixi and Emperor Guangxu died in 1908, and three years later the Qing dynasty fell. In 1912, the Republic of China was founded, with Sun Zhongshan 孫中山 (or Sun Yat-sen, 1866–1925) being the provisional president, who was soon replaced by Yuan Shikai 袁世凱 (1859–1916), the former Qing minister who supplied the Western music band that accompanied Yu's court concert. Yuan failed miserably in holding the new republic together, and provincial warlords became the dominant power brokers in China from the late 1910s to late 1920s. In the meantime, foreign imperialist influences continued to grow in China, with Japan emerging as the most aggressive threat from the north, especially after the Japanese occupation of Manchuria in 1933. Despite the escalating tension between the two countries, Japan, as the major cultural mediator between the West and East Asia, had been a popular destination for Chinese students to study abroad since the turn of the century until mid-1930s.

   Frustrated by a series of less-than-effective attempts to modernize China, many Chinese intellectuals, since the mid-1910s, came to agree that a major obstacle to China's modernization and self-strengthening was the "feudalist ideology" deeply rooted in the minds of the masses. Therefore, they proposed to establish and disseminate a "new culture" (mainly western or westernized cultures) to replace or reform the "old culture." This is generally known as the "May Fourth Movement." Some of the leading May Fourth intellectuals turned to Marxist socialism for a solution, and the Chinese Communist Party (CCP) was founded in 1921.

   Towards the common goal of battling warlordism, landlordism, and foreign imperialism, the Communists and the Sun Zhongshan-led Nationalists (or Guomindang) formed an alliance to establish a new military and political base in Guangzhou, south China. After Sun's death in 1925, the leadership of the alliance was seized by the Nationalist leader Jiang Jieshi 蔣介石 (or Chiang Kai-shek, 1887–1975). In 1926, the Nationalist-Communist alliance launched a successful military campaign, known as the Northern Expedition or the Great Revolution, to reunify China under a single central government, a goal achieved nominally in 1928. However, due to irreconcilable disagreements over social policy and power struggle, the alliance broke up in 1927 and the Communists were purged. Forced out of big cities, the Communists established their own military and political bases in southern rural China but had to give those up in 1934 under sustained military attacks by the Jiang-led Nationalists. After the Long March, the Communists reestablished their stronghold in the barren north in 1935. Under the pressure of the looming Japanese invasion and a public tired of endless civil wars, the two sides renewed their alliance in 1937. The alliance lasted until the end of WWII, when a new civil war broke out in 1945, which ended in 1949 with the victorious Communists founding the People's Republic of China and the Nationalists retreating to Taiwan.

2. Wu, *Wo de wudao*, 18.

3. Ibid., 93. For a brief introduction to the May Fourth Movement, see footnote 1, or Spence, *The Search for Modern China*, 286–95. Among other dance practitioners who contributed to this enduring endeavor, Dai Ailian, who studied central European modern dance and ballet in England, is another important figure. Dai participated in this cause only after 1940 and her major contribution was primarily concentrated on ethnic and folk dance and, later, ballet. See chapter 4 in this book and also Richard Glasstone, *The Story of Dai Ailian: Icon of Chinese Folk Dance, Pioneer of Chinese Ballet* (Alton: Dance Books Limited, 2007); Wang Kefen 王克芬 and Long Yinpei 隆蔭培, eds., *Zhongguo jinxiandai dangdai wudao fazhanshi* 中國近現代當代舞蹈發展史 [The development history of modern and contemporary Chinese dance] (Beijing: Renmin yinyue chubanshe, 1999), 72–80; Tong Yan 仝妍, *Minguo shiqi wudao yanjiu* 1912–1949 民國時期舞蹈研究 1912–1949 [Research on the dance of the Republican era 1912–1949] (Beijing: Zhongyang minzu daxue chubanshe, 2013), 69–71, 88–89; Emily Wilcox, *Revolutionary Bodies: Chinese Dance and the Socialist Legacy* (Oakland: University of California Press, 2019), 13–47. For other secondary yet non-negligible forces shaping the new dance movement in China, see Wang and Long, *Zhongguo jinxiandai*; Tong, *Minguo shiqi*.

4. Lu Xun 魯迅, *Jottings under Lamplight*, ed. Eileen J. Cheng and Kirk A. Denton (Cambridge: Harvard University Press, 2017), 20–21.

5. Ibid., 21.

6. Emily Wilcox discusses some artistic practices of Wu Xiaobang in the period under study here, but neither Wu nor the transnational travel and adaptation of modern dance in China is her primary focus; see Emily Wilcox, "Dancers Doing Fieldwork: Socialist Aesthetics and Bodily Experience in the People's Republic of China," *Journal for the Anthropological Study of Human Movement* 17, no. 2 (Fall 2010): 6–16; Wilcox, *Revolutionary Bodies*, 24–32.

As for the Chinese scholarship on Wu, his endeavor of learning and performing modern dance in Japan and China in this period is too often hastily subsumed into a "leftist" narrative characterized by a linear transition from the "bourgeois" (modernism) to the "revolutionary" (leftism, realism), rather than being treated as a complicated transnational and transcultural phenomenon in its own right, fraught with problems and dilemmas. Moreover, the issues associated with the unique characteristic of dance—using the physical body and its movement as the primary artistic medium—has not yet been explicitly and adequately addressed. This chapter aims to overcome these two major shortcomings. Also, the existing Chinese historiography on Wu tends to overly identify him with the leftist artistic camp in the 1930s, largely a result of retrospectively extrapolating Wu's experience as a CCP member since 1949 to his earlier life (so did Wu himself too, to some extent) under ideological imperative. The current study shows that, just as in the cases of many contemporary artists, the "bourgeois" aspect of Wu coexisted uneasily yet symbiotically with his "leftist" aspect during this period (actually throughout his whole life), and thus complicated the image of Wu in the current Chinese dance historiography. See, for example, Wang and Long, *Zhongguo jinxiandai*, 64–72; Tong, *Minguo shiqi*, 57–59, 67–69.

7. Susan L. Foster, "Movement's Contagion: the Kinesthetic Impact of Performance," in *The Cambridge Companion to Performance Studies*, ed. Tracy C. Davis (Cambridge: Cambridge University Press, 2008), 46–59; Susan L. Foster, "Dancing with the 'Mind's Muscles': A Brief History of Kinesthesia and Empathy," keynote address, presented at the conference "Kinesthetic Empathy: Concepts and Contexts," University of Manchester, April 2010, http://www.watchingdance.ning.com; Susan L. Foster, *Choreographing Empathy: Kinesthesia in Performance* (New York: Routledge, 2011).

8. John Martin, *The Dance* (New York: Tudor Publishing Company, 1946), 105, quoted in Foster, "Movement's Contagion," 2008, 49.

9. For example, see Jing Jiang, "From Foot Fetish to Hand Fetish: Hygiene, Class, and the New Woman," *Positions: East Asia Cultures Critique* 22, no. 1 (2014): 131–59.

10. Carrie Preston, *Modernism's Mythic Pose: Gender, Genre, Solo Performance* (Oxford: Oxford University Press, 2011), 17–18, 174–75.

11. According to the statistics provided by the Ministry of Education of the Republican government, in 1926, the rate of illiteracy among adults in the Zhabei District 閘北 區 of Shanghai, where the labor class was concentrated, was as high as 78 percent. The percentage of school-age children that were not in school was about 80, and these figures should be at the lower end compared with those of other areas in China, which were typically much less developed than metropolitan Shanghai. See Shanghai shi defang zhi bangongshi上海市地方志辦公室 [Office of the Local Chronicles of Shanghai], *Shanghai chengren jiaoyu zhi* 上海成人教育志 [The chronicle of adult education in Shanghai], http://www.shtong.gov.cn/node2/node2245/node82368/node82374/index.html.

12. Andrew Hewitt, *Social Choreography: Ideology as Performance in Dance and Everyday Movement* (Durham and London: Duke University Press, 2005), 6–11, 117–23. Hewitt is careful to note that his division of the literate and the postliterate is highly schematic and he uses it only to highlight this particular strategy of modern dance to establish its legitimacy in the United States.

13. Mark Franko, *Dance as Text: Ideologies of the Baroque Body* (revised edition) (New York: Oxford University Press, 2015), xix.

14. Elizabeth Francis, "From Event to Monument: Modernism, Feminism, and Isadora Duncan," *American Studies* 35, no.1 (1994): 25–45, 44.

15. Wu Xiaobang, "Queli xin de wudao yishuguan" 確立新的舞蹈藝術觀 [Establishing a New Artistic View of Dance] [1985], reprinted in *Wu Xiaobang wudao wenji*, vol. 3, 54–61, 55.

16. For example, Andrew F Jones, *Yellow Music: Media Culture and Colonial Modernity in the Chinese Jazz Age* (Durham: Duke University Press, 2001); Xiaobing Tang, *Origins of the Chinese Avant-garde: The Modern Woodcut Movement* (University of California Press, 2008); Siyuan Liu, *Performing Hybridity in Colonial-Modern China* (New York: Palgrave MacMillan, 2013); Liang Luo, *The Avant-Garde and the Popular in Modern China: Tian Han and the Intersection of Performance and Politics* (Ann Arbor: University of Michigan, 2014).

17. Wang and Long, *Zhongguo jinxiandai*, 43–51; Tong, *Minguo shiqi*, 8–14; Andrew D. Field, *Shanghai's Dancing World: Cabaret Culture and Urban Politics, 1919–1954* (Hong Kong: The Chinese University of Hong Kong, 2010); Wilcox, *Revolutionary Bodies*, 119–55.

18. In 1939, Wu indeed attempted to appropriate the influence of ballet by advertising his first dance drama *Yingsu hua* 罌粟花 (The poppy flower) as a "modern ballet." This strategy—which tried to exploit the common conflation of "ballet" with all kinds of "dance drama" in the Chinese popular perception—backfired, as reflected in the harsh reviews by the advocates of ballet. For example, Si San 思三 criticizes Wu for his "over-publicizing" the dance drama by illegitimately associating his "naïve" work with the mature genre of ballet. It seems that, since then, Wu had forsaken this strategy for good. See Qin Tailai 秦泰來 and Du Ao 杜鰲, "Zhongguo zhi xinxing wuyong ju" 中國之新型舞踊劇 [China's new dance drama], *Liang you huabao* 良友畫報, no. 141 (1939): 38–39; Si San 思三, "Ballet yu zhongguo wu ju de qiantu" Ballet 與中國舞劇的前途 [Ballet and the future of China's dance drama], *Zuo Feng* 作風, no.1 (1941): 114–20.

19. Kusaka Shirō 日下四郎, *Modan dansu shukkō: Takada Seiko to tomo ni* モダン・ダンス出航: 高田せい子とともに [Starting the journey of modern dance with Takada Seiko] (Tōkyō: Mokujisha, Shōwa, 1976), 78–100.

20. Wu Xiaobang, *Wudao xue yanjiu* 舞蹈學研究 [Research on dance] (Beijing: Zhongguo wenlian chubanshe, 1991), reprinted in *Wu Xiaobang wudao wenji*, vol. 2, 223–316, 228; Wu, *Wo de wudao*, 21.

21. Wu, *Wo de wudao*, 23.

22. For general studies on modern Japanese dance, see Michiko Toki 土岐迪子, *Kindai Nihon josei shi: geinō* 近代日本女性史: 芸能 [The history of Japanese women: performance arts] (Tōkyō: Kajima Kenkyujo Shuppankai, 1970); Kuniyoshi Kazuko 國吉和子, *Yumeo no ishō kioku no tsubo: buyō to modanizumu* 夢の衣裳・記憶の壺: 舞踊とモダニズム [The clothes of dreams and the jar of memories: dance and modernism] (Tōkyō: Shinshokan, 2002); Nishimiya Yasuichirō 西宮安一郎, ed., *Modan dansu Eguchi Takaya to geijutsu nendaishi* モダンダンス江口隆哉と芸術年代史: 自1900年至1978年 [Modern dance and the chronicle of the arts of Eguchi Takaya: from 1900 to 1978] (Tōkyō: Tokyo Shinbun Shuppankyoku, 1989); Nishikata Setsuko 西形節子, *Kindai Nihon buyōshi* 近代日本舞踊史 [The history of modern Japanese dance] (Tōkyō: Engeki Shuppansha, 2006).

23. Wei Bu 葦布, "Wangshi nanwang" 往事難忘 [The unforgettable past] [1982], reprinted in *Wu Xiaobang wudao wenji*, vol. 1, 183–97, 189–90.

24. Nishimiya, *Modan dansu Eguchi Takaya to geijutsu nendaishi*, 1989; Sondra Fraleign and Tamah Nakamura, *Hijikata Tatsumi and Ohno Kazuo* (New York: Routledge, 2006), 14.

25. Ibid.

26. Carol-Lynne Moore, *The Harmonic Structure of Movement, Music, and Dance According to Rudolf Laban: An Examination of His Unpublished Writings and Drawings* (Lewiston: The Edwin Mellen Press, 2009).

27. Ibid.

28. Susan Manning, *Ecstasy and the Demon: The Dances of Mary Wigman* (Minneapolis: University of Minnesota Press, 2006), 47–84.

29. For detailed technicality of the training content, see Wu, *Wo de wudao*, 23–34.

30. Nikaido Akiko, "Takada Eguchi's Creative Methodology and Ideas through the Influence of M. Wigman," Taipei DRST paper, April 5 (2010); Manning, *Ecstasy and the Demon*, 44; Dee Reynolds, *Rhythmic Subjects: Uses of Energy in the Dances of Mary Wigmany, Martha Graham and Merce Cunningham* (UK: Dance Books, 2007), 4; Lucia Ruprecht, "Gesture, Interruption, Vibration: Rethinking Early Twentieth-Century Gestural Theory and Practice in Walter Benjamin, Rudolf Von Laban, and Mary Wigman," *Dance Research Journal* 47, no. 2 (2015): 23–41, 25.

31. Eguchi Takaya 江口隆哉, *Wudao chuangzuo fa* 舞蹈創作法 [Buyō Sōsakuhō 舞踊創作法, Methodology of dance creation], trans. Jin Qiu 金秋 (Beijing: Xueyuan chubanshe, 2005), 6–7.

32. Wu, *Wo de wudao*, 30.

33. Ibid., 28, 32.

34. Nikaido, "Takada Eguchi's Creative Methodology"; Manning, *Ecstasy and the Demon*, 47.

35. Takaya, *Wudao chuangzuo fa*, 3–5.

36. Wu, *Wo de wudao*, 27.

37. Ibid., 28.

38. Ibid., 38, 45–9; Wu Xiaobang 吳晓邦, "Guanyu *Yingsu hua* de yanchu" 關於罌粟花的演出 [On the performance of *The Poppy Flower*], *Wenxian* 文獻, no. 6 (1939): 215–18; Shide 拾得, "Xinxing wuyong ju *Yingsu hua* de yanchu (fu tupian) shi ren shifen xingfen" 新型舞踊劇"罌粟花"的演出(附圖片)使人十分興奮 [The performance of the new dance drama *The Poppy Flower* (with pictures) was very exciting], *Shen bao* 申報 (February 23, 1939): 18.

39. For Wu's system of training methods and theory, see Wu Xiaobang 吳曉邦, *Xin wudao yishu chubu jiaocheng* 新舞蹈藝術初步教程 [An elementary textbook for the art of new dance] (Wuhan: Huazhong Xinhua shudian, 1949); Wu Xiaobang 吳曉邦, *Xin wudao yishu gailun* 新舞蹈藝術概論 [A brief introduction to the art of new dance] [1950, 1951, 1982], reprinted in *Wu Xiaobang wudao wenji*, vol. 2, 3–222.

40. Wu, *Wo de wudao*, 25.

41. Wu formed many personal connections with both established and young artists based in Shanghai, such as the painter Ye Qianyu 葉淺予, the musician and composer Chen Gexin 陳歌辛, and the playwright and theater actor Ouyang Yuqian 歐陽予倩. Many of these connections turned into lifelong friendships and played a crucial role later in Wu's dance career. See Wu, *Wo de wudao*, 20–23.

42. Isadora Duncan, *My Life* (Garden City: Garden City Publishing Company, 1927), 175; Wu, *Wo de wudao*, 27.

43. Francis, "From Event to Monument," 37.

44. For Duncan's earlier conceptualization of the relationship among body, movement, mind, and spirit, see Ann Daly, *Done into Dance: Isadora Duncan in America* (Bloomington: Indiana University Press, 1995), 27–38, 67, 128–9, 152–3; Preston, *Modernism's Mythic Pose*, 161–62.

45. Daly, *Done into Dance*, 152–53.

46. Eguchi Takaya, "Buttai buyō no teishō: odori te no inai buyō," 物體舞踊の提唱: 踊リ手のいない舞踊 [Promoting the object dance: dance without a dancer], in Nishimiya, *Modan dansu Eguchi Takaya to geijutsu nendaishi*, 231.

47. Wu Xiaobang, "Wuyong yishu jianghua" 舞踊藝術講話 [A talk on the art of dance] [1940], reprinted in *Yidai wudao dashi: jinian Wu Xiaobang wenji* 一代舞蹈大師：紀念吳曉邦文集 [The great dance master: an anthology in memorial of Wu Xiaobang], ed. Jia Zuoguang 賈作光 (Beijing: Wudao zazhi chubanshe, 1996), 272–8.

48. This is based on a survey of the frequencies of the two words appearing in *Shenbao* 申報 since the 1910s.

49. Wu, "Wuyong yishu," 272.

50. Mark Franko, *Dancing Modernism/Performing Politics* (Bloomington: Indiana University Press, 1995), 2.

51. Wei, "Wangshi," 190.

52. Wu Xiaobang 吳曉邦, "Wo duiyu *Xishi* zhong pailian ju de wuyong de yidian yijian" 我對於 "西施" 中排練劇的舞踊的一點意見 [My opinion on the choreography of dramatic dance in *Xishi*], *Xinren zhoukan* 新人周刊 2, no. 4 (1935): 63; Wu, *Wo de wudao*, 22; Jia, *Yidai wudao dashi*, 334; Xiang Yang 向陽, "Cong yue ju *Xishi* kan zuoyouyi juren de yichang lunzheng" 從樂劇《西施》看左右翼劇人的一場論爭 [A debate between the leftist and rightist practitioners of theater: the musical drama *Xishi* as a case], *Xiju yishu* 戲劇藝術, no.3 (2013): 70–81.

53. Xiang, "Cong yue ju *Xishi*."

54. Wu, "Wo duiyu *Xishi*."

55. Wu Xiaobang 吳曉邦, "Zai kangzhan zhong shengzhang qilai de wuyong yishu" 在抗戰中生長起來的舞踊藝術 [The dance art growing up in the war of resistance], *Zhong Su wenhua* 中蘇文化 9, no. 1 (1941): 96–98, 96.

56. Wu, *Wo de wudao*, 55.

57. Wu, "Wuyong yishu," 273. The word "dancing" is written in English in the original text.

58. See Wu Xiaobang 吳曉邦, "Wutai renti yundong xunlian fa de guoqu he xianzai" 舞臺人體運動訓練法的過去和現在 [The past and present of the training method of human bodily movement onstage], *Kangzhan xiju* 抗戰戲劇 2, no. 10 (1938): 3–6. In the same article, Wu stated that "dance training has become a required course for not just dancers but also all stage artists . . . as long as being well trained in this method, [stage performers] can play any role onstage," and that "the maturing scientific training method of [central European modern] dance has gradually attracted attention in China. Because it [the method] can enable the talented stage performers to

shorten the time needed to achieve technical maturity, and, at the same time, without groping blindly." See Wu, "Wutai renti yundong," 5–6.

59. Wu, "Zai kangzhan zhong," 97.

60. Wu, *Wo de wudao*, 55.

61. Wu, "Wuyong yishu," 275.

62. Daly, *Done into Dance*, 2.

63. Manning, *Ecstasy and the Demon*, 34.

64. Ibid., 209.

65. Eguchi, *Wudao chuangzuo fa*, 9–12.

66. Feng and Yu, *Wu Xiaobang wudao wenji*, vol. 5, 4.

67. Wu, "Queli xin," 55.

68. Wu, *Xin wudao yishu gailun*, 39–40.

69. Lu Jiabin 盧家彬, "Shige duan ping wuyong" 詩歌短品舞踊 [Poetic short dance], *Qingnian shenghuo* 青年生活 1, no. 4 (1939): 14.

70. Wu had recorded the audience's reactions to his public performance of this work: "I choreographed a dance with the theme 'perpetual motion' . . . however, at the end, people all shook their heads and did not understand it." See Wu, *Wudao xue yanjiu*, 229.

71. Ellen Graff, *Stepping Left: Dance and Politics in New York City, 1928–1942* (Durham: Duke University Press, 1997).

72. Manning, *Ecstasy and the Demon*, 131–66, 221–54.

73. Daly, *Done into Dance*, 115, 148, 152–53, 184.

74. Franko, *Dancing Modernism*, 57–64; Gay Morris, *A Game for Dancers: Performing Modernism in the Postwar Years, 1945–1960* (Middletown: Wesleyan University Press, 2006), 20–4; Mark Franko, *Choreographing Discourses: A Mark Franko Reader*, ed. Mark Franko with Alessandra Nicifero (New York: Routledge, 2019), 30–31.

75. Susan Manning, "The Female Dancer and the Male Gaze: Feminist Critiques of Early Modern Dance," in *Meaning in Motion: New Cultural Studies of Dance*, ed. Jane Desmond (Durham: Duke University Press, 1997), 153–66, 146.

76. See, for example, Liu, *Performing Hybridity*, 150–53; Luo, *The Avant-Garde and the Popular*, 114–8; Joshua Goldstein, *Drama Kings: Players and Publics in the Re-creation of Peking Opera, 1870–1937* (Berkeley: University of California Press, 2007).

77. This may be ascribed to Chinese audience's "habit" of viewing traditional drama *xiqu* which integrates music and dance; see Xiang, "Cong yue ju *Xishi*," 70–81; Liu, *Performing Hybridity*, 150–53; Goldstein, *Drama Kings*.

78. Wang and Long, *Zhongguo jinxiandai*, 61–62; Tong, *Minguo shiqi*, 75–76, 89–90.

79. The difference between *yue ju* and Avshalomov's musical is that the former is first and foremost a drama, with music being only a supplement, while in the latter music is of primacy.

80. These introductions of Wu's dance works are not anything like advertisements for public performances, or program guidelines for audience. They are materials prepared by Wu purposefully for the historiography of his dance works and career. For this reason, it would have been reasonable to include accounts of dance movements. Wu's other writings, like dance textbooks and theories, show that he was fully capable of writing movement analyses. However, this part is not included in his collected writings. See Feng and Yu, *Wu Xiaobang wudao wenji*, vol. 5.

81. Dance works mentioned here include: *Kuilei* 傀儡 (The puppet, 1933), percussion music, first performed in Tokyo, Japan; *Wu jingzhi de dong* 無靜止的動 (Perpetual motion, 1933), performed in Tokyo, Japan; *Songzang qu* 送葬曲 (Funeral march, 1935), music by Frédéric Chopin, performed in Shanghai; *Huangpu Jiang bian* 黃浦江畔 (By the Huangpu River, 1935), music by Chopin, performed in Shanghai; *Ai de bei'ai* 愛的悲哀 (Love's Sorrow, 1935), music by Fritz Kreisler, performed in Shanghai. See Feng and Yu, *Wu Xiaobang wudao wenji*, vol. 5.

82. Wu Xiaobang 吳曉邦, "Ertong changge wudao shuoming" 兒童唱歌舞蹈説明 [An introduction to the singing-dance for children], *Yue feng* 樂風 1, no. 10 (1941): 15–16.

83. Patrick Carnegy, *Wagner and the Art of the Theatre* (New Haven: Yale University Press, 2006), 46–49; Daly, *Done into Dance*, 145.

84. For example, Liu, *Performing Hybridity*, 150–3; Luo, *The Avant-Garde and the Popular*, 115.

85. Wu, *Wo de wudao*, 21–22; Feng and Yu, *Wu Xiaobang wudao wenji*, vol. 5, 3.

86. Wei, "Wangshi," 189, 195.

87. Ibid., 195–96.

88. Feng and Yu, *Wu Xiaobang wudao wenji*, vol. 5, 3.

89. Ibid.

90. Wei Bu 韋布, "Ji Wu Xiaobang" 紀念吳曉邦 [In memorial of Wu Xiaobang] in *Yidai wudao dashi*, 43–4.

91. Wei, "Wangshi," 189.

92. For similar considerations, see, for example, Hannah Kosstrin, *Honest Bodies: Revolutionary Modernism in the Dances of Anna Sokolow* (New York: Oxford University Press).

93. Wu, *Wo de wudao*, 33–4.

94. Feng and Yu, *Wu Xiaobang wudao wenji*, vol. 5, 11–2.

95. Ibid.

96. Wu, *Wo de wudao*, 8–11.

97. Ibid., 10.

98. Ibid., 8.

99. Ibid., 14–5.

100. See Chen Gexin 陳歌辛, "Zuo yi" 作揖 [Taking a bow], *Xinren zhoukan* 新人周刊 2, no.4 (1935): 64.

101. Ibid.

102. Wu, "Wo duiyu *Xishi*," 63.

103. Ibid.

104. Jones, *Yellow Music*, 112.

105. See also Luo, *The Avant-Garde and the Popular*, 145–76.

106. Chen Gexin 陳歌辛, "*Yingsu hua* de yinyue, dengdeng" "罌粟花"的音樂, 等等 [The music of *The Poppy Flower*, etc.], *Wenxian* 文獻 no. 6 (1939): 218.

107. Ibid.

108. Wu, *Wo de wudao*, 36–9.

109. Feng and Yu, *Wu Xiaobang wudao wenji*, vol. 5, 14.

110. Jones, *Yellow Music*, 121–22.

111. Feng and Yu, *Wu Xiaobang wudao wenji*, vol. 5, 16.

112. Ibid.; See also Tang, *Origins of the Chinese Avant-garde*.

113. Wu, *Wo de wudao*, 37; Feng and Yu, *Wu Xiaobang wudao wenji*, vol. 5, 16.

114. Wu, *Wo de wudao*, 37–8.

115. Du Xuan 杜宣, "Cong pannizhe dao tuohuangzhe" 從叛逆者到拓荒者 [From a rebel to a pioneer] [1982]; He Minshi 何敏士, "Liangshi. Yaolan: Yi Wuxiaobang laoshi zaonian zai Guangdong banxue" 良師, 搖籃: 憶吳曉邦老師早年在廣東辦學 [Good mentor, cradle: recollecting Teacher Wu Xiaobang's teaching early in Guangdong] [1982]; Chen Ming 陳明, "Yi Wuxiaobang laoshi zai 'Xinlü' de jiaoxue yu yishu huodong" 憶吳曉邦老師在"新旅"的教學與藝術活動 [Teacher Wu Xiaobang's teaching and artistic activities in "Xinlü"] [2006]; Bu He 布赫, "Wu Xiaobang yu Nei Menggu xin wudao yishu" 吳曉邦與內蒙古新舞蹈藝術 [Wu Xiaobang and the art of New Dance in Inner Mongolian] [2001], reprinted in *Wu Xiaobang wudao wenji*, vol. 1, 178, 181; 199; 216; 222.

116. Jones, *Yellow Music*, 122.

117. Matthew Reason and Dee Reynolds, "Kinesthesia, Empathy, and Related Pleasures: An Inquiry into Audience Experiences of Watching Dance," *Dance Research Journal* 42, no. 2 (Winter 2010): 49–75.

118. Thus, kinesthesia has a close affinity with the concept of "performativity." In particular, kinesthesia provides a bodily mechanism through which a sense of collective identity is not only formed and embodied but also "activated" by the bodily movements of the individual performer(s), and the ideological discourse is not only materialized but also "animated" by the bodily performance.

119. Wu, *Wo de wudao*, 37.

120. Ibid., 37–8.

121. Ibid., 38.

122. Wu Xiaobang 吳曉邦, "Jinjun wu de chuangzuo ji yanchu de zongjie (jielu)" 進軍舞的創作及演出的總結 (節錄) [A summary of the creation and performance of the *Dance of the Strategic Offense* (excerpt)], *Wenyi bao* 文藝報 1, no. 9 (1949): 10–12.

123. Feng Shuangbai 馮霜白, "Xin wudao yishu de xianqu: Wu Xiaobang" 新舞蹈藝術的先驅 [The pioneer of the art of new dance: Wu Xiaobang], in *Yidai wudao dashi*, 223.

124. Wu, "Jinjun wu," 10.

125. Ibid., 11–12; Yan Ke 彥克, "Xian gei renmin he shidai de wudao: yi Wu Xiaobang de Jinjun wu chuangzuo" 獻給人民和時代的舞蹈——憶吳曉邦的《進軍舞》創作 [Dance presented to the people and the times: a recollection of Wu Xiaobang's creation of the *Jinjun wu*] [1982], reprinted in *Wu Xiaobang wudao wenji*, vol. 5, 108–9.

126. Feng and Yu, *Wu Xiaobang wudao wenji*, vol. 5, 43–94. For a detailed analysis of one of the works mentioned here, *Si fan* 思凡, see chapter 3 in this book and "The Conflicted Monk: Choreographic Adaptations of *Si fan* in Japan's and China's New Dance Movements," in *Corporeal Politics: Dancing East Asia*, ed. Emily Wilcox and Katherine Mezur (Ann Arbor: The University of Michigan Press, 2020), 60–77.

127. See Lu, "Shige duan ping," 14.

Chapter 3

1. The Beijing Dance School held its first class in Beijing's Xiang Er Alley in 1954 and was later moved to the Baijia Zhuang in Beijing in the same year. It was relocated to #19 Taoran Road in 1955. See *Xuanwu wenshi* 宣武文史 [The culture and history of the Xuanwu district] (Beijing: Zhongguo zhengzhi xieshang weiyuanhui xuanwuqu wenshi ziliao weiyuanhui, 1997), vol. 6, 117.

2. For an account of the founding of the Beijing Dance School and the development of its curriculum, see Emily Wilcox, *Revolutionary Bodies: Chinese Dance and the Socialist Legacy* (Oakland: University of California Press, 2019), 48–77.

3. "Beijing wudao xuexiao fangwenji" 北京舞蹈學校訪問記 [A record of visiting the Beijing Dance School], *Wudao* 舞蹈, no. 1 (1958): 22–24; see also the journal *Wu xiao jianshe* 舞校建設, no. 1 (1957).

4. Following Alan J. Berkowitz, throughout this chapter, the orthography "Taoist" (and Taoism) is reserved for "the general philosophical bent (often called 'philosophical Taosim') that has found expression in such texts as the *Zhuangzi* and the *Laozi*. The orthography 'Daoist' (and Daoism) is used when referring to China's indigenous system of religious beliefs whose codification began in the second through fourth centuries of the Common Era." See Alan J. Berkowitz, *Patterns of Disengagement: The Practice and Portrayal of Reclusion in Early Medieval China* (Stanford: Stanford University Press, 2000), 2–3n.

5. Pu Yimian 蒲以勉, "Wudao de bieyang nianhua: shenghuo zai tianma wudao gongzuoshi" 舞蹈的別樣年華：生活在天馬舞蹈工作室 [A special time of dance: living in the Tianma dance studio] [2006], in *Wu Xiaobang wudao wenji* 吳曉邦舞蹈文集 [Anthology of Wu Xiaobang on Dance], ed. Feng Shuangbai 馮霜白 and Yu Ping 余平 (Beijing: Zhongguo wenlian chubanshe, 2007), vol. 1, 268–78, 272.

6. Li Shan 李山, "Wu Xiaobang tongzhi zhuchi de Tianma Wudao Gongzuoshi jijiang chengli" 吳曉邦同志主持的天馬舞蹈工作室即將成立 [Tianma Dance Studio, headed by Comrade Wu Xiaobang, will soon be founded], *Wudao tongxun* 舞蹈通訊, no. 12 (1956): 2.

7. In fact, Wu advocated the corporatization of state-owned song-and-dance ensembles nationwide. See Wu Xiaobang 吳曉邦, "Ge wu yishu fazhan shang de jige wenti" 歌舞藝術發展上的幾個問題 [Several problems concerning the development of the arts of singing and dance], *Renmin ribao* 人民日報 (March 22, 1957): 3; Wu Xiaobang, "Yige xin wudao qimengzhe de zibai" 一個新舞蹈啟蒙者的自白 [The confession of an enlightener of New dance] [ca. 1980], in *Wu Xiaobang wudao wenji*, vol. 1,163–74; Wu Xiaobang, *Wo de wudao yishu shengya* 我的舞蹈藝術生涯 [My artistic career of dance] (Beijing: Zhongguo xiju chubanshe, 1982), reprinted and expanded in *Wu Xiaobang wudao wenji*, vol. 1, 1–174, 129–54.

8. Shen Zhihua 沈志華, *Sikao yu xuanze: cong zhishifenzi huiyi dao fan youpai yundong* 思考與選擇：從知識分子會議到反右派運動 (1956–1957) [Reflections and choices: from the Conference on the Issues of Intellectuals to the Anti-Rightist Campaign (1956–1957)], *Zhonghua renmin gongheguo shi, di san juan* 中華人民共和國史, 第三卷 [The history of the People's Republic of China, Volume 3] (Hong

Kong: Research Centre for Contemporary Chinese Culture, The Chinese University of Hong Kong, The Chinese University Press, 2008); Lin Yunhui 林蘊暉, *Wutuobang yundong: cong Da yue jin dao Da jihuang* (1958–1961) 烏托邦運動: 從大躍進到大饑荒 (1958–1961) [The utopian movement: from The Great Leap Forward to the Great Famine (1958–1961)], *Zhonghua renmin gongheguo shi, di san juan* 中華人民共和國史, 第四卷 [The history of the People's Republic of China, Volume 4] (Hong Kong: Research Centre for Contemporary Chinese Culture, The Chinese University of Hong Kong, The Chinese University Press, 2008)

9. Ibid., 278; Feng and Yu, *Wu Xiaobang wudao wenji*, vol. 5, 209.

10. Wu, *Wo de wudao*, 129–54.

11. Gay Morris, *A Game for Dancers: Performing Modernism in the Postwar Years, 1945–1960* (Middletown: Wesleyan University Press, 2006), xiv–xix.

12. The more "natural sounding" term "new classical dance" (*xin gudian wu* 新古典舞) has different denotations in the field of Chinese dance studies. First, it could refer to the "classical dance" itself, which was created in the Beijing Dance School in the mid-1950s. The qualifier "new" is used to distinguish the newly invented "classical dance" from the real ancient (or classical) dances lost in history; see Long Yinpei 隆蔭培, Xu Erchong 徐爾充, Ou Jianping 歐建平, eds., *Wudao zhishi shouce* 舞蹈知識手冊 [Handbook of dance knowledge] (Shanghai: Shanghai yinyue chubanshe, 1999), 99–100. Second, the term could also refer to a large group of classical-styled dance works choreographed after the end of the Cultural Revolution in the late 1970s and 1980s, which diverged from the *xiqu*-based code of the earlier "classical dance" and later coalesced into a new codified system; see Mu Yu 慕羽, *Zhongguo dangdai wudao de chuangzuo yu yanjiu* 中國當代舞蹈的創作與研究 [The composition and study of contemporary Chinese dance] (Beijing: Zhongguo wenlian chubanshe, 2009), 111. Third, as Wu Xiaobang's Tianma dances shared similar motivations with, and provided inspirations for, the "new classical dance" of the 1980s (some of the major choreographers were Wu's students), Wu's classical-themed dances of Tianma are also called "new classical dance"; see Zi Huajun 資華筠, *Wu yi wu li* 舞藝, 舞理 [Dance art and dance theory] (Shenyang: Chunfeng wenyi chubanshe, 1998), 159. Fourth, to distinguish Wu's "new classical dance" from its successor in the 1980s (and further from the "classical dance" of the 1950s), the former is sometimes called Gudian xin wu 古典新舞 [literally, classical new dance] to further stress its lineage from Wu's new (or modern) dance (Wu himself also used this term); see Mu, *Zhongguo dangdai wudao de chuangzuo yu yanjiu*, 58–59. This study uses "classical new dance" to refer to Wu's classical-themed Tianma dances. In fact, the qualifier "new" turns out to be somewhat anachronistic, because the so-called classical dance (*gudian wu* 古典舞)—the competitor of Wu's "new" version—was being constructed contemporaneously in the Beijing Dance School in the 1950s. All the elements needed to justify "classical dance" as a coherent discipline and genre—such as vocabulary, repertoire, methodology of choreography, training curriculum, and underlying aesthetics—were quite fluid and under incessant debate. Thus, what Wu intended to suggest by the adjective "new" is not so much temporality as the superiority of the ideological underpinnings of his approach over those of the classical dance.

13. Wu Xiaobang 吳曉邦, "Chengqing wo de sixiang" 澂清我的思想 [Clarifying my thoughts], *Wenyi bao* 文藝報, no. 3 (1952): 13–15; Luo Zhang 駱璋, "'Yige wudao yishu jiaoyu xin tixi de niyi' duhou" "一個舞蹈藝術教育新體系的擬議"讀後 [Comments on "Proposal of a new system of dance art education"], *Wudao congkan* 舞蹈叢刊, no. 2 (1957): 70–77, 71; Wu, *Wo de wudao*, 119; Si Xiaobing 司小兵, "Tan Wu Xiaobang tongzhi duidai minzu chuantong de cuowu taidu" 談吳曉邦同志對 待民族傳統的錯誤態度 [On the wrong attitudes of Comrade Wu Xiaobang toward national tradition], *Wudao* 舞蹈, nos. 8–9 (1960): 59–65, 64–65.

14. Ann Daly, *Done into Dance: Isadora Duncan in America* (Bloomington: Indiana University Press, 1995), 91; Carrie Preston, *Modernism's Mythic Pose: Gender, Genre, Solo Performance* (Oxford: Oxford University Press, 2011), 5–6, 182.

15. Jens Richard Giersdorf, *The Body of the People: East German Dance since 1945* (Madison: The University of Wisconsin Press, 2013), 7.

16. Ibid., 12–25.

17. Christina Ezrabi, *Swans of the Kremlin* (Pittsburgh: University of Pittsburgh Press, 2012); Janice Ross, *Like a Bomb Going Off: Leonid Yakobson and Ballet as Resistance in Soviet Russia* (New Haven: Yale University Press, 2015).

18. Giersdorf, *The Body of the People*, 7.

19. Ibid., 49–84; Ezrabi, *Swans of the Kremlin*, 30–33; Ross, *Like a Bomb Going Off*, 21–25.

20. Daly, *Done into Dance*, 10, 128–29, 136–39, 137; Preston, *Modernism's Mythic Pose*, 12, 161.

21. Owen Hulatt, "Introduction," in *Aesthetic and Artistic Autonomy*, ed. Owen Hulatt (London: Bloomsbury Academic, 2013), 6.

22. For an account of the process of creating the "Chinese classical dance" (which actually started earlier than the Beijing Dance School's project), see Wilcox, *Revolutionary Bodies*, 48–118; Emily Wilcox, "Han-Tang Zhongguo Gudianwu and the Problem of Chineseness in Contemporary Chinese Dance: Sixty Years of Controversy," *Asian Theatre Journal* 29, no. 1 (2012): 206–32.

23. For Mao's various observations regarding this notion, see Mao Zedong毛澤東, *Mao Zedong xuan ji* 毛澤東選集 [Selected works of Mao Zedong] (Beijing: Renmin chubanshe, 1969), vol. 3, 804–35 ("Talks at the Yan'an Forum," 1942); vol. 3, 787–803 ("Opposing Stereotyped Party Writing," 1942); vol. 2, 623–70 ("On New Democracy," 1940).

24. Wilcox, "Han-Tang Zhongguo Gudianwu," 224.

25. Eric Hobsbawm, "Introduction: Inventing Tradition," in *The Invention of Tradition*, ed. E. Hobsbawm and T. Ranger (Cambridge: Cambridge University Press, 1983), 7–8.

26. Joshua Goldstein, *Drama Kings: Players and Publics in the Re-creation of Peking Opera, 1870–1937* (Berkeley: University of California Press, 2007), 4–5.

27. Wilcox, *Revolutionary Bodies*, 7.

28. Mao, "Talks at the Yan'an Forum," 818–19; Robert E. Hegel, "Making the Past Serve the Present in Fiction and Drama: From the Yan'an Forum to the Cultural Revolution," in *Popular Chinese Literature and Performing Arts in the People's Republic of China, 1949–1979*, ed. Bonnie S. McDougall (Berkeley: University of California Press, 1984), 198–99.

29. Mao, "Talks at the Yan'an Forum," 812.

30. Ibid., 822–3.

31. Xiaobing Tang, *Visual Culture in Contemporary China: Paradigms and Shifts* (Cambridge: Cambridge University Press, 2015), 11, 24–33; Wilcox, "Han-Tang Zhongguo Gudianwu," 214–15.

32. Louis Althusser, "Ideology and Ideological State Apparratuses (Notes towards an Investigation)," in *Cultural Theory: An Anthology*, ed. Imre Szeman and Timothy Kaposy (UK: Wiley-Blackwell, 2011), 204–22.

33. Mao, "Talks at the Yan'an Forum," 806–7.

34. In Tang, *Visual Culture in Contemporary China*, 21–22, Tang sees the politics of the socialist regime as part of a radical, concerted, and systematic experiment of "striving for a profound cultural transformation," which is "a continuation of the project to achieve cultural modernity." This approach is informed by Tang's main perspective—"with regard to the political culture of socialist China, it should be more revealing to see politics as a forceful response to cultural issues, than to see culture as being exploited for political purpose." That is, Tang reverses the common conception of the "means-end" relation between culture (or art) and politics. Despite the fresh and generative insights, this approach is not suited for explicating the phenomenon under study here. Viewing the socialist cultural campaigns as a "concerted" and "systematic" project of socio-cultural transformation risks suppressing the diverging undercurrents that exposed the inconsistencies and contradictions beneath the united front of the project. Individuals, groups, and organizations with different and even conflicting interests often appropriated these campaigns and exploited the inconsistencies thereof to advance their own, sometimes subversive, political and/or artistic agendas, which is the focus of this chapter.

35. Wang Lili 王麗麗, *Zai wen yi yu yishixingtai zhijian: Hu Feng yanjiu* 在文藝與意識形態之間: 胡風研究 [Between literature-arts and ideology: a study of Hu Feng] (Beijing: Zhongguo renmin daxue chubanshe: 2003).

36. Ibid.

37. Hu Feng 胡風, *Lun minzu xingshi wenti* 論民族形式問題 [On issues of the national form] (Shanghai: Haiyan shudian, 1947).

38. Quoted in Si Xiaobing, "Tan Wu Xiaobang tongzhi duidai minzu chuantong," 64; Zhongguo wudao yishu yanjiu hui 中國舞蹈藝術研究會, *Wudao tongxun* 舞蹈通訊 [Dance communication], no. 3 (1955): 2–9. Wu had been consistently advocating this May-Fourth attitude. For example, as Wu observes in the early 1940s, "the entire artistic field was engaged in the debate on the national form [in 1940 and 1941]; many people believed that folk forms are the only source of the national form, and thus turned history backwards. Since the time of our departure, [I] had been determined not to be a slave of folk forms, not to be fettered by the old forms . . ." See Wu Xiaobang 吳曉邦, "Zai kangzhan zhong shengzhang qilai de wuyong yishu" 在抗戰中生長起來的舞踊藝術 [The dance art growing up in the war of resistance], *Zhong Su wenhua* 中蘇文化 9, no. 1 (1941): 96–98, 97. As another example, in Wu's 1949 summary of his experiences of creating the *Jinjun wu* 進軍舞 (Dance of the strategic offense, see chapter 2), he maintains that "as for the issue of the national form, we . . . felt that,

concerning the representation of the life content of soldiers, if [we] can manage to [let the dance] be realistic and liked and accepted by the soldiers—in other words, when we achieve [the goal of] representing the rich content of the nation—[the dance] would be guaranteed to obtain a realistic, national form of our own nation. Therefore, as for the issue of the national form, we were determined to not cut the feet to fit the shoes to contain the cut feet, but must create forms according to the content . . ." See Wu Xiaobang 吳曉邦, "Jinjun wu de chuangzuo ji yanchu de zongjie (jielu)" 進軍舞 的創作及演出的總結 (節錄) [A summary of the creation and performance of the *Dance of the Strategic Offense* (excerpt)], *Wenyi bao* 文藝報, no. 9 (1949): 10–12, 10.

39. In an international context, the United States, also in the 1950s, promoted dance modernism as a major representative of the new American ideology of international universalism in fighting the "war of ideas" against the Soviet bloc during the Cold War. In some sense, the invention of the Chinese national dance form, by emphasizing cultural distinctiveness, was a political response to this rising American universalism. However, this nationalist project itself became hegemonic in the Chinese dance world, and this is the context within which Wu's subversion occurred. See Rebekah Kowal, *How to Do Things with Dance: Performing Change in Postwar America* (CT: Wesleyan University Press, 2010), 19–51; Wilcox, "Han-Tang Zhongguo Gudianwu."

40. Goldstein, *Drama Kings*, 1–13.

41. Si Xiaobing, "Tan Wu Xiaobang tongzhi duidai minzu chuantong," 64.

42. Wu, *Wo de wudao*, 120–28.

43. Si Xiaobing, "Tan Wu Xiaobang tongzhi duidai minzu chuantong," 64.

44. Ibid., 61; Wu Xiaobang 吳曉邦, "Tan wudao chuangzuo huodong shang de fanwei jiqi xianghu guanxi" 談舞蹈創作活動上的範圍及其相互關係 [On the scopes of the activity of dance choreography and their mutual relationship], *Wudao tongxun* 舞 蹈通訊, nos. 8–9 (1956): 43.

45. Wu Xiaobang 吳曉邦, "Gudian wu he gudian jingshen" 古典舞和古典精神 [Classical dance and the classical ethos] [1987], reprinted in *Wu Xiaobang wudao wenji*, vol. 3, 159–63, 162. Wu had not published his idea of the relationship between classical dance and the "classical ethos" until the end of the Cultural Revolution (1966–1976), but this idea took shape in the Tianma period.

46. Wu's idea about the relationship between classical dance and the "classical ethos" was later appropriated by some practitioners/scholars of classical dance to justify that the "classical dance" indeed captures the classical ethos, while Wu's original intention of using the classical ethos to liberate his classical new dance from the formal restriction of the "classical" codes was dismissed. For a quoted example of this kind of appropriation, see Wilcox, "Han-Tang Zhongguo Gudianwu," 218.

47. Wu, "Gudian wu he gudian jingshen," 163; Wu Xiaobang, 1957, quoted in Si Xiaobing 司小兵, "Tan Wu Xiaobang tongzhi de chuangzuo qingxiang" 談吳曉邦同志的創 作傾向 [On Comrade Wu Xiaobang's Predilections in Choreography], *Wudao* 舞蹈, no. 10 (1960): 28–34, 33.

48. Wu Xiaobang, "Shi lun shehuizhuyi wudao yishu de duoyanghua fazhan" 試論社會 主義舞蹈藝術的多樣化發展 [A tentative discussion on the diversifying development of socialist dance art] [1982], reprinted in *Wu Xiaobang wudao wenji*, vol. 3,

3–9, 6; "Zai lun wudao yishu de duoyanghua" 再論舞蹈藝術的多樣化 [Continued discussion on the diversification of dance art] [1982], reprinted in *Wu Xiaobang wudao wenji*, vol. 3, 17–25, 19, 21; "Yao chuantong, bu yao chuantong zhuyi" 要傳統, 不要傳統主義 [Hold tradition, not traditionalism] [1986], reprinted in *Wu Xiaobang wudao wenji* vol. 3, 153–58, 156–58; "Leitong, liupai he xiongxin" 雷同, 流派和雄心 [Repetition, style, and ambition] [1980], reprinted in *Wu Xiaobang wudao wenji*, vol. 4, 390–96.

49. Eguchi Takaya 江口隆哉, *Wudao chuangzuo fa* 舞蹈創作法 [The Methodology of Dance Creation], translated by Jin Qiu 金秋 (Beijing: Xueyuan chubanshe, 2005), 5; Si Xiaobing, "Tan Wu Xiaobang tongzhi duidai minzu chuantong," 65; Susan Manning, *Ecstasy and the Demon: The Dances of Mary Wigman* (Minneapolis: University of Minnesota Press, 2006), 44; Dee Reynolds, *Rhythmic Subjects: Uses of Energy in the Dances of Mary Wigmany, Martha Graham and Merce Cunningham* (UK: Dance Books, 2007), 4; Lucia Ruprecht, "Gesture, Interruption, Vibration: Rethinking Early Twentieth-Century Gestural Theory and Practice in Walter Benjamin, Rudolf Von Laban, and Mary Wigman," *Dance Research Journal* 47, no. 2 (2015): 23–41, 25.

50. Wu, "Ge wu yishu," 3.

51. Wilcox, "Han-Tang Zhongguo Gudianwu," 208–9.

52. Feng and Yu, *Wu Xiaobang wudao wenji*, vol. 5, 215; Xiao Sai 蕭賽, "Jiu meng chong wen" 舊夢重溫 [Re-dream an old dream], *Chengdu ribao* 成都日報 (June 22, 1957).

53. Wu, *Wo de wudao*, 120–28; See also, Emily Wilcox, "Dancers Doing Fieldwork: Socialist Aesthetics and Bodily Experience in the People's Republic of China," *Journal for the Anthropological Study of Human Movement* 17, no. 2 (Fall 2010): 6–16.

54. Wang Kefen 王克芬 and Long Yinpei 隆蔭培, eds., *Zhongguo jinxiandai dangdai wudao fazhanshi* 中國近現代舞蹈發展史 (1840–1996) [A Developmental History of Dance in Modern China] (Beijing: Renmin yinyue chubanshe, 1999), 223–24.

55. The division of the two camps is only schematic—the two did have some personnel, organizational, and disciplinary overlaps.

56. "Dai Ailian deng zai zuotan hui shang tanshuai piping: wudao jie jiaotiaozhuyi zongpaizhuyi yanzhong" 戴愛蓮等在座談會上坦率批評: 舞蹈界教條主義宗派主義嚴重 [Dai Ailian etc. criticized at the discussion session that dogmatism and fractionism are serious in the field of dance], Renmin ribao 人民日報 (May 18, 1957).

57. Wu Xiaobang, "Yige xin wudao," 169–71; *Wo de wudao*, 129–54.

58. Ibid.

59. Wang Tao 王濤, "Xiqu biaoyan rencai peiyang de xiandai xuetuzhi tansuo" 戲曲表演人才培養的現代學徒制探索 [The exploration of modern apprenticeship in cultivating talents of *xiqu* performance], *Guangming ribao* 光明日報 (June 24, 2013): 16.

60. "Dai Ailian deng zai zuotan hui."

61. Wu, "Yige xin wudao," 173.

62. Pu, "Wudao de bieyang," 273.

63. Ibid.

64. Ibid., 270–72; Li, "Wu Xiaobang tongzhi zhuchi de Tianma," 2.

65. Pu, "Wudao de bieyang," 270.

66. Ibid., 271; Si Xiaobing, "Tan Wu Xiaobang tongzhi de chuangzuo," 32.

67. Si Xiaobing 司小兵, "Cong Wu Xiaobang tongzhi dui 'Bai hua qi fang, Bai jia zheng ming' de cuowu lijie tanqi'" 從吳曉邦同志對"百花齊放, 百家爭鳴"的錯誤理解談起 [A discussion starting from Comrade Wu Xiaobang's misunderstanding of "Let a hundred flowers bloom and a hundred schools of thought contend"], *Wudao* 舞蹈, no. 7 (1958): 28–34, 65.

68. Pu, "Wudao de bieyang," 273.

69. Wu Xiaobang, *Wu lun ji* 舞論集 [Writings on dance theory] (Chengdu: Sichuan wenyi chubanshe, 1985), 64.

70. Wu Xiaobang, "'Wu Xiaobang wudao yishu sixiang yanjiu hui' de bimu ci" "吳曉邦舞蹈藝術思想研究會"的閉幕詞 [The closing speech of the research conference on Wu Xiaobang's thoughts on the art of dance] [1985], reprinted in *Wu Xiaobang wudao wenji*, vol. 3, 134–45, 142–43.

71. Lin, *Wutuobang yundong*, 7–13; Shen, *Sikao yu xuanze*, 373–422; Kimberley Ens Manning and Felix Wemheuer, "Introduction," in *Eating Bitterness: New Perspectives on China's Great Leap Forward and Famine*, ed. Kimberley Ens Manning and Felix Wemheuer (Vancouver: The University of British Columbia Press, 2011), 1–27.

72. Manning and Wemheuer, "Introduction," 1; Frank Dikötter, *Mao's Great Famine: The History of China's Most Devastating Catastrophe, 1958–62* (New York: Bloomsbury, 2010).

73. Julia F. Andrews, *Painters and Politics in the People's Republic of China, 1949–1979* (Berkeley: University of California Press, 1994), 211.

74. King, "Romancing the Leap: Euphoria in the Moment before Disaster," in *Eating Bitterness*, 52.

75. For example, see Yu Taishang 于太賞, "Yuejin zhong de Shandong wudao shiye" 躍進的山東舞蹈事業 [The dance enterprise of Shandong in leap forward], *Wudao* 舞蹈, no. 2 (1960): 17–18; Zi Jian 子堅, "San hu wan sui de ge wu huiyan" 三呼萬歲的歌舞會演 [An assorted performance of songs and dances that hailed "Long-live" thrice], *Wudao* 舞蹈, no. 2 (1960): 19–21; Shao Bing 哨兵, "Zai geng da yuejin Zhong de qunzhong wudao yishu" 在更大躍進中的群衆舞蹈藝術 [The dance art of the masses in greater leap forward], *Wudao* 舞蹈, no. 2 (1960): 21–22; Xiao Wei 肖偉, "Shandong sheng yuejin gehu huiyan guan hou" 山東省躍進歌舞會演觀後 [After watching the assorted performance of songs and dances in leap forward of the Shandong province], *Wudao* 舞蹈, no. 2 (1960): 23; Lu Jing 陸靜 et al., "Huan wu yuejin de xin shidai" 歡舞躍進的新時代 [A new time of joyfully dancing and leaping forward], *Wudao* 舞蹈, no. 4 (1960): 4–13; Wang Gong 王恭 et al., "Qunzhong chuangcuo fang yicai" 群衆創作放異彩 [Creations of the masses shine with distinct colors], *Wudao* 舞蹈, no. 4 (1960): 14–17; Fu Zechun 傅澤淳, "Shengchan yuejin, huan wu fengshou: xi kan Hunan sheng sanjie zhigong yeyu wenyi hui yan" 生產躍進, 歡舞豐收: 喜看湖南省三屆職工業餘文藝會演 [Production in leap forward, joyful dances in harvest: pleasantly watching the third assorted amateur artistic performance by workers of the Hunan province], *Wudao* 舞蹈, no. 5 (1960): 34.

76. Jie Li, *Utopian Ruins: A Memorial Museum of the Mao Era* (Durham: Duke University Press, 2020), 105.

77. Among the twenty-seven dance works Wu choreographed for Tianma within the four years, there are only six with themes more or less related to the Great Leap. Six of the rest are re-staging, with only limited adaptation, of the religious and court ritual dances Wu collected during his national field work before 1957. The remaining fifteen works are all inspired by and choreographed according to traditional Chinese musical pieces, which are called by Wu *gu qu xin wu* 古曲新舞 (literally, ancient music new dance). However, *gu qu xin wu* should not be seen as a dance genre, as it only refers to the fact that these dances are all kinestheticization of "ancient music." Among these fifteen "new dances with old music," there are four with modern themes (or themes with no clear temporal context). Therefore, only the rest eleven or so are representative "classical new dance."

78. Wu Xiaobang, "Wo he wudao (houji): wo de wudao guan" 我和舞蹈 (後記): 我的舞蹈觀 [Dance and me (epilogue): my view of dance] [1985], reprinted in *Wu Xiaobang wudao wenji*, vol. 3, 127; Wu, "Yige xin wudao," 169–70.

79. See Wu Xiaobang, "Jingxin tansuo, du pi xi jing" 精心探索, 獨闢蹊徑 [Carefully explore and independently blaze a new trail] [1985], reprinted in *Wu Xiaobang wudao wenji*, vol. 4, 81–83, 82; Berkowitz. *Patterns of Disengagement.*

80. Lin, *Wutuobang yundong*, 205–206.

81. At the beginning, Wu was also affected by the frenzy. He once led his students to farm in the countryside in the leap-forward way, hoping to achieve food self-sufficiency. However, Wu became disillusioned in the late 1958 after his own failure and seeing the harsh reality in the countryside. See Wu, *Wo de wudao*, 141–47.

82. Frederick C. Teiwes, "Establishment and Consolidation of the New Regime" in Roderick MacFarquhar and John K. Fairbank, eds., *The Cambridge History of China* (NY: Cambridge University Press, 1987), vol. 14, 51–143, 83–88, 110–22; Lin, *Wutuobang yundong*, 9.

83. Lin, *Wutuobang yundong*, 167, 211.

84. Ibid., 154–86, 212–16; Manning and Wemheuer, "Introduction," 6; Kimberley Ens Manning, "The Gendered Politics of Woman-Work: Rethinking Radicalism in the Great Leap Forward," in *Eating Bitterness*, 72–106; Wang Yanni, "An Introduction to the ABCs of Communization: A Case Study of Macheng County," in *Eating Bitterness*, 148–70.

85. Lin, *Wutuobang yundong*, 181; Manning and Wemheuer, "Introduction," 7.

86. Merlie Goldman, "The Party and the Intellectuals," in *The Cambridge History of China*, vol. 14, 218–58, 234–36.

87. Ibid., 257; Shen, *Sikao yu Xuanze*, 523–673, 661–62.

88. Merlie Goldman, "The party and the intellectuals: phase two" in *The Cambridge History of China*, vol. 14, 432–77, 432; Lin, *Wutuobang yundong*, 226–61.

89. This schizoid state of Wu was representative of the mentality of many Chinese intellectuals in the early years of the socialist regime. See Goldman, "The party and the intellectuals," 235–36; Shen, *Reflections and Choices*, 661–73.

90. Pu, "Wudao de bieyang," 277.

91. Ibid.

92. Kun opera originated in southeast China in the late 1300s and enjoyed its greatest popularity from the mid-sixteenth to late eighteenth centuries. While the performance of Kun opera centers on singing with a refined and subtle vocal style, it is an integrative art that incorporates rich, smooth, and elegant dance movements. For a detailed performance history of the Kun opera, see Lu O-t'ing 陸萼庭, *Kun ju yanchu shigao* 昆劇演出史稿 [The performance history of Kun opera] (Taiwan: Guojia chubanshe, 2002).

93. For Mei's interactions with early modern dance in the West and the "new dance movement" (*xin wuyong yundong* 新舞踊運動) in Japan, see Catherine Yeh, "Experimenting with Dance Drama: Peking Opera Modernity, Kabuki Theater Reform and the Denishawn's Tour of the Far East," *Journal of Global Theatre History* 1, no. 2 (2016): 28–37; Catherine Yeh, "Mei Lanfang, the Denishawn Dancers, and World Theater," in *A New Literary History of Modern China*, ed. David Wang (Cambridge, MA: Harvard University Press, 2017), 311–18; Catherine Yeh, "Mei Lanfang and Modern Dance: Transcultural Innovation in Peking Opera, 1910s–1920s," in *Corporeal Politics: Dancing East Asia*, ed. Katherine Mezur and Emily Wilcox (Ann Arbor: The University of Michigan Press, 2020), 44–59.

94. Mei Lanfang, *Mei Lanfang tan yi lu* 梅蘭芳談藝錄 [Mei Lanfang's discussions on art] (Changsha: Hunan daxue chubanshe, 2010), 123–37; For different performance versions of *Si Fan*, see Andrea S. Goldman, "The Nun Who Wouldn't Be: Representations of Female Desire in Two Performance Genres of 'Si Fan,'" *Late Imperial China* 22, no. 1 (2001): 71–138; for a short summary of the performance history of *Si fan* in the Chinese theatrical tradition, see Nan Ma, "The Conflicted Monk: Choreographic Adaptations of *Si fan* in Japan's and China's New Dance Movements," in *Corporeal Politics: Dancing East Asia*, ed. Emily Wilcox and Katherine Mezur (Ann Arbor: The University of Michigan Press, 2020), 60–77, 64–66, and "*Si fan* zai zhong ri 'xin wudao yundong' zhong de kuaguojie chuanbo" 《思凡》在中日"新舞蹈运动"中的跨国界传播 [The transnational adaptations of *Si fan* (Longing for the mundane) in China's and Japan's new dance movements], *Journal of Beijing Dance Academy*, no. 4 (2019): 73–81.

95. Wu, *Wo de wudao*, 56.

96. Fujikagekai 藤蔭會, ed., *Fujikage Shizue* 藤蔭静枝 (Tōkyō: Fujikagekai, 1934), in Tsubōuchi Memorial Theater Museum of Waseda University 早稲田大學演劇博物館, Tōkyō, Japan.

97. Nishikata Setsuko 西形節子, *Kindai nihon buyōshi*近代日本舞踊史 [The history of modern Japanese dance] (Tōkyō: Engeki Shuppansha, 2006), 108–109.

98. It was celebrated as an experiment that finally appeared about seventeen years after Tsubōchi Shōyo坪内逍遥's call for the reform of traditional Japanese dance in his *Shin gakugekiron*新楽劇論 [On the new musical drama] in 1904. See Kuniyoshi Kazuko 國吉和子, *Yumeo no ishō kioku no tsubo: buyō to modanizumu* 夢の衣裳・記憶の壺: 舞踊とモダニズム [The clothes of dreams and the jar of memories: dance and modernism] (Tōkyō: Shinshokan, 2002), 119; Nishikata, *Kindai nihon buyōshi*, 108; Chao Chi-Fang趙綺芳, "Quanqiu xiandaixing,

guojiazhuyi yu 'xinwuyong:' yi 1945 nian yiqian riben xiandaiwu de fazhan wei li zhi fenxi" 全球現代性, 國家主義與"新舞踊": 以1945 年以前日本現代舞的發展為例之分析 [Global modernity, nationalism and the "New dance": an analysis using the development of modern dance in pre-1945 Japan as a case], *Yishu pinglun* 藝術評論, no. 18 (Taipei: Taipei National University of Arts, 2008): 27–55, 42.

99. Perhaps because Wu intended to position his *Si fan* as a work of new dance and of a Chinese origin, he never confirmed any direct connection between his version and either Mei's "old" *kunqu* opera or Fijikage's Kabuki adaptation. Instead, he attributed the inspiration to Huang Youdi 黃友棣 (1912–2010)'s violin solo *Dinghu shang de huanghun* 鼎湖上的黃昏 (Dusk on the Dinghu Mountain), which became the accompanying music for Wu's *Si fan*. See Wu, *Wo de wudao*, 59.

100. Feng and Yu, *Wu Xiaobang wudao wenji*, vol. 5, 74; Kuniyoshi, *Yumeo no ishō kioku no tsubo*, 119; Mei, *Mei Lanfang tan yi lu*, 123–37.

101. See Ma, "The Conflicted Monk" and "*Si fan* zai zhong ri" for a transnational, comparative adaptation study of the multilayered, varied, and counterbalancing meanings of modernity (or modernities) associated with the *Si fan* theme, and their different and even opposite manifestations in the choreographies of Mei, Wu, and Fujikage in relation to the particular historical, socio-cultural contexts of early-twentieth-century East Asia.

102. Feng and Yu, *Wu Xiaobang wudao wenji*, vol. 5, 74.

103. *Si fan* has long been recognized as one of the most difficult works to perform in the *kunqu* repertoire, especially the dance solo of the female lead. See Liu Jianchun 劉建春, *Zhongguo kunqu ditu* 中國昆曲地圖 [The map of Chinese *kunqu*] (Shanghai: Shanghai wenhua chubanshe, 2010), 89.

104. Feng and Yu, *Wu Xiaobang wudao wenji*, vol. 5, 71–74.

105. Ibid.

106. Mei, *Mei Lanfang tan yi lu*, 128.

107. Wu Xiaobang, "Jiekai zhongguo xin wudao de xumu" 揭開中國新舞蹈的序幕 [Draw up the curtain of China's New dance] [1985], reprinted in *Wu Xiaobang wudao wenji*, vol. 3, 44–53, 46; Wu, "Wo he wudao," 121–33, 121–22.

108. Wu Xiaobang, "Wudao chuangzuo yao geng shang yi ceng lou" 舞蹈創作要更上一層樓 [Dance choreography must arise to a new level] [1982], reprinted in *Wu Xiaobang wudao wenji*, vol. 4, 153–65, 164.

109. In the Kun opera repertoire, there is a sequel to *Si fan*, named *Seng ni hui* 僧尼會 (The rendezvous between the monk and the nun). After running away from the convent, the nun Zhao Sekong meets a young monk who has likewise abandoned his religious faith, and the two become lovers. Wu's *Si fan* may thus be seen as related to the story of the monk in *Seng ni hui* as well. However, the story of *Si fan* is much more popular than *Seng ni hui*. Goldman, "The Nun Who Wouldn't Be," 72–73.

110. Feng and Yu, *Wu Xiaobang wudao wenji*, vol.5, 71.

111. Goldstein, *Drama Kings*, 118–28.

112. Ibid., 10.

113. Wu, "Wo he wudao," 124.

114. Wu, "Zai kangzhan zhong," 96.

115. Wu Xiaobang, "Zhongguo xiandai wudao de lilun yu shijian" 中國現代舞蹈的理論 與實踐 [The theory and practice of modern Chinese dance] [1987], reprinted in *Wu Xiaobang wudao wenji*, vol. 3, 164–69, 166.

116. Feng and Yu, *Wu Xiaobang wudao wenji*, vol.5, 72.

117. Wu, *Wo de wudao*, 55.

118. Ibid., 54–56.

119. Ibid., 56.

120. He Minshi 何敏士, "Liang shi, yaolan: yi Wu Xiaobang laoshi zaoqi zai Guangdong banxue" 良師, 搖籃: 憶吳曉邦老師早期在廣東辦學 [Good mentor, cradle: recollecting Teacher Wu Xiaobang's teaching early in Guangdong] [1982], reprinted in *Wu Xiaobang wudao wenji*, vol. 1, 198–205, 202–203.

121. Ibid., 203.

122. Wu, *Wo de wudao*, 61; Du Xuan 杜宣, "Cong pannizhe dao tuohuangzhe" 從叛逆 者到拓荒者 [From a rebel to a pioneer] [1982], reprinted in *Wu Xiaobang wudao wenji*, vol. 1, 175–97, 180; Pu, "Wudao de bieyang," 269.

123. Lin, *Wutuobang yundong*, 159; Manning and Wemheuer, "Introduction," 6.

124. Xiao, "Shandong sheng yue jing," 23; A Ying 阿瑩, "Ba qunzhong wudao chuangzuo shuiping tigao yi bu" 把群眾舞蹈創作水平提高一步 [Elevate one step higher the level of choreographing dances of the masses], *Wudao* 舞蹈, no. 4 (1960): 10; Xiaochun 曉春, "Wudao yishu jinmi fanying xianshi de yidian tihui" 舞蹈藝術緊 密反映現實的一點體會 [Some thoughts on the art of dance's close reflection of reality], *Wudao* 舞蹈, no. 4 (1960): 9–10; Guo Bingling 郭冰玲, "Nuli suzao gongren jieji de yingxiong xingxiang" 努力塑造工人階級的英雄形象 [Striving to create the heroic image of the proletarian class], *Wudao* 舞蹈, no. 12 (1960): 19.

125. Goldman, "The party and the intellectuals: phase two," 434; King, "Romancing the Leap," 52.

126. Wu Xiaobang, "Tan huiyan zhong youguan wudao yishu de jige wenti" 談匯演中有 關舞蹈藝術的幾個問題 [On several problems concerning the art of dance in the performance] [1959], reprinted in *Wu Xiaobang wudao wenji*, vol. 4, 149–52, 150; Si Xiaobing, "Cong Wu Xiaobang tongzhi dui 'Bai hua qi fang, Bai jia zheng ming,'" 32.

127. Wu, "Tan huiyan," 150. Note that Wu did not consistently devalue the amateur dances that "simplistically imitate the reality." For example, in 1952, Wu comments on this issue: "this shortcoming is a necessary phase of the process of development . . . the simplistic imitation of life is indeed inadequate; yet from another perspective, this is the consequence of proceeding from the reality of life." However, by the late 1950s, the rise of manual labor into primacy and the fast decline of the status of intellectuals and professionals seem to have exacerbated Wu's anxiety on this matter. See Wu Xiaobang 吳曉邦, "Cong 'ba yi' jianjun jie jingsai yanchu kan xin wudao yishu zai budui zhong de fazhan" 從 "八一" 建軍節競賽演出看新舞蹈藝 術在部隊中的發展 [Evaluate the development of the art of New dance in the military according to the contest performance of the "August 1st" Army Day], *Xinhua yuebao* 新華月報, no. 9 (1952): 228–29.

128. Xiao, "Shandong sheng yue jing," 23; A Ying, "Ba qunzhong wudao chuangzuo shuiping tigao yi bu," 10.

129. Ellen Graff, *Stepping Left: Dance and Politics in New York City, 1928–1942* (Durham: Duke University Press, 1997); Mark Franko, *The Work of Dance: Labor, Movement, and Identity in the 1930s* (Middletown: Wesleyan University Press, 2002); Mark Franko, *Choreographing Discourses: A Mark Franko Reader*, ed. Mark Franko with Alessandra Nicifero (New York: Routledge, 2019), 197–204.

130. Franko, *Choreographing Discourses*, 197, 199–200.

131. Wu, "Tan huiyan," 151.

132. Dance works mentioned here are *Yufu le*, *Ju lao* 菊老 (The old chrysanthemum man), *Yangchun baixue*, and *Yizhi chun* 一枝春 (A branch of spring); for details of these dances, see Feng and Yu, *Wu Xiaobang wudao wenji*, vol. 5, 132–44, 188–89, 151–57, 181–83.

133. His last one was twelve years earlier, also in Chongqing, before he left for Yan'an in 1945.

134. Wu, *Wo de wudao*, 131–32.

135. Feng and Yu, *Wu Xiaobang wudao wenji*, vol. 5, 132.

136. Lin Lang 林浪, "Ping *Yufu le* de cuowu sixiang qingxiang" 評《漁夫樂》的錯誤思想傾向 [Comments on the wrong ideological tendency of *Yufu le*], *Wudao* 舞蹈, no. 4 (1960): 28–29, 28.

137. Feng and Yu, *Wu Xiaobang wudao wenji*, vol. 5, 132.

138. Ibid.

139. Zhuang Zhou莊周, "Qi wu lun" 齊物論 (On the identity of things) in Guo Qingfan 郭慶藩, annotated, *Zhuangzi jishi*莊子集釋 [Collected commentaries on *Zhuangzi*] (Beijing: Zhonghua shuju, 1969), vol. 1, 133. As the allegory goes, Zhuang Zhou once had a dream in which he turned into a butterfly. The feeling of being a flying butterfly in the dream was so real that Zhuang forgot himself being Zhuang Zhou. He then woke up suddenly and found that he was still Zhuang Zhou, but his feeling of being Zhuang Zhou in reality was no more real than his feeling of being a butterfly in the dream. He got confused: "Is he now, as the butterfly-turned Zhuang Zhou, in the dream of a butterfly, or was he then, as a Zhuang Zhou-turned butterfly, in the dream of Zhuang Zhou?"

140. Feng and Yu, *Wu Xiaobang wudao wenji*, vol. 5, 132.

141. Ibid. This reaction of the fisherman allows for different interpretations. It could suggest that he has reestablished the absolute distinction between dream and reality and thus expresses his self-ridicule toward his previous confusion. Or it could also be the case that the old fisherman, still under the influence of alcohol, has given up any serious effort to figure out the "butterfly paradox" and, in a cynical way, put his confusion in suspension. Here, Wu still leaves some uncertainty in his choreography.

142. The theme of "fish" and "joy" in *Yufu le* may also allude to another famous Taoist allegory, *Hao liang zhi bian*濠梁之辯 [The debate at the Hao Bridge]. One day, Zhuangzi and his philosopher friend Hui Shi惠施 had a tour on a bridge across the Hao River. Zhuangzi saw the fish in the river and said: "The fish swim so leisurely, which is the joy of the fish." Hui Shi challenged Zhuangzi: "You are not the fish. How can you know the joy of the fish?" Zhuangzi asked back: "You are not me. How can you know that I do not know the joy of the fish?" Hui Shi answered: "I am not you,

so I indeed cannot know you. However, you are not the fish either, so you cannot know the joy of the fish. That's it." Here is Zhuangzi's final rejoinder: "Let's return to the beginning of our conversation. You asked: 'How can you know the joy of the fish'? This means that you had already known that I had known, and then you asked me. I had already known [this] on the Hao Bridge." This playful, mind-bending allegory once again demonstrates the epistemological paradox inherent in any definite knowledge based on the distinction between the self and the other, the subject and the object. See Zhuang Zhou, "Qiu shui" 秋水 [Autumn water] in Guo, *Zhuangzi jishi*, vol. 6, 606–7.

143. Feng and Yu, *Wu Xiaobang wudao wenji*, vol. 5, 132–33.

144. See Si Ji 思集, "Zenyang caineng 'Jingli wei geming fuwu'" 怎樣才能"盡力爲革命服務" [How can one "Do the best to serve the revolution"], *Wudao* 舞蹈, no. 6 (1960): 24–25, 24.

145. See Lin, "Ping *Yufu le*," 28.

146. Wen Shan 文山, "Yao zhenzheng de zhichi he guli" 要真正的支持和鼓勵 [In need of true support and encouragement], *Wudao* 舞蹈, no. 4 (1960): 29–31.

147. See Si Ji, "Zenyang caineng," 24.

148. Goldman, "The party and the intellectuals," 254.

149. Shen, *Sikao yu xuanze*, 523–616.

150. Ibid.; Goldman, "The party and the intellectuals," 242–58.

151. Wu, *Wo de wudao*, 130.

152. Wang Yu 王余, "Huanying ni, Chongqing de lao pengyou" 歡迎你, 重慶的老朋友 [Welcome! Old friend of Chongqing], *Chongqing ribao* 重慶日報 (June 6, 1957); Wang Ke 王克, "Chongman le rendaozhuyi jingshen, chuchu biaoxian le yishujia de liangxin" 充滿了人道主義精神, 處處表現了藝術家的良心 [Filled with the humanistic spirit, expressing the conscience of the artist everywhere], *Chongqing ribao* 重慶日報 (June 21, 1957); 蕭賽, "Jiu meng chong wen" 舊夢重溫 [Reliving the old dream], Chengdu ribao 成都日報 (June 22, 1957); Si Xiaobing, "Tan Wu Xiaobang tongzhi de chuangzuo," 29.

153. Si Ji, "Zenyang caineng,'" 24.

154. Wu, *Wo de wudao*, 151; Feng and Yu, *Wu Xiaobang wudao wenji*, vol. 5, 203.

155. Fang Xuanling 房玄齡 et al., "Jikang zhuan" 嵇康傳 [Biography of Ji Kang] in *Jin Shu* 晉書 [Book of Jin] (Beijing: Zhonghua shuju, 1974), vol. 49, 1369–74.

156. Wang Shixiang 王世襄, "Guqin qu Guangling san shuoming" 古琴曲《廣陵散》說明 [Explication of the guqin piece Guangling san] in Wang Shixiang, *Jin hui dui* 錦灰堆 [A pile of brocade ashes] (Beijing: *San lian shu dian*, 1999), vol. 2, 513.

157. Shima Qian 司馬遷, "Cike liezhuan" 刺客列傳 [Biographies of assassins] in *Shiji* 史記 [The grand scribe's records] (Beijing: Zhonghua shuju, 1959), vol. 86, 2515–38, 2522–26.

158. *Wudao* 舞蹈, nos. 1, 3, 4, 5, 6, 7, 8, 9, 10 (1960).

159. Ibid.

160. "Wu dai hui jianbao digao (yi) (er) (san)" 舞代會簡報底稿 (一) (二) (三) [Original drafts of abbreviated minutes of the meetings in the third National Representatives Conference of the Chinese Dance Art Research Association (*Disanjie Zhongguo*

wudao yishu yanjiu hui huiyuan daibiao dahui 第三屆中國舞蹈藝術研究會會員代表大會) (Part I) (Part II) (Part III)], July 30–31, 1960; "Wu dai hui zhuxi tuan huiyi jilu" 舞代會主席團會議記錄 [Minutes of the presidential board meeting of the National Conference of Representatives of the Chinese Dance Art Research Association], July 31, 1960, uncatalogued archival documents in the Chinese Dance Collection at the University of Michigan Library; Wu, "Yige xin wudao," 172.

161. Pu, "Wudao de bieyang," 278.

162. Ibid.; Wu, "Yige xin wudao," 172.

163. Wu, "Yige xin wudao," 173.

164. Wu, *Wo de wudao*, 1.

165. For this psychoanalytic interpretation of *Don Giovanni*, see Slavoj Žižek, *Absolute Recoil: Towards a New Foundation of Dialectical Materialism* (London: Verso), 120–25. Wu, *Wo de wudao*, 129–54.

Chapter 4

1. Peng Song 彭松, "Cai wu ji: yi 1945 nian Chuan-Kang zhi xing" 采舞記: 憶1945年川康之行 [A record of collecting dances: a recollection of the 1945 journey to Sichuan and Xikang], *Xin min bao* 新民報 (1947), reprinted in Peng Song 彭松, *Wudao xuezhe Peng Song quan ji* 舞蹈學者彭松全集 [The complete works of the dance scholar Peng Song] (Beijing: Zhongyang minzu daxue chubanshe, 2011), 3–5.

2. Gao Du 高度 and Huang Yihua 黃奕華, eds., *Zhongguo minzu minjian wu koushu shi (diyi ce)* 中國民族民間舞口述史 (第一冊) [Oral histories of Chinese ethnic folk dances (vol. 1)] (Shanghai: Shanghai yinyue chubanshe, 2015), 53.

3. Some other pioneers in this endeavor are, for example, Wu Xiaobang 吳曉邦 (1906–1995), Qemberxianim 康巴爾汗 (aka Qambarkhan, 1914–1994), Liang Lun 梁倫 (b. 1921), and Choe Seung-hui 崔承喜 (aka, Choi Seunghee, 1911–1969), see Wang Kefen 王克芬 and Long Yinpei 隆蔭培, eds., *Zhongguo jinxiandai dangdai wudao fazhanshi* 中國近現代舞蹈發展史 [The development history of modern and contemporary Chinese dance] (Beijing: Renmin yinyue chubanshe, 1999), 77–78,132–33; Emily Wilcox, *Revolutionary Bodies: Chinese Dance and the Socialist Legacy* (Oakland: University of California Press, 2019), 40–43.

4. Wang Mingke 王明珂, *Qiang zai Han Zang zhijian: chuan xi qiang zu de lishi renleixue yanjiu* 羌在漢藏之間: 川西羌族的歷史人類學研究 [The Qiang between the Han and the Tibetan: a historical anthropological study of the Qiang ethnicity in Western Sichuan] (Beijing: Zhonghua shuju, 2008), 221.

5. Peng, "Cai wu ji," 4.

6. The well-known American missionary-anthropologist David Crokett Graham (aka Ge Weihan 葛維漢), who conducted ethnological research in the same area in the 1940s, also recorded a similar version of the story in another Qiang settlement in the region. His transliteration of the two ancient nations was Gu La and Tzu La, and he explicitly explained that Tzu La was the old name of China, similar to the Japanese word *shina* 支那. See David Crokett Graham, *The Customs and Religions of the Ch'iang* (Washington D.C.: Smithsonian Institution, 1958), 7–8.

7. In Peng's account, it is Gula that defeated Zila, while in Graham's record, it is the other way around. However, in both versions, it is the ancestors of the Qiang people that were vanquished, which led to the legendary long migration. Here, I adopt Graham's version because the pronunciations of "Zila" and "China" are closer.

8. Wang, *Qiang zai Han Zang*, 189.

9. Peng, "Cai wu ji," 4.

10. Ibid.

11. Joseph Fletcher, "The heyday of the Ch'ing order in Mongolia, Sinkiang and Tibet," in *The Cambridge History of China* (vol. 10, Late Ch'ing, 1800–1911, Part I), ed. John K. Fairbank (Cambridge: Cambridge University Press, 1978), 351–408.

12. Peng, "Cai wu ji," 5.

13. Ibid.

14. Wilcox, *Revolutionary Bodies*, 2–4.

15. Peng, "Cai wu ji," 3; Dai Ailian 戴愛蓮, *Wo de yishu yu shenghuo* 我的藝術與生活 [My Art and Life], recorded and edited by Luo Bin 羅斌 and Wu Jingshu 吳靜姝 (Beijing: Huayue chubanshe, 2003), 127–28; Gao and Huang, *Zhongguo minzu minjian wu*, 54; Wilcox, *Revolutionary Bodies*, 34.

16. Wang and Long, *Zhongguo jinxiandai dangdai wudao*, 64–80; Richard Glasstone, *The Story of Dai Ailian: Icon of Chinese Folk Dance, Pioneer of Chinese Ballet* (Binsted: Dance Books Ltd., 2007); Wilcox, *Revolutionary Bodies*, 8–10, 13–47.

17. Dai, *Wo de yishu*, 127; Wang and Long, *Zhongguo jinxiandai dangdai wudao*, 77; Wilcox, *Revolutionary Bodies*, 14–15.

18. Peng, "Cai wu ji," 5; Dai, *Wo de yishu*, 127–29; Wang and Long, *Zhongguo jinxiandai dangdai wudao*, 77–80; Wilcox, *Revolutionary Bodies*, 32–34.

19. Wilcox, *Revolutionary Bodies*, 61–65, 74–77.

20. Zi Huajun資華筠, "Enshi Dai Ailian Xiansheng" 恩師戴愛蓮先生 [My teacher Dai Ailian], in *Dai Ailian jinian wenji* 戴愛蓮紀念文集 [The Anthology in Memorial of Dai Ailian]), ed. Jiang Dong 江東 and Wang Kefeng 王克芬 (Guangzhou: Linnan meishu chubanshe, 2011), 103.

21. Wang and Long, *Zhongguo jinxiandai dangdai wudao*, 72–80; Jiang and Wang, *Dai Ailian jinian wenji*.

22. Shu-Mei Shih, "Against Diaspora: The Sinophone as Places of Cultural Production," in *Global Chinese Literature: Critical Essays*, ed. Jing Tsu and David Der-wei Wang (London: Brill, 2010), 32.

23. Jana Braziel and Anita Mannur, eds., *Theorizing Diaspora: A Reader* (Blackwell, 2003), 4.

24. No later than the late 1940s, the Chinese intellectual and artistic circle began to use terms like *xin de zhongguo minjian wu* 新的中國民間舞 (new Chinese folk dance) to "nationalize" Dai's ethnic dance works. See "Dai Ailian zai Beiping" 戴愛蓮在北平 [Dai Ailian in Beiping], *Hua shang bao* 華商報, no. 755 (1948): 3.

25. Emily Wilcox, "Diasporic Moves: Sinophone Epistemology in the Choreography of Dai Ailian," in *Corporeal Politics: Dancing East Asia*, ed. Katherine Mezur and Emily Wilcox (Ann Arbor: The University of Michigan Press, 2020), 115–34; Shih, "Against Diaspora," 38–39.

26. I refrain from using the term "cosmopolitan" to describe Dai's experiences because the Chinese national identity became so dominant in Dai's self-perception and portrayal of her identity after she went to China in the 1940s that, perhaps partly due to her diasporic background, Dai sometimes behaved as if she was more "Chinese" than the native Chinese. See, for example, Jiang Qing 江青, *Shuo Ailian* 說愛蓮 [Eileen] (Beijing: Renmin chubanshe, 2016), 216–18, 239–40.

  I also avoid using the term "Sinophone" for the following reasons. The case of Dai exposes a major limitation of the Sinophone—its "lingua-centrism" that predicates cultural identity and "the notion of 'belonging' to the Sinophone community on the act of speaking (or not speaking) the language of one's ancestors." Thus, the Sinophone is not applicable to the case of Dai, because she, as a fourth-generation Cantonese immigrant, spoke only English and learned Mandarin as a second language only after traveling to China at the age of twenty-four, and more importantly, her work is the wordless dance. I also do not intend to simply extend the Sinophone to encompass dance as some generalized "language," which would reinforce the implied lingua-centrism. Rather, I position dance in a critical (yet not oppositional) relation to language, both spoken and written.

  Wilcox points out similar limitations of applying the Sinophone to Dai's case and uses the term "Sinophone epistemology" instead to circumvent the Sinophone's lingua-centrism. However, I choose to stick to the conceptual framework of (multi-) diaspora, because the recent development in the scholarship on diaspora has retooled the concept to challenge the hegemony of Sinocentrism, nationalism, and the essentialist view of "Chineseness"—the very target of the Sinophone studies. My usage of the term is in line with this latest development.

  See Andrea Riemenschnitter and Deborah L. Madsen, eds., *Diasporic Histories: Cultural Archives of Chinese Transnationalism* (Hong Kong: Hong Kong University Press, 2009); Rainer Baubock and Thomas Faist, eds., *Diaspora and Transnationalism: Concepts, Theories and Methods* (Amsterdam: Amsterdam University Press, 2010); Shu-Mei Shih, "Against Diaspora," 29–48; Glen Peterson, *Overseas Chinese in the People's Republic of China* (London: Routledge, 2012); Olivia Khoo, "Singapore, Sinophone, Nationalism: Sounds of Language in the Films of Tan Pin Pin," in *Sinophone Cinemas*, ed. Audrey Yue and Olivia Khoo (UK: Palgrave McMillan, 2014), 77–97; Shelly Chan, *Diaspora's Homeland: Modern China in the Age of Global Migration* (Durham: Duke University Press, 2018); Wilcox, "Diasporic Moves."

27. Emily Wilcox, "Dancers Doing Fieldwork: Socialist Aesthetics and Bodily Experience in the People's Republic of China." *Journal for the Anthropological Study of Human Movement* 17, no. 2 (2012): 6–16.

28. Wilcox, *Revolutionary Bodies*, 40–43.

29. Wang, *Qiang zai Han Zang*, 211.

30. Gao and Huang, *Zhongguo minzu minjian wu*, 10–11; Dai Ailian 戴愛蓮, *Wo de yishu*, 127; "Dai Ailian zai Beiping," 3.

31. Edward Said, *Orientalism* (London and Henley: Routledge and Kegan Paul, 1978).

32. Thomas S. Mullaney, *Coming to Terms with the Nation: Ethnic Classification in Modern China* (Berkeley: University of California Press, 2011), 56–57;

Chang-tai Hung, *Going to the People: Chinese Intellectuals and Folk Literature, 1918–1937* (Cambridge: Harvard university Press, 1985), 171–72; Chow Tse-tsung, *The May Fourth Movement: Intellectual Revolution in Modern China* (Stanford: Stanford University Press, 1967); Vera Schwarcz, *The Chinese Enlightenment: Intellectuals and the Legacy of the May Fourth Movement of 1919* (Berkeley: California University Press, 1986).

33. For example, see Yang Chengzhi 楊成志, "Yunnan minzu diaocha baogao" 雲南民族調查報告 [A report on the investigation of the ethnicities in Yunnan], *Guoli Zhongshan daxue yuyan lishi yanjiu suo zhoukan* 國際中山大學語言歷史研究所周刊 11, nos. 129–32 (1930); Li Lie 李列, *Minzu xiangxiang yu xueshu xuanze: yi zu yanjiu xiandai xueshu de jianli* 民族想象于學術選擇: 彞族研究現代學術的建立 [Ethnic imagination and intellectual choice: reflection on the foundation of modern scholarship on Yi studies in China] (Beijing: Renmin chubanshe, 2006), 62–63.

34. Dru C. Gladney, "Representing Nationality in China: Refiguring Majority/Minority Identities." *Journal of Asian Studies* 53, no. 1 (1994): 92–123; Louisa Schein, "Multiple Alterities: The Contouring of Gender in Miao and Chinese Nationalisms," in *Women Out of Place: The Gender of Agency and the Race of Nationality*, ed. Brackette Williams (New York: Routledge, 1996); Louisa Schein, *Minority Rules: The Miao and the Feminine in China's Cultural Politics* (Durham, NC: Duke University Press, 2000).

35. For critiques of the internal orientalist framework, see Uradyn Bulag, *The Mongols at China's Edge: History and the Politics of National Unity* (Lanham, MD: Rowman & Littlefield (2002); Uradyn Bulag, *Collaborative Nationalism: The Politics of Friendship on China's Mongolian Frontier* (Lanham: Rowman & Littlefield, 2010); Uradyn Bulag, "Seeing Like a Minority: Political Tourism and the Struggle for Recognition in China," *Journal of Current Chinese Affairs* 41, no. 4 (2012): 133–58; Emily Wilcox, "Beyond Internal Orientalism: Dance and Nationality Discourse in the Early People's Republic of China, 1949–1954," *The Journal of Asian Studies* 75, no. 2 (2016): 363–86.

36. Peter Perdue, *China Marches West: The Qing Conquest of Central Eurasia* (Cambridge: Harvard University Press, 2005); Mark Elliott, *The Manchu Way: The Eight Banners and Ethnic Identity in Late Imperial China* (Stanford: Stanford university Press, 2001); James Millward, *Beyond the Pass: Economy, Ethnicity, and Empire in Qing Central Asia, 1759–1864* (Stanford: Stanford University Press, 1998); Nicola Cosmo, "Qing Colonial Administration in Inner Asia," *International Historical Review* 20, no. 2 (June 1998): 287–309; Peter Perdue, "Empire and Nation in Comparative Perspective: Frontier Administration in Eighteenth-Century China," *Journal of Early Modern History* 5, no. 4 (November 2001): 282–304; Pamela Crossley, *A Translucent Mirror: History and Identity in Qing Imperial Ideology* (Berkeley: University of California Press, 1999); Evelyn Rawski, "Presidential Address: Reenvisioning the Qing: The significance of the Qing in Chinese history," *Journal of Asian Studies* 55 (November 1996); C. Patterson Giersch, *Asian Borderlands: The Transformation of Qing China's Yunnan Frontier* (Cambridge: Harvard University Press, 2006); David Bello, "To Go Where No Han Could Go for Long: Malaria and the Qing Construction of Ethnic Administrative Space in Frontier Yunnan," *Modern China* 31, no. 3 (July 2005): 283–317; Kai-wing Chow, "Imagining Boundaries of Blood: Zhang Binglin and the Invention of the Chinese Race in Modern China," in *Racial Identities in*

East Asia, ed. Barry Sautman (Hong Kong: Hong Kong University of Science and Technology, 1995).

37. Chiang Kai-shek 蔣介石, *Zhongguo zhi mingyun* 中國之命運 [China's destiny], rev. ed. (reprint, Taipei: Zhongzheng shuju, [1947] 1986), 73; Mullaney, *Coming to Terms with the Nation*, 28–30.

38. Mullaney, *Coming to Terms with the Nation*, 28–30; Wilcox, *Revolutionary Bodies*, 36–37.

39. Wilcox, *Revolutionary Bodies*, 23–33.

40. Joseph Fletcher, "Ch'ing Inner Asia c. 1800," in *The Cambridge History of* China, vol. 10, 35–106; Paul Cohen, "Christian Missions and Their Impact to 1900," in *The Cambridge History of China*, vol. 10, 543–90; Immanuel C. Y. Hsu, "Late Ch'ing Foreign Relations, 1866–1905," in *The Cambridge History of China* (vol. 11, *Late Ch'ing, 1800–1911*, Part II), ed. John K. Fairbank and Kwang-Ching Liu (Cambridge: Cambridge University Press, 1978), 70–141; Kwang-Ching Liu and Richard Smith, "The Military Challenge: the North-West and the Coast," in *The Cambridge History of China*, vol. 11, 202–73.

41. Graham Dunlop, *Military Economics, Culture and Logistics in the Burma Campaign, 1942–1945* (New York: Routledge, 2015); Lloyd E. Eastman, *The Nationalist Era in China, 1927–1949* (Cambridge: Cambridge University Press, 1986), 145, 280; Hsaio-ting Lin, *Tibet and Nationalist China's Frontier: Intrigues and Ethnopolitics, 1928–49* (Vancouver: UBC Press, 2006), 105–56.

42. Dunlop, *Military Economics*; Lin, *Tibet and Nationalist China's Frontier*, 105–56.

43. Li, *Minzu xiangxiang*, 22–30; Mullaney, *Coming to Terms with the Nation*, 46–48.

44. Thomas Torrance, *The History, Customs and Religion of the Ch'iang* (Shanghai: Shanghai Mercury Ltd., 1920); Wang, *Qiang zai Han Zang*, 138.

45. Thomas Torrance, China's First Missionaries: Ancient Israelites (London: Thynne & Co. Litd., 1937); Wang, *Qiang zai Han Zang*, 138.

46. Graham, *The Customs and Religion*, 45–46; Wang, *Qiang zai Han Zang*, 274.

47. Wang, *Qiang zai Han Zang*, 167.

48. Henry Davies, *Yün-nan, the Link Between India and the Yangtze* (Cambridge: Cambridge University Press, 1909).

49. Mullaney, *Coming to Terms with the Nation*, 45.

50. Ibid., 47–48.

51. Ibid., 48–51.

52. Ibid., 63–65.

53. Li, *Minzu xiangxiang*, 44–45.

54. Wen You 聞宥, "Chuan xi qiang yu de chubu fenxi" 川西羌語的初步分析 [A preliminary analysis of the Qiang language in West Sichuan], *Hua xi daxue zhongguo wenhua yanjiu suo ji kan* 華西大學中國文化研究所集刊 *Studia Serica* 2 (1941), 60; Wang, *Qiang zai Han Zang*, 137.

55. Li, *Minzu xiangxiang*, 44–45.

56. Yang, "Yunnan minzu diaocha"; Li, *Minzu xiangxiang*, 44.

57. Gregory Eliyu Guldin, *The Saga of Anthropology in China: From Malinowski to Moscow to Mao* (Armonk: M. E. Sharpe, Inc., 1994).

58. Li, *Minzu xiangxiang*, 53, 58, 67–8, 70, 80; Wang, *Qiang zai Han Zang*, 167–70, 270–71, 276.

59. Yang, "Yunnan minzu diaocha," 1–4; "Guoli Zhongshan daxue xinan yanjiu hui chengli xuanyan" 國立中山大學西南研究會成立宣言 [The manifesto for the founding of the Southwest Research Association of the National Zhongshan University], *Guoli Zhongshan daxue xinan yanjiu hui zhuan kan* 國立中山大學西南研究會專刊 (January 1932); Li, *Minzu xiangxiang*, 67, 70–71.

60. Li, *Minzu xiangxiang*, 51.

61. See for example, Cen Jiawu 岑家梧, "Xinan minzu zhi yue wu" 西南民族之樂舞 [The music and dance of southwest nationalities], *Wen xun* 文訊 4, no. 1 (1943); Hu Jianmin 胡鑒民, "Qiang zu de xinyang yu xiwei" 羌族的信仰與習爲 [The religions, customs, and behaviors of the Qing nationality], *Bianjiang yanjiu lun cong* 邊疆研究論叢 (1941), reprinted in *Xinan minzu yanjiu lunwen xuan* 西南民族研究論文選 [Selected research essays on the southwest nationalities], ed. Li Shaoming 李紹明 and Cheng Xianmin 程賢敏 (Chengdu: Sichuan daxue chubanshe), 194; Li, *Minzu xiangxiang*, 257–58; Wang, *Qiang zai Han Zang*, 275.

62. John Israel, *Lianda: A Chinese University in War and Revolution* (Stanford: Stanford University Press, 1998); Wang and Long, *Zhongguo jinxiandai dangdai wudao*, 75–76,139–50; Emily Wilcox, "Dance in Wartime China: Liang Lun's Choreographic Migrations of the 1940s," 무용역사기록학 (The Journal of Society for Dance Documentation and History of South Korea) 52 (March 2019): 45–75.

63. Li, *Minzu xiangxiang*, 180–1, 215–28; Hu Hongbao 胡鴻保, ed., *Zhongguo renleixue shi* 中國人類學史 [The history of Chinese anthropology] (Beijing: Zhongguo renmin chubanshe, 2006), 78–90; Guldin, *The Saga of Anthropology*, 57–70; Mullaney, *Coming to Terms with the Nation*, 61–63.

64. Peng, "Cai wu ji"; Guldin, *The Saga of Anthropology*, 60, 63; Hu, *Zhongguo renleixue shi*, 87–88; Fang-Kuei Li, "Linguistics East and West: American Indian, Sino-Tibetan, and Thai," interview with Ning-Ping Chan and Randy La Polla, 1986, accessed April 26, 2019, http://content.cdlib.org/view?docId=hb3489n99m&brand=calisphere&doc.view=entire_text.

65. Peng, "Cai wu ji," 3.

66. Ibid., 4–5.

67. For more detailed biographical information of Dai, see Dai, *Wo de yishu*; Glasstone, *The Story of Dai Ailian*. For a nice summary and additional newly found information and analysis of Dai's life and career before moving to mainland China, see Wilcox, *Revolutionary Bodies*, 16–23.

68. Chan, *Diaspora's Homeland*, 1–16; see also Peterson, *Overseas Chinese*.

69. Walton Look Lai, "The Chinese Indenture System in the British West Indies and Its Aftermath," in *The Chinese in the Caribbean*, ed. Andrew Wilson (Princeton: Markus Wiener Publishers, 2004), 21–3.

70. Dai, *Wo de yishu*, 1–2; Lai, "The Chinese Indenture System," 3–4; Walton Look Lai, *Indentured Labor, Caribbean Sugar: Chinese and Indian Migrants to the British West Indies, 1838–1918* (Baltimore: The Johns Hopkins University Press, 1993), 37–49.

71. Anne-Marie Lee-Loy, "Kissing the Cross: Nineteenth-Century Representations of Chinese and Indian Immigrants in British Guiana and Trinidad," in *The Chinese in the Caribbean*, 25–39.

72. Ibid., 35.

73. Ibid., 25–39.

74. Lai, *Indentured Labor*, 189–95; Lai, "The Chinese Indenture System," 18.

75. Dai, *Wo de yishu*, 1–2; Wilcox, *Revolutionary Bodies*, 16–8; Jiang, *Eileen*, 318, 320.

76. Dai, *Wo de yishu*, 12; Wilcox, *Revolutionary Bodies*, 16–18.

77. Ibid.

78. Dai, *Wo de yishu*, 6, 12.

79. Ibid., 17.

80. Ibid., 6.

81. Ibid., 19.

82. Ibid., 14, 18; Lai, "The Chinese Indenture System," 17–18; Lee-Loy, "Kissing the Cross," 38–39.

83. Ibid; Jiang, *Eileen*, 321.

84. Dai, *Wo de yishu*, 26–27.

85. Wilcox, *Revolutionary Bodies*, 18; Dai, *Wo de yishu*, 17; Glasstone, *The Story of Dai Ailian*, 7–10.

86. Dai, *Wo de yishu*, 40–41; Wilcox, *Revolutionary Bodies*, 18–19.

87. Anna Kisselgoff, "China's Dance Doyenne Brings Troupe to U.S.," *The New York Times* (March 4, 1986), C15.

88. There was only once when Dai, as a ballet dancer, joined the modern dance studio of Lesley Burrows-Goossens, she felt the hostility held by some fellow dancers toward her. However, this was due to the confrontation between ballet and modern dance in general, and Dai explicitly explains in her oral history that it was not because she was Chinese. Dai quickly used her choreography to convince the other dancers that she can compose and perform modern dance too. Later, she got expelled from the studio, because the idea she held about the relationship between ballet and modern dance was vastly different from the doctrine of the modern dance studio, not due to her race. See Dai, *Wo de yishu*, 37.

89. Dai, *Wo de yishu*, 26–73.

90. Ibid., 38–39, 76.

91. "Dai Ailian zai Beiping," 3; Wang and Jiang, *Dai Ailian jinian wen ji*, 80.

92. "Yansu de wudaojia Dai Ailian" 嚴肅的舞蹈家戴愛蓮 [The serious dancer Dai Ailian], *Funü wenhua* 婦女文化 2, no. 19 (December 1947): 80.

93. Dai, *Wo de yishu*, 74; Glasstone, *The Story of Dai Ailian*, 19.

94. Dai, *Wo de yishu*, 12.

95. Glasstone, *The Story of Dai Ailian*, 19–20; Wilcox, *Revolutionary Bodies*, 21.

96. Dai, *Wo de yishu*, 125; Wilcox, *Revolutionary Bodies*, 20.

97. Glasstone, *The Story of Dai Ailian*, 19.

98. Dai, *Wo de yishu*, 56; Wilcox, *Revolutionary Bodies*, 19.

99. Dai, *Wo de yishu*, 56, 66–67.

100. Ibid., 66–67.

101. Ibid., 77–80; Glasstone, *The Story of Dai Ailian*, 19–20; Wilcox, *Revolutionary Bodies*, 21–22.

102. Ibid.

103. Dai, *Wo de yishu*, 87–103; Wilcox, *Revolutionary Bodies*, 32–33.

104. Reprinted in Jiang, *Eileen*, 43.

105. Dai, *Wo de yishu*, 88–81; Wilcox, *Revolutionary Bodies*, 21–22.

106. Dai, *Wo de yishu*, 92.

107. Ibid., 83–84; Wilcox, *Revolutionary Bodies*, 22.

108. Dai, *Wo de yishu*, 76, 87–88.

109. Chan, *Diaspora's Homeland*, 16, 146–84; See also Peterson, *Overseas Chinese*, 15.

110. Dai, *Wo de yishu*, 152, 179, 197; Jiang, *Eileen*, 167–71, 223–25, 238–39, 295.

111. Wang and Jiang, *Dai Ailian jinian wenji*, 135–8; Jiang, *Eileen*, 309–11.

112. Dai, *Wo de yishu*, 197; Jiang, *Eileen*, 223.

113. Jiang, *Eileen*, 249–51.

114. Dai, *Wo de yishu*, 219–46.

115. Jiang, *Eileen*, 275.

116. Zhang Minchu 張敏初, "Dai Ailian xiansheng rensheng zuihou de shike zai mang sha?" 戴愛蓮先生人生最後的時刻在忙啥? [What was Teacher Dai doing during the last days of her life?], in *Dai Ailian jinian wenji*, 151–52.

117. Jiang, *Eileen*, 310.

118. Ye Qianyu, *Xi xu cangsang ji liunian* 細敘滄桑記流年 [Narrate in detail the vicissitudes and record the passing years] (Beijing: Qunyan Shubanshe), 163–75.

119. Ibid., 163; Dai, *Wo de yishu*, 127.

120. Danzhu Angben 丹朱昂奔, "Xu yi: yige ren dui guojia minzu de shiming gan he zeren gan" 序一: 一個人對國家民族的使命感和責任感 [Preface I: a man's sense of destiny and responsibility towards the country and nation] in Zhuang Xueben 莊學本, *Zhuang Xueben quan ji* 莊學本全集 (上冊) [Complete works of Zhuang Xueben (vol. 1)] (Beijing: Zhonghua shuju, 2009).

121. In 1941, Zhuang Xueben was elected to serve on the board of directors of the *Zhongguo bianjiang xue hui* 中國邊疆學會 [Chinese academic association of borderlands] founded by the famous historian Gu Jiegang 顧頡剛 (1893–1980) and hired by the Huaxi Union University as an honorary consultant. In the same year, he held three exhibitions of *Photography of Xikang* in Chongqing, Chengdu, and Ya'an, which attracted over 200,000 viewers in total. Among the viewers were top-ranking Nationalist officials and influential artists, intellectuals, and scholars. See Zhuang, *Zhuang Xueben quan ji* (vol. 2), 561–70, 760–61; Wang, *Qiang zai Han Zang*, 207, 269; Li, *Minzu xiangxiang*, 288.

122. Wang Huangsheng 王璜生, "Xu er: Huan lishi yi zunyan" 序二: 還歷史以尊嚴 [Preface II: return dignity to history], in *Zhuang Xueben quan ji* (vol. 1).

123. Zhuang, *Zhuang Xueben quan ji* (vol. 2), 762.

124. Lin, *Tibet and Nationalist China's Frontier*, 129.

125. Dai, *Wo de yishu*, 127–28.

126. Ye, *Xi xu cangsang*, 146–54, 524; Ye Qainyu 葉淺予, *Ye Qianyu* 葉淺予 (Shijiazhuang: Hebei jiaoyu chubanshe, 2002).

127. André Migot, *Tibetan Marches*, trans. Peter Fleming (New York: E. P. Dutton & Co. Inc., 1955), 101; Melvyn Goldstein, *A History of Modern Tibet, 1913–1951: The Demise of the Lamaist State* (Berkeley: University of California Press, 1989).

128. Dai, *Wo de yishu*, 128.

129. Ye, *Xi xu cangsang*, 166–68.

130. Dai, *Wo de yishu*, 131–39; Wang and Jiang, *Dai Ailian jinian wenji*, 48, 50, 81, 85, 94–95, 97, 155, 232–33.

131. Ibid.; Wilcox, *Revolutionary Bodies*, 32–40.

132. Dai, *Wo de yishu*, 125–38; Guo Qinfang 郭琴舫, "Wudaojia Dai Ailian" 舞蹈家戴愛蓮 [The Dancer Dai Ailian], *Qingming* 清明, no. 2 (1946): 9–12.

133. Ibid.; Wilcox, *Revolutionary Bodies*, 32–40.

134. Dai Ailian 戴愛蓮, "Fazhan Zhongguo wudao de yi bu" 發展中國舞蹈的第一步 [The first step in developing the Chinese dance], *Zhongyang ribao* 中央日報 (April 10, 1946); Wilcox, *Revolutionary Bodies*, 9–10, 39–40.

135. Note that Dai also had continuous connection with the Communists, although the *Plenary* was mainly sponsored by Nationalist Institutions. See Wilcox, *Revolutionary Bodies*, 38.

136. Lin, *Tibet and Nationalist China's Frontier*, 141–45.

137. Ibid., 121–56.

138. Zhuang, *Zhuang Xueben quan ji* (vol. 2), 670.

139. Lin, *Tibet and Nationalist China's Frontier*, 129.

140. Ibid., 141–45.

141. Ye, *Xi xu cangsang*, 168.

142. Lin, *Tibet and Nationalist China's Frontier*, 129.

143. Ye, *Xi xu cangsang*, 173.

144. Dai, *Wo de yishu*, 125–27; Dai, "Fazhan zhongguo wudao."

145. Dai, "Fazhan zhongguo wudao."

146. Ibid. Note that in the manifesto, Dai does admit that the dances in Xinjiang had Indian influences. However, as her argument goes, since the dance forms there are closer to Russian and Indian than to Chinese, the dances in Xinjiang, unlike Tibetan dances, are placed at a relative "peripheral" position in Dai's lineage of ethnic dances. Therefore, admitting foreign influences on a "peripheral" dance is less problematic for Dai's dance lineage.

147. Dai, *Wo de yishu*, 199; "Dai Ailian zai Beiping," 3.

148. Dai, *Wo de yishu*, 128–29.

149. Ibid., 129.

150. Wang, *Qiang zai Han Zang*, 1, 121–42.

151. Dai Ailian, "The Development of Chinese Dance," *The Dancing Times* (March 1947), 302–4.

152. Ibid., 304.

153. Feng Ren 锋刃, "Dai Ailian he ta de wudao" 戴愛蓮和她的舞蹈 [Dai Ailian and Her Dance], *Minjian* 民間, no. 5 (1946): 10.

154. Ye, *Xi xu cangsang*, 161–62.

155. Wilcox, *Revolutionary Bodies*, 180–82.

156. Dai, "The Development of Chinese Dance," 302–4.

157. Xiao Kun 蕭鯤, "Dai Ailian zhi wu" 戴愛蓮之舞 [Dance of Dai Ailian], *Wen cui* 文萃 1, no. 45 (1946): 22.

158. Qin Sheng 勤生, "Dai Ailian zhi wu" 戴愛蓮之舞 [Dance of Dai Ailian], *Jia* 家 10 (November 1946): 19–20.

159. Jiang, *Eileen*, 113; Wang and Jiang, *Dai Ailian jinian wen ji*, 98.

160. Dai, *Wo de yishu*, 134; Jiang, *Eileen*, 113.

161. For Dai, the dance forms of Xinjiang are closer to Russian and Indian than to Chinese. See Dai, "Fazhan zhongguo wudao."

162. Jiang, *Eileen*, 113; Wang and Jiang, *Dai Ailian jinian wen ji*, 98.

163. Wang and Jiang, *Dai Ailian jinian wen ji*, 98.

164. Gao and Huang, *Zhongguo minzu minjian wu*, 61.

165. Dai, *Wo de yishu*, 140–3; Ye, *Xi xu cangsang*, 193–261; Kisselgoff, "China's Dance Doyenne."

166. Dai, *Wo de yishu*, 140.

167. Kisselgoff, "China's Dance Doyenne."

168. Ye, *Xi xu cangsang*, 230–31.

169. The other dance filmed is *Yazi bei feng* 啞子背瘋 (The mute carries the cripple), adapted by Dai from a play of the Han-ethnic Gui opera (*gui ju* 桂劇) popular in the Guangxi province in southern China. The film is also likely to be part of the materials used in Situ Huimin's documentary *Zhongguo minzu wudao* 中國民族舞蹈 [Chinese ethnic dances], which won an award in the 1948 Edinburgh International Film Festival, see Zang Jie 臧傑, Minguo ying tan de jijing zhenying: diantong yingpian gongsi mingxing qun xiang 民國影壇的激進陣營: 電通影片公司明星群像 [The radical camp in the Republican film world: A group portrayal of the stars of the Tiantong film company] (Beijing: Zhongyang bianyi chubanshe, 2011), 187–203; Wilcox, *Revolutionary Bodies*, 13–14; John Martin, "The Dance: Notes: Plans and Programs in the Summer Scene," *The New York Times* (August 10, 1947), X5; "Notes and Programs," *The New York Times* (June 13, 1948), X6; John Martin, "The Dance: On Summer Schedule," *The New York Times* (June 20, 1948), X6; "Of Local Origin," *The New York Times* (May 13, 1954), 34.

170. Wilcox, *Revolutionary Bodies*, 15, https://doi.org/10.1525/luminos.58.2.

171. Ye, *Xi xu cangsang*, 231.

172. Dai Ailian, "Introducing Tibetan Dance" in *Gift of Dr. Ann Hutchinson Guest* from the Special Collection of New York Public Library Jerome Robbins Dance Division, July 1980, MGRN 80–3221 D [no. 7]. Hutchinson was Dai's classmate at Dartington Hall. She was living in New York and Dai met her during her 1946–47 visit. That is probably when Dai gave the notes to her. See Dai, *Wo de yishu*, 249.

173. Rebekah Kowal, *Dancing the World Smaller: Staging Globalism in Mid-Century America* (New York: Oxford University Press, 2020), 72–119.

174. Ibid., 88.

175. Ibid., 91–2.

176. Ibid., 77.

177. "This Week's Events: Original Ballet Russe at Metropolitan," *The New York Times* (March 16, 1947), X12; Kowal, *Dancing the World Smaller*, 104–9.
178. Martin, "The Dance: On Summer Schedule."
179. Here, I do not intend to comprehensively cover the history of the Oriental dance class at Beijing Dance School, or Oriental dances in general in socialist China. Rather, I focus only on how Dai's diasporic identity is related to the founding of the class and the genre. For more historical details, see Wilcox, *Revolutionary Bodies*, 75; "Performing Bandung: China's Dance Diplomacy with India, Indonesia, and Burma, 1953–1962," *Inter-Asia Cultural Studies* 18, no. 4 (2017): 518–39; "Crossing Over: Choe Seung-hui's Pan-Asianism in Revolutionary Time," 무용역사기록학 (The Journal of Society for Dance Documentation and History of South Korea) 51 (December 2018): 65–97.
180. Dai, *Wo de yishu*, 190.
181. Ibid., 192.
182. Ibid.
183. Ibid., 182–83; For more details, see Wilcox, "Performing Bandung."
184. Dai, *Wo de yishu*, 190–93; Zhang Jun 張均, "Dai Ailian, Yige chuncui de yishujia" 戴愛蓮, 一個純粹的藝術家 [Dai Ailian, A Pure Artist], in *Dai Ailian jinian wenji*, 122–27.
185. Dai, *Wo de yishu*, 190–93; Wilcox, "Performing Bandung," 533–34.
186. Dai, *Wo de yishu*, 192.
187. Ibid., 186; Zhang, "Dai Ailian," 122–24; Wilcox, "Performing Bandung," 531.
188. Zhang, "Dai Ailian," 122–23.
189. Ibid., 186.
190. Zhang, "Dai Ailian," 123–5; Wilcox, "Performing Bandung."
191. Dai, *Wo de yishu*, 191.
192. Ibid., 193; Wilcox, "Performing Bandung," 520, 531–32.
193. Ibid.
194. Dai, *Wo de yishu*, 135.
195. Ann Hutchinson, *Labanotation: The system of Analyzing and Recording Movement*, *2nd edition* (New York: Theatre Arts Books, 1970); Carol-Lynne Moore, *The Harmonic Structure of Movement, Music, and Dance According to Rudolf Laban: An Examination of His Unpublished Writings and Drawings* (Lewiston: The Edwin Mellen Press, 2009); Rudolf Laban, *Laban's Principles of Dance and Movement Notation, 2nd edition* (Boston: Plays, Inc., 1975); Rudolf Laban, *A life for Dance: Reminiscences*, trans. Lisa Ullmann (London: MacDonald & Evans Ltd., 1975).
196. Dai, *Wo de yishu*, 135, 182–86.
197. Hutchinson, *Labanotation*, 20–27.
198. For different dance notations in history, see Ann Hutchinson, *Choreographics: A Comparison of Dance Notation Systems from the Fifteenth Century to the Present* (Philadelphia: Gordon and Breach, 1989), 177.
199. Rudolf von Laban, "Foreword" in Hutchinson, *Labanotation*, xiii–xvi, xiii.
200. Hutchinson, *Labanotation*, 17–19.
201. Peng, "Cai wu ji."

202. Dai, *Wo de yishu*, 135, 253.

203. Ibid., 183–85.

204. Ibid., 185.

205. Ann Hutchinson Guest, "The Jooss-Leeder School at Dartington Hall," *Dance Chronicle* 29 (2006): 181–82.

206. Wang and Jiang, *Dai Ailian jinian wen ji*, 254–55; Zi Huajun 資華筠, "Guan yu 'ding wei fa wu pu' de zhexue sikao" 關於定位法舞譜的哲學思考 [Philosophical reflection on the *Ding wei fa* dance notation], *Wudao yishu* 舞蹈藝術 24, no. 3 (1988): 17–26.

207. Dai, *Wo de yishu*, 105.

208. Wang and Jiang, *Dai Ailian jinian wen ji*, 256–57.

209. Wilcox, *Revolutionary Bodies*, 178, 180–81.

210. Zi Huajun 資華筠, *Wudao he wo* 舞蹈和我 [Dance and me] (Chengdu: Sichuan wenyi chubanshe, 1987), 55–64.

211. Dai, *Wo de yishu*, 66.

212. Ibid., 173.

213. Ibid., 173–74; Glasstone, *The Story of Dai Ailian*, 42–43.

214. William C. Reynolds, "Film versus Notation in Dance: Basic Perceptual and Epistemological Differences," in *The 5th Hong Kong International Dance Conference/ The Second International Congress on Movement Notation: Notation Papers* (Hong Kong: The Hong Kong Academy for Performing Arts, 1990), 151–64; Sheila Marion, "Authorship and Intention in Re-created or Notated dances," in *The 5th Hong Kong International Dance Conference/The Second International Congress on Movement Notation: Notation Papers*, 106–22.

215. Michel Foucault, *The Order of Things: An Archaeology of the Human Sciences* (New York: Taylor and Francis e-Library, 2005), 147.

216. Gregoria Baty-Smith, "Tinkling in Labanotation: A Search for Transcribing a Non-Western Dance" in *The 5th Hong Kong International Dance Conference/The Second International Congress on Movement Notation: Notation Papers*, 1–12, 8.

217. Dai Ailian, "Introducing Tibetan Dance"; Dai, *Wo de yishu*, 249; Wang and Jiang, *Dai Ailian jinian wen ji*, 206; Hutchinson, "The Jooss-Leeder School at Dartington Hall," 185; Hutchinson, *Labanotation*, 10; "Finding Aid: World Dance at the DNB," accessed May 6, 2019, http://www.dancenotation.org/library/bib/folkdance/folkda nce.html.

218. John Martin, "The Dance: Script: Bureau of Notation Plans Increased Activities," *The New York Times* (December 21, 1947), X11.

219. Dai, *Wo de yishu*, 251–66; Wang and Jiang, *Dai Ailian jinian wen ji*, 165, 182.

220. Dai Ailian 戴愛蓮 and Feng Bihua 馮碧華, *Zhongguo shaoshu minzu minjian jiti wu* 中國少數民族民間集體舞 [Collective folk dances of ethnic minorities in China] (Beijing: Zhongguo wudaojia xiehui Laban wupu xuehui, 1986).

221. Dai, *Wo de yishu*, 259; Baty-Smith, "Tinikling in Labanotation," 7.

222. Dai Ailian, *Dance On with Billie Mahoney, Dai Ailian*, interview with Billie Mahoney (Kansas City: Dance On Video, 1983), accessed May 6, 2019, https://search.alexande rstreet.com/preview/work/bibliographic_entity%7Cvideo_work%7C609047.

223. *Hua ren shijie* 華人世界 [The world of overseas Chinese], CCTV 4, December 21, 2011, accessed May 6, 2019, http://tv.cntv.cn/video/C17604/73f045813c024b6ab 9243a27046d0c7a.

224. Marion, "Authorship and Intention," 106–22.

225. Dai, *Wo de yishu*, 194, 266; Jiang, *Eileen*, 285–88.

226. Dai, *Dance On with Billie Mahoney*; Dai, *Wo de yishu*, 294.

227. Wang and Jiang, *Dai Ailian jinian wen ji*, 205.

228. Dai, *Wo de yishu*, 254.

229. Dai, *Dance On with Billie Mahoney*.

230. Dai, *Wo de yishu*, 251.

231. Dai, *Dance On with Billie Mahoney*.

232. Dai, *Wo de yishu*, 256–60.

233. Dai, "Fazhan Zhongguo wudao."

234. Wang and Jiang, *Dai Ailian jinian wen ji*, 152–3; Jiang, *Eileen*, 223.

235. Dai, *Wo de yishu*, 153; Wang and Jiang, *Dai Ailian jinian wen ji*, 153, 172–73, 221.

236. Dai, *Wo de yishu*, 262–63.

237. Dai, Ailian, "On '3-Step-Plus,'" in *The 5th Hong Kong International Dance Conference/ The Second International Congress on Movement Notation: Notation Papers*, 53–8, 54.

238. Dai, "On '3-Step-Plus,'" 53.

239. Ibid., 54.

240. Ibid., 53–58.

241. Rey Chow, *Writing Diaspora: Tactics of Intervention in Contemporary Cultural Studies* (Bloomington: Indiana University Press, 1993).

242. Dai, *Wo de yishu*, 262.

Epilogue

1. Zhongguo wudao yishu yanjiu hui 中國舞蹈藝術研究會 [Chinese dance art research association], "Wudao yanjiu hui biangeng qingkuang" 舞蹈研究會變更情況 [A summary of the historical changes in the Dance Research Association, 1949–1959], December 8, 1959, uncatalogued archival documents in the Chinese Dance Collection at the University of Michigan Library (hereafter, UM Chinese Dance Collection for short).

2. "Wu dai hui jianbao digao (yi) (er) (san)" 舞代會簡報底稿 (一) (二) (三) [Original drafts of abbreviated minutes of the meetings in the Dance Representatives Conference, i.e., the Third National Representatives Conference of the Chinese Dance Art Research Association (*Disanjie Zhongguo wudao yishu yanjiu hui huiyuan daibiao dahui* 第三屆中國舞蹈藝術研究會會員代表大會) (Part I) (Part II) (Part III)], July 30–31, 1960, uncatalogued archival documents in the UM Chinese Dance Collection.

3. "Huibao, diyi hao" 彙報: 第一號 [Briefing: no. 1], in "Wu dai hui qijian difang ge danwei dui xiehui de yijian" 舞代會期間地方各單位對協會的意見 [Comments made by local units to the Association during the Dance Representatives Conference], July 21, 1960, uncatalogued archival documents in the UM Chinese Dance Collection.

4. "Wu dai hui hexin zu changwei hui jilu" 舞代會核心組常委會記錄 [Minutes of the meeting of the standing committee of the Dance Representatives Conference's core group], July 23, 1960, uncatalogued archival documents in the UM Chinese Dance Collection.

5. "Huibao, diyi hao."

6. "Wu dai hui jianbao digao (yi) (er) (san)."

7. "Wu dai hui jianbao digao (yi)."

8. Ibid.

9. Ibid.

10. Ibid.

11. Ibid.

12. "Wu dai hui jianbao digao (er)."

13. "Wu dai hui jianbao digao (yi)."

14. "Wu dai hui jianbao digao (er)"; "Wu dai hui Beijing daibiaodui fenzu taolun hui jilu" [舞代會北京代表隊分組討論會記錄] (Minutes of the group discussion of Beijing representatives during the Dance Representatives Conference), July 30, 1960, uncatalogued archival documents in the UM Chinese Dance Collection.

In the meeting on July 30, 1960, Dai first admitted her own Trinidadian bourgeois background and individualistic past: in 1945, after she collected ethnic dances from China's southwestern borderlands (see chapter 4), someone used the materials without her permission; this incident upset her because it contradicted her Western "bourgeois," "individualistic" understanding of intellectual property. Dai then claimed, "with the help of the Party and the masses" and "through a series of [political] movements, especially the Anti-Rightist Campaign," she had willingly accepted thought reform, "woken up," and realized that she "walked down the wrong path in the past," and now, being transformed into a "revolutionary dance worker," she "can work pleasantly." Therefore, for Dai, condemning Wu of his bourgeois background, individualism, and resistance to thought reform may be a timely reconfirmation of her "successful"—yet, in the eyes of others, perhaps dubious—transformation.

Moreover, compared with Wu, Dai had a deeper modernist lineage and stronger American tie. While the modernist foundation of Wu's new dance was a three-week course of the Laban-Wigman system taught by Eguchi Takaya in Tokyo (see chapter 2), Dai received more direct and comprehensive training in the Laban system at Dartington Hall in England (see chapter 4). Whereas Wu's American connection was a largely symbolic one through his reception of Duncan's autobiography (chapter 2) and he never went to the United States, Dai had many American friends and colleagues and stayed in the United States from 1946 to 1947 as a cultural ambassador representing the Nationalist government (chapter 4). In fact, the modern dance Dai watched in mid-century America had become quite distanced from Duncan's early-century predecessor. Nevertheless, in the general anti-American political climate, by forcing an American modernist tie onto Wu's new dance and identifying herself entirely with the classical dance and ballet camp—in political opposition to Wu's modern/new dance—Dai could shift the focus of public attention from her own problematic past to Wu and his Tianma as the main target in the conference.

15. "Huibao, diyi hao"; "Wu dai hui jianbao digao (san)"; "Wu dai hui zhuxi tuan huiyi jilu" 舞代會主席團會議記錄 [Minute of the presidential board meeting of the

NT

Dance Representative Conference], July 21, 1960, uncatalogued archival documents in the UM Chinese Dance Collection.

16. "Wu dai hui zhuxi tuan huiyi jilu."

17. The "president" Guo was waiting for could be Dai Ailian or, more likely, Chen Jinqing 陳錦清 (1921–1991), then the vice president of the Beijing Dance School, since Chen was the one who had the true authority of making personnel and staffing decisions.

18. Liu Qingyi 劉青弋, "Lu zhong fei nan jin, feng duo xiang yi chen: Zhongguo wudao lilunjia Guo Mingda yu Zhongguo xiandai wu" 露重飛難進, 風多響易沉: 中國舞蹈理論家郭明達與中國現代舞 [Soaked by heavy dew, birds struggle with flying; Against strong winds, sounds are easy to be muffled: The Chinese dance theorist Guo Mingda and modern dance in China], Beijing Wudao Xueyuan xue bao 北京舞蹈學院學報, no. 1 (2007): 49–59; Wang Hui 王輝, "Cong Guo Mingda de yishu lichen kan ta dui Zhongguo wudao de gongxian" 從郭明達的藝術歷程看他對中國舞蹈的貢獻 [Evaluation of Guo Mingda's contributions toward Chinese dance] (M.A. thesis, Zhongguo yishu yanjiu yuan 中國藝術研究院 Chinese National Academy of Arts, 2009), 22.

19. Liu, "Lu zhong," 50; Wang, "Cong Guo Mingda," 6.

20. Wang, "Cong Guo Mingda," 10.

21. Liu, "Lu zhong," 50; Wang, "Cong Guo Mingda," 11.

22. Wang, "Cong Guo Mingda," 11.

23. Liu, "Lu zhong," 50; Wang, "Cong Guo Mingda," 12.

24. Wang, "Cong Guo Mingda," 13–14.

25. Liu, "Lu zhong," 50–53; Wang, "Cong Guo Mingda," 12–13.

26. Liu, "Lu zhong," 51; Wang, "Cong Guo Mingda," 15; Guo Mingda 郭明達, "Zai tan 'Yige wudao yishu jiaoyu xin tixi de niyi:' da Luo Zhang tongzhi" 再談 "一個舞蹈藝術教育體系的擬議": 答駱璋同志 [Further discussion on "Proposal of a new system of dance art education": a reply to Comrade Luo Zhang], Wudao congkan 舞蹈叢刊, no. 2 (1957): 77–86, 80; See also Stacey Prickett, "From Workers' Dance to New Dance," Dance Research: The Journal of the Society for Dance Research 7, no. 1 (Spring 1989): 47–64; Ellen Graff, Stepping Left: Dance and Politics in New York City, 1928–1942 (Durham: Duke University Press, 1997).

27. Guo, "Zai tan," 80; Liu, "Lu zhong," 61–62; Wang, "Cong Guo Mingda," 15–17.

28. Wang, "Cong Guo Mingda," 17.

29. Ibid.; Liu, "Lu zhong," 51.

30. Ibid.

31. Wang, "Cong Guo Mingda," 17.

32. Ibid., 18.

33. Ibid., 18–19; Liu, "Lu zhong," 52.

34. Liu, "Lu zhong," 53; Wang, "Cong Guo Mingda," 20.

35. Wang, "Cong Guo Mingda," 22.

36. Liu, "Lu zhong," 54; Wang, "Cong Guo Mingda," 22.

37. Liu, "Lu zhong," 54; Wang, "Cong Guo Mingda," 21.

38. For a description of the four works Guo performed, see Liu, "Lu zhong," 54–55; Wang, "Cong Guo Mingda," 21–22.

39. Liu, "Lu zhong," 55; For three agitprop works Guo choreographed with modern dance elements, see also Wang, "Cong Guo Mingda," 22–23.

40. Guo Mingda 郭明達, "Yige wudao yishu jiaoyu xin tixi de niyi" 一個舞蹈藝術教育新體系的擬議 [Proposal of a new system of dance art education], *Wudao tongxun* 舞蹈通訊, no. 12 (1956): 12–14.

41. Luo Zhang 駱璋, "'Yige wudao yishu jiaoyu xin tixi de niyi' duhou" "一個舞蹈藝術教育新體系的擬議"讀後 [Comments on "Proposal of a new system of dance art education"], *Wudao congkan* 舞蹈叢刊, no. 2 (1957): 70–77.

42. Rebekah Kowal, *How to Do Things with Dance: Performing Change in Postwar America* (CT: Wesleyan University Press, 2010), 32.

43. Ibid., 20–21, 32–42.

44. Ibid., 21, 29–30, 32–49.

45. Emily Wilcox, "Han-Tang Zhongguo Gudianwu and the Problem of Chineseness in Contemporary Chinese Dance: Sixty Years of Controversy," *Asian Theatre Journal* 29, no. 1 (2012): 206–32, 224.

46. Liu, "Lu zhong," 53–54.

47. Ibid., 54.

48. Guo, "Zai tan," 83–85.

49. Ibid., 86.

50. Ibid., 82, 86.

51. Wang, "Cong Guo Mingda," 23; "Wu dai hui zhuxi tuan."

52. Liu, "Lu zhong," 55.

53. Ibid., 57–58; Wang, "Cong Guo Mingda," 7.

54. Liu, "Lu zhong," 57–59.

55. Yu Rongling, in her late eighties, was beaten by the Red Guards, and as a result her both legs were broken and she died in misery in 1973; Wu Xiaobang, in his sixties, classified as a "reactionary academic authority," was verbally and physically abused numerous times; Dai Ailian, labeled as an "American spy" due to her "connection" with the American sinologist John Fairbank, was forced to receive long-term labor reform, which seriously damaged her health; Guo Mingda also received long-term labor reform, which permanently injured his right wrist and thus impaired his ability to write. See Ye Zufu 葉祖孚, "Xi taihou yuqian nüguan Yu Rongling (qi)" 西太后御前女官裕容齡(七) [Yu Rongling: Lady in waiting of the West Empress Dowager (VII)], *Zongheng* 縱橫, no. 7 (1999): 50–53, 53; Zhou Weizhi 周巍峙, "Dai xu: huainian Xiaobang" 代序: 懷念曉邦 [Preface: in memory of Xiaobang], in *Wu Xiaobang wudao wenji* 吳曉邦舞蹈文集 [Anthology of Wu Xiaobang on Dance], ed. Feng Shuangbai 馮霜白 and Yu Ping 余平 (Beijing: Zhongguo wenlian chubanshe, 2007), vol. 1, 1–8, 5–6; Dai Ailian 戴愛蓮, *Wo de yishu yu shenghuo* 我的藝術與生活 [My Art and Life], recorded and edited by Luo Bin 羅斌 and Wu Jingshu 吳靜姝 (Beijing: Huayue chubanshe, 2003), 196–218; Liu, "Lu zhong," 55; Wang, "Cong Guo Mingda," 7.

56. Liu, "Lu zhong," 57–59; Wang Tianbao 王天保, "Xiwang" 希望 [Hope], *Wudao* 舞蹈, no.1 (1981): 6–7, 7.

57. Shang Huizhen 尚慧貞 and Shang Jiaxiang 尚家驤, "Yishaduola Dengken (lishi renwu jieshao)" 伊莎多拉·鄧肯 (歷史人物介紹) [Isadora Duncan (introducing a historical figure)], *Wudao* 舞蹈, no. 5 (1978): 39–42.

58. Han Yi 涵逸, "Dengken Zizhuan zai Zhongguo de yi chuanuan ji qita" 《邓肯自传》 在中國的譯傳及其它 [The translation and dissemination of Duncan's autobiography in China], *Wudao Yishu* 舞蹈藝術 15, no. 2 (1986), 135–45.

59. Guo Mingda 郭明達, "Ludaoerfu Laban de shengping jiqi youguan 'dongzuo kexue fenxi he yishu yanjiu' de xueshuo" 魯道爾夫·拉班的生平及其有關"動作科學分析 和藝術研究"的學說 [Rudolf Laban's life and his theory related to the "scientific analysis of movement and research on art"], *Wudao* 舞蹈, no. 3 (1979).

60. "Dai Ailian fang oumei guilai da benkan jizhe wen" 戴愛蓮訪歐美歸來答本刊記 者問 [Dai Ailian answering questions from our journal's journalist after her visit to Europe and America], *Wudao* 舞蹈, no. 2 (1980): 8–10.

61. Wu Xiaobang 吳曉邦, "Xuexi xiandai wu de kai duan" 學習現代舞的開端 [The beginning of learning modern dance], *Wudao* 舞蹈, no. 4 (1979).

62. Fangfei Miao, "Dancing Cross-Cultural Misunderstandings: The American Dance Festival in China's New Era" (PhD diss., University of California, Los Angeles, 2019), 27–34.

63. Liu, "Lu zhong," 56; Wang, "Cong Guo Mingda," 24–26.

64. Wang, "Cong Guo Mingda," 24.

65. Ibid.

66. Emily Wilcox, *Revolutionary Bodies: Chinese Dance and the Socialist Legacy* (Oakland: University of California Press, 2019). Another formal discussion within the Chinese dance circle on the legitimacy of developing modern dance in China happened around the same time in 1980 Beijing; see Miao, "Dancing Cross-Cultural Misunderstandings," 53–54.

67. Guo, "Zai tan," 81.

68. Guo Mingda 郭明達, "Xiandai wudao jixun he Chuangzuo wenti mantan" 現代舞 蹈基訓和創作問題漫談 [A discussion of issues concerning modern dance training and choreography], *Wudao yishu congkan* 舞蹈藝術叢刊 5 (June 1983), 74–85, 76.

69. For example, see Wang, "Cong Guo Mingda," 35–36.

70. Guo Mingda 郭明達, "Zhongguo xiandai wu fazhan zhi wojian" 中國現代舞發展之 我見 [My vision for developing modern dance in China], *Wudao luncong* 舞蹈論叢, no. 2 (1980), 17–20; Wang, "Cong Guo Mingda," 38–40.

71. Ibid.

72. Liu, "Lu zhong," 56–57; Wang, "Cong Guo Mingda," 24–26.

73. There were several other modern dance technique workshops offered in China by foreign-based dancers around the same time. Yet, Guo's workshop was the earliest one that systematically taught histories, theories, and practices of modern dance after the Cultural Revolution and resulted in modern dance choreographies that caused wide discussion in China's dance circle. See Miao, "Dancing Cross-cultural Misunderstandings," 31–37.

74. Ibid.

75. Wang, "Xiwang."

76. Ibid.

77. Yu Zengxiang 于增湘, "Cong *Xiwang* xiangdao de" 從《希望》想到的 [What I think of *Hope*], *Wudao* 舞蹈, no. 1 (1981): 18–19; Cuncao 寸草, "Cong *Xiwang* tanqi" 從《希望》談起 [Talking about *Hope*], *Wudao* 舞蹈, no. 1 (1981), 19.

78. Yu, "Cong *Xiwang* xiangdao," 18.

79. Wang, "Xiwang," 6.

80. Ibid.

81. Liu, "Lu zhong," 57; Wang, "Cong Guo Mingda," 26; Miao, "Dancing Cross-Cultural Misunderstandings," 51–52.

82. For the development of modern dance in China after *Hope* throughout the 1980s and early 1990s and the intercultural exchanges concerning the genre between the United States and China, see Miao, "Dancing Cross-Cultural Misunderstandings."

Index